Ageing Masculinities in Contemporary European and Anglophone Cinema

This volume offers a unique exploration of how ageing masculinities are constructed and represented in contemporary international cinema.

With chapters spanning a range of national cinemas, the primarily European focus of the book is juxtaposed with analysis of the social and cultural constructions of manhood and the "anti-ageing" impulses of male stardom in contemporary Hollywood. These themes are inflected in different ways throughout the volume, from considering how old age is not the monolithic and unified life stage with which it is often framed, to exploring issues of queerness, sexuality, and asexuality, as well as themes such as national cinema and dementia.

Offering a diverse and multifaceted portrait of ageing and masculinity in contemporary cinema, this book will be of interest to scholars and students of film and screen studies, gender and masculinity studies, and cultural gerontology.

Tony Tracy is Lecturer in Film and Media Studies and Co-founder of the Huston School of Film & Digital Media, University of Galway, Ireland. His research centres on film history and Irish cinema with a particular interest in masculinities. His monograph *White Cottage, White House: Irish American Masculinities in Classical Hollywood Cinema* was published in 2022.

Michaela Schrage-Früh is Lecturer in German and Comparative Literature at the University of Galway, Ireland. She is the author of *Emerging Identities: Myth, Nation and Gender in the Poetry of Eavan Boland, Nuala Ní Dhomhnaill and Medbh McGuckian* (2004) and *Philosophy, Dreaming and the Literary Imagination* (2016). She has published widely on representations of gender and ageing in literature and culture, and is co-editor of five essay collections on the theme.

Routledge Advances in Film Studies

Philosophical Theories of Political Cinema
Angelo Emanuele Cioffi

Breaking Down Joker
Violence, Loneliness, Tragedy
Edited by Sean Redmond

Film, Environment, Comedy
Eco-Comedies on the Big Screen
Robin L Murray and Joseph K. Heumann

Space and Time in African Cinema and Cine-scapes
Kenneth W. Harrow

Decline and Reimagination in Cinematic New York
Cortland Rankin

Digital Space and Embodiment in Contemporary Cinema
Screening Composite Spaces
Jennifer Kirby

Emotion Pictures
Movies and Feelings
Lucy Fischer

Gender, Power, and Identity in The Films of Stanley Kubrick
Edited by Karen A. Ritzenhoff, Dijana Metlić and Jeremi Szaniawski

Ageing Masculinities in Contemporary European and Anglophone Cinema
Edited by Tony Tracy and Michaela Schrage-Früh

For more information about this series, please visit: www.routledge.com/

Ageing Masculinities in Contemporary European and Anglophone Cinema

Edited by Tony Tracy and Michaela Schrage-Früh

LONDON AND NEW YORK

Designed cover image: © Getty Images

First published 2023
by Routledge
4 Park Square, Milton Park, Abingdon, Oxon OX14 4RN

and by Routledge
605 Third Avenue, New York, NY 10158

Routledge is an imprint of the Taylor & Francis Group, an informa business

© 2023 selection and editorial matter, Tony Tracy and Michaela Schrage-Früh; individual chapters, the contributors

The right of Tony Tracy and Michaela Schrage-Früh to be identified as the authors of the editorial material, and of the authors for their individual chapters, has been asserted in accordance with sections 77 and 78 of the Copyright, Designs and Patents Act 1988.

All rights reserved. No part of this book may be reprinted or reproduced or utilised in any form or by any electronic, mechanical, or other means, now known or hereafter invented, including photocopying and recording, or in any information storage or retrieval system, without permission in writing from the publishers.

Trademark notice: Product or corporate names may be trademarks or registered trademarks, and are used only for identification and explanation without intent to infringe.

British Library Cataloguing-in-Publication Data
A catalogue record for this book is available from the British Library

Library of Congress Cataloging-in-Publication Data
Names: Tracy, Tony, editor. | Schrage-Früh, Michaela, editor.
Title: Ageing masculinities in contemporary European and Anglophone cinema / edited by Tony Tracy and Michaela Schrage-Früh.
Description: Abingdon, Oxon ; New York : Routledge, 2023. | Series: Routledge advances in film studies | Includes bibliographical references and index.
Identifiers: LCCN 2022042343 (print) | LCCN 2022042344 (ebook) | ISBN 9781032302287 (hardback) | ISBN 9781032306636 (paperback) | ISBN 9781003306146 (ebook)
Subjects: LCSH: Masculinity in motion pictures. | Older people in motion pictures.
Classification: LCC PN1995.9.A433 A4325 2023 (print) | LCC PN1995.9.A433 (ebook) | DDC 791.43/65211—dc23
LC record available at https://lccn.loc.gov/2022042343
LC ebook record available at https://lccn.loc.gov/2022042344

ISBN: 978-1-032-30228-7 (hbk)
ISBN: 978-1-032-30663-6 (pbk)
ISBN: 978-1-003-30614-6 (ebk)

DOI: 10.4324/9781003306146

Typeset in Sabon
by Apex CoVantage, LLC

Contents

Acknowledgements   vii
List of Figures   viii
Notes on Contributors   ix

1 Introduction: Ageing Masculinities in Contemporary European and Anglophone Cinema   1
TONY TRACY AND MICHAELA SCHRAGE-FRÜH

2 The Ageing of Men on Film: Concepts and Perspectives   11
MICHAEL KIMMEL

3 "Using the Difficulty": Michael Caine as Ageing Rebel   17
ROBERT SHAIL

4 "A Porcelain Feeling": Performance and Ageing in the Very Late Films of John Gielgud   29
JONATHAN STUBBS

5 Ageing Disgracefully: Depardieu, Hallyday, Luchini, and Silver Linings in Recent French Cinema   43
PHIL POWRIE

6 Jean Rochefort as Ageing Star: Masculinity and Masquerade   60
PHILIP DINE

7 From Mustang to 2CV: Ageing in Claude Lelouch's *Un homme et une femme* Trilogy   75
ÉAMON Ó COFAIGH

8 Ageing Male Melodrama and Post-Soviet Generational Conflict in Contemporary Estonian Cinema   88
TEET TEINEMAA

9 Restitution and Ageing Masculinities in Post-1989
   Czech Cinema   101
   MATTHEW SWENEY

10 The (Im-)Possibility of Solidarity: Narratives of Ageing,
   Masculinity, and Intergenerational Relationships in the
   German Comedies *We Are the New Ones* (2014) and
   Granny Nanny (2020)   119
   LISA-NIKE BÜHRING

11 Ageing, Masculinity, and the Absurd in *Toni Erdmann*
   (2016)   134
   MICHAEL STEWART

12 "What Makes Us Alive": The Ageing Artist in Paolo
   Sorrentino's *The Great Beauty* (2013) and *Youth* (2015)   148
   MANUEL BARBERÁ

13 Masculinity, Creativity, and Successful Ageing in Pedro
   Almodóvar's *Pain and Glory* (2019)   160
   HEATHER JERÓNIMO

14 Ageing Myths and Dark Romanticism in Albert Serra's
   Story of My Death (2013)   175
   ESTHER ZAPLANA

15 Male Ageing and Retribution in Contemporary Action
   Thrillers   189
   THOMAS BRITT

16 De-ageing and Denying the "Older Man" in Recent
   Hollywood   204
   TIMOTHY SHARY

17 Our Fathers: Ageing Masculinities and Dementia
   in Contemporary Film   213
   TONY TRACY

   Index   229

Acknowledgements

This collection developed from research and symposia undertaken as part of the international research project "Gendering Age: Representations of Masculinities and Ageing in Contemporary European Literatures and Cinemas" ("MASCAGE"). We gratefully acknowledge the Irish Research Council and the Gender-Net Plus ERA-Net Cofund for supporting this work. Special thanks are due to project leaders Professor Josep M. Armengol (Spain) and Professor Roberta Maierhofer (Austria), as well as to all participating researchers, and especially our fellow team members at the University of Galway, Dr Margaret O'Neill and Dr Áine Ní Léime. Sincere thanks to our Routledge editors Suzanne Richardson and Tanushree Baijal for their invaluable support and guidance throughout the publication process. The project began just before global COVID-19 restrictions were implemented, and so we are above all especially grateful to the contributors to this volume for participation in online events and for their ongoing commitment to developing their ideas against the backdrop of often uncontested assumptions about social, cultural, and biological meanings of age and ageing.

Figures

4.1	Gielgud mentors his pupil from a sedentary position in *Shine* (1996)	38
4.2	Gielgud raises his head towards the audience in *Catastrophe* (2000)	40
5.1	The sculpture of Serge constructed from soft toys	46
5.2	The cover of *Innocent*	47
5.3	The strip search in *Welcome to New York* (2014)	48
5.4	Franck tries to recognize his hired killers from photos	50
5.5	The man-free utopia of an extended family	50
5.6	The extended family of *Salaud, on t'aime* (2014)	51
5.7	Germain fantasizes that he is in the room described in Claude's story	53
5.8	Martin spies on Gemma	54

Notes on Contributors

Manuel Barberá earned his PhD in Literature (cum laude and with an international mention) at Universitat de València, Spain, in 2020. He works as a post-doctoral researcher at Universidad de Castilla–La Mancha, Spain, where he analyses representations of ageing masculinities in European literatures and cinemas. He is author of *Making the Best of a Bad Job: Representations of Disability, Gender and Old Age in the Novels of Samuel Beckett* (Peter Lang, 2021).

Thomas Britt is Professor of Film and Video Studies at George Mason University, USA, where he teaches ethics and is the head of the screenwriting concentration. He is a recipient of the university's Teaching Excellence Award. He writes about film, television, and music for various publications. His short film screenplays have been selected or awarded by more than 100 film festivals and competitions internationally.

Lisa-Nike Bühring is a research assistant at the University of Applied Sciences Fresenius, Germany, where she lectures in qualitative research and media and cultural studies. Her research focuses on the analysis of the socio-cultural frames of ageing and gender in the West and on gaining a better understanding of how these narratives affect older people and particularly older men. She has contributed to the *Encyclopaedia of Gender, Media and Communication* and is a member of the *Centre for Women, Ageing and Media* (WAM); the *European Network in Ageing Studies* (ENAS); *Ageing + Communication + Technologies* (ACT); the *North American Network of Ageing Studies* (NANAS); and the Gender-Net Plus ERA-Net project "MASCAGE – Gendering Age: Representations of Masculinities and Ageing in Contemporary European Literatures and Cinemas" (2019–2022).

Philip Dine is Personal Professor Emeritus at University of Galway, Ireland. He has been a pioneering figure internationally in the cultural history of French sport and the literary and cinematographic representations of colonial conflict. He has published widely on representations of the French empire and its cultural legacies in fields ranging from children's literature to professional sport. Further projects targeted sport and identity construction in France and the Francophone world. He is the author of *Images of the Algerian War: French Fiction and Film, 1954–1992* (Clarendon Press/OUP, 1994); *French Rugby Football: A Cultural History* (Berg, 2001); and *Sport and Identity in France: Practices, Locations, Representations* (Peter Lang, 2012).

Éamon Ó Cofaigh lectures in French at the University of Galway, Ireland. His research interests include 20th-century French culture, tourism, and recreation, the French and Francophone Chanson, and French cinema. He is author of *A Vehicle for Change: Popular Representations of the Automobile in 20th-century France* (Liverpool University Press, 2022).

Heather Jerónimo is Associate Professor of Spanish at the University of Northern Iowa, USA. She specializes in contemporary Spanish literature and film with an emphasis on non-normative families, ageing studies, and queer theory, often with a transatlantic focus. She has published on these topics in several book chapters and articles in peer-reviewed journals, such as *Letras Femeninas, Bulletin of Spanish Studies, Revista Canadiense de Estudios Hispánicos*, and *Hispanófila*. Her most recent publication was a co-authored article in *Foreign Language Annals* (2021) on the use of Twitter to create an educational community in the Spanish literature classroom.

Michael Kimmel is one of the world's leading experts on men and masculinities. He is Distinguished Professor of Sociology and Gender Studies at Stony Brook University, USA. Among his many books are *Manhood in America* (Free Press, 1996); *Angry White Men* (Nation Books, 2013); *The Politics of Manhood* (Temple University Press, 1984); *The Gendered Society* (Oxford University Press, 2000); and the bestseller *Guyland: The Perilous World Where Boys Become Men* (Harper Perennial, 2009). With funding from the MacArthur Foundation, he founded the Center for the Study of Men and Masculinities at Stony Brook in 2013. A tireless advocate of engaging men to support gender equality, he has lectured at more than 300 colleges, universities, and high schools. He has delivered the International Women's Day annual lecture at the European Parliament, the European Commission, and the Council of Europe, and he has worked with the Ministers for Gender Equality of Norway, Denmark, and Sweden in developing programs for boys and men. He consults widely with corporations, non-governmental organizations, and public sector organizations on gender equity issues. He was recently called "the world's most prominent male feminist" in the *Guardian* newspaper in London.

Phil Powrie is Professor Emeritus of Cinema Studies at the University of Surrey, UK, and former Chair of the British Association for Film, Television and Screen Studies and Chief General Editor of *Studies in French*

Cinema. He is one of the world's leading authorities on French cinema and has published more than 90 articles and book chapters and published 20 books as author or editor, including his most recent monographs *The French Film Musical* and *Music in Contemporary French Cinema: The Crystal-Song* (Palgrave, 2017). Among his notable publications as editor is *The Trouble With Men: Masculinities in European and Hollywood Cinema* (Wallflower Press, 2004).

Michaela Schrage-Früh is Lecturer in German and Comparative Literature at the University of Galway, Ireland. She is the author of *Emerging Identities: Myth, Nation and Gender in the Poetry of Eavan Boland, Nuala Ní Dhomhnaill and Medbh McGuckian* (WVT, 2004) and *Philosophy, Dreaming and the Literary Imagination* (Palgrave Macmillan, 2016). She has published widely on representations of gender and ageing in literature and culture, and is co-editor of five essay collections on the theme, most recently (with Tony Tracy) *Ageing Masculinities in Irish Literature and Visual Culture* (Routledge, 2022). She was part of the Irish research team of the Gender-Net Plus ERA-Net project "MASCAGE – Gendering Age: Representations of Masculinities and Ageing in Contemporary European Literatures and Cinemas" (2019–2022).

Robert Shail is Professor of Film and Director of Research in the Leeds School of Arts at Leeds Beckett University, UK. He is widely published on stardom and masculinity in British cinema including his study of Welsh star/producer Stanley Baker, for which he was awarded an AHRC fellowship. His more recent work has widened his focus to children's cinema and media in the UK.

Timothy Shary has published extensively on ageing representation in cinema. His studies of youth include *Generation Multiplex: The Image of Youth in Contemporary American Cinema* (2002; revised 2014) and *Teen Movies: American Youth on Screen* (2005), and he edited *Youth Culture in Global Cinema* (2007) with Alexandra Seibel. He co-authored *Fade to Gray: Aging in American Cinema* (2016) with Nancy McVittie. He has also edited *Millennial Masculinity: Men in Contemporary American Cinema* (2013) and is the co-editor of *The Films of Amy Heckerling* (2016) and *The Films of John Hughes* (2021), both with Frances Smith. He authored a volume on the film *Boyhood* in 2017, and his next book is an edited collection called *Cinemas of Boyhood: Masculinity, Sexuality, Nationality*. He teaches at Eastern Florida State College, USA.

Michael Stewart is Senior Lecturer in Film and Media at Queen Margaret University, UK. His main areas of research are film genre, film melodrama, and adaptation. He has published on these topics in various journals and books, most recently *Calvary* (2014); in *Studies in European Cinema* (2019); and "Whisky Galore" (2016), with Robert Munro, in *European Film Remakes* (EUP, 2021). He has also edited Melodrama in *Contemporary Film and Television* (Palgrave Macmillan, 2014), and co-edited (with Robert Munro) *Intercultural Screen Adaptation: British and Global Case Studies* (EUP, 2020). He is a peer reviewer for various film, media, and culture journals and is on the editorial board of *Film Criticism*.

Jonathan Stubbs is Professor in the Faculty of Communication at Cyprus International University. His research focuses on historical cinema and the representation of history in film, the cultural and economic relationships between Hollywood and the British film industry, British film policy, and the history of media in Cyprus during the British colonial period. He is the author of *Hollywood and the Invention of England: Projecting the English Past in American Cinema, 1930–2017* (Bloomsbury Academic, 2019) and *Historical Film: A Critical Introduction* (Bloomsbury Academic, 2013). His work has also appeared in various journals, including the *Historical Journal of Film and Television*, *Journal of British Cinema and Television*, and *International Journal of Cultural Policy*.

Matthew Sweney is a teacher, editor, and translator, currently working for the Rector's Office of Palacký University Olomouc, Czech Republic. He was a researcher on the Gender-Net Plus ERA-Net project "MASCAGE: Representations of Masculinities and Ageing in Contemporary European Literatures and Cinemas." Recent publications include Sylva Fischerová's collection *A Church for Smokers: Prague Poems* (Novela Bohemica 2019; as translator) and *Ageing Masculinities, Alzheimer's and Dementia Narratives* (Bloomsbury Academic 2022; as co-editor).

Teet Teinemaa is Lecturer in Film Studies at Tallinn University, Estonia. He received his PhD from the University of Warwick, UK. Teinemaa serves as the co-editor of *Baltic Screen Media Review*, and his articles have appeared in journals such as *Film International, Journal of Aging Studies*, and *Studies of Art and Architecture*. He is the head of the international MA programme Literature, Visual Culture, and Film Studies. His research interests are post-Soviet masculinities, ageing, and nostalgia in Eastern European film. He was part of the Estonian research team of the Gender-Net Plus ERA-Net project "MASCAGE: Representations of Masculinities and Ageing in Contemporary European Literatures and Cinemas."

Tony Tracy is Lecturer in Film and Media Studies and co-founder of the Huston School of Film and Digital Media, University of Galway, Ireland. His research centres on film history and Irish cinema with a particular interest in masculinities. His monograph is *White Cottage, White House: Irish American Masculinities in Classical Hollywood Cinema* (SUNY, 2022). He has authored numerous articles and co-edited a number of collections, including *Ageing Masculinities in Irish Literature and Visual Culture* (co-edited with Michaela Schrage-Früh; Routledge, 2022);

Irish Masculinity and Popular Culture: Tiger Tales (Palgrave Macmillan, 2014); and *John Huston: Essays on a Restless Director* (McFarland, 2010). He is founding editor of the annual Irish film review for *Estudios Irlandeses* (www.estudiosirlandeses.org) and co-author (with Roddy Flynn) of *The Historical Dictionary of Irish Cinema* (Rowman & Littlefield, 2019). He was part of the Irish research team of the Gender-Net Plus ERA-Net project "MASCAGE – Gendering Age: Representations of Masculinities and Ageing in Contemporary European Literatures and Cinemas" (2019–2022).

Esther Zaplana completed her PhD at the International Centre for Music Studies, Newcastle University, UK. Her research covers cultural, feminist, and theoretical approaches to aesthetic questions in musical performance, with emphasis on the female voice and the relationship between the visual and the auditory. As a cultural analyst, she is also interested in filmic and literary representations of gender, including masculinity. She specializes in French feminism and the work of Luce Irigaray, contributing a chapter on feminine musical performance and Irigaray's thinking in *Luce Irigaray: Teaching* (2008), edited by Irigaray herself. Her publications include work on gender and music (*Repercussions*, 2014), ideal masculinity (*Masculinity and Western Musical Practice*, 2009), and feminist literature (*Bulletin of Spanish Studies*, 2005). Currently, she teaches English literature at the University of Castilla–La Mancha, Spain.

1 Introduction
Ageing Masculinities in Contemporary European and Anglophone Cinema

Tony Tracy and Michaela Schrage-Früh

A June 2022 article in the online magazine *The Ringer* offered a variety of statistical and industry perspectives on a phenomenon that has been increasingly obvious to viewers of contemporary film and TV: mainstream (American) screen actors are ageing. Accompanying the piece were images of Kevin Costner, Denzel Washington, Jeff Bridges, Viola Davis (the only woman), Val Kilmer, Ed Harris, and, of course, Tom Cruise, whose 60th birthday coincided with his latest action-packed box-office smash *Top Gun: Maverick* (2022) – a film, the article noted, that also features 50-somethings Cruise, Jennifer Connelly, and Jon Hamm. Noting the trend across a range of films and TV shows, the writers opined that "the era of old actors has no end in sight" (Lindbergh and Arthur, n.p.).

On the face of it, this seems good news, a challenge to the ingrained ageism that Hollywood and popular culture generally have done so much to shape and sustain. Is it a sign, perhaps, that age is (finally) gaining mainstream recognition as an identity category shaped by its cultural constructions and taking its place within the diversity and inclusion agenda? Maybe. While the writers provided evidence that, indeed, the "top stars" are getting older, there may be more prosaic reasons for why this might be the case. Certainly, feminism has had an impact – though arguably not nearly enough – on how cinema and society regard older women. But another is that target audiences – and in particular the "boomer generation" – are also ageing and staying loyal to actors, and indeed genres, they know. With this target audience in mind, Josephine Dolan rightly draws our attention to "the dual meanings of 'silvering' – profit and the signs of ageing" (Dolan 1). With the splintering and fragmentation of media consumption across platforms and devices, younger audiences are also elsewhere (and everywhere) in comparison to earlier mass audiences. At the same time the significance of a medium such as Netflix for older actors, both male and female, seeking to carve out a space for sustained and diverse representations of later life cannot be underestimated. Successful recent Netflix shows such as *Grace and Frankie* (2015–2022), starring Jane Fonda (b. 1937) alongside Lily Tomlin (b. 1939), and *The Kominsky Method* (2018–2021) starring Michael Douglas (b. 1944) and Alan Arkin (b. 1934), are cases in

DOI: 10.4324/9781003306146-1

point and have reached and enthralled both older and younger audiences. Finally, these older actors, thanks to advances in healthcare, lifestyle, and in some cases cosmetic surgery, are perceived to be in better shape than their predecessors and are thus more palatable to audiences as examples of "successful ageing."[1]

Cinematic representations are instrumental not only in reflecting and exploiting but in constructing and challenging popular images, narratives, and ideologies of ageing. As Julia Twigg and Wendy Martin have noted, studying such representations is crucial not least because the "rise of the visual and virtual . . . has exposed the ways in which age itself is a visual phenomenon, a process whereby older people are caught in and defined by their appearance" (2015, 5). It is thus not surprising that studies of ageing in cinema have gathered apace in recent years, albeit in sporadic and often disparate contexts. The field – as in many other areas of humanities scholarship – nonetheless remains at a relatively early stage, particularly in comparison to scholarship on themes of identity and representation such as gender, race, class, or sexuality. The emergence and development of cultural gerontology has certainly been a central factor in developing the field in recent years but so too has been the ageing of the post-war "boomer generation" as both cinema stars and audiences. The implications of such demographic shifts have most frequently been explored regarding their effect on women, whose cultural and social value is still often conflated with their youthful outward appearance (Sontag 1972; Woodward 1999; Swinnen and Stotesbury 2012; Jermyn and Holmes 2015; McGlynn, O'Neill and Schrage-Früh 2017; Liddy 2020). However, recent studies have begun to explore the impact of ageing (or lack thereof) on male actors, the roles and genres they are cast in (or not), and representations of older male characters on screen, though often with an emphasis on Anglophone and Hollywood cinema (Chivers 2011; Gravagne 2013; Shary and McVittie 2016; Bolton and Wright 2016; Dolan 2017).

While the present collection of chapters is indebted to and builds on this pioneering body of work, what sets it apart from previous studies on ageing and film is not just its focus on ageing *masculinities* but also its emphasis on *European* cinemas. In recent years narratives of ageing have gained special pertinence in view of the "greying of Europe," the demographic shift to older populations across European countries. By bringing together chapters on Czech, Estonian, Belgian, French, German, Spanish, Italian, and British cinema – alongside, to a lesser extent, Hollywood productions – we hope to broaden, complement, and enrich the emerging debate on ageing masculinities in film by offering a comparative and European perspective. While the chapters are arranged according to geographic location, they speak to each other across national and geographical boundaries in drawing on and combining the insights from masculinity studies and age studies to provide new perspectives on stardom and ageing; overviews of national cinematic traditions; transnational reappraisals of traditional and recent genres; and case studies of individual actors and/or films in their national contexts.

As the contributions assembled here demonstrate, a European perspective on ageing masculinities can lead to more nuanced insights into the gendered constructions of ageing across national cinemas, including ways in which male actors and the characters they embody can function as signifiers of and metaphors for political and social change or the ways in which these changes are viewed through the prism of such characters' subjective experience. They also demonstrate the ways in which ageing intersects not only with gender but with other markers of identity such as class, race, ethnicity, sexuality, and disability. Many of the chapters in this collection engage with what Margaret M. Gullette has identified as the "master narrative of decline" (1997), which views ageing as "a linear and chronological biological, psychological, and social process of deterioration" (Gravagne 12) and therefore an undesirable one-way street towards frailty, deficiency, dependency, and ultimately death. In doing so they, for instance, explore how and to what effect this narrative of decline is presented, challenged, resisted, or eschewed in cinematic representations of older men and these characters' renegotiations of masculinity as they age. As Aagje Swinnen points out:

> Hegemonic masculinity scripts are connected to physical strength, sexual prowess and power. Contrarily, later life is delineated as the period wherein all these traits are in decline. This puts older men at risk of being "othered," prompting them to resort to strategies to keep ageing at a distance.
>
> (2015, 72–73)

However, many of the case studies provided here paint a more nuanced picture of the myriad forms in which ageing masculinities are imagined and inhabited by actors, filmmakers, and film characters in later life. These range from depictions of ageing as decline to representations of successful ageing to more nuanced portrayals of what Linn Sandberg (2013) calls "affirmative old age," in which both the losses and gains involved in the process of ageing are acknowledged in all their (often contradictory) complexity.

Michael Kimmel has been a foundational figure and scholarly presence in masculinities studies for over 30 years. In his prefatory comments to this collection he explores the theme of ageing masculinities in relation to three life stages, which he identifies as "Boyhood," "Guyland," and "Elderly." In doing so, he argues that the "project" of masculinity is a relational process rather than a state of being and thus changes over the life course. Using a selection of mainstream films to explore these themes and stages, Kimmel laments the contemporary "one last" tendency of contemporary genre and "geriaction" cinema (Crossley and Fisher 2021) foregrounding ageing male movie stars keen to prove their conception of masculinity one final time. Instead of characters in franchises such as *Taken* or *The Expendables* trying to prove their manhood to the point of parody, Kimmel suggests that an understanding of masculinity as process can allow men to accept and "act their age." Mainstream cinema, as well as other cultural constructions, can play a central role in progressing such work and hence arguably bring forth more varied, relatable, and interesting portrayals of men in their later years.

Reflecting the central importance of the visual in cultural constructions of ageing, the collection begins with a number of chapters dealing with late male stardom across a range of contexts. Returning to a subject he first explored some 20 years ago (Shail 2004), Robert Shail focuses on the indomitable Michael Caine (b. 1933) and considers how the actor's star persona developed over the course of a remarkably prolific late career. Shail examines "Caine as Ageing Rebel" and argues that while Caine has negotiated growing older with agility and a high degree of professional activity that readily embraces his ageing persona, this has stopped short of depicting the perceived deficiencies and detrimental effects of old age, instead encouraging his older audiences to "use the difficulty." His performances can thus be understood as a resistance to rather than genuine engagement with the infirmities of ageing.

Jonathan Stubbs' chapter on "Performance and Ageing in the Very Late Films of John Gielgud" takes up precisely this theme. Focusing on another institution of the British acting establishment, Stubbs pushes beyond the traditional limits of stardom studies in consideration of Gielgud's persona in what gerontologists describe as "deep old age," "frail old age," or "the fourth age" (Gilleard and Higgs 2011; Lloyd 2015), a life stage typically ignored, hidden away, or presented as either "abject" or grotesque in Western societies. Yet, as Stubbs' astute analysis of Gielgud's rare but significant screen performances between 1994 and his death in 2000 at the age of 96 highlights, the actor's performance of bodily frailty in combination with his "enduring vocal prowess" and the British stage acting tradition he represented served to avert "commonplace associations between old age and cognitive decline," as well as with the grotesque. Stubbs' appraisal of Gielgud's late-life performances as a culmination of his long screen acting career provides an important reminder of the need to view old age as part of the life course rather than as an isolated life stage.

The next three chapters offer a sustained engagement with ageing male stardom in a specific national context: France. Phil Powrie has written widely on French cinema and stardom and here turns his attention to the later careers of three stalwarts of the French silver screen – Gerard Depardieu, Johnny Hallyday, and Fabrice Luchini – and their late career portrayals of ageing "losers." His perceptive reading of these actors' personas and recent roles finds a developing wistfulness in which the ageing male's narrative of decline becomes a "nostalgic celebration." Powrie argues that because audiences know these actors and their personas over an extended period of time, their roles and performances in the films under consideration cut both ways; to be sure, an acknowledgement and acceptance of the passage of time but also something "subversive because they valorize age, turning what might seem to be a decline into a virtue." Thus, while on the one hand male ageing is understood in such films in terms of loss – of youth, mind, and voice – on the other we have elements of celebration, what Powrie calls a kind of silver lining to the dark clouds of loss. Encompassing a range of actors and narratives, this chapter demonstrates how cinema can play an important role in reflecting but also (intertextually) inflecting cultural discourses and attitudes towards ageing in a specific national context.

The following two chapters take up themes of Powrie's enquiry and his observation that post-war French cinema's sustained relationship between producers and audiences – through narratives, directors, and especially stars – offers rich territory for considering filmic constructions of ageing. In his chapter, Phil Dine considers Jean Rochefort (1930–2017), whose distinctive acting style and choice of roles would make ageing – his own, as well as that of the assorted characters he brought to life – integral to an ongoing exploration of male identities. In an inspired move, Dine argues that Rochefort be considered as "an ageing text" whose "performances foregrounded the social pretensions and psychological artifices" of French masculinities across eras and contexts. Read in this way, the performer offers a lens for studying how a national cinema operates at the intersection of society's construction and understanding of gender and ageing.

Bringing these themes and arguments into even tighter focus, Éamon Ó Cofaigh explores Claude Lelouch's *Un homme et une femme* (A Man and a Woman) trilogy and traces the on-screen ageing of a single character (Jean-Louis Duroc) and the actor who played him (Jean-Louis Trintignant) across three films and more than half a century: *Un homme et une femme* (1996), *Un homme et une femme: vingt ans déjà* (1986), and *Les plus belles années d'une vie* (1995). While the recurring appearance of a character across multiple film texts is not unique (Francois Truffaut's Antoine Doinel series being perhaps the most celebrated in French cinema), there are few – if any – cases that so consciously foreground themes of masculinity and ageing across such an extended time frame. One benefit of a sustained case study such as this is that it allows Ó Cofaigh to raise and engage with the theme of age transitions, the passage from one phase of the life course to another. Taking his cue from the three decades of post-war French prosperity known as "les trente glorieuses" and the gender ideals fostered under its discourses of speed and modernity, Ó Cofaigh argues that Duroc remains firmly trapped in memories of a "glorious" past.

While French cinema (and its stars) is well known beyond its national borders and has inspired a rich critical literature in English, the same cannot be said of Eastern European film. The next two chapters bring us insights into the post-Soviet cinemas of Estonia and the Czech Republic, respectively, through their analysis of the representations and broader sociological functions of ageing masculinities on screen. Addressing a perceived lacuna in scholarship around masculinities in post-Soviet European cinemas, Teet

Teinemaa focuses on the Estonian film *Rohelised kassid* (Green Cats; 2017), framing it as a male melodrama in which its older central protagonists function to illustrate and illuminate post-Soviet society and the intergenerational tensions it has produced. The film's central characters were imprisoned in Soviet times and are granted an amnesty after over 20 years to find themselves released into European Estonia – an utterly changed world. As revealed in Teinemaa's deft analysis, the film seeks not only to bring into focus these older masculinities – ones closely linked to Soviet-era norms – and contrast them with present-day practices but also to call into question contemporary, neoliberal constructions of how to age "successfully." As such, he argues, *Green Cats* underlines the relationality and socio-cultural dimension of ageing and runs counter to Estonia's official liberal discourse of the primacy of self-reliance.

In a complementary analysis, Matthew Sweney offers a critical overview of ageing masculinities in Czech cinema. Recognizing that film and politics became inseparable in the wake of the Prague Spring of 1968, Sweney focuses on works produced in the aftermath of the so-called Velvet Revolution of 1989 and identifies restitution as a core theme in a representative corpus of films in which "ageing Czech masculinities are not only topical but also central to the films' themes." As Sweney notes, the international success of the Oscar-winning *Kolja* (Kolya; 1996, dir. Jan Svěrák) aside, these films were not produced for international audiences and rely on the viewer's insider knowledge and understanding of socio-cultural and political references. Embedding his overview firmly within this national context, Sweney shows how older film characters often serve as "a kind of shorthand" for political and social changes "which shaped the lives of such men and made them who they are."

Older characters and intergenerational conflict have received heightened attention in recent German-language film productions. Interestingly, comedy seems to be the genre of choice for German and Austrian filmmakers wishing to address the everyday challenges and opportunities of an ageing society through the lens of their characters' individual experiences. Lisa-Nike Bühring analyses two recent commercially successful German mainstream comedies, *We are the New Ones* (2014) and *Granny Nanny* (2020), both of which tackle constructions of ageing masculinity in the context of intergenerational and gender relationships. Her close analysis shows that both films seemingly challenge prevalent stereotypes about older people but ultimately are informed by "reductive and stereotypical understandings of generational differences." These stereotypes, she argues, are shaped by specific post-war German cultural and historical contexts and not only "foster ageism" but ultimately "thwart the possibility for constructive intergenerational relationships."

Michael Stewart's chapter focuses on one of the critically acclaimed and award-winning recent German-Austrian productions, Maren Ade's *Toni Erdmann* (2016). The film's concerns with intergenerational conflict and ageing masculinity are explored through the lens of a strained father-daughter relationship: divorced and recently retired Winfried Conradi (Peter Simonischek) and his career-focused daughter Ines (Sandra Hüller), from whom he is estranged but who he nevertheless decides to visit in Bucharest. Stewart's astute reading of the film in light of theories of the absurd reveals how Winfried's transformation into his alter ego Toni Erdmann constitutes an attempt to challenge and rethink the cultural constructions of ageing masculinity. This, he argues, is done "through a variety of means, including an excessive embodied performance; the affective use of time and space; a certain type of world openness; and the production of embarrassment, discomfort and comedy."

The next section brings together ageing and auteur studies in discussions of recent portraits of ageing masculinities in films by three of southern Europe's most original and daring writers/directors. Framing his discussion within a consideration of constructions of masculinity in the oeuvre of Paolo Sorrentino, Manuel Barberá offers a compelling analysis of how the director explores male ageing in the films *The Great Beauty* (2013) and *Youth* (2015). Old age here, he argues, is presented as a time to look back, to (re-)define and accept oneself, and as a gendered process. He identifies the protagonists' determination to choose desire over horror in old age as central to Sorrentino's artistic message and deeply personal vision. As Barberá concludes, Sorrentino's films can be considered as progress narratives, in which the "grief, sadness, and obsolescence" inherent in the ageing process find an outlet in art and can be overcome through creativity. As such, they are an example of what Margaret M. Gullette refers to as "resistant fictions" (2011, 209).

Heather Jerónimo's chapter approaches one of the most successful of recent cinematic portraits of male ageing – Pedro Almodóvar's *Pain and Glory* (2019) – from a number of critical perspectives including auteur theory, stardom, and most importantly the controversial concept of "successful ageing" (Rowe and Kahn, 1987). As noted by many critics, and indeed the supporting publicity, the film's narrative has clear parallels to the life (and work) of Almodóvar. Jerónimo notes however that while the film is to be celebrated in bringing a queer, disabled representation of ageing to the screen and demonstrates the powerful potential of creativity, Salvador – as alter ego and in the casting of Antonio Banderas – is a character who struggles against being perceived as old, rather than critically investigating and rejecting negative stereotypes of male ageing.

Esther Zaplana's chapter turns to one of European cinema's most enigmatic auteurs, the Catalan director Albert Serra, and his ongoing fascination with older male characters from literature and history. Such figures – Don Quixote, Louis XIV, Casanova – occupy quasi-mythical importance in European (particularly southern) cultures and reveal how understandings and attitudes to ageing masculinities are shaped but also haunted by representations over hundreds of years. Zaplana here explores Serra's 2013 film

Story of My Death, which tracks the final days of the infamous 18th-century Italian writer, adventurer, and lover Giacomo Casanova (1727–1803); the title is a fictional extension to Casanova's famous 12-volume autobiography *Story of My Life*. Describing it as an "anti-period" film that re-utilizes the clichés of dark romanticism and the Gothic sublime in a postmodern context, Zaplana identifies an "ugly" aesthetics at work in the film's portrayal of Casanova in old age in which he encounters a mythical version of Count Dracula. Recognizing the film's grounding in avant-garde traditions, Zaplana sees Serra's often confrontational portrait of male old age as subverting conventional, hegemonic thinking about ageing and masculinities in ways meant to shock and challenge.

The final three chapters focus on trends in recent Anglophone cinemas. As mentioned, in recent years Hollywood has attracted a good deal of critical attention for its engagement with ageing masculinities with a growing literature, focusing particularly on specific actors and genres (Crossley and Fisher 2021; Donner 2016; Gates 2010). Thomas Britt's chapter traces the development of cinematic narratives of retribution that foreground ageing masculinities in characters that resist the narrative of decline. Tracing a generic line from the post-war Hollywood cowboy – especially John Ford's *The Searchers* (1956) – through the *Death Wish* and *Taken* franchises to contemporary examples from three national contexts (Belgium, Ireland, the United States), Britt argues that the trope of retribution in which gnarly experience and a knowledge of violence combine has a long, transnational history that evolves and persists across cultural and production contexts. As Britt argues, contemporary action thrillers thus provide

> a space for ageing male actors and characters in both national and international cinema to return to and re-work themes of the post-classical Western model, and in so doing assert a model of masculinity that has, in many respects, become otherwise outmoded.

Timothy Shary turns to the recent developments in "de-ageing" in Hollywood cinema to argue that for all the visibility of ageing male stars, they may be the last. Despite the presence of ageing men in American business and politics and the ongoing careers of a handful of "boomer" actors discussed at the beginning of this chapter, he contends that there are precious few men over 60 in American cinema today. For Shary, this is not only because Hollywood tends to ignore the interests of older audiences but also because it continues to promote the idea that "young lives are the most worthwhile, the most fulfilling, and even the most common."

In the final chapter Tony Tracy identifies a shift away from an earlier phase in mainstream representations of dementia – which foregrounded carers, exceptional individuals and a "neuro-normative gaze" – to more recent films that focus on ageing male characters. Identifying an intertextual resonance with recent productions of Shakespeare's *King Lear* in these narratives of ageing and widowed fathers, Tracy reads these films as contemporary expressions of attitudes and anxieties around dementia. They also however, to varying degrees, use dementia to comment on ageing white masculinity in the #MeToo era. While there is a danger in such portraits that dementia can too easily become reduced to the level of metaphor, there emerges nonetheless across all the films a palpable and topical anxiety around questions of care and the capacities of adult children to look after ageing parents in distant settings.

Aagje Swinnen has noted that film does "cultural work" in negotiating "the often-contradictory meanings of ageing and later life that shape our specific historical moment" (Swinnen 2015, 74). This collection builds on and contributes to the growing scholarship in cultural gerontology and film studies that explores how ageing manhood is imagined in contemporary cinema. While "ageism" has been a touchstone and central concern of the former approach (Butler, 1969),[2] as the chapters gathered here attest, this is but one way to approach the how and why of older characters. A focus on gender reveals how masculinities themselves are not only constructed within specific socio-historical contexts but how ideas of what is normative (such as assumptions of hegemonic masculinity) may change with both age and time. This is especially visible in the discussions of post-war and post-Soviet European contexts where, as a number of the authors show, representations often reveal intergenerational shifts in gender and ideological values and are frequently mobilized as a means of understanding (and questioning) such transformations. Ageing masculinities offer a particularly valuable lens through which such shifts can be traced and contextualized in national contexts, whether in thematically explicit ways (the "I'm too old for this" trope of genre cinema, for instance) or more implicitly in the ageing of individual actors and the intertextuality of their roles across a career. Whether approached as portraits of individuals, in terms of socio-historical contexts or within frameworks of film theory and history (genre, stardom, audiences), we propose that such representations offer much scope for future research.

Notes

1 The term "successful ageing" was coined by Rowe and Kahn (1997) to indicate psychological, physical, and social wellbeing and functioning in later life. It is now often used interchangeably with terms such as "positive ageing" or "ageing well."
2 In his 1969 article, Butler defined "age-ism" as reflecting "a deep-seated uneasiness on the part of the young and middle-aged – a personal revulsion to and distaste for growing old, disease, disability; and fear of powerlessness, 'uselessness,' and death" (Butler 1969, 243).

Works Cited

Bolton, Lucy, and Julie Lobalzo Wright. *Lasting Screen Stars: Images that Fade and Personas that Endure*. Palgrave Macmillan, 2016.

Butler, Robert. "Age-Ism: Another Form of Bigotry." *The Gerontologist* 9.4 (1969): 243–246.

Chivers, Sally. *The Silvering Screen: Old Age and Disability in Cinema*. U Toronto P, 2011.

Crossley, Laura, and Austin Fisher. "Geriaction Cinema: Introduction." *Journal of Popular Film and Television* 49.3 (2021): 130–135.

Dolan, Josephine. *Contemporary Cinema and 'Old Age': Gender and the Silvering of Stardom*. Palgrave Macmillan, 2017.

Donner, Glen. "Narratives of Cultural and Professional Redundancy: Ageing Action Stardom and the 'Geri-action' Film." *Communication, Politics & Culture* 49.1 (2016): 1–18.

Gates, Philippa. "Acting His Age? The Resurrection of the 80s Action Heroes and their Ageing Stars." *Quarterly Review of Film and Video* 27.4 (2010): 276–289.

Gilleard, Chris, and Paul Higgs. "Ageing Abjection and embodiment in the Fourth Age." *Journal of Aging Studies* 25.2 (2011): 135–142.

Gravagne, Pamela H. *The Becoming of Age: Cinematic Visions of Mind, Body and Identity in Later Life*. McFarland, 2013.

Gullette, Margaret Morganroth. *Declining to Decline: Cultural Combat and the Politics of the Midlife*. U Virginia P, 1997.

Gullette, Margaret Morganroth. *Agewise: Fighting the New Ageism in America*. U Chicago P, 2011.

Jermyn, Deborah, and Susan Holmes, eds. *Women, Celebrity and Cultures of Ageing: Freeze Frame*. Palgrave Macmillan, 2015.

Liddy, Susan, ed. *Women in the International Film Industry: Policy, Practice and Power*. Springer, 2020.

Lindbergh, Ben, and Rob Arthur. "The Golden Age of the Aging Actor." *The Ringer*, 27 June 2022. www.theringer.com/movies/2022/6/27/23181232/old-actors-aging-tom-cruise-top-gun-maverick

Lloyd, Liz. "The Fourth Age." *Routledge Handbook of Cultural Gerontology*. Ed. Julia Twigg and Wendy Martin. Routledge, 2015. 261–268.

McGlynn, Cathy, Margaret O'Neill, and Michaela Schrage-Früh, eds. *Ageing Women in Literature and Visual Culture: Reflections, Refractions, Reimaginings*. Palgrave Macmillan, 2017.

Rowe, J. W., and R. L. Kahn. "Successful Aging." *The Gerontologist*, 37.4 (1997): 433–440. https://doi.org/10.1093/geront/37.4.433

Sandberg, Lynn. "Affirmative Old Age – The Ageing Body and Feminist Theories on Difference." *International Journal of Ageing and Later Life* 8.1 (2013): 11–40. https://journal.ep.liu.se/IJAL/article/view/1237

Shail, Robert. "Masculinity and Class: Michael Caine as Working-Class Hero." *The Trouble with Men: Masculinities in European and Hollywood Cinema*. Eds. Phil Powrie, Ann Davies, and Bruce Babington. Wallflower, 2004.

Shary, Timothy, and Nancy McVittie: *Fade to Gray: Aging in American Cinema*. UT Press, 2016.

Sontag, Susan. "The Double Standard of Aging." *The Saturday Review*, 23 Sept. 1972: 29–38.

Swinnen, Aagje. "Ageing in Film." *The Routledge Handbook of Cultural Gerontology*. Eds. Julia Twigg and Wendy Martin. Routledge, 2015. 69–76.

Swinnen, Aagje, and John A. Stotesbury, eds. *Aging, Performance, and Stardom: Doing Age on the Stage of Consumerist Culture*. LIT, 2012.

Woodward, Kathleen M. *Figuring Age: Women, Bodies, Generations*. Indiana UP, 1999.

2 The Ageing of Men on Film
Concepts and Perspectives

Michael Kimmel

Let's start with a story, archetypal and familiar. In Sophocles' great play *Oedipus Rex*, Oedipus must answer the riddle posed to him by the Sphinx:

> What goes on four feet in the morning, two feet at noon, and three feet in the evening?

Oedipus is the first to get it right: "A man," he says, thus becoming King and also, not incidentally, ending the plague that was decimating the population of Thebes. As an infant, a man crawls on all four feet. An adult man walks on two feet. And an older man needs a cane to walk, thus three "feet."

It would be both a conceptual and a political mistake to fail to listen to the Sphinx on this question.

To be sure, it's natural to hear a phrase like "ageing masculinities" and immediately think of older men. After all, who thinks about ageing but the old? If, as the saying goes, "youth is wasted on the young," then thinking about ageing is often the domain of the old.

To steer us back towards Oedipus's answer, though, I'd like to offer a few orienting concepts to help organize any inquiry into ageing masculinities. I'll illustrate these concepts by referring to some recent films.

In essence, I offer these framing concepts to potentially guide our inquiries:

(1) ageing is a process, not a state of being;
(2) ageing masculinities are relational (to other men, to women);
(3) the "project" of masculinity changes over the life course;
(4) masculinity often needs to be "redeemed" in those relationships.

1. Ageing as a process. There is a difference between what we might call "aged" masculinities and "ageing" masculinities. To be "aged" is to occupy a seemingly fixed stage, and cinematically that means images of older men whose identifying characteristic is, in fact, their age. "Ageing," by contrast, refers to a process, and is thus illustrated by images of men and boys at different moments of the life cycle. In that sense,

DOI: 10.4324/9781003306146-2

a man of any age can be studied within the framework of "ageing masculinities."
2. Masculinities are relational. If masculinity is relational, then to what is it related? Other men? Women? Older men? Younger men? Media images? Stereotypes?

   It is, by now, axiomatic in gender studies that gender does not arise in a vacuum, but rather we define gendered identities in relation to others – to other men, to women. And the salience of both of those references varies across the life course. To the boy, for example, masculinity is defined largely through interaction with other boys. It is other boys who teach boys what it means to be a man, often through gender policing.
3. Masculinity changes over the life course. As with ageing, masculinity is not a state of being but a social process. What it means to be a man will vary over the course of a life: what it means at age 20 will be different from what it might mean at age 40, which is again different from what it might mean at age 80. To speak of "ageing masculinities" is to remain attentive to these shifts.
4. The circumstances may change, but the project of masculinity is often a project of redemption. This begs the question: Why do men need to be redeemed in the first place? And who is capable of doing the redeeming?

Let's use the riddle of the Sphinx to illustrate these points. I'll look at ageing masculinities at three life stages and point out some of the relational aspects of each stage. I'll point to one film that illustrates the relational aspects of ageing masculinities.

Boyhood: Boys With Boys

Boyhood is often imagined as a homosocially pure moment, a moment when relations with other boys are paramount, before puberty, before preoccupation with girls and sex "corrupt" the relations among boys. True boyhood – "deep boyhood" we might say – is redemptive: we must return to it.

Take, for example, the 1986 film *Stand by Me*. Here are four sixth-grade boys off for their last summer adventure, that last weekend before school begins. That means it is the last summer before middle school, before puberty, before adolescence, before girls. It is the last gasp of homosocial purity and innocence.

In the very last scene of the film, the narrator, the adult male narrator, now a father himself, writes the last lines of his memoir. "I never had any friends later on like the ones I had when I was twelve. Jesus, does anyone?"

Of course, there are many examples of a mirror image of this homosocial purity. Indeed, if boyhood is not the domain of homosocial innocence, then it is a Hobbesian horror, the war of each against all, as in *Lord of the Flies* (1990), where a group of English schoolboys, stranded by themselves with no rules or any adults to keep them in line, can only bond through torture and intimidation.

What prevents that homosocial innocence from disintegrating, or, perhaps better stated, what transforms that homosocial heaven into that Hobbesian hell, is hierarchy. Once the boys discover inequality, using whatever factor they can use – race, class, body size, strength, sexuality – the pure bonds of boyhood dissolve, and the more ephemeral pleasures of domination take its place.

Guyland: Young Men With Other Young Men and With Women

Hierarchy is the core principle of gender policing, at once validating one's actions and problematizing the actions of others. Where cooperation was, now competition resides. With puberty comes the possibility of sexuality, and when girls enter the picture, the relations among boys are again transformed. The bonds of the brothers may be broken or at least strained; relations among men become competitive, impure.

In some cases, the dominance bonding of the *Lord of the Flies* becomes the dominant model. Homophobia is the currency of bullying, adolescent violence, hierarchy. Even at best, left to themselves, adolescents and young men will be immature, sexually feckless slackers.

Take, for example, the 2007 film *Knocked Up*. Here, a group of postpubescent slackers spend their days smoking weed, loafing, and fantasizing about creating clever pornographic websites they can monetize.

Just who are these guys who wear their pajamas all day, play video games, and think that cold, day-old pizza is haute cuisine? Clearly, this version of "ageing masculinities" cries out for redemption. But who can redeem these young male slackers?

Previous generations may have had solutions, but they may no longer work for contemporary men. Once upon a time in America, the hero would redeem himself, entirely by himself. Like Ulysses, or any of the heroes of Joseph Campbell's recitation, the hero rides off into the sunset, in search of another adventure that will test his manhood again, each time against other men.

Well, that myth may continue to hold resonance for some, but it is increasingly clear that modern men can't do it alone. Most young people have never even heard of John Wayne, let alone sought to emulate him.

If the hero's journey is less appealing as a form of redemption, perhaps they can embrace a more Freudian model, and see women as a civilizing force. After all, women represent family and domesticity. But in *Guyland* (cf. Kimmel 2008), that same civilizing force is seen not as civilizing but as constraining. There is a world of difference between domesticity and domestication, the latter tethering men to home, sexual boredom, and the negation of freedom.

Even in *Knocked Up* it is not the mature romance between the woman and man that will eventually transform Seth Rogan into a "good man."

And since domestication emasculates men, it becomes difficult for men to turn to their fathers for mentorship and advice. The poet Robert Bly writes that with the collapse of hierarchical relations that characterize traditional societies, patriarchy is no longer a source of order and coherence. Instead, he argues that we have become a "sibling society," in which everyone is equal. (He believes this is a bad thing, and that the traditional rule of the fathers needs to be restored. I do not share his prescription.)

Take perhaps the most telling archetype of that story of the emasculation of the fathers. In *Rebel Without a Cause* (1955), James Dean is anguished and confused, and goes home to seek his father's advice. His father is washing the dishes, wearing an apron, the epitome of emasculation. Obviously, fathers cannot be relied upon for masculine redemption.

So what is the answer? Boys! Boys can redeem fallen manhood. By their innocence and homosocial purity, boys are the new saviors of masculinity. (This purity and innocence can be so easily perverted into the motivation of pedophile priests who may seek to purify their impurities through the innocence of the boy.) Boys enable adult men to return to that pristine purity, before they themselves were corrupted. The boy is father to the man.

Think of what a common theme this has become from the 1979 touchstone text of *Kramer vs. Kramer* to the 1997 confection *Liar, Liar* to the more recent (and quite hilarious) 2008 film *Role Models*, in which two ageing slacker-reprobates are assigned as "bigs" (big brother, mentors) to two troubled boys who, in their turn, become the role models that enable all to achieve a more authentic manhood.

Elderly Masculinities

Everyone knows that passage in 1 Corinthians 13:11: "When I was a child I spoke as a child, I understood as a child, I thought as a child; but when I became a man, I put away childish things."

Seriously? I think the problem is that no matter the stage of life, no matter the "project" of our age, we never completely put away those childish things. We still seek validation of our masculinity from other men, still assemble and disassemble hierarchies, using the same currencies of homophobia, racism, and sexism. What could be more "childish," after all, than seeking that validation of our masculinity in the first place? At what point do men finally get to give it a rest?

In several recent films, the answer is "after one more." One more bank heist. One more dangerous adventure. One more sexual fling. One more test. If ageing is a process of progressive emasculation – also of vigor, strength, sexual potency – how many films depict ageing stars, once the rugged heroes of our youthful fantasies, now refusing to "go gentle into that good night" but rather gathering together for one last hurrah, one last adventure, one last time you settle your ageing body on an oversized motorcycle, trade in the minivan for a muscle car, and head out for one more rodeo before that "last roundup"?

The past decade – and the coming one – will provide a never-ending series of films depicting ageing male stars forming that last posse, a forced reunion, the over-the-hill gang of yesteryear. And what could be more parodic, and thus more poignant, than the series *The Expendables*, whose first three iterations (2010, 2012, 2014) gathered a virtual who's who of ageing male action stars into one film for that masculinity's last stand.

Just look who's in the house: Banderas, Ford, Gibson, Stallone, Lundgren, Statham, Schwarzenegger, Snipes, Willis, Chan, Rourke.

Expendables 4 was released in 2022. The film drops the Roman numerals for Arabic numbers, but adds Jackie Chan, Lou Ferrigno, Steven Seagal, Hulk Hogan, Chuck Norris, Liam Neeson, Pierce Brosnan, Tom Hardy, Hugh Jackman, Vin Diesel, Daniel Craig, John Travolta, Danny Trejo, Denzel Washington, and even Clint Eastwood!

It's as if any male actor over 60 who has ever done one of their own stunts is in the film, suddenly returned for a veritable fraternity reunion of male action heroes of the last half century, all decked out in black leather. If history repeats itself, the first time as tragedy and the second time as farce, by the fourth installment we're in the realm of a parody so desperate that it will make us wince.

Perhaps there is another route to masculine redemption for ageing men. Perhaps it's been sitting there all this time and we just didn't know it. It's called "acting your age."

Take, for one last example, *Something's Gotta Give*, a 2003 rom-com starring Jack Nicholson, Amanda Peet, and Diane Keaton. In the film, Harry (Nicholson) is dating a woman (Peet) more than 30 years his junior – as in, old enough to be his daughter – when a pre-sex heart attack forces him to confront his mortality. And, in true rom-com fashion, he falls for his girlfriend's mother (Keaton), and they, we are led to believe, will live happily ever after – at least for the years they have left.

After decades as the leading male reprobate, Nicholson "succumbs" to his mortality by finally growing up, seeking happiness not in asymmetrical conquest but in egalitarian partnership. Gone, finally, is the hierarchy – between women and men, among men – that men believed would enable them to feel like real men but instead traps them in an endless cycle of proving manhood at every turn.

From the time men exit from boyhood, they are required to prove their masculinity. Finally, as they accept their age, they can exhale, their mission accomplished, their manhood no longer a question, and thus no longer a quest.

Filmography

The Expendables 1. Dir. Sylvester Stallone. 2010.
The Expendables 2. Dir. Simon West. 2012.
The Expendables 3. Dir. Patrick Hughes. 2014.
The Expendables 4. Dir. Scott Waugh. 2022.
Knocked Up. Dir. Judd Apatow. Universal Pictures, 2007.
Kramer vs. Kramer. Dir. Robert Benton. Columbia Pictures, 1979.
Liar, Liar. Dir. Tom Shadyac. Universal Pictures, 1997.
Lord of the Flies. Dir. Harry Hook. Columbia Pictures, 1990.
Rebel Without a Cause. Dir. Nicholas Ray. Warner Bros., 1955.
Role Models. Dir. David Wain. Universal Pictures, 2008.
Something's Gotta Give. Dir. Nancy Meyeres. Warner Bros. Pictures, Columbia Pictures, 2003.
Stand by Me. Dir. Rob Reiner. Columbia Pictures, 1986.

Works Cited

Bly, Robert. *The Sibling Society: An Impassioned Call for the Rediscovery of Adulthood*. Vintage, 1997.

Kimmel, Michael. *Guyland: The Perilous World Where Boys Become Men*. Harper, 2008.

Sophocles. *The Three Theban Plays: Antigone, Oedipus the King, Oedipus at Colonus*. Penguin Classic, 1984.

3 "Using the Difficulty"
Michael Caine as Ageing Rebel

Robert Shail

Introduction

In the autumn of 2021 various international media outlets loudly announced the retirement of veteran actor and film star, Michael Caine. The *Daily Express*, for example, quoted him as saying "I can't walk very well," in reference to an ongoing spinal problem, and went on to report that he had not had the offer of a film role in over two years (Simpson). However, these reports of his impending retirement proved something of an exaggeration as indicated by an interview he gave for BBC Radio 5 Live (which turned out to be the original source for much of the subsequent media speculation), when he said that although his latest film release was likely to be his last, he intended to continue working, albeit writing books (Griffin). He subsequently tweeted: "I haven't retired and not a lot of people know that" (16 October 2021) and distanced himself still further from the reports by telling *Variety*: "regarding retirement, I've spent over 50 years getting up at 6 a.m. to make movies and I'm not getting rid of my alarm clock" (Hailu). Apart from indicating the remarkable amount of media excitement that can be generated by a popular British actor in his late eighties, these celebrity news stories also point to underlying discourses around issues of ageing and the desire to define, celebrate, or even denigrate a public person on the basis of their age. Not only does this coverage prove that the request received by this author some years ago to contribute to a press obituary of Caine was considerably premature, but it also offers an opportunity to consider Caine's late career as a distinctive – perhaps unique – case study in British male stardom.

I first wrote about Michael Caine in 2004 in an essay called "Masculinity and Class: Michael Caine as 'Working-Class Hero,'" which appeared in the edited collection *The Trouble With Men: Masculinities in European and Hollywood Cinema* (Powrie, Babbington and Davies). The collection broadly adopted an analytical approach which foregrounded the reading of stars, and of gender identity, within defined socio-cultural contexts, as well as in relation to prevalent production trends in cinema. Much of the work in the collection inevitably drew on Richard Dyer's landmark study,

DOI: 10.4324/9781003306146-3

Stars (first published 1979), where social typologies are employed to make culturally specific readings of the representational functions of individual stars (Dyer). In my essay I charted the rise of Caine during the 1960s and early 1970s. In this period, he established himself firstly as a star in the UK and then gradually in America through a series of critical and box office successes. Key films in this development of his career and persona are: *Zulu* (Cy Endfield, 1964), *Alfie* (Lewis Gilbert, 1966), *The Ipcress File* (Sidney J. Furie, 1966), *The Italian Job* (Peter Collinson, 1968), and *Get Carter* (Mike Hodges, 1971). Caine's star persona was, perhaps, most associated by the public with *Alfie*; the advertising campaign suggested that Caine *is* Alfie. In the film he plays a working-class lothario on the make in Swinging London. In Dyer's terms, Caine's persona in this period can be seen as fitting with the "Rebel," one of two anomic star types he identifies, alongside the "Independent Woman." These types embody disquiet, or even resistance, to the dominant social values of their time and location (Dyer 47–52). Dyer contrasts them with the "Good Joe," "Tough Guy," and "Pin-up" who uphold and reinforce dominant values.

In the context of the 1960s in Britain, class was frequently central to the representation of the rebel as the period was marked by an explosion of working-class talent right across the arts; Caine often played heavily in interviews on his childhood background as the son of a porter at Billingsgate Fish Market and a char lady, exhibiting a proudly proletarian bravado that was then expressed through his roles of the period. As Bruce Babbington suggests, with particular reference to Michael Caine: "There is also a sense in which, whatever he, or other stars, mean in the larger cinema, they signify more complexly in relation to their original environment" (Babington 22). To be publicly identified as working-class was to be seen as part of a process of change that had started with the angry young men of the late 1950s, an act of rebellion against the perceived middle-class complacency of the established British film industry and of the older generation: "the acceptance, and indeed success, of so defiantly proletarian a star indicates the kind of social changes that had taken place in Britain in the 1960s" (Shail 68).

During the 1970s and 1980s Caine based himself in America and established his status as a Hollywood leading man and international star with major commercial and critical successes like *The Man Who Would Be King* (John Huston, 1975), *Dressed to Kill* (Brian DePalma, 1980), and *Hannah and Her Sisters* (Woody Allen, 1986) before following a familiar path for male stars as they enter middle age with a shift into supporting "character" roles. This development provides the first critical lens through which to consider Caine's persona as an older man, akin to the tribal elder type as defined by Andrew Spicer but also highly distinctive. A second analytical framework draws on the field of cultural gerontology in order to consider the impact of the extended life span on Caine's public and film persona, particularly in light of dominant concepts of active ageing. The final section of the chapter continues in this vein, drawing on what many cultural gerontologists have described as a final stage of the life cycle associated with infirmity and abjection – all the more appropriate as recent press reports about Caine have dwelt on his use of a walking stick. Here the analysis will explore how Caine's late-life film persona has conformed to a wider cultural resistance to reflecting the uncomfortable realities and challenges of the ageing process, preferring instead a heroic image of age resistance. Throughout, we follow the way in which Caine's career and screen persona can be seen as ciphers for dominant discourses of male ageing in Western – particularly Anglophone – societies.

Caine as "Tribal Elder"

Michael Caine's transition from leading man to more character-centred and supporting roles began towards the end of the 1990s, at a time when he was already well into his sixties. Three releases in consecutive years mark this change: *Little Voice* (Mark Herman, 1998), *The Cider House Rules* (Lasse Hallstrom, 1999), and *Miss Congeniality* (Donald Petrie, 2000). Following a well-established path for male stars, these roles tend to occupy less screen time than Caine was previously able to command, typically provide moral and emotional support to a more central character in the narrative, and attract a lower billing in the film's promotional materials and credits. Andrew Spicer's essay, "Sean Connery: Loosening His Bonds," charts a comparable trajectory through the later career of the former James Bond. Connery was three years older than Caine and hailed from a comparative working-class background, albeit in Scotland. Spicer sees him entering into this phase of his career in the late 1980s, as he was approaching 60, with two key films: *The Untouchables* (Brian DePalma, 1987) and *Indiana Jones and the Last Crusade* (Steven Spielberg, 1989). In the first, Connery has second billing to the emergent Hollywood star Kevin Costner, and plays an older police officer who acts as a moral counsellor and father figure to the younger detective, drawing on years of hard-won experience and street knowledge to impart wisdom and provide guidance. This proves invaluable, even if it costs the life of the older man, in securing victory over the villainous Al Capone (Robert DeNiro). In the third instalment of the Indiana Jones franchise, Connery plays Indiana's father, and much humour is derived from revelations regarding his prowess, even to the extent of having had an earlier physical relationship with the film's leading female character, Elsa Schneider (Alison Doody), who is now involved with Indiana (Harrison Ford) himself. His son is somewhat astounded to discover that there is life in the old man yet. Despite lifelong resentments towards his father, he ends up appreciating his masculine – and thus paternal – qualities.

For Spicer, the tribal elder persona "gains cumulative force from each new embodiment" (Spicer 227) as it is developed across a succession of films, creating a character that is as recognizable for audiences of the period as Connery's James Bond had been in the 1960s. These older men make room for a younger hero to carry the main narrative action of the film, and usually the romantic aspects as well, but offer the benefits of knowledge that can only be won with the experience of age. In addition, the later persona consistently reminds audiences of the earlier one. For Connery, this means drawing on his established reputation for independence, irascibility, and Celtic non-conformism, as well as for physicality and an authority based on a clear code of integrity. Caine similarly reevokes qualities from his earlier work in his characterizations of late middle age, although these often differ from Connery, particularly in relation to an acknowledgement of character frailties. In Spicer's analysis, leading roles belong to younger actors who are able to embody a highly physical version of masculinity identified with action and romantic love; with age, the need for these qualities is perceived to fade and therefore cannot be embodied in the older star who instead becomes the tribal elder, leaving behind physicality for a more cerebral function. At the same time, this reflects the received wisdom of the film industry that prefers to invest in a public identification with youth, acknowledging the demographic of their global audience.

Perhaps the first role in which Caine's version of the tribal elder begins to appear is *Little Voice*, directed by Mark Herman and based on the popular 1992 stage play "The Rise and Fall of Little Voice" by Jim Cartwright. The film stars Jane Horrocks as the gifted Laura Toffs, whose talents as singer and performer are stifled by her own shyness and an overbearing mother, played by Brenda Blethyn. She finds herself managed by the seedy and largely unsuccessful promotor, Ray Say, played with disreputable oiliness by Caine. Although Caine is clearly ranked third in terms of the narrative importance of each character, his star status at this stage was still considerably higher than his two female co-stars, who were mainly known only to UK audiences, and consequently he has top billing on the main poster used for the publicity campaign. The role itself evokes memories of the crafty double-dealing of Alfie, with Ray always on the lookout for a quick win. In a way, he is another working-class man dreaming of a better life. The sense of melancholy and self-doubt that marks the climax of *Alfie* is intensified here by age. Ray is certainly a father figure in his attempts to coax Laura to success, but he is also burdened with a lingering sense of failure – rather like Alfie but more so, his working-class ambition having led to little. Caine is given one barnstorming scene in which he performs the song "It's Over" to a deeply unappreciative nightclub audience. The performance is marked by a combination of pathos and defiance, but the passing of time seems to have made the act of rebellion against Britain's class system more pyrrhic than it is effective. The interpretation of tribal elder offered by Caine here also differs distinctly from the marked heroism of Connery in its more open acknowledgement of weaknesses and failings.

For *Miss Congeniality* Caine has obvious second billing to the film's star and producer, Sandra Bullock, both in the credits and the advertising campaign and in the film's narrative. She plays an FBI agent who is working undercover at a beauty pageant, with Caine in a relatively small role as Victor Melling, her coach for the event. Initially aggrieved by the triviality of the whole proceeding, she gradually comes at least to see the value of the older man's knowledge and experience, even if the relationship is played largely for comic effect. Whatever the shallow nature of the world of beauty pageants, the skills which have been honed by Melling from life experience are to be acknowledged. Here Caine is demonstrably the "tribal elder" by dispensing wisdom and life lessons to the apprentice.

A more complex representation of the type is to be found in *The Cider House Rules*, adapted from John Irving's novel and directed by Lasse Hallström. Public recognition of Caine's new star status and persona was confirmed by his second Academy Award as Best Supporting Actor for his role as Dr Wilbur Larch. However, in the film's billing he is ranked fifth behind Tobey Maguire (the male lead), Charlize Theron (female lead), Delroy Lindon, and Paul Rudd. Nonetheless Caine's character is the dominant figure in the narrative for the opening 30 minutes of the film before retreating into a supporting role, as Tobey Maguire's Homer Wells carries the narrative action and the central romantic interest. Homer grows up in a benevolent orphanage run by Dr Larch and, on reaching adulthood, finds himself still at the institution where he is in the process of becoming Larch's assistant and heir apparent. Throughout the opening section of the film Caine's role conforms to the tribal elder type, as he is shown to be wise, drawing on a lifetime of experience to offer guidance to the younger man and to everyone else at the orphanage. However, the film gradually complicates this role. Homer and Larch clash over the illegal abortions which the doctor performs, with Homer unwilling to assist. Larch himself is shown to be a conflicted character, retreating from the strains of his role through an addiction to ether which will eventually take his life. Homer decides to leave the orphanage in a rebellion against his surrogate father and makes his own way in the world, much to Larch's disappointment and irritation. Again, differences are evident here from Connery's embodiment of the tribal elder in that Caine's persona admits more in the way of character frailties and imperfections. Nonetheless, for all these complications, the narrative finally returns Caine/Larch to his rightful position, even if this is in death. In the end he is proved right in the ethical position he has taken. Homer finally returns home and takes up his predestined role as head of the orphanage as Larch/Caine always knew he would. This forms the final uplift of the narrative circle and confirms the value of the paternal role model.

Probably the most impactful example of this transitional stage in Caine's career in both commercial and audience terms is the role of Alfred, unflappable butler and assistant to Bruce Wayne/Batman in Christopher Nolan's trilogy of Batman films: *Batman Begins* (2005), *The Dark Knight* (2008), and *The Dark Knight Rises* (2012). Alfred is much more than just an avuncular, ageing servant (previous versions tend to use him as a largely comic figure): he proves equally adept as strategist both for Batman's heroic exploits and

Wayne's personal life. He can handle himself in almost any social context and always provides thoughtful advice. In virtually every interaction with Bruce Wayne/Batman, Alfred's function is to reflect on the situation and offer a considered opinion. That his views are invariably proven to be correct becomes the subject of a running joke in *The Dark Knight*, delivered with a slightly sardonic wit by Caine that will remind older viewers of the insolence of Harry Palmer in *The Ipcress File* and its sequels. There is also no attempt to suppress Caine's London accent and the role is reminiscent of Charlie Croker in *The Italian Job*, full of keen judgement and an individual moral compass, even if the actor is no longer performing the action stunts or winning the heroine. The early star persona has been absorbed into the new one but with a different narrative function. If Caine increasingly found himself some way down the credits, his appearances were nonetheless greeted with both affection and admiration in the positive critical response.

These roles indicate Caine's career at this stage of his life as falling closely into line with Spicer's analysis of the tribal elder role, albeit with specific nuances that fit with Caine's established screen persona. The following decade, however, was to take Caine's on-screen persona into less well-established territory.

The Mythologies of Active Ageing

The field of cultural gerontology has been largely concerned with how the biological and physical processes of ageing intersect with wider social aspects of this process, including its cultural representations. This takes gerontology beyond the field of biological sciences and health care into interdisciplinary areas where science connects with the social sciences and humanities. At this intersection, as influential theorist Margaret Morganroth Gullette puts it, "Human beings are aged by culture" (Gullette 12), as well as by physical developments. Although cultural gerontology, in principle, can be concerned with the whole ageing process throughout life, it is reasonable to note that the main area of focus for discussion and debate has been the cultural and social representation created around later life. For Lynne Segal, this has meant that "scholars in the field have sought above all to affirm the diversity, significance, and challenge of old age" (Segal 31). The emphasis has often been on the challenge.

For Higgs and Gilleard, the cultural narrative of ageing in Western societies is rooted in an understanding of worth which is directly related to discourses of economic productivity (Higgs and Gilleard). In this respect, ageing is equated to a decrease in usefulness within a capitalist socio-economic system of value. Older age then becomes culturally equated with no longer working or contributing economically to the wider society but being a probable drain on resources as the need for a financial and health support increases. The narrative is one of decline and loss. For Gullette, this loss is especially associated with becoming less visibly youthful or as Kathleen Woodward puts it: "we are not judged by how old we are, but by how young we are not" (quoted in Twigg 61). Part of this discourse is an association of ageing bodies with failure and unattractiveness. The ageing body itself becomes taboo and stigmatized. Peter Laslett has suggested that the decline narrative can be broken into four distinct stages. The first is characterized by "dependence, socialisation, immaturity and education", while the second is marked by "independence, maturity, responsibility and earning" (Laslett 134–135). The economic sense of usefulness is apparent in these definitions of childhood and young adulthood. In Laslett's essay, the third age is a key area of focus in that it is here that the requirement to work potentially ceases and, in principle, the individual is freed to focus on their own fulfilment. For Higgs and Gilleard, this stage is typified by "the freedom to choose and the freedom to spend money in the pursuit of individual lifestyle goals" (Higgs and Gilleard 153). This positive narrative is particularly associated with the so-called baby boomer generation growing up in the post-war era for whom stars like Caine can be viewed as aspirational role models.

However, a further dimension of this narrative of opportunity and self-fulfilment is its association with continued youthfulness. For Higgs and Gilleard, this means the attempted exclusion of any acknowledgement of the physical effects of ageing, where middle age becomes stretched out into much later life. So-called successful ageing becomes a process whereby personal fulfilment is made possible only by maintaining a youthful lifestyle and sustaining its physical and mental attributes for as long as possible. Ageing itself is seen as an impediment to a successful old age, with a consequent emphasis on a whole range of products and services designed to keep the physical symptoms of old age at bay. The third age is therefore one in which ageing itself is denied. In this narrative, an active lifestyle becomes an imperative for self-fulfilment and inactivity is equated with passive decline. Little allowance is made for differences in experience which can often be traced to economic factors, meaning that although this active ageing lifestyle is not as easily available to all, it still remains the ideal in cultural and media discourses.

The work of Josephine Dolan has been particularly useful in applying the characteristics of the third age, and indeed the fourth (to be discussed later), to discourses of stardom culminating in her key work *Contemporary Cinema and "Old Age": Gender and the Silvering of Stardom* (2017). Her focus has been on the specific impact of the active ageing ethos on female stars where the emphasis on physical attributes, and particularly beauty and desirability, is usually more marked than for their male equivalents. However, her work also points to the universality of a narrative of decline and resistance to it through continued youthfulness, even for male stars.

For Caine, the acknowledgement of this wider context is marked by his appearance in the 2009 crime drama *Harry Brown* (Daniel Barber, 2009).

In some ways the film refers back to his role as the avenging criminal/investigator in *Get Carter* and also links to Don Siegel's controversial American "vigilante cop" film, *Dirty Harry* (1971). This Harry is an elderly Royal Marine veteran now living in a flat on a run-down council estate, where residents are terrorized by violent gangs and drug trafficking. He consoles himself through his friendship with fellow pensioner Len (David Bradley), but his attitude darkens following the murder of Len by gang members and the death alone in hospital of his wife. The failure of the police to take effective action against the gang members prompts Harry into action himself (although the first violent incident is purely in self-defence). There is clear acknowledgement throughout the film of Harry's growing infirmity and lack of mobility, and other challenges of ageing are represented such as bereavement and the increasing isolation and loneliness he suffers. Much of this is handled with Caine's characteristic humour, but other scenes evoke a sense of pathos. However, Harry is nonetheless an extreme embodiment of active ageing. He has all of his mental faculties and remains remarkably agile and forceful. In a key sequence he rescues a young woman from a violent assault before burning down a drug den and despatching a number of gang members. Despite being hospitalized by an attack of emphysema, Harry discharges himself and then plays a central role in the final destruction of the drug gang in the midst of a near apocalyptic riot on the estate. There can be few more extreme images of the triumph of successful ageing than Harry dragging himself out of hospital into the middle of the violent conflagration where his actions will bring comparative peace to the area.

The final images of *Harry Brown* depict the now recovered Harry stalking the quiet estate, his presence seemingly enough to keep order; the review in *The Times* described Harry as "a superannuated killing machine" (Maher). Although far from the excesses of Harry, Caine's own memoir, *Blowing the Bloody Doors Off; And Other Lessons in Life* (2018), sees the actor very much adopting the role of both tribal elder and defiant silver star. The book itself is designed as a kind of self-help manual aimed not just at aspiring actors but at anyone facing challenges in life. He offers wisdom based on his own experiences under headings like "learn what you can from life" and "reinvent yourself," but he always strikes a note of defiance against ageing: "I don't regret that I am no longer young. It's a waste of time anyway, I've done being young. I had a great time but now I'm having a great time being old" (Caine 269–270). Far from struggling to find roles, he suggests that he gets as many offers as before and that although he may not get the lead, the characters are actually more interesting:

> every decade has been an improvement on the last and it just keeps getting better. . . . I don't feel I have had a good innings just yet. I feel like I've just stepped up to the crease. Pass me the bat: there's a few more overs in me yet.
>
> (Caine 269–270)

The Final Act

The fourth stage of ageing identified by gerontologists is the most challenging of all, not just in terms of life experience but also in the cultural responses it seems to generate, or even in the failure to generate any fictive representations at all. This stage is frequently described by gerontologists, and the wider society, in terms of infirmity, ill health, gradual physical and mental deterioration, and eventual death. This is "deep old age" and its narrative is characterized by the accumulation of elements typically excised from the account of active ageing which dominates in the third stage. It manifests all the fears and social anxieties which the preceding phase seeks to mitigate against. As such, theorists like Twigg have seen it as a form of social imaginary, a collective site of societal unease particularly associated with a lack of personal agency. Here, the definitions of self are not taken by the individual but imposed as a form of "otherness" (Twigg 64) by the wider society. For Higgs and Gilleard, its markers are frailty, abjection, and the event horizon. Frailty here is associated with a loss of personhood via physical decline, with a subsequent drift into social exclusion, whilst abjection embodies fears of physical and mental disintegration themselves. Whilst in the third age it remains possible to regain some of these losses via active ageing, the impending "event horizon" suggests the impossibility of this for the fourth age (Higgs and Gilleard 15). Decline into death is not to be avoided, at least in the real world. The language used indicates an entirely negative cultural conception of extreme old age.

In *Blowing the Bloody Doors Off*, Caine mirrors many of the social taboos that have led to this stage being so frequently omitted from cultural discourses. He concedes that he has to choose roles more carefully now to ensure that shooting schedules are not too taxing and that locations are easily reachable – planning becomes imperative and recognizes the unwillingness of some production companies to insure a much older performer. At one point he admits that "even if on the inside you feel sprightly, on the outside everything starts falling apart. Your looks fade, your eyesight goes, your hearing, your back, your memory" (Caine 264). At the same time, he still argues that his own infirmities can provide a form of imaginary connection for audience members who see themselves, or someone they know, reflected in his public persona. However, defiance of ageing still remains central to this public persona, as evidenced by the media coverage of his apparent retirement. Josephine Dolan has characterized this phase for men as one in which there is a marked emphasis in film representations on failing sexual potency and subsequent resistance to this, as identified in a series of Viagra-related romantic comedies where male stars are rescued from impotence and abjection (Dolan; see the chapter "A Hard Story to Tell: Silvering Abjection and the Gendered Prosthetics of the Fourth Age Imaginary").

The taboo nature of representations of the fourth age is apparent by its absence in many media discourses of ageing – and similarly, with Caine's own filmography, where more recent roles have often been brief cameos or voice work. The only film to more openly acknowledge the infirmities of age is probably *King of Thieves* (James Marsh, 2018). The film is based on the real-life Hatton Garden safe deposit burglary of 2015, which itself provoked widespread coverage in the British media with reports finding considerable humour, as well as a touch of defiance, in an ambitious heist undertaken by a geriatric group of would-be robbers. Caine plays the gang's mastermind, Brian Reader, a 77-year-old rebelling against the tedium of suburban retirement and defying society's stigmatization of him as somebody who is "past it." Caine is supported by a cast of similarly ageing British actors including Tom Courtenay, Jim Broadbent, and Michael Gambon. If press coverage of the original robbery seemed consumed with concern regarding the age of the thieves, then reporting of the film adopted a similar preoccupation with the cast members, with the *Daily Express* noting concerns for Caine's health in the run-up to production and following his appearance at the premiere in a wheelchair having suffered an accident (Sheldon), although even here the reporting is deliberately recuperative, with the report keen to emphasize that the actor was actually in good health and fine spirits.

The poster campaign for the film depicts the gang as smart and stylish (with Michael Gambon as the dishevelled exception right at the far edge of the image), evoking previous sharp-suited gangsters from the public imagination. Caine's own role evokes his masterminding of a similarly ambitious caper in *The Italian Job*. Similarly, the main trailer, whilst including a few jokes at the expense of the elderly characters, also places considerable emphasis on their continued ability to pull off "the crime of the century." The film's only real concession to the fears and anxieties of the fourth age is in Michael Gambon's character, who is visually frail, exhibiting memory loss and physical uncertainty. Even this is treated as charmingly humorous rather than alarming or even important, stripping much of the anxiety from the possible representations. Gambon's character is relatively marginal and doesn't speak a line in the principal trailer. There are several humorous scenes in the film that play on the infirmities of the gang members, with one character being gently mocked for his deafness and another falling asleep whilst they are discussing the planning of the robbery; one of them suggests that it's a case of "blind leading the deaf." However, Caine's character seems largely unaffected by the ageing process and is still capable of considerable physical and mental exertion. The gang's descent into the vault down a lift shaft using wires and then smashing their way through the walls of the vault using a formidable drilling device is evidence of their age-defying youthfulness. Despite all the evident afflictions of the fourth age, nothing really prevents them from exerting masculine prowess.

The most recent phase of Caine's career tends to confirm the rejection of cultural discourses relating to the fourth age. The opportunity to address issues of frailty, abjection, and the event horizon are largely ignored or sidestepped. *King of Thieves* fits this pattern with its view of the final age of its characters as something that can be managed with black humour or simply defied by the superhuman restatement of age-defying physical and mental strength. The reality remains taboo.

Conclusion

Michael Caine's star persona has broadly followed the pathway described in the four ages identified by cultural gerontologists. From the 1950s (when he first took up acting) through to the 1970s (when he confirmed his status as a major international star), he can be seen moving through periods of apprenticeship and growing maturity, rising from walk-on roles, to key supporting ones such as in *Zulu* (1964), to his recognition by audiences as an embodiment of British working-class rebellion and aspiration, something acknowledged in the celebratory documentary *My Generation* (David Batty, 2017), which Caine narrated and co-produced. The transition in his career to the third age is to be found in roles like Alfred in the Batman franchise where he comfortably occupies the position of tribal elder, whilst performances like that in the title role of *Harry Brown*, alongside his public statements on ageing, endorse the active ageing agenda. Here the rebel against the stifling British class system has become an agent of defiance against limiting definitions of the ageing process.

Even more striking, however, is the degree to which the realities of the fourth age remain forbidden in large portions of Western culture. The impact of frailing, abjection, and the inevitable arrival of the final event horizon are to be mocked or ignored. The filmography of Michael Caine tends to confirm the prevalence of this discourse. Perhaps this is simply an acknowledgement of popular culture's role in providing compensation, offering a reassuring fantasy to stand against confronting the reality of experience. Caine's work lies within the cultural mainstream and adheres to its dominant value systems. In his own memoirs, Caine certainly sees no positive advantage in accepting that reality himself, any more than mainstream cinema seems to want to:

> Find what you love and do it as well as you can. Pursue your dream and even if you never catch it, you'll enjoy the chase. The rest comes down to luck, timing and God. And if all of that runs out, use the difficulty.
> (Caine 288)

Works Cited

Babington, Bruce. *British Stars and Stardom: From Alma Taylor to Sean Connery*. Manchester University Press, 2001.

Caine, Michael. *Blowing the Bloody Doors Off; And Other Lessons in Life*. Hodder and Stoughton, 2018.

Dolan, Josephine. *Contemporary Cinema and 'Old Age': Gender and the Silvering of Stardom*. Palgrave Macmillan, 2017.

Dyer, Richard. *Stars*. Bloomsbury, 1998.

Griffin, Louise. "Sir Michael Caine 'Not Retiring' from Acting." *Metro*, 16 Oct. 2021. https://metro.co.uk/2021/10/16/sir-michael-caine-says-hes-retiring-from-acting-after-next-role-15432125/.

Gullette, Margaret Morganroth. *Aged by Culture*. U Chicago P, 2004.

Hailu, Salome. "Michael Caine is not Retiring from Acting." *Variety*, 16 Oct. 2021. https://variety.com/2021/film/news/michael-caine-not-retiring-best-sellers-1235090863/.

Higgs, Paul, and Chris Gilleard. "Frailty, Abjection and the 'Othering' of the Fourth Age." *Health and Sociology Review* 1.23 (2014): 10–14.

Laslett, Peter. "The Emergence of the Third Age." *Ageing and Society* 2.7 (1987): 133–160.

Maher, Kevin. "Review of *Harry Brown*." *The Times*, 13 Nov. 2019. www.thetimes.co.uk/article/harry-brown-kqrl2m9j6gb.

Segal, Lynne. "The Coming of Age Studies." *Age Culture Humanities* 1 (2014): 31–34.

Shail, Robert. "Masculinity and Class: Michael Caine as 'Working-class' Hero." *The Trouble with Men: Masculinities in European and Hollywood Cinema*. Eds. Phil Powrie, Ann Davies, and Bruce Babington. Wallflower Press, 2004.

Sheldon, Jess. "Michael Caine Health Update: Star, 85, Returns in Heist Film *King of Thieves*." *Daily Express*, 8 Aug. 2018. www.express.co.uk/celebrity-news/1000709/Michael-Caine-health-update-films-movies-new-film-King-of-Thieves-Hatton-Garden-video.

Simpson, George. "Michael Caine, 88, Retires from Acting due to Spine Problem." *Daily Express*, 17 Oct. 2021. www.express.co.uk/entertainment/films/1506742/Michael-Caine-retirement-last-film-Best-Sellers.

Spicer, Andrew. "Sean Connery: Loosening His Bonds." *British Stars and Stardom from Alma Taylor to Sean Connery*. Ed. Bruce Babington. Manchester UP, 2001.

Twigg, Julia. "The Body, Gender and Age: Feminist Insights in Social Gerontology." *Journal of Ageing Studies* 1.18 (2004): 59–73.

4 "A Porcelain Feeling"
Performance and Ageing in the Very Late Films of John Gielgud

Jonathan Stubbs

Introduction

In the 2006 film *Venus* Peter O'Toole plays actor Maurice Russell, a fading, somewhat rakish figure who, we surmise, once had a significant career in British theatre. In between treatments for prostate cancer Russell maintains a low-key but rewarding professional life by taking small roles in film and television dramas. In the first of these, Russell appears in a hospital bed surrounded by grieving family. A second role, in a Regency-era heritage drama filmed in a stately home, is more substantial and dignified. Russell initially falters while delivering his speech but he completes the scene with aplomb, an achievement rather cruelly undercut when he is later shown wearing a catheter and a urinary bag beneath his costume. Throughout the film, Russell is associated with death, doomed sexual desire, and the unravelling of masculine self-control. As his female companion (and the object of his futile infatuation) tells him, "there's always bits of you where there shouldn't be." At the film's denouement, Russell is mourned by his friends and his death is marked by a full-page obituary in *The Guardian*, illustrated with a striking photo of O'Toole in his youth. The plot of *Venus* takes inspiration from the late careers of many distinguished actors who plied their trade in British film and television. Indeed, O'Toole himself remained active and in demand until his retirement in 2012 at the age of 80. More than anyone, perhaps, *Venus* recalls the career of John Gielgud, who prolonged his remarkable acting career in a series of film and TV performances until his death in 2000 at the age of 96. These roles were rather less blunt than *Venus* in their representation of male old age, but they provide an unusual insight into the complicated representational functions of ageing masculinity in contemporary screen fictions.

John Gielgud is known primarily as a stage actor, and he is particularly celebrated for his part, alongside Laurence Olivier and Ralph Richardson, in modernizing British drama during the 1930s, inaugurating what has been described as a "golden age" of classical theatre. He gave his final stage performance in 1988 at the age of 84, and in the years that followed he acted principally for the screen. *Prospero's Books*, his 1991 collaboration with

DOI: 10.4324/9781003306146-4

Peter Greenaway, was by far the most substantial of these post-theatrical performances. Among other innovations, Gielgud performed the dialogue for every character on screen, giving free reign to what Greenaway called his "powerful and authoritative ability to speak text" (qtd. in Croall 646). In *Prospero's Books* Gielgud is presented as a venerable patriarch who renounces his art and appeals to the audience to be set free. The parallel to the actor's own career was clear to many commentators. Russell Jackson called the film "an act of homage to Gielgud" (56); for Geoff Andrew it was "an acknowledgement of the imminent end of Gielgud's career" (n.p.). But although Gielgud never took another role of this size, the end of his career was certainly not imminent: he remained prolific in a series of small but often prominent roles in popular, well-funded period dramas, as well as longer performances for the radio and audiobook recordings.

This late-career activity has often been characterized in condescending terms as the whim of a fading star to "stay busy" in his twilight years. In an obituary, the *Financial Times* stated that "he claimed he needed the money to maintain his elegant seventeenth century house in Buckinghamshire, but he probably enjoyed being active more" ("A Life" 20). There is much evidence to suggest that Gielgud felt the same way. In a letter to a friend shortly after his 90th birthday, he professed that the "completely insignificant parts" that were available to him "suffice to pass the time and keep my hand in" (qtd. in Mangan 488). In a 1996 interview he seemed more resigned, saying "I don't care much whether I play leading parts or small parts, now. As long as I work" (qtd. in Hutchinson T6). Gielgud's late career choices have also been perceived to be haphazard and undiscerning, in stark contrast to the run of theatrical performances in which he established his reputation. As David Thomson put it, he "plunged into film with a magnificent, indiscriminate zest" (335). According to biographer Sheridan Morley, Gielgud was willing "to accept everything on offer, so long as the money and the dates were roughly suitable" (432). However, these characterizations undermine the quality that Gielgud brought to his roles in this advanced stage of his career and the value he provided to the many filmmakers eager to cast him. It is worth emphasizing that these roles were relatively well paid. According to contract data, Gielgud's rate for film and TV in the late 1990s was around £10,000 a day.[1] He earned significantly more acting in commercials, including £165,000 in 1996 for two short TV advertisements for Union Bank of Switzerland.[2] This is rather less than his commercial peak in the early 1980s, after winning an Academy Award for his role in *Arthur* (1981), but it indicates the high economic value that was placed on his work. It is also a significant departure from *Venus*, in which Maurice Russell took his salary in small envelopes of cash.

Moreover, if Gielgud was less than discriminating about the roles he took, the filmmakers who sought him out were not: he was employed for quite deliberate purposes, to embody specific qualities in films and television dramas. As Jane Campion, his director in *The Portrait of a Lady*, put it, "because he was ninety-two there was a porcelain feeling, a mixture of delicacy and strength. He had that beautiful sense of being very open" (qtd. in Croall 663). In this chapter I examine exactly what these qualities were. What did this highly distinguished, nonagenarian, predominantly stage actor provide as a production value? What did he represent as a screen persona? How were his connections to British theatrical tradition deployed in film and TV? And how did his final performances accommodate his advanced age and bodily frailty? I will address these questions by considering the 12 films and television dramas that Gielgud appeared in after his 90th birthday, between 1994 and 2000. He performed as a miserly grandfather in *Scarlett* (1994), a village elder in *First Knight* (1995), a family doctor in *Haunted* (1995), a piano teacher in *Shine* (1996), a delusional professor in *Gulliver's Travels* (1996), a dying king in *Hamlet* (1996), a dying patriarch in *The Portrait of a Lady* (1996), an aristocratic novelist in *A Dance to the Music of Time* (1996), a ruthless judge in *The Tichborne Claimant* (1998), another dying king in *Merlin* (1998), a scheming pope in *Elizabeth* (1998), and the enigmatic "Protagonist" in the Samuel Beckett adaptation, *Catastrophe* (2000).[3] These roles were brief, but Gielgud was often featured prominently in marketing materials. He was billed in fourth position – ahead of several well-known actors who had considerably more screen time – on the posters for *Elizabeth*, in fifth position in *The Tichborne Claimant*, and in third position in *Haunted*.

This chapter begins by examining Gielgud's screen persona in relation to his association with stage acting, both as a style of performance and as an embodiment of British cultural capital. As the last survivor – the last actor standing, in a sense – in a generation of venerated stage performers who emerged in the 1930s, Gielgud embodied a sense of continuity with this cultural heritage. His presence on screen thus invoked historical traditions of performance which legitimized and elevated his material while also associating it with the past. Secondly, this chapter examines Gielgud's late-career performances more specifically by focusing on *Shine* and *Catastrophe*. Appraisals of Gielgud's acting have consistently centred on the precision and musicality of his voice; the physical aspect of his performances was often found lacking by comparison. As he aged, however, the prominence of Gielgud's voice over his body may in fact have extended his career, allowing him to maintain a level of acting prowess as his mobility declined. Nevertheless, his visible frailty in his late performances carries a distinctly melancholy dimension, and in many of these productions his roles are directly associated with decline, decrepitude, and death.

The Gielgud Persona: Heritage, Theatre, and Performance

Gielgud could hardly be regarded as a major star – on film, at least – but his extensive screen work during the 1980s and 1990s generated a distinctive and marketable persona of sorts. His role in *First Knight* as a wise village elder offering marriage advice to Guinevere owes something to his performance as Dudley Moore's acerbic but devoted valet in *Arthur*, a persona he reprised in various adverts for Paul Masson wines during the 1980s. His casting opposite Moore's immature lead in *Arthur* was also reproduced in later appearances, notably *Shine* and *Portrait of a Lady*, where he provided counsel and mentoring to much younger characters at the beginning of their narrative journeys. The priggish martinets Gielgud played in other late films – notably as Pope Pius V in *Elizabeth* and the Lord Chief Justice in *The Tichborne Claimant* – also reflect a persona constructed in earlier roles, including as Charles Ryder's vindictive father in *Brideshead Revisited* (1981), as the antisemitic Master of Trinity College in *Chariots of Fire* (1981), and as the disdainful colonist Lord Irwin in *Gandhi* (1982). Finally, and perhaps inevitably, Gielgud's performances were strongly associated with dying and death. He complained that "most of the scripts I get sent nowadays are all about men at death's door" (qtd. in Croall 565), and indeed he dies on screen in *Hamlet*, *Merlin*, and *The Portrait of a Lady*. In *Haunted*, a ghost story, his character is already dead. This aspect of his persona was likewise established in numerous earlier screen roles. Most notably, the illness and death of his character in *Arthur* provide a turning point in the film, while in Alain Resnais' *Providence* (1977) Gielgud plays a dying, bedridden novelist who, much like Prospero, claims control over his family through his writing.

On the surface, the characters Gielgud played in the final years of his career reflect a persona built up on screen during the 1980s rather than in his earlier theatrical performances. These roles also depend on commonplace dramatic associations between old age, wisdom, and mentoring on the one hand and frailty, corruption, and death on the other. However, Gielgud's screen persona very much built on his aura as an actor and his commanding position in the venerated tradition of British theatrical performance. In a 1952 profile, Kenneth Tynan outlined his vaunted status: "Gielgud is not so much an actor, as *the* actor ... a theatrical possession, an inscription, a figurehead and a touchstone" (Tynan 46). His acting peers included Laurence Olivier, Ralph Richardson, Michael Redgrave, Edith Evans, and Peggy Ashcroft, but Gielgud outlasted them all. By the 1990s he was perhaps unique in providing a link, delicate but still tangible, to this rich cultural heritage. The filmmakers who cast him were often eager to attach their work to this tradition. In *Hamlet*, Gielgud took the tiny, wordless role of Priam, in which he essentially mimes action described in a speech delivered by Charlton Heston's Player King. In a promotional feature included on the DVD of the film, director Kenneth Branagh stated that "to have the greatest Hamlet of the century in the film ... would be a particular blessing, and so as much as anything [the scene] is there as a kind of tribute to him and a blessing for us." In this way, the presence of Gielgud conveys prestige and tradition, rooting films and TV dramas in the past and tying them to his own distinguished career on the stage. For productions which sought to bolster their cultural capital, this function was particularly valuable.

Acting has been acknowledged as a distinctive element in British film and TV, particularly the stage tradition associated with Britain's drama schools, its theatre companies, and the mainly Shakespearean roles in which acting prowess is demonstrated. According to Robert Gordon, stage acting in Britain began to centre on Shakespearean performance as early as the 17th century. As a result,

> An unbroken theatrical tradition was dominated by definitive performances in the major Shakespearean roles, successive generations of actors seeking to challenge the pre-eminence of their predecessors by establishing new approaches to well-known roles.
>
> (146)

Theatrical training was formalized by the emergence of London drama schools in the early 20th century, and from the outset the performance of Shakespeare was privileged above other texts (Gordon 147). Textual interpretation and vocal practice, particularly the speaking of verse, were among the formative principles of British acting in this era (Cochrane 86; Gordon 146). However, an emphasis on the voice reinforced the social exclusivity of British theatre acting as Received Pronunciation (RP) became institutionalized as the "neutral" voice of British acting and "the vocal starting point of classical acting practice" (Friedman et al. 1004). As Claire Cochrane notes, the relatively high cost of formal training had a similar impact, further narrowing the class base of the British acting profession (86). The emergence of cinema and television later in the 20th century provided British actors with new creative and economic opportunities. According to Cochrane, film enabled established performers such as Gielgud and Olivier to maintain national profiles without needing to leave London to tour regional theatres (98). British acting was thus entrenched even more deeply in the nation's capital. The geographical concentration of Britain's theatrical and filmmaking industries came with many practical advantages, but it also marginalized acting traditions which emerged outside London, stifling the class and regional diversity of the British acting profession (Cochrane 98).

The new generation of stage performers which emerged in the 1950s promised to broaden the narrow demographics of Britain's theatre. Actors from northern England, such as Albert Finney, Alan Bates, and Peter O'Toole, who studied together at RADA, introduced a more modern style of performance which stood apart from earlier generations and transferred effectively to the cinema. The middle-class, RP-inflected vocal style associated with Gielgud and his peers came to be regarded as affected and anachronistic. In his influential discussion of screen acting, John Caughie stated "the theatrical – the stagy – has been a term of abuse, formally, culturally and politically, at least since the late 1950s" (144). Gielgud was certainly conscious of these perceptions, noting "when I saw *Look Back in Anger*

I thought my number was up. I didn't know anything about those people. One loses confidence. One is afraid of being old-fashioned and hammy" (qtd. in Apple 35). However, the scale of this demographic and stylistic shift should not be overstated. The British film and theatre industries did not abandon their metropolitan base, and actors from the new generation were still able to perform in refined RP, as O'Toole demonstrated in *Lawrence of Arabia* (1962). Moreover, the dominant forms of stage training and performance did not break entirely with the past. According to Gordon, although influential directors such as Peter Hall and John Barton abandoned the "excessively musical style" of verse speaking which was associated with pre-war theatre, their approach was still rooted in vocal work and textual interpretation, emphasizing "an unsentimental and muscular approach to speaking the text that stressed *sense* over *sound*" (170). It should also be noted that Gielgud and his acting peers were able to adapt to this new climate, taking significant professional risks in the process. Olivier sensed the changing mood and sought out a role in John Osborne's *The Entertainer* in 1957. Gielgud's introduction to modern theatre came later, with acclaimed performances alongside Ralph Richardson in David Storey's *Home* (1970) and in Harold Pinter's *No Man's Land* (1975), directed by Lindsay Anderson and Peter Hall, respectively. Thus, even as cultural fashions changed, British theatrical acting maintained ties to the cultural heritage of the past.

By the 1980s and 1990s, British stage actors – including the new generation of the 1950s – were widely associated with heritage film and television. In a discussion of *Brideshead Revisited* and *The Jewel in the Crown* (1984), starring Gielgud and Peggy Ashcroft, respectively, Charlotte Brunsdon highlights the "best of British acting" as a "component" denoting quality in discourses around British television (85). Appraising the heritage film cycle of the 1980s and 1990s, Andrew Higson notes that the presence of older actors invokes "the qualities and conventions of the British theatre tradition" (98). Higson goes on to describe space in the heritage film as being organized around "the display of heritage properties rather than the enactment of drama" (99). This ostensibly refers to the familiar heritage film iconography of stately homes and ornate set design, but the idea of "heritage property" can be extended to describe the ways in which other elements of British culture are put on display, including actors associated with the stage tradition. Higson also links the heritage film to an implicitly nationalistic desire to assert "continuity with the past" and to preserve "values and traditions" (95). The casting of actors tied to the British theatre certainly serves this purpose as well. Heritage films and TV thus functioned as showcases for a certain type of British actor and for the spectacle of British stage acting more generally. Gielgud was not alone in his ability to evoke this cultural heritage on screen, but his pre-eminence as a stage performer, as well as the length and richness of his career, allowed him to embody these qualities in a particularly focused and refined form.

The long history of stage performance in Britain has generated a certain received wisdom about British acting in general. Most conspicuously, British acting has been regarded as primarily logocentric, based on speech and the "correct" interpretation of literary texts. In his history of method acting, Isaac Butler describes the "English approach" as "largely external, based on physical and vocal transformation and careful attention to the rhythms and sounds of the text" (n.p.). As such, British acting has often been regarded as a function of the mind first and the body second – intellectual and technical rather than physical and intuitive. This notion has often been extrapolated to draw broad distinctions between British and American actors, as Carole Zucker reveals in her interviews with British and American stage actors. According to Eileen Atkins, British actors are "head-based, and not gut-based" (qtd. in Zucker, *In the Company* 10). For the British actor Jane Lapotaire,

> The physical side of our theatre is sadly way down the priority list. I'm ashamed when I direct English actors. Their sense of spatial relationships, their sense of the picture they create on stage is zero!
> (qtd. in Zucker, *In the Company*, 90)

The American actor Lindsay Crouse spells out the binary opposition:

> What we're great at is this kind of organic, shoot-from-the-hip, react-off-the-other person, casual arena of acting. What we're not so good at is the control – voice-work, interpretation, clarity, being able to use the text. . . . It's what the English are so good at, and also why we love their theater.
> (qtd. in Zucker, *Figures of Light* 17)

Summarizing these nationally inflected positions, Simone Knox and Gary Cassidy suggest that American acting is seen as "organic, inside out, 'from the guts,' concerned with 'emotional truth' and more suitable for the screen," whereas British acting is conceived as the opposite, being "disciplined, outside in, text based, concerned with technique and more suitable for the stage" (181). In practice, as Knox and Cassidy among others have noted, the relationship between British and American acting is more complex: gut-based and head-based acting can be found on both sides of the Atlantic, in addition to acting styles not accommodated within this binary. Nevertheless, Gielgud's performance style surely exemplifies the conventional conception of British acting as technical, externalized and language-centred, emphasizing vocal performance over physical expression. On screen, he evoked the heritage of the British stage not only by historical association but also in the aesthetic qualities of his performance style. Moreover, as Gielgud aged and became frailer the characteristic discrepancy between his vocal and physical performance took on an even greater significance.

"A Kind of Liberation": Frailty, Virtuosity, and the Voice

Gielgud's voice attracted attention and acclaim throughout his career. The class associations of his RP accent were unmistakable, but so too was a vocal technique frequently likened to musical performance. Alec Guinness compared Gielgud's voice to "a silver trumpet muffled in silk" (qtd. in Hutchinson T6), while the obituary published in the *Times* described it as "an instrument of spellbinding purity, unrivalled in its speed and sensitivity of articulation" ("Sir John" 20). According to Russell Jackson, Gielgud was able to "negotiate rapidly through clusters of consonants but maintaining a *legato* that carried through and across verse lines" (15). Gielgud wrote at length about his method in his book *Stage Directions*:

> I try to phrase correctly for breathing, punctuation and emphasis, and then, conforming to this main line, I experiment within it for modulation, tone, and pace, trying not to drag out the vowels, elongate syllables, or pounce on opening phrases, and being very careful not to drop the ends of words and sentences to pronounce the final consonants.
>
> (5)

In counterpoint, Gielgud was sometimes criticized for his lack of physical presence. His expressivity of movement could be limited, leading Tynan to call him "the finest actor on earth from the neck up" (qtd. in Gussow, "Sir John" 1). Gielgud's comments on the physical aspects of performance in *Stage Directions* are limited to a few references to "deportment" and the wearing of costumes. Reminiscing in 1993, he stated,

> I had terrible trouble with my movement when I was young because I never did any sports. I can't swim, I can't ride. I should have forced myself. And I got much too fond of my voice. I sang all my parts.
>
> (qtd. in Gussow, "At Home" C1)

Lightly built and less conventionally masculine than many of his peers – notably Olivier – Gielgud's physicality may have limited his opportunities in mainstream cinema during much of his career. It is certainly hard to imagine him in the romantic roles which made Olivier a Hollywood star in the late 1930s and early 1940s. But as Gielgud grew older, this ceased to be such an encumbrance. In his nineties, he stated that he was no longer so concerned with his looks or his movement, noting "the only thing that old age gives you is a kind of liberation" (qtd. in Croall 652). As Elizabeth W. Markson argues, "aging and old age have been understood primarily in relationship to bodily changes" (79). Mike Featherstone and Mike Hepworth suggest that "deep old age is personally and socially disturbing" due to the way that the "loss of bodily control" is stigmatized (376). But it should be noted that the ageing process affected Gielgud's voice much less markedly than his body. Indeed, it can be argued that old age separated – or even liberated, to use Gielgud's term – his virtuosic voice from the less virtuosic instrument of his body, allowing him to perform through his physical frailty. Gielgud's enduring vocal prowess also averted commonplace associations between old age and cognitive decline. Aside from *Gulliver's Travels*, in which he plays a professor who has gone mad after dedicating his life to extracting sunlight from cucumbers, his late performances were not associated with mental infirmity. Indeed, he was typically presented as intellectually acute in professionally distinguished roles which included a judge, a doctor, a music teacher, and the pontiff of the Roman Catholic Church. As Sadie Wearing has suggested, representations of male old age in film often highlight anxieties over "how cognitive frailty and impairment trouble masculine identifications, gendered roles and the related ability to author[ise] the self" (139). Despite his evident physical frailty, this is not the case in Gielgud's late performances. His on-screen body may have faltered, but the fluency of his voice denoted a high level of mental acuity.

The union of fluent voice and frail body is apparent in many of Gielgud's late performances. In *The Portrait of a Lady* Gielgud plays the wealthy banker Mr Touchett, the wise and generous uncle of Isabel, played by Nicole Kidman. Touchett is conveyed in a wheelchair in their first scene together; his inability to move independently echoes Isabel's reluctance to lose autonomy by marrying. In their second scene he is prostrate in bed and dies silently in front of her, having previously secured her financial independence in his will. In *Shine*, a biopic depicting the life of the Australian pianist David Helfgott, Gielgud plays Cecil Parkes, an inspirational teacher at the Royal College of Music. Parkes mentors the young Helfgott, who has begun to show signs of disorganized speech and thinking. But Parkes recognizes the young pianist's genius and he serves as a nurturing surrogate for Helfgott's tyrannical father. The film clearly links Helfgott's increasingly disordered state with his musical brilliance. According to director Scott Hicks, in a personal letter to Gielgud, "Parkes sees the damage in David as the shadow of the spark of genius he knows the genuine artist must carry" (n.p.). As in *The Portrait of a Lady*, Parkes is physically weak: the screenplay states that he has been "crippled by a stroke" and thus is no longer able to play the piano (Sardi 60). The screenplay also specifies that Parkes is in his sixties – some 30 years younger than Gielgud at the time – suggesting that the actor's more advanced age was used to accentuate the frailty of the character. The onset of Helfgott's mental illness is thus placed in counterpoint with the physical infirmity of Parkes, the fluent delivery of the latter contrasting with the halting speech of the former. But teacher and pupil are bonded by their virtuosity, with the musicality of Parkes' voice complementing the expressive dynamism of Helfgott's playing. Parkes is also able to bring Helfgott into a grand cultural lineage. Just as Gielgud the actor connects the film to a cultural heritage of stage acting, Parkes the character is able to induct Helfgott into a venerable tradition of musical performance.

Gielgud's scenes in *Shine* centre on preparations for the Royal Academy contest, in which Helfgott has elected to perform Rachmaninoff's Third Piano Concerto. Parkes describes the piece as "monumental" and "dangerous," noting that no student has "ever been mad enough" to attempt it. In the film's distinctly romantic conception of musical self-expression, the emotional toll of the music, culminating in a triumphant performance in the contest, hastens Helfgott's psychological collapse and his subsequent institutionalization. *Shine* dramatizes their rehearsals in a series of rapidly edited scenes which contrast the dynamism and volatility of Helfgott's playing and Rachmaninoff's music with the lucid calmness of Parkes' mentoring. As the piece begins, the camera orbits around David and the piano in a swerving, unstable trajectory. Beside him, Parkes is anchored to the spot, captured in a locked-off, medium close-up as he issues fragmentary commands to his pupil, describing the piece as "two separate melodies jousting for supremacy" and exhorting him to "tame the piano" (Figure 4.1). The writing is unsubtle, reflecting Helfgott's interior torment and the overwhelming effort of his creative endeavour rather too neatly. Parke's instruction to master the piece while blindfolded recalls, intentionally or otherwise, Luke Skywalker's "force" training in *Star Wars* (1977). However, Gielgud's actorly declamation and his pre-eminence as an interpreter of complex texts (Shakespeare, in place of Rachmaninoff) elevates the sequence. As the rehearsals continue, Gielgud's voice takes centre stage and his body appears less and less on screen. His words are layered over images of Helfgott's playing, and in one passage Parkes sings in tandem with the piano as the camera tracks away from the rehearsal towards a window. In this way, Parkes becomes almost a voice without a body, a cerebral counterpoint to the precarious but exhilarating physicality of Helfgott's playing.

Figure 4.1 Gielgud mentors his pupil from a sedentary position in *Shine* (1996)

"A Porcelain Feeling" 39

Gielgud's performances became fewer and briefer as his health declined. The death of his partner, Martin Hensler, in 1999 was deeply felt and it further curtailed his appearances (Croall 667). His role in the short Samuel Beckett play, *Catastrophe*, in 2000 was to be his very last, performed "at the very limit of life," as Normand Berlin put it (97). Directed by David Mamet for the "Beckett on Film" TV series, *Catastrophe* features an autocratic Director (played by Harold Pinter) and a deferential Assistant who conduct a rehearsal for a play consisting of a man, referred to as the Protagonist and played by Gielgud, standing motionless on a pedestal. The dynamic of *Shine* is thus inverted, with Gielgud cast as the performer instead of the instructor. As the Protagonist, Gielgud is almost entirely passive, more victim than collaborator. The Director and the Assistant do not speak or engage with him directly but rather inspect, discuss, manipulate and partially expose his body. Gielgud plays an actor who is not permitted to act, whose autonomy is negated by the apparatus which encloses him. The Protagonist is also silent, and thus Gielgud is deprived of the principal instrument in his armoury. Inverting *Shine* once again, he is made into a body without a voice. Even more than the prior roles discussed in this article, this performance depends on the audience's knowledge of Gielgud's acting career – awareness of the voice which has been suppressed heightens the power and tragedy of the Protagonist's muteness. The overt theatricality of *Catastrophe*'s setting is significant, as is Gielgud's presence alongside Pinter and Mamet in a play written by Beckett. Returning to a stage in this final appearance, Gielgud was able to underscore his place among the major figures of 20th-century theatre.

Catastrophe can be understood as a depiction of totalitarianism, the overbearing Director manipulating a silent, docile public into an image of submission. The play was dedicated to the dissident Czech playwright Václav Havel, who was imprisoned at the time, and in its original staging in 1982 the Director was costumed to resemble a member of the Soviet bureaucratic elite (Rae 313). The Protagonist may thus be seen as a kind of political prisoner, disciplined by a totalitarian state in what Paul Rae calls "a microspectacle of repressive power" (313). According to Beckett's final stage direction, the Protagonist "raises his head and fixes the audience," causing a "distant storm of applause" to falter and die (461). It is a tiny, optimistic gesture of defiance: the Protagonist resists the Director's tyrannical, dehumanizing vision, but the diegetic audience is unsure how to react. As Rae suggests, this ending serves to implicate the non-diegetic theatre audience in the oppressive spectacle on the stage, conflating them with the Director's anticipated audience as they are confronted with an "irresistible nub of human spirit" (313). In Mamet's version, however, the Protagonist does not "fix" the audience. Instead, Gielgud is framed in a close, heavily shaded, high-angle shot (Figure 4.2). Rather than making eye contact with the viewing audience via the camera, his gaze is directed towards the empty theatre stalls. And instead of hearing the applause of an audience, we hear only the

Figure 4.2 Gielgud raises his head towards the audience in *Catastrophe* (2000)

isolated, unfaltering applause of the dutiful Assistant. There is no interplay between real and imagined audiences, the Protagonist's resistance seems to go unnoticed, and the overall tone is far from defiant. Beckett stated in his text that the "age and physique" of the Protagonist was "unimportant" (457), but for Mamet this was clearly not the case. In this final role, Gielgud's advanced age seems absolutely crucial to his performance, his physical frailty and uncharacteristic muteness providing a critical element in this highly pessimistic interpretation of Beckett's play.

Conclusion

Gielgud spent his 96th birthday on the set of *Catastrophe* and he died just five weeks later, ending a remarkable acting career which began in the early 1920s. The screen roles he took between 1994 and 2000 were often insignificant, at least as scripted, but they were magnified by his extraordinary talent and aura as an actor and by the cultural heritage which he embodied. His late performances present a body in advanced stages of decline, associated with death and sometimes with corruption. But in contrast to common representations of female ageing, this body was never made to appear grotesque (Markson 98). His voice, moreover, remained strong until the very end of his career, embodying the refined class associations of British stage acting and reflecting his technical prowess as a speaker of dramatic text. Indeed, Gielgud's vocal talent allowed him to continue performing even as his body became frail. More broadly, Gielgud's late performances served to identify the films and TV dramas in which he starred with a sense of pastness, both through his association with historical stage traditions and in his expression of a historical mode of performance. Caughie has written that "the body of the actor is stubborn: the furniture may be authentic nineteenth century, but the body of the actor and its gestures are our contemporary." Taking *Pride and Prejudice* (1995) as an example he notes that the movement of Jennifer Ehle (as Elizabeth Bennet) "*feels* like the present" (151). The observation can be applied to numerous historical dramas: the recent performances of Elle Fanning and Nicholas Hoult in *The Great* (2020–21) come to mind. However, the performances of older actors, not least Gielgud, do not necessarily convey this sense of anachronistic contemporaneity. In his final performances, I would suggest, Gielgud's body and gestures do not "feel like the present" in the least. Instead, he was able to connect to an alternate temporality, outside the here and now and grounded in his own long history of performance.

Notes

1 Information collated from various contracts in the John Gielgud Papers, Add MS 81339, British Library, London.
2 British Actor's Equity Association Client Ledger Card for John Gielgud, 21 March 1996. John Gielgud Papers, Add MS 81339, British Library, London.
3 This list excludes the wholly vocal performances given by Gielgud in the same period: acting for radio (notably a full performance as King Lear directed by Kenneth Branagh for BBC Radio 4 in 1994), recording documentary narration and audiobooks, and voice acting in animated films.

Works Cited

"A Life Devoted to Acting: Obituary, Sir John Gielgud." *Financial Times*, 23 May 2000: 20.
Andrew, Geoff. "Prospero's Books." *Time Out*, 30 Aug. 1991. Web. www.timeout.com/movies/prosperos-books.
Apple, R.W. "At 75, John Gielgud Looks Back and to the Future." *The New York Times*, 15 Apr. 1979: 35.
Beckett, Samuel. *The Complete Dramatic Works*. Faber and Faber, 1986.
Berlin, Normand. "Traffic of our Stage: Gielgud." *Massachusetts Review* 42.1 (2001): 97–120.
Brunsdon, Charlotte. "Problems with Quality." *Screen* 31.1 (1990): 67–90.
Butler, Isaac. *The Method: How the Twentieth Century Learned to Act*. Bloomsbury, 2022.
Caughie, John. "What Do Actors Do When They Act?" *British Television: Past, Present and Future*. Ed. Jonathan Bignell and Stephen Lacey. Palgrave Macmillan, 2014. 143–155.

Cochrane, Claire. *Twentieth-Century British Theatre: Industry, Art and Empire*. Cambridge UP, 2014.

Croall, Jonathan. *John Gielgud: Matinee Idol to Movie Star*. Bloomsbury, 2011.

Featherstone, Mike, and Mike Hepworth. "The Mask of Ageing and the Postmodern Life Course." *The Body: Social Process and Cultural Theory*. Ed. Mike Featherstone, Mike Hepworth, and Bryan S. Turner. Sage Publications, 1991. 371–389.

Friedman, Sam, Dave O'Brien, and Daniel Laurison. "'Like Skydiving Without a Parachute': How Class Origin Shapes Occupational Trajectories in British Acting." *Sociology* 51.5 (2017): 992–1010.

Gielgud, John. *Stage Directions*. Sceptre, 1992.

Gordon, Robert. *The Purpose of Playing: Modern Acting Theories in Perspective*. U Michigan P, 2006.

Gussow, Mel. "At Home With: John Gielgud." *New York Times*, 28 Oct. 1993: C1. Print.

Gussow, Mel. "Sir John Gielgud, 96, Dies: Beacon of Classical Stage." *New York Times*, 23 May 2000: A1.

Hicks, Scott. Letter to John Gielgud, 24 January 1994. John Gielgud Papers, Add MS 81383, British Library, London.

Higson, Andrew. "Re-presenting the Past: Nostalgia and Pastiche in the Heritage Film." *British Cinema and Thatcherism: Fires Were Started*. Ed. Lester Friedman. 2nd ed. Wallflower Press, 2007. 91–109.

Hutchinson, Mike. "The Gielgud Factor." *The Guardian*, 8 Nov. 1996: T6.

Jackson, Russell. *Gielgud, Olivier, Ashcroft, Dench: Great Shakespeareans Vol XVI*. Bloomsbury, 2013.

Knox, Simone, and Gary Cassidy. "*Game of Thrones*: Investigating British Acting." *Transatlantic Television Drama: Industries, Programs, and Fans*. Ed. Matt Hills, Michele Hilmes, and Roberta E. Pearson. Oxford UP, 2019. 181–200.

Mangan, Richard, ed. *Gielgud's Letters: John Gielgud in His Own Words*. Weidenfeld & Nicolson, 2010.

Markson, Elizabeth W. "The Female Aging Body Through Film." *Aging Bodies: Images and Everyday Experience*. Ed. Christopher A. Faircloth. AltaMira Press, 2003. 77–101.

Morley, Sheridan. *The Authorised Biography of John Gielgud*. Hodder and Stoughton, 2001.

Rae, Paul. "A Chinese *Catastrophe*? The Moving Target of Political Theatre." *The Routledge Companion to Theatre and Politics*. Ed. Peter Eckersall and Helena Grehan. Routledge, 2019. 313–316.

Sardi, Jan. *Shine: The Screenplay*. Bloomsbury, 1997.

"Sir John Gielgud." *The Times*, 23 May 2000: 20.

Thomson, David. *The New Biographical Dictionary of Film*. 4th ed. Little, Brown, 2002.

Tynan, Kenneth. *Profiles*. Nick Hern Books, 2020.

Wearing, Sadie. "Troubled Men: Ageing, Dementia and Masculinity in Contemporary British Crime Drama." *Journal of British Cinema and Television* 14.2 (2017): 125–142.

Zucker, Carole. *Figures of Light: Actors and Directors Illuminate the Art of Film Acting*. Plenum, 1995.

Zucker, Carole. *In the Company of Actors: Reflections on the Craft of Acting*. Routledge, 2001.

5 Ageing Disgracefully
Depardieu, Hallyday, Luchini, and Silver Linings in Recent French Cinema

Phil Powrie

There has been considerable interest in ageing stars over recent years.[1] As might be expected, most case studies focus on American and British film stars. Where French stars are the subject, the majority of case studies focus on women, the only man being Gérard Depardieu (1948–).[2] It is for this reason that I have chosen to focus on several ageing male actors. I could have chosen Jean-Paul Belmondo (1933–2021), Alain Delon (1935–), Jean-Pierre Léaud (1944–), Jean Rochefort (1930–2017), or Jean-Louis Trintignant (1930–2022), all of whom have significant careers and who should therefore be of interest to researchers. [Two of these are subjects of Chapters 6 and 7 in this collection. Eds.] Depardieu will be the first of my case studies because as France's most significant male star, he is the main focus of interest in academic studies, and because his decline has been very visible in the media. I will also explore Johnny Hallyday (1943–2017), France's great rock star who frequently appeared in films, and who was given a state funeral on his death; and Fabrice Luchini (1951–), well known for his frequent stage and TV appearances reading the classics of French literature.

My focus on male actors is conditioned by a specifically French interest in the decline of the male or "loser" (the English term has been appropriated by the French). A conference on the topic was organized by French anthropologists and sociologists in Paris at the same time that there was a flurry of Anglophone research into ageing stars (Rivoal and De Sales 2012), leading to considerable media interest with web lists of these loser characters in French cinema, for example Jean-Claude Duss (played by Michel Blanc) in Patrice Leconte's *Bronzés* films, or the François Pignon character in Francis Veber's films, played by a range of actors over the years.[3] These films are all comedies, but the loser as a phenomenon appears in other genres, as we shall see in this chapter. The conference organizers stated that a key criterion for being a loser is desynchronization and disassociation from the present and from the community; the loser, they say, is "en arrière, à côté, en-deçà" (behind, disconnected, falling short). This is a convenient way of thinking about the performances of many ageing male actors in French cinema, given that the characters they play tend to be losers, and that their off-screen activities frequently parallel the characters they play. The ageing male actor and his film characters are disconnected, out of kilter. This, however, raises the question of what they might be out of kilter with.

Our view of the ageing loser combines both his representation as a film character and what we know of the actor who plays the character, something that studies of ageing female actors have explored, for example Susan Smith on Elizabeth Taylor (2012), or William Brown on Charlotte Rampling (2012). The actor performs a character in the narrative, performs the persona of the star in and outside of the film, and performs the star's real body in and outside of the film. What we experience as spectators is therefore respectively textual, paratextual, and metatextual. At all three of these levels, the ageing actor embodies the passage of time and the decline of the body, all the more so in the case of male actors who regularly play losers. Because we recognize the decline and degradation of the ageing actor's body, the character they embody contains both the past and the present in a configuration of loss. The actor who plays losers has lost youth, beauty, memory, intellect, and so on, and is as a result out of kilter with himself. The past lies like an archaeological layer in the present of viewing, a tectonic plate that shifts our experience of the present. What we see on screen is always already a body degraded by time; we are forced to see the past (body) of the actor as a ghost in the faulty machine of the narrative's present character. The actor's performance is therefore a complex palimpsest: he is both himself as a real person and as the character he plays informed by his star persona; that persona is itself formed over time by a series of performances, both on screen and off screen. But the palimpsest is not only visual, it is also temporal, an overlaying of performances over time resulting in the one we see on screen: a cumulative series of lost personas which the star's performance re-actualizes while undermining them because of his physical decline.

The performance therefore holds in tension two apparently contradictory movements, one regressively restorative, the other subversive. For the first, Aagje Swinnen reprises Anne Basting's work on theatrical performance (Swinnen citing Basting, 1998, 7–8). Basting cites Richard Schechner's view that the performance gives actors the "chance to rebecome what they once were, or even, and most often, to rebecome what they never were but wish to have been or wish to become" (cited in Basting, 1998, 7). Basting contrasts this position with that of Judith Butler, who argues that hyperbolic display – which we could argue is what happens in films where the actor plays a loser – is subversive of norms. The narratives of these films function to revalorize loss, to recover and reposition lost personas, so that from being "out of kilter" the ageing actor is back "into kilter" in spite of the physical or mental decline displayed by the character he plays.

The three actors I have chosen come back into kilter in their recent films which are narratives of male decline. Their performances, based in their past personas, are transformed. They are regressively restorative because they reprise and replay what we know of them. But those performances are also at the same time subversive because they valorize age, turning what might seem to be a decline into a virtue. Briefly characterized, Depardieu transforms his persona into an innocent Candide figure; Hallyday valorizes the enclosed and fantasied space of the family; and Luchini takes refuge in literature.

Depardieu: The Candide Effect

The main focus of scholars investigating ageing in the stars of French cinema has been Gérard Depardieu, not least because of the global media coverage of his provocative and problematic activities: he was removed from a plane in 2011 for urinating in a plastic bottle; he was derided for moving to Belgium in 2012 so as to avoid taxes; and he was ridiculed in 2013 for taking on Russian nationality. These activities, coupled with a bloated physique denoting undisciplined excess led French commentators to see him as an extreme example of the loser as defined above, not least in comparison with his younger self. Sue Harris explores "the incomprehension, inarticulacy and emasculation" of Depardieu (2015, 330). I suggest that there is a more positive way of thinking through Depardieu's ageing: the kinds of loss associated with ageing are held in tension with core values related to the star persona, something that Raphaëlle Moine (2015) has done for Depardieu. As she points out (2015), echoing Harris, Depardieu is playing into the idea of the *monstre sacré*, who ignores social norms, seeks out attention to display his "monstrousness," and thereby places himself beyond criticism.

Depardieu has lost the lithe and athletic body of his young rebel characters, seen for example in *Les Valseuses* (Going Places; Bertrand Blier, 1974) or *Loulou* (Maurice Pialat, 1980), and has also lost his more imposing physique of the heritage films of the 1980s and 1990s, where his weight, in both senses of the word, supported the weight of French history, almost as if his imposing but not yet bloated body was a guarantor of the weightiness of historical events. A gourmet (he owns several restaurants) and a wine producer, as he describes himself on his passport, he has over the years spread out both concretely and figuratively. His body has ballooned and overflowed. This might suggest that he and we have lost all sense of proportion in relation to his persona; but Moine and Harris's perceptive analyses demonstrate how he has rather *transformed* his image, making the grotesque acceptable.

This is very clear in *Mammuth* (Gustave Kervern et Benoît Delépine, 2010) in which Depardieu plays a long-haired innocent, Serge Pilardosse, who has retired from work in an abattoir. He realizes that he does not have the required points for a full pension and so starts a quest for his previous salary slips on his treasured motorbike, a German Mammuth from the 1970s. The film clearly gestures, if ironically, to *Easy Rider* (Dennis Hopper, 1969): Serge meets a range of off-kilter characters (a gravedigger, a beachcomber, a hooker with a broken ankle, his deranged niece, a cousin with whom he masturbates). One of his former employers says that he is, "con," dumb, and Depardieu plays up the stupidity and destitution of his character, undermining his own star persona as the foremost male star of the French cinema. Harris pinpoints Serge's off-kilterness:

> Serge's new state of idleness . . . is characterized by incomprehension, inarticulacy and emasculation. . . . He is the last of his kind, a mammoth on the brink of extinction. As his journey through France progresses, he is faced with the realization that social and technological progress has rendered him, and the industries that defined his life, obsolete, calling his whole past life into question.
>
> (2015, 330)

Depardieu's performance emphasizes his abject body, his obscenely bloated paunch frequently on display. And yet this abjectness is held in tension with Serge's often emphasized naïve and sensitive approach to life; for example, his niece has created a sculpture of him from stuffed toys (connoting childhood and softness; see Figure 5.1), saying "This is you, a giant on the outside, all soft inside. The elephant is your heart, the rabbits are your hands, and the marmoset your willy."[4] And at the end of the film there is a surreal sequence where we see Serge sitting his *baccalauréat* alongside schoolkids. Instead of writing an essay, he writes a poem saying that he has worked all his life and is now committed to love. This confirms the "suffering macho" persona identified by Ginette Vincendeau (1993, 353). It also chimes with the persona that Depardieu has been cultivating in his published autobiographical work, such as the aptly titled *Innocent* whose cover shows Depardieu semi-naked behind a table, as he was in the infamous strip-search scene of *Welcome to New York* (Abel Ferrara, 2014; see Figures 5.2 and 5.3). The film is about

Figure 5.1 The sculpture of Serge constructed from soft toys

Ageing Disgracefully 47

Figure 5.2 The cover of *Innocent*

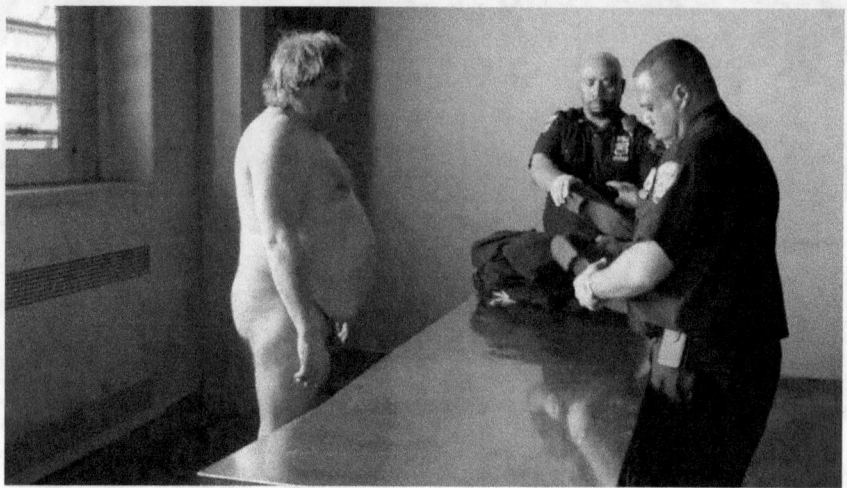

Figure 5.3 The strip search in *Welcome to New York* (2014)

the arrest in New York in 2011 of the former chief of the International Monetary Fund, Dominique Strauss-Kahn, for assault and attempted rape. We see Depardieu as Strauss-Kahn being fellated by a call girl, and later engaging in a steamy threesome, then being arrested and strip-searched, ending up naked, his bloated paunch on display. Discourse around the film focused largely on the display of Depardieu's body, as is evident from the following review, which baldly states that the film is

> An intimate metaphor of monstrousness, of the addiction to the body, of decline . . . Depardieu is the main character. His body becomes the main character. Vast, excessive. Deformed even, compared with what we might have seen of him over the years.
>
> (Pudlowski 2014)[5]

Indeed, the contrast with Depardieu's naked body in *Les Valseuses* or in *La dernière femme* (The Last Woman; 1976) is shocking. As Harris says, Depardieu "offers a grotesque counterpoint to the codes of youth, beauty and charisma on which the Depardieu star persona was first constructed, and which lives on in popular memory in France" (2015, 320).

Depardieu's book is to an extent a counter-attack justifying the grotesque display of his body. The blurb appeals to the idea of innocence underlying his many gaffes:

> I take full responsibility for my screw-ups and gaffes. Because there's something truthful in them. And if you never make mistakes, it's often

because you're an asshole. I don't control anything . . . I'm not trying to be a saint. It's not that I'm against it, it's just hard. A saint's life is shitty. I prefer me as I am. I want to carry on as I am. An innocent.
(Depardieu 2015, back cover)[6]

Depardieu may have aged disgracefully in many different ways, but the implication is that at heart he is an innocent, a Candide, a sensitive child, who has managed to retain a childlike innocence as his overriding value. Coupled with this innocence however is monstrousness, but paradoxically a monstrousness stripped of individuality to become Everyman, according to the right-wing commentator Richard Millet. Depardieu is for Millet the archetypal Rabelaisian Frenchman: "He is the French body burping, farting, sniffing, vomiting, and bursting with laughter, as one does in the French provinces"(2014, 22).[7] His physical decline is a metaphor for France's decline: "He shows (reveals) the France of the last 40 years, which has changed more in four decades than in two centuries of post-revolutionary degradation" (2014, 27).[8] Depardieu's grotesque body may carve out a space of innocence which is beyond critique, but that innocence is compromised because it is possible to see it as a metaphor for the apolitical Everyman, the individual as exception submerged and (literally) incorporated in a kind of transcendent zeitgeist – which like the notion of the *monstre sacré* serves to mitigate excess and to exonerate it as a kind of new and (at least in Millet's eyes) unwelcome normal. As Millet provocatively says, Serge and Strauss-Kahn may be two extremes, but they gesture to the same thing: "The wish to lose or to lose oneself, the Frenchman as loser/la volonté de perdre ou de se perdre, le Français comme *looser*" (2014, 99; Millet's italics and misspelling).

Johnny Hallyday: Fantasizing the Family

In the blood-spattered Hong Kong thriller *Vengeance*, Hallyday plays Franck Costello, a former assassin whose daughter and her family have been massacred in Hong Kong by hired killers. Franck goes to Hong Kong to exact vengeance. He gradually loses his memory in the course of the film, because of a bullet lodged in his brain, as we see in an extraordinary rain-soaked sequence that echoes *Memento* (2000) when he tries to remember the identity of his team of hired killers from photos he has taken and annotated (Figure 5.4). He loses his memory completely once he has exacted his revenge, returning to a kind of prelapsarian innocence alongside women and children who provide him with an ersatz family to replace the one he lost (Figure 5.5). He is therefore out of kilter with the present, the past lodged in his brain like the bullet, an inert and unrecognizable mass, as he forgets the past in the timeless present of a redemptive amnesiac innocence.

There is a second way in which he is out of kilter. His name, Costello, is also the name of another well-known cinematic killer, Jef Costello, played by Alain Delon in *Le Samouraï* (1967). Indeed, director Johnnie To wanted

Figure 5.4 Franck tries to recognize his hired killers from photos

Figure 5.5 The man-free utopia of an extended family

Delon originally for the Franck Costello role. Costello the character and Hallyday the actor are therefore both out of kilter, the character by his loss of the past and the actor by the inevitable intertextual and haunting recollection of Delon. Franck Costello and Johnny Hallyday are both palimpsests overlaid on a lost but dimly recollected past. Unlike Jef Costello in *Le Samouraï*, however, Franck Costello does not die: after a gory and bloodspattered shootout he returns to a colony of women and children in a kind of Edenic fantasy. Hallyday insisted on this conclusion, emphasizing the importance of family to him personally: "I really wanted to use what I am currently going through with my own family and to put it into the film. I'm totally scared by loneliness, I didn't want to end up alone, but surrounded by kids."[9]

Hallyday's personal life was complicated (five marriages, two children by different women, and adopted children), so the film's closure on an Edenic community would have been understood by spectators as a palliative fantasy contrasting with his off-screen personal life. This is emphasized in *Salaud, on t'aime* (2014), in which Hallyday plays Jacques, a famous photographer and philanderer who has just bought a mountain retreat and wants his four daughters by different marriages to be with him. But he has not been a good father, so the daughters do not see the need. Jacques's best friend, Frédéric, who is a doctor, is played by another veteran actor and rock star, Eddie Mitchell. Tasked with resolving the problem, Frédéric pretends that Jacques is about to die, which brings his daughters running to the house. In what is no doubt supposed to be a poignantly nostalgic scene, Hallyday and Mitchell sing along to Dean Martin and Ricky Nelson in *Rio Bravo* (1959) as they talk about Jacques dying. The insistent intercutting between the two old men and the youngster crooning "My Rifle, My Pony and Me" suggests connotations of nostalgia and regret for a long-lost youth. Claude Lelouch, the film's director, insisted on representing time passing (2013, 4), and the song manages to do this convincingly. The lyrics are about retirement: "Gonna hang my sombrero. . . . No more cows to be roping"; it is taken from an old film which the two characters are watching on TV; and the two characters who sing along to it are played by two ageing rock stars, Hallyday and Mitchell, who sang together in their youth and both acted in the Elvis Presley inspired *yéyé* films of the 1960s (e.g., *Les Parisiennes* [Tales of Paris; 1962] and *Cherchez l'idole* [The Chase; 1964]). In this film, they sing very badly, which serves, like Depardieu's grotesque body, to emphasize the decline of old age. Like Serge, Jacques has lost his youth, he does not sing (he is a photographer in the film), or if he does he does it badly (which we might not have expected given Hallyday's credentials as France's foremost rock star), and in *Vengeance* he is losing his memory. Held in tension with these instances of loss and physical decline, in both of these films Hallyday's character finds comfort in a return to the innocence of a fantasized paradisiacal family, whether the symbolic family of *Vengeance* or the more concrete but fractured family of *Salaud, on t'aime* (see Figure 5.6), gesturing

Figure 5.6 The extended family of *Salaud, on t'aime* (2014)

at one of the familiar tropes of ageing masculinity, that of paternity in old age (Hamad 2014).

Fabrice Luchini and the Fetishization of Literary Culture

With Luchini, we move away from compromised innocence to a more complex representation of male decline characterized by loss of intellect and of the hold over reality rather than immediately obvious physical decline. But like the characters played by Depardieu and Hallyday, Luchini's take refuge in a fantasy world. In *Jean-Philippe* (2006), for example, the title referring to Johnny Hallyday's real name, Jean-Philippe Smet, Luchini plays one of Hallyday's fans who one day finds himself in an alternate reality in which Johnny Hallyday the star does not exist. Luchini's engagement with popular culture in the form of Hallyday's rock star is unusual, however, because he is more often associated with high-cultural literature. In the film following *Jean-Philippe*, for example, *Molière* (2007), Luchini plays one of Molière's most famous characters, Monsieur Jourdain from the social satire *Le Bourgeois Gentilhomme* (1670), and as if to insist on "classical" literature, a few years later he plays a grumpy thespian who lives like a hermit and who refuses to play another of Molière's great characters, Alceste from *Le Misanthrope* (1666), in *Alceste à bicyclette* (Bicycling With Molière; 2013). These films trade on Luchini's relationship with literature in his public readings in theatres and on radio, whether of Céline (who is mentioned in *Dans la maison*), or others such as La Fontaine or Flaubert who are gestured at in both of the films I will be exploring.

In *Dans la maison*, Luchini plays Germain, a bored French teacher, who once published a novel and who coaches his star pupil, Claude, in creative writing. Claude is fascinated by the family of one of his schoolmates, Rapha, and gradually insinuates himself into his family, all the while writing about it. Germain, increasingly obsessed by the instalments Claude gives him, and not realizing that the story is in fact reality, treats the story as fiction and encourages Claude to make the story more dramatic, more literary – to "follow his desires," as he says. We see him intervening in the story and commenting on Claude's seduction of Rapha's mother Esther (Figure 5.7). The film enacts Claude's story, and the framing of each instalment becomes less and less clear so that by the end we are not sure whether what we are seeing is his fiction or the reality of the film: at one point he is in the room voyeuristically watching what we assume is fiction. Rapha commits suicide in the real world, and Germain loses his job as a result of his obsession. His wife shows him the latest instalment of the story, which recounts how Claude has seduced Germain's wife. Germain thinking that this has really happened, beats his wife, who leaves him. In the final Hitchcockian scene, we see him and Claude imagining different stories as they look at distant flats from the retirement home in which Germain has been put. The film

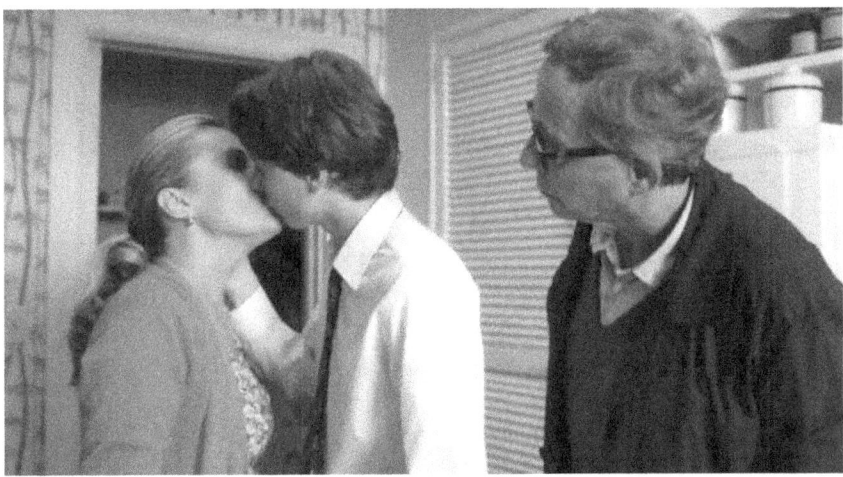

Figure 5.7 Germain fantasizes that he is in the room described in Claude's story

has been about Germain acting like a literary critic, removed from the real world and living in a world of literary fantasy, but falling into a trap set by the precocious Claude, who we understand by the end of the film is a deeply disturbed psychopath.

We find a similar framework in the other two films I want to consider. *Gemma Bovery* is an adaptation of Posy Simmonds's graphic novel, itself is a pastiche based on Flaubert's great novel. The Luchini character, Martin Joubert, is such a lover of literature that he sees life imitating art everywhere. When Gemma Bovery and her husband arrive as neighbours, the husband whose name is Charles, as in the Flaubert novel, he begins to imagine that the same things will happen to Gemma as Emma. They do to some extent: she falls for a young and very spoiled chateau brat, Hervé, paralleling the role of Rodolphe in the Flaubert novel, and she dies at the end, although not through taking arsenic, but because she unintentionally chokes on Martin's bread. As in the Ozon film, Martin is a voyeur, spying on Gemma whenever he can (Figure 5.8). As was the case in the previous film, he interferes, sending pages from the Flaubert novel anonymously to Gemma and others in an effort to prevent the worst from happening, and actually making things worse – life does not simply imitate art; he makes it so. *Le Mystère Henri Pick* confirms the association with high literature and off-kilterness of the ageing male. Luchini again plays a failed author, now a TV literary critic who, rightly as it turns out, believes a hit novel by a village pizzeria owner to be by someone else. After vituperatively attacking the supposed author's wife on his TV show, he loses his job, and sets out on a personal quest to prove that the book is a fraud.

Figure 5.8 Martin spies on Gemma

In all of these films Luchini sports a two-day stubble. While this is clearly not of the same order as Depardieu's bloated paunch and puffy complexion, nonetheless there is the same physical and mental decline. Luchini's characters lose all sense of reality, become obsessed with fiction, and end up living in a fantasy world, cut off from others, spying on them or investigating them voyeuristically, disassociated and desynchronized, as Rivoal and De Sales point out in their analysis of the loser. In both *Dans la maison* and *Gemma Bovery* his characters twist reality so that it can conform to their fantasy, nourished by literary fiction. This has tragic consequences: in *Dans la maison* Germain loses his job, his wife and his freedom, as well as being in part responsible for the suicide of Claude's friend, Rapha; and in *Gemma Bovery*, what might in his fantasy have been a suicide resembling that of Flaubert's Emma Bovary, is a tragic accident brought about, ironically and not a little comically, by Gemma choking on his bread. Whether the end result is tragic, as in *Dans la maison*, or comic, we know that Luchini's characters cannot escape. At the end of *Gemma Bovery*, Martin meets new neighbours, and his son makes him think that they are Russian because their surname begins with a K. "Karenina" murmurs Martin, as he addresses the very French neighbour in pidgin French, much to her consternation. Comical though this may be, it is, like Germain in *Dans la maison*, indicative of his disassociation and desynchronization. It is perhaps no surprise that Germain's full name is a repetition – Germain Germain – emphasizing his solipsistic disassociation from reality.

Men and women age differently in French films. Women become powerful, for example Catherine Deneuve (1943–), who ends up as a Member of Parliament in *Potiche* (Trophy Wife; 2010), the characters played by Depardieu and Luchini in that film being sidelined. We find a powerful Deneuve again as company director in *L'Homme qu'on aimait trop* (In the Name of

My Daughter; 2014), and juvenile court judge in *La Tête haute* (Standing Tall; Emmanuelle Bercot, 2015). Actors who play old men play up surliness and grumpiness, and generally turn to younger women to save them from themselves, as is the case for Michel Serrault (1928–2007) in *Une hirondelle a fait le printemps* (The Girl from Paris; 2001), Jean-Paul Belmondo in *Un homme et son chien* (A Man and His Dog; 2009), Claude Brasseur (1936–2020) in *L'Étudiante et Monsieur Henri* (The Student and Monsieur Henri; 2015), and André Dussollier (1946–) in *Adopte un veuf* (2015). The trope of the older man in a relationship with a younger woman is a familiar one in French cinema, as Vincendeau pointed out some time ago (1989 and 1992). The difference with more contemporary films is that the men have got older and the women have become younger, which only serves to emphasize the men's physical decline.

However, in the films I have discussed in this chapter, the relationship with the young woman is generally not the focus of the narrative. Serge in *Mammuth* appears to have a close relationship with his niece, but it is not clear whether it is sexual; the poem he writes at the end of the film talks in general about "love," but it is not clear whether this sentiment relates to his wife, with whom he also has a close relationship, or his niece. In *Salaud, on t'aime*, Jacques enters into a sexual relationship with the younger estate agent who has sold him the house, but despite the character being played by an A-list actor, Sandrine Bonnaire, this is a very subsidiary subplot which is less the point of the narrative than his relationship with his daughters. Martin in *Gemma Bovery* is fascinated by the younger woman but watches her from a distance. The focus in these films is resolutely on the ageing male, his fear of death and the fantasies he creates to sustain himself.

Physical decline is accompanied by moral decline, and the films display both so as to evoke nostalgically the actor's youthful body hidden beneath the sagging paunch, the wrinkled skin, the turkey neck, and the mandatory greying stubble. Whatever the narrative premise – Depardieu's road movie quest, Hallyday's quest for an unfractured family, Luchini's quest for an alignment between reality and fiction – their films all gesture towards something lost and the nostalgic quest to replace that loss with fantasy.

The films of these actors all focus on loss and destitution, whether physical for Depardieu and Hallyday or psychological for Luchini. But in each case the narratives work hard to counterbalance that loss and destitution with what I have called core values, in the sense that these are values that are closely linked to the star personas. This might be sensitivity and innocence related to the suffering macho persona of Depardieu; it might be the importance of family for Hallyday, at odds with his personal life; or it might be the importance of literature in the case of Luchini, conforming to his patrician literary associations. In each case, these core values are the silver linings kept in tension with the inevitability of loss and the choice to age disgracefully.[10]

Notes

1. There have been books (Dolan and Tincknell 2012; Swinnen and Stotesbury 2012; Whelehan and Gwynne 2014; Jermyn and Holmes 2015), and several conferences: "Age Spots and Spotlights: Celebrity, Ageing and Performance" (Birkbeck, University of London, 2011); "Revisiting Star Studies" (Newcastle University, 2013); "L'Âge des stars" (Université de Bordeaux-Montaigne, 2015); and "Ageing Film Stars" (Queen Mary University of London, 2015). The journal *Celebrity Studies* has devoted two special issues to ageing stars (Jermyn 2012; Jerslev and Petersen 2018), as well as a dossier (McCabe 2012).
2. Brigitte Bardot, Catherine Deneuve, Gérard Depardieu (Harris 2015; Moine 2016); Bernadette Lafont (Günther 2015); Charlotte Rampling (Brown 2012); Emmanuelle Riva, Simone Signoret (Leahy 2006); and Agnès Varda (Beugnet 2006).
3. Jacques Brel (*L'Emmerdeur* [A Pain in the Ass], 1973); Pierre Richard (*Les Compères* [The ComDads], 1983 and *Les Fugitifs* [The Fugitives], 1986); Jacques Villeret (*Le Dîner de cons* [The Dinner Game], 1998); Daniel Auteuil (*Le Placard* [The Closet], 2001); Gad Elmaleh (*La Doublure* [The Valet], 2005); and Patrick Timsit (*L'Emmerdeur* [A Pain in the Ass], 2008).
4. "C'est toi, un géant à l'extérieur, tout doux à l'intérieur. L'éléphant c'est ton coeur, les lapins ce sont tes mains, et l'ouistiti c'est ton zizi."
5. "Une métaphore intimiste de la monstruosité, de la dépendance au corps, de la déchéance . . . Depardieu devient le personnage principal. Son corps devient le personnage principal. Immense, démesuré. Déformé même, par rapport à ce que l'on a pu voir de lui au fil des années."
6. "Je revendique complètement ma connerie et mes dérapages. Parce qu'il y a là quelque chose de vrai. Et si on ne dérape jamais, c'est souvent qu'on est un peu con. . . . Je ne cherche pas à être un saint. Je ne suis pas contre, mais être un saint, c'est dur. La vie d'un saint est chiante. Je préfère être ce que je suis. Continuer à être ce que je suis. Un innocent."
7. "Le corps français éructant, pétant, humant, vomissant, et riant aux éclats, comme on le fait dans la province française."
8. "Il nous montre (révèle) la France des quarante dernières années, qui a plus changé en quatre décennies qu'en deux siècles de dégradation postrévolutionnaire."
9. "Je tenais tellement à me servir de ce que je vis aujourd'hui avec ma famille et l'insérer à l'écran. La solitude me fout la trouille, je ne voulais pas terminer seul, mais entouré de gamins."
10. This chapter is a revised version of " 'Losing the plot': le loser français et les masculinités à l'écran." *La figure du loser dans le film et la littérature d'expression française*, edited by Carole Edwards and Françoise Cévaër, Presses universitaires de Limoges, 2018, pp. 31–52.

Filmography

Adopte un veuf. Directed by François Desagnat, Nac Films/Someci, 2015.

Cherchez l'idole. Directed by Michel Boisrond, Union Générale Cinématographique/Adelphia Cinematografica, 1964.

Dans la maison. Directed by François Ozon, Mandarin Films/Mars Films/France 2 Cinéma/FOZ, 2012.

Easy Rider. Directed by Dennis Hopper, Pando/Raybert, 1969.

Gemma Bovery. Directed by Anne Fontaine, Albertine Productions/Ciné@/Gaumont/Cinéfrance 1888/France 2 Cinéma, 2014.

Jean-Philippe. Directed by Laurent Tuel, Fidélité Productions/Bankable, 2006.

L'Emmerdeur. Directed by Édouard Molinaro, Les Films Ariane/Mondex Films/Oceania Produzioni Internazionali Cinematografiche/Rizzoli Film, 1973.
L'Emmerdeur. Directed by Francis Veber, Pulsar Productions/TF1 International/TF1 Films Production/Téléma/EFVE 2008.
L'Étudiante et Monsieur Henri. Directed by Ivan Calbérac, Mandarin Films/StudioCanal/France 2 Cinéma/Les Belles Histoires Productions, 2015.
L'Homme qu'on aimait trop. Directed by André Téchiné, Fidélité Films/VIP Cinéma 1/Mars Films/Caneo Films, 2014.
La dernière femme. Directed by Marco Ferreri, Flaminia Produzioni Cinematografiche/Les Productions Jacques Roitfeld, 1976.
La Doublure. Directed by Francis Veber, Gaumont/EFVE/TF1 Films Production, 2005.
La Tête haute. Directed by Emmanuelle Bercot, Les Films du Kiosque/France 2 Cinéma/Wild Bunch/Rhône-Alpes Cinéma/Pictanovo Nord-Pas-de-Calais, 2015.
Le Dîner de cons. Directed by Francis Veber, Gaumont/EFVE/TF1 Films Production, 1998.
Le Mystère Henri Pick. Directed by Rémi Besançon, Manadrin Films/Gaumont/France 2 Cinéma/Scope Pictures, 2019.
Le Placard. Directed by Francis Veber, Gaumont/EFVE/TF1 Films Production, 2001.
Le Samouraï. Directed by Jean-Pierre Melville, Compagnie Industrielle et Commerciale Cinématographique/Fida Cinematografica/Filmel/T.C. Productions, 1967.
Les Compères. Directed by Francis Veber, Fideline Films/DD Productions, 1983.
Les Fugitifs. Directed by Francis Veber, Fideline Films/DD Productions/EFVE/Orly Films, 1986.
Les Parisiennes. Directed by Marc Allégret, Francos Films/Incei Films, 1962.
Loulou. Directed by Maurice Pialat, Action Films/Gaumont, 1980.
Mammuth. Directed by Gustave Kervern et Benoît Delépine, GMT Productions/No Money Productions/Arte France Cinéma/DD Productions/Monkey Pack Films, 2010.
Memento. Directed by Christopher Nolan, Newmarket Capital Group/Team Todd/I Remember Productions/Summit Entertainment, 2000.
Potiche. Directed by François Ozon, Mandarin Films/FOZ/France 2 Cinéma/Mars Films/Wild Bunch/Scope Pictures, 2010.
Rio Bravo. Directed by Howard Hawks, Armada Productions, 1959.
Salaud, on t'aime. Directed by Claude Lelouch, Les Films 13/Rhône-Alpes Cinéma, 2014.
Un homme et son chien. Directed by Francis Huster, F Comme Film/France 2 Cinéma/Fidela SAP, 2009.
Une hirondelle a fait le printemps. Directed by Christian Carion, Artémis Productions/Canal+/Centre Européen Cinématographique Rhône-Alpes/Cofimage 12/M.S. Productions/Mars Films/Nord-Ouest Films/Rhône-Alpes Cinéma/Société des Producteurs de Cinéma et de Télévision/StudioCanal, 2001.
Vengeance. Directed by Johnnie To, ARP Sélection/Milky Way Image Company, 2009.
Welcome to New York. Directed by Abel Ferrara, Belladonna Productions, 2014.

Works Cited

Basting, Anne Davis, *The Stages of Age: Performing Age in Contemporary American Culture*. The U Michigan P, 1998.

Beugnet, Martine. "Screening the Old: Femininity as Old Age in Contemporary French Cinema." *Studies in the Literary Imagination*, 39.2 (2006): 1–20.

Brown, William. "Channel Hopping: Charlotte Rampling in French Cinema of the Early 2000s." *Celebrity Studies* 3.1 (2012): 52–63.

Chivers, Sally. *The Silvering Screen: Old Age and Disability in Cinema*. U Toronto P, 2011.

Cohen-Shalev, Amir. *Visions of Ageing: Images of the Elderly in Film*. Sussex Academic Press, 2009.

Depardieu, Gérard. *Innocent*, Cherche-midi, 2015.

Dolan, Josephine. *Contemporary Cinema and 'Old Age': Gender and the Silvering of Stardom*. Palgrave Macmillan, 2018.

Dolan, Josephine, and Estella Tincknell, eds. *Aging Femininities: Troubling Representations*, Cambridge Scholars, 2012.

Dubois, Régis. "Les losers magnifiques du cinéma américain." *Le sens des images: cinéma, pop-culture et société*, 24 Apr. 2016. http://lesensdesimages.com/2016/04/24/les-losers-magnifiques-du-cinema-americain/. Accessed 15 Sept. 2016.

Gravagne, Pamela H. *The Becoming of Age: Cinematic Visions of Mind, Body and Identity in Later Life*. McFarland, 2013.

Günther, Renate. "Cross-generational Companionship: Representations of Ageing in Contemporary French Cinema." *French Cultural Studies*26.4 (2015): 439–447.

Hamad, Hannah. "Paternalising the Rejuvenation of Later Life Masculinity in Twenty-First Century Film." *Ageing, Popular Culture and Contemporary Feminism*. Eds. Imelda Whelehan and Joel Gwynne. Palgrave Macmillan, 2014. 78–92.

Harrington, C. Lee, Denise D. Bielby, and Anthony R. Bardo, eds. *Aging, Media and Culture*. Lexington Books, 2014.

Harris, Sue. "Degraded Divinity? Sacred Monstrosity? Gérard Depardieu and the Abject Star Body." *Screen* 56.3 (2015): 319–334.

Jermyn, Deborah, ed. "Back in the Spotlight: Female Celebrity and Ageing." *Celebrity Studies* 3.1 (2012).

Jermyn, Deborah, and Susan Holmes. *Women, Celebrity and Cultures of Aging: Freeze Frame*. Palgrave Macmillan, 2015.

Jerslev, Anne, and Line Nybro Petersen, eds. "Ageing Celebrities, Ageing Fans, and Ageing Narratives in Popular Media." *Celebrity Studies* 9.2 (2018).

Leahy, Sarah. "Simone Signoret: Aging and Agency." *Studies in the Literary Imagination* 39.2 (2006): 21–42.

Lelouch, Claude. "Entretien avec Claude Lelouch." *Salaud, on t'aime, Les Films* 13.4. www.lesfilms13.com/wp-content/uploads/2013/05/SALAUD_DP-A5-WEB.pdf

McCabe, Jane, ed. "Grey Matters: Male Ageing, Performance and Celebrity." *Celebrity Studies* 3.2 (2012).

Millet, Richard. *Le corps politique de Gérard Depardieu*. Pierre-Guillaume de Roux, 2014.

Moine, Raphaëlle. "Gérard Depardieu, star 'hénaurme': vieillir en monstre sacré." Conference programme 'L'Âge des stars: des images à l'épreuve du vieillissement', 2016. http://mica.u-bordeaux-montaigne.fr/images/stories/seminaires/07-2015-livret_age_des_stars.pdf. Accessed 17 Sept. 2016.

Pudlowski, Charlotte. "*Welcome to New York* n'est pas un film sur DSK mais sur Depardieu." *Slate*, 18 May 2014. www.slate.fr/culture/87237/welcome-new-york-dsk-depardieu. Accessed 19 Sept. 2016.

Richardson, Niall. *Ageing Femininity on Screen: The Older Woman in Contemporary Cinema*. Bloomsbury Academic, 2019.

Rivoal, Isabelle, and Anne De Sales. "Anthropologie de la Lose." Conference programme, December, Paris 10.2012. www.mae.u-paris10.fr/lesc/IMG/pdf/Anthropologie-Lose-programme.pdf. Accessed 15 Sept. 2016.
Shary, Timothy, and Nancy McVittie. *Fade to Gray: Ageing in American Cinema.* U Texas P, 2016.
Smith, Susan. " 'Get Off Your Asses for These Old Broads!': Elizabeth Taylor, Ageing and the Television Comeback Movie." *Celebrity Studies* 3.1 (2012): 25–36.
Swinnen, Aagje. "Introduction: *Benidorm Bastards*, or the Do's and Don'ts of Aging." *Aging Performance and Stardom: Doing Age on the Stage of Consumerist Culture.* Eds. Aagje Swinnen and John Stotesbury. LIT, 2012. 7–14.
Swinnen, Aagje, and John Stotesbury, eds. *Aging Performance and Stardom: Doing Age on the Stage of Consumerist Culture.* LIT, 2012.
Vincendeau, Ginette. "Daddy's Girl: Oedipal Narratives in 1930s French Films." *Iris* 8 (1989): 71–80.
Vincendeau, Ginette. "Family Plots: The Fathers and Daughters of French Cinema." *Sight & Sound* 1.11 (1992): 14–17.
Vincendeau, Ginette. "Gérard Depardieu: The Axiom of Contemporary French Cinema." *Screen* 34.4 (1993): 343–361.
Whelehan, Imelda, and Joel Gwynne, eds. *Ageing, Popular Culture and Contemporary Feminism: Harleys and Hormones.* Palgrave Macmillan, 2014.

6 Jean Rochefort as Ageing Star
Masculinity and Masquerade

Philip Dine

This chapter focuses on a range of films drawn from the extensive career of Jean Rochefort (1930–2017), one of France's best-loved and most lauded stage and screen actors. The works examined cover five decades, dating from 1977 to 2015, while their subjects range from decolonization to dementia. Through his evolving star persona, and particularly his regular engagement with the processes of ageing, Rochefort offered French audiences a distinctive variety of on-screen masculinity, and, in important respects, an enduring image of France itself. His roles frequently foregrounded individuals in perceived decline, whether physical, psychological, professional or even political in nature. Examined as an "ageing text," this star performer offers a lens both for studying a national cinema culture and for exploring how a given society understands growing old. More specifically, Rochefort's frequently, but by no means exclusively, whimsical variety of cinematic masculinity highlights how the on-screen depiction of diverse forms of individual retreat, retirement or other age-related withdrawal may provide opportunities for the expression of personal resilience and even clues towards collective redemption.

A key feature of the following analysis will be Lisa Downing's insights into Rochefort's extended association with filmmaker Patrice Leconte, for whom he became an acknowledged alter ego. Through this partnership, the pair were to present what Downing has identified as a critical reflection on "ways in which cinematic masculinity functions as a masquerade" (2004, 54). This scholar notes that Rochefort's physical characteristics, including his spare frame, drooping moustache and hangdog expression, made him the ideal focus for Leconte's high-spirited contemplation of variously challenged, and not infrequently conflicted, masculine identities. This aspect of the pair's work together would, over time, become firmly associated with illness and ageing, culminating in their collaboration with national music icon Johnny Hallyday (1943–2017) in *L'Homme du train* (Man on the Train, 2002). The release, and combined critical acclaim and commercial success, of this film fed into the exceptionally public, and overtly state-endorsed, celebration of (male) ageing that occurred in June 2003 when Hallyday turned 60, and which included prime-time retrospectives every evening for 60 days on national television, together with a series of sold-out concerts at the Parc des Princes stadium in Paris (Tinker 2007, 67–68).

While subject to less spectacular manifestations of collective adulation, Rochefort was also undoubtedly "a French national treasure" (Guardian 2017). However, he may not be the first actor who suggests himself for a case study of ageing on the French screen, belonging as he does to a generation of male stars remarkable for their personal and professional longevity. In fact, Rochefort's peer group itself followed in the footsteps of Jean Gabin (1904–1976), whose first screen role came in 1930, while his final film appeared in the year of his death. Gabin's later career saw him co-star alongside a particularly rich post-war cohort of masculine leads, who would prove to be similarly expansive in their output. These celebrated figures include Jean-Paul Belmondo (1933–2021), Alain Delon (1935-present) and Michel Piccoli (1925–2020). Like Gabin, Belmondo and Delon, Piccoli often played tough-guy police officers and gangsters. However, Piccoli's exceptional range distinguishes him in this regard, in a career that included collaborations with eminent directors as varied as Jean Renoir and Alain Resnais, and as Luis Buñuel and Alfred Hitchcock. In contrast, in Guy Austin's analysis, "Along with [Italian-born, Lino] Ventura [1919-1987] and the mature Gabin, Belmondo and Delon are the key macho stars in modern French film," throughout their careers conforming to "ultra-masculine archetypes, most notably expressing the ideals of independence and authority" (2003, 49).

Crucially, as Austin argues, we may identify "a historical specificity fuelling such archetypes" (2003, 49), namely the rapid and radical transformation of French society that resulted from the post-war reconstruction made possible by Marshall Aid, together with the ensuing Americanization of the country's cultural sphere. One celebrated cinematic evocation of this unprecedented reordering and the new mobility to which it gave rise – Jean-Luc Godard's *À bout de souffle* (Breathless, 1960) – is hinted at by Kristin Ross when she highlights "the headlong, dramatic, and breathless" quality of the twin narratives of modernization and decolonization that prevailed in the France of this period (1995, 4). While the former articulated the reorganization of the country during the *Trente Glorieuses* (the 30 years of sustained economic growth that followed World War II), the latter included the experience of successive military defeats in Indo-China (1946–1954) and Algeria (1954–1962). These processes forcefully combined, with the result that "French society was transformed after the war from a rural, empire-oriented, Catholic country into a fully industrialized, decolonized, and urban one" (Ross 1995, 4).

Constructions of masculinity were central to the self-conscious modernity of this period:

> an examination of the discursive production of the time shows that the noun most often modified by the adjective "new" was in fact that of

"man": . . . the arrival of the "new man," of a new construction of (male) subjectivity was proclaimed from all sides, celebrated, analysed, and debated.

(Ross 1995, 157–158)

In their different ways, Belmondo, Delon and Piccoli all offered incarnations of this new man.[1] In contrast, and although a member of this same cinematic generation, Jean Rochefort was to configure himself as an antidote to the frenetic modernization of the *Trente Glorieuses*, together with the socio-political uncertainties both of that age and of the decades that followed. He did this by making ageing, and diverse forms of age-related social withdrawal, central aspects of his on-screen persona, finding strength in a variety of expressions of retreat and retirement. In the process, Rochefort's work would encourage a re-evaluation of the symbolic legacies of this pivotal period: the end of empire, the changing face of the broadcast media, the vanishing charm of provincial towns and villages, and the threatened rituals of everyday life in such socially and cinematically cherished locations. The actor would also become the focus for expressions of individual and collective memory, from the contested to the nostalgic, together with attendant representations of decline, regret and loss, typically leavened by his trademark blend of playfulness and paradoxical resilience. In this way, Rochefort's later filmic repertoire offered French audiences a vicarious experience of the vicissitudes of the individual life course that would cumulatively prove to be of abiding value.

In the first of the above-mentioned memorial spheres, we may draw attention to Pierre Schoendoerffer's *Le Crabe-Tambour* (1977). In this film, the elegiac evocation of the colonial recollections of a dying naval officer foregrounds individual frailty as a metaphor for collective dysfunction, linking France's historic failure of accountability as regards its former territories to an ongoing crisis of masculinity in the post-imperial era. The work may thus be considered a precursor of the broader questioning of established gender roles that would play out on the nation's screens in the 1980s (Powrie 1997). At a more personal level, Schoendoerffer's film was just one expression of his career-long engagement with the French wars of decolonization, notably informed by his own experience as a veteran of the Indo-China conflict. However, for our purposes here, the production is primarily remarkable for Rochefort's performance in the lead role as the ship's commander. Significantly, this character is never named, being referred to by his rank of "Commandant" or, both respectfully and affectionately, by crewmembers who appreciate his professional expertise but from whom he nevertheless always keeps his distance, as "le Vieux" or "the old man." Rochefort received a César award for his contribution to the film, as did its celebrated cinematographer, Raoul Coutard, another Indo-China veteran and formerly a key figure in the emergence of the New Wave.

Much of the film's action takes place on a fishery protection vessel in the North Atlantic, with extended sequences of icy seas underscoring the isolation of the ship, its crew, and above all their ailing captain. Playing against type, Rochefort remains stoically and silently watchful for much of the film, until forced to give up this final command as his health declines during the return voyage to the vessel's home port of Lorient. Increasingly essential consultations between the commander and the ship's doctor (Claude Rich) reveal the senior officer's terminal cancer, which he had not disclosed, while also allowing the gradual emergence of his hidden history. This centres on the perceived dishonour that resulted from the naval authorities' rejection of his offered resignation in the wake of the failed Algiers putsch of April 1961, to which he had promised support. This involvement reflected his then friendship with a seditious fellow officer, Lieutenant Willsdorff (Jacques Perrin, another regular collaborator of the director), now a fisherman on a Breton trawler, whom he will speak to briefly by ship-to-ship radio before returning home to die. The Commandant's parting message – "Adieu – il n'y a rien à dire" (Farewell – there is nothing to say) – is the culmination of the film's predominant sense of loss, both personal and political, which is underlined by the melancholy images of rotting vessels that open and close the film.

While Rochefort was only in his forties when he made *Le Crabe-Tambour*, he was in his fifties by the time he worked with Patrice Leconte on *Tandem* (1987). This collaboration was possible despite the well-documented clash of personalities that had occurred a decade earlier when the two worked together on Leconte's first full-length feature, the zany police comedy, and commercial and critical flop, *Les vécés étaient fermés de l'intérieur* (The Toilets Were Locked from the Inside, 1976). Their altogether more fruitful collaboration on *Tandem* would lay the ground for later successes including *Le Mari de la coiffeuse* (The Hairdresser's Husband, 1990) and *L'Homme du Train* (The Man on the Train, 2002), both of which are considered here. They also worked together to good effect on productions ranging from the widely lauded costume drama *Ridicule* (1996) to the knockabout comedy *Les Grands Ducs* (The Grand Dukes, also 1996), which features a trio of ageing and impecunious actors who attempt to salvage their careers with one last repertory tour.

A similar combination of low-rent road movie and artistic last bow also characterized *Tandem* (1987), in which Rochefort played an elderly game show host, based on the real-life figure of Lucien Jeunesse (1918–2008). Jeunesse presented over 10,000 editions of the weekday radio quiz *Le Jeu des mille francs* (The Thousand Francs Game) between 1957 and 1995, when he announced his retirement. The show that Jeunesse had made famous would subsequently relaunch in response to the ensuing public clamour, still existing today as *Le Jeu des mille euros* (The Thousand Euros Game). In Leconte's version of this story, which Jeunesse himself strongly disliked (Harang 1995), Rochefort's character, Michel Mortez, is a complex figure. His frequently disagreeable personality reveals itself in irritability and self-importance, neither of which is improved by his alcoholism and a gambling addiction. However, the character's redeeming qualities include periodic self-parody and an always-consummate professionalism, despite his increasingly apparent illness, in both of which he is unstintingly supported by his long-suffering sound engineer Rivetot (Gérard Jugnot). The physical disparity between the elegant and angular Rochefort and the rumpled and stocky Jugnot is verbally underscored by their respective use of the familiar *tu* and the respectful *vous* forms of address as they criss-cross France in an ageing Ford Granada estate.

Sharing the confined space of the car as they traverse uniformly dull byways between insignificant localities, their trip is punctuated by overnight stays in the similarly constricted spaces of twin bedrooms in cheap hotels. However, as they drive, bicker, then reconcile, the two men experience moments of warmth and even freedom in shared expressions of relaxation and amusement, developing a mutual affection that overcomes the constitutional arrogance of the presenter and the learnt subservience of the sound engineer.[2] Their evolving friendship comes to the fore with Rivetot's ultimately vain attempt to prevent Mortez from finding out that his show is due to be axed and that this is consequently his swan song. Suggestions earlier in the film of the ageing star's mental, as well as physical, fragility are reinforced by Rivetot's discovery that his regular and impassioned calls to his wife from public telephones have throughout been play-acting in reply to the speaking clock. This revelation's punctual insistence on temporality underlines the broader theme of time passing and, indeed, of its passing the pair by, as France moves on and public tastes change.

Having discovered the truth about the show's future, Mortez disappears in the course of his final live transmission. His increasingly evident breakdown culminates in a remarkable scene where he wanders aimlessly across a landfill site, surrounded by thousands of scavenging seagulls that take to the air as he passes, like some junkyard King Lear. The regularly elegiac qualities of this tragi-comedy are here particularly in evidence. In a final plot twist, permitting a shift of tone that amounts to a happy ending, the down-at-heel Rivetot discovers Mortez working as a successful, and again self-parodic, itinerant hawker in that commercial cathedral of "les trente glorieuses," the out-of-town hypermarket, and the two men renew their nomadic partnership in a new car and with a fresh optimism. They may have left, or been left behind by, the constantly shifting world of the French broadcast media, but their reinvigorated odd-couple friendship now offers them fresh horizons for ironizing self-discovery as they continue their journey through their still fundamentally recognizable homeland.

Having enjoyed success with this focus on male bonding in *Tandem*, Leconte would seek to explore male-female relations in a subsequent trilogy of films, characterized by Lisa Downing as "a tripartite self-referential reflection on the mechanisms of cinematic voyeurism" (2004, 83). This cycle opens with *Monsieur Hire* (1989) and concludes with *Le Parfum d'Yvonne*

(Yvonne's Perfume, 1993), neither of which features Jean Rochefort. However, the actor did take on the role of the eponymous protagonist in the central element of this directorial triptych, *Le Mari de la coiffeuse* (The Hairdresser's Husband, 1990). Downing notes the key function played in this "idiosyncratic and semi-autobiographical" film (2004, 15), and in others directed by Leconte, by the star's determinedly non-macho performance of masculinity. According to this analysis, Rochefort is of particular value to the director as

> a figure whose persona (a combination of diegetic character and off-screen reputation) suggests mental instability or fragility (*Tandem*), loss and melancholy (*Le Mari de la coiffeuse*) and . . . the frailty of ill health and encroaching old age (*L'Homme du train*).
>
> (Downing 2004, 68)

Moreover, as Downing explains:

> In placing Rochefort, rather than some glamorous or macho figure, as the directorial alter ego, Leconte admits an awareness of the constructedness of cinematic masculinity and the fragility of the masquerade into his filmmaking with the very gesture that usually masks and disavows them.
>
> (2004, 68)

Where Rochefort's physically declining but psychologically maturing game show host was initially constrained and eventually liberated by geographical mobility in *Tandem*, Antoine, the protagonist of *Le Mari de la coiffeuse* (1990), draws upon varieties of locational stability to achieve an objectively implausible but artistically coherent expression of happiness. Critics have varied widely in their assessment of this film, with accusations of misogyny (such as from Guy Austin) contrasting with praise for its psychological complexity as a study of sexual fetishism and deferred mourning (notably by Paul Sutton; Downing 2004, 89–91). These differing interpretations have their roots in the central narrative, which begins by retracing, in flashback, Antoine's adolescent fascination with the voluptuous local hairdresser, Madame Sheaffer (Anne-Marie Pisani). Her suicide appears to have fixed this obsession in the boy's mind, with his lifetime ambition, as declared to his appalled father, becoming to marry a hairdresser. While the intervening years of his life remain unclear, in his fifties Antoine does, indeed, meet and marry the vivacious and much younger Mathilde (Anna Galiena), living an idyllic existence in her barbershop for a decade before she too commits suicide, ostensibly because she does not want their happiness to end.

An erotic male fantasy that turns on this repetition of female self-sacrifice, Leconte's tragicomedy reveals its constitutive ambiguity on closer inspection. In her analysis, Marie-Claude Loiselle stresses the contrast between the two central figures, evoking "the serene immobility of Antoine" and the "silent and eminently more down-to-earth anguish" that characterizes Mathilde's personality; significantly, the hairdresser is the sole breadwinner of the married couple (Loiselle 1991, 64). While he revels languidly in their belated love affair, combining a passionate present with fond recollections of youthful carnality, she cannot escape the daily signs of the passage of time and with it the inevitability of physical decline and death. The steadily worsening stoop of one of her regular customers, of which Mathilde alone takes note, serves to trace the evolution of her own, altogether more negative, outlook on ageing (Loiselle 1991, 64).

Leconte's film undoubtedly has a dreamlike quality, and one in which the sensual depiction of the two female figures, and of the married couple's May–September love affair, may reasonably be regarded as voyeuristic, in line with the erotic perspective of the protagonist. However, as Claude Evans has argued: "Even if *Le Mari de la coiffeuse* seems to be the perfect illustration of Laura Mulvey's theory of the masculine gaze on the feminine object . . . the director's misogyny is open to question" (2004, 144). She makes this argument because Mathilde, in common with a number of other female characters in Leconte's films, possesses

> a strength of mind that their partners sorely lack. They have the courage to jump because of their desire for an absolute that real life does not offer them. . . . Mathilde ends her days alone, which puts into question the image of the idealized couple she makes with Antoine.
>
> (Evans 2004, 144)

Thus, rather than taking his own life, the bereaved Antoine seeks solitary refuge in the now abandoned small-town hairdressing salon that forms the film's primary location, there to submerge himself anew in the fantasy world that he has created. This psychic immersion takes on a physical dimension through Antoine's previously displayed penchant for Arab dancing, indulged in one final time as the film closes in a parting, and characteristically self-deprecating, performance of a playfully exotic sexual identity. At once comedic and poignant, this strange ritual is a key element in the film's resolutely provincial continuity, functioning as a "bizarre leitmotif . . . in which the very French, very middle-aged Rochefort undulates incongruously to the accompaniment of Eastern music" (Downing 2004, 94–95). As Evans argues, in an increasingly open-minded and multicultural France, "Oriental dance is the caricature of a provocative sexuality which has become the norm. Performed by Antoine, who shows off his paunch and sometimes has a cigarette hanging from his mouth, it becomes grotesque" (2004, 137). As embodied by Rochefort, the amused self-acceptance of an ageing male's misshapen body, together with his irredeemable fetishism, would appear to offer a suitable tribute to Eros and at least a temporary refuge from Thanatos (Downing 2004, 89–96).

Although nominated for seven César awards, *Le Mari de la coiffeuse* was ultimately unsuccessful at an annual ceremony dominated by Jean-Paul Rappenau's costume drama *Cyrano de Bergerac* (1990), starring Gérard Depardieu (1948–present), himself an acknowledged *monstre sacré* of the French screen. Nevertheless, the film was Leconte's first international success, as reflected by its nomination in 1992 for the British Academy of Film and Television Arts prize for best foreign-language film. Although Rappenau's film was also nominated, neither French production took the award. Yet the reception of Leconte's film marked an important expansion of Rochefort's visibility, with his most significant fan in the English-speaking world being Terry Gilliam. This exceptionally innovative director went on to cast the actor as the eponymous knight errant in his notoriously troubled film *The Man Who Killed Don Quixote*, for which pre-production began in 1998 but which finally made it to the screen in 2018. Rather than being "a marriage made in heaven" (Kermode 2013), as the actor's back catalogue might reasonably have suggested, this casting decision contributed significantly to Gilliam's creative woes. Filming began in Spain in 2000, but was catastrophically difficult from the outset, ending when the 70-year-old Rochefort was obliged to pull out of the project due to illness. The actor had been selected by Gilliam as the perfect incarnation of Cervantes's "knight of the sorrowful countenance" both because of his distinctive physical appearance and for his skill as a horseman, reflecting a lifelong passion that included distinguished service as an equestrian sports commentator for French national television (Guérand 2017). Nor could there be any doubting the seriousness of Rochefort's preparation for the role, which involved practising his part in English for seven months (Adriaensen 2009, 253). However, a combination of prostate problems and a herniated spinal disc, both exacerbated by riding in an unfamiliar period saddle – and, in the actor's estimation, on a wholly unsuitable mount – were to end his participation in the seemingly doomed venture (Guérand 2017).

However, Rochefort would shortly return to less taxing subversions of masculine archetypes, moving from the age of chivalry to the tradition of hard-boiled detective fiction and its reflection in both American and French *film noir*. As Guy Austin argues, in their later careers, even such confirmed macho men as Belmondo and Delon were to inflect their characters with pathos and comedy (2003, 59–62). Both of these elements are amply in evidence in Leconte's *L'Homme du train* (2002), in which the director renewed his collaboration with Rochefort. In addition, Leconte mobilized, and playfully undermined, the self-consciously Americanized machismo of national music icon Johnny Hallyday, in such a way as to generate an engaging cinematic meditation "whose key thematic preoccupations can be said to be maturation, demystification and reflection on the past" (Downing 2004, 126).

Returning to the trope of the odd couple, Leconte deftly handles the chance encounter between Rochefort's retired poetry teacher, Manesquier, and Hallyday's mysterious gangster, Milan, in what is an undoubted high point in the careers of all three artists. Filmed in Annonay in the tranquil southern department of the Ardèche, the film's unassuming provincial location establishes an initial mood of permanence, and associated boredom. This predictability will be disrupted by the arrival of Milan, to whom Manesquier offers a place to stay as the small town's single hotel is closed. Apparent certainties about their contrasting varieties of masculinity dissolve as the two men eat, drink and converse, learning about each other and their differences, both real and imagined. In the course of these exchanges, they swap ironically stereotypical aspects of their lives: Milan learns the proper way to wear a pair of slippers, while Manesquier receives tuition in how to handle a gun. For all their superficial disparity, the two men are both marking time, reflecting on their retreating pasts, unsatisfactory presents, and uncertain futures as they await critical moments in their lives: "The narrative reaches its climax as the two men both face a day of reckoning: Manesquier's triple bypass operation and Milan's bank robbery" (Downing 2004, 126). Ambiguity, both narrative and ontological, is the most striking feature of the film's final scenes:

> As both protagonists lie apparently dying – Manesquier from a failed surgical operation, Milan from a shoot-out – we cut to scenes of Milan returning to his friend's house to take up the life of the retired school teacher, while Manesquier prepares to board the train on which Milan arrived, to seek out the limitless adventures his previous life of comfort and confinement had precluded.
>
> (Downing 2004, 127)

Whether or not these images are simply the fantasies of dying men, their lack of diegetic closure encourages reflection on the vagaries of the life course, and of life choices, with particular regard not only to the challenges but also to the opportunities of ageing. This unforeseen denouement thereby suggests the experiential, and even existential, doors that may open, as well as those that are sure to close, in the latter stages of that inevitable process.

The ambiguities of life and the certainties of death, and the imbrication of both with individual itineraries embarked upon in youth and completed in old age, are also foregrounded in Fernando Trueba's *L'Artiste et son modèle* (The Artist and the Model, 2012). A Franco-Spanish coproduction filmed in the two languages and on both sides of the international border, this work makes the crossing of frontiers – personal, geographical, and aesthetic – an integral part of its narrative. Situated in the French Catalan region in the summer of 1943, Trueba's film sets the lyrical evocation of the seasonal rhythms of rural life against the jarring backdrop of the Nazi Occupation. The plot centres on an elderly but celebrated sculptor, Marc Cros, played by the then octogenarian Jean Rochefort. Having lost his interest in artistic endeavour, Cros reawakens to his vocation when his wife Léa (Claudia Cardinale), for many years his inspirational model, takes in a young Spanish refugee, Mercé (Aida Folch), on condition that she should pose unclothed for her husband. Trueba largely avoids the voyeuristic potential of this arrangement through black-and-white filming and sensitive framing, notably including shots in the artist's studio of sketches and sculptures previously generated as part of his obsessive preoccupation with the female form. The resulting contemplation of the process of imaginative creation culminates in Cros's achievement of his life's ambition in the form of a neo-classical masterpiece inspired by his young muse. This objective finally reached, the film closes with Mercé heading off on her bicycle for a new life in Marseille, avoiding the Occupation forces by following the backroads of the lovingly filmed Mediterranean landscape. For his part, Cros applies the final touches to his magnum opus before taking his life with an old shotgun in the sunlit garden of his hillside studio.

On one level, this narrative is an obvious reworking of the Pygmalion myth, as well as one more variation on the May–September love affair, which, in this case, is generally platonic in nature, with the exception of a single ambiguous sequence. This episode follows on from one the previous day, in which Cros is troubled for the first time by sexual arousal while sculpting Mercé's naked form. Having left the studio abruptly, he returns home and confesses his discomfiture to his amused wife as they lie together that night, notably rejecting Léa's own playful advances. Early the next morning, finding Mercé still in bed at the studio, he goes into her room and proceeds to stroke her reclining body, seemingly with the young woman's tacit acceptance as she turns her bare back towards him. Then, turning to face him once again, she cradles his face in her hands in what appears to be a display of filial affection rather than a sexual embrace, moving the old man to tears. However, the following scene, in which the pair share an al fresco meal, and in which Mercé almost stereotypically smokes and drinks wine, while Cros questions her gently about her previous sexual encounters, certainly leaves scope for doubt. In contrast, Mercé's affair with a wounded young *maquisard*, whom she takes in and nurses before guiding him to safety across the Spanish border, is both overt and clearly accepted by Cros, who commits himself to the pair's Resistance work despite his initial reluctance to be drawn into the war.

Here, as in other aspects of the film, "Jean Rochefort is deeply moving [*bouleversant*] in his role as the elderly artist who understands neither the absurdity of war nor the folly of men" (Degroult et al. 2014, 16). British critic Mark Kermode underlines the actor's crucial contribution to the originality of Trueba's film, which, in other respects, reproduces a variety of philosophical commonplaces and familiar cinematic tropes. In Kermode's formulation (2013):

> With Jean-Claude Carrière sharing screenwriting credits,[3] this holds few surprises in its revelatory conclusions about old men and young

women, war and peace, art and reality, God and the devil. Still, Daniel Vilar's handsome monochrome photography is very easy on the eye, and Rochefort remains one of the few performers who can make the act of pouring olive oil on to bread seem significant, even metaphysical.

In the French press, Sandrine Marques (2013) similarly hailed the star's underpinning of the production's thematic coherence and aesthetic precision: "this constrained film is reliant on the internalized performance of the excellent Jean Rochefort to enable it to stick to the clear line of its subject." Comparing the film's overall effect to that of a still life painting – evocatively rendered in French as "une nature morte" – this critic also highlights the pivotal contribution made to the film by Aida Folch as the ageing artist's youthful muse: "By the grace of her incandescent presence, the character of Mercé contrasts with the film's ambient morbidity" (Marques 2013). This broader impression reinforces the striking contrast, as the film closes, between her joyful mobility and the now permanent immobility of Cros, with suicide once again firmly in the narrative mix, but this time paradoxically reflecting the rediscovered free will of the male protagonist.

Three years later, Rochefort would produce his most fully developed performance of the linked themes of ageing and illness as Claude Lherminier, the protagonist of Philippe Le Guay's *Floride* (Florida, 2015). Having regularly played the older lover, in his final screen role Rochefort was destined to bear out Aagje Swinnen's shrewd observation on the cinematic representation of ageing: "If we have late-life romances at one end of the film spectrum, on the other we find plots propelled by the impact of dementia on individual lives" (2015, 71). Dreaming throughout of the titular American state and its familiar retirement idyll, Rochefort's character offers a powerful depiction of the devastating impact of Alzheimer's disease on the protagonist himself and on those around him, including most dramatically his devoted daughter Carole (Sandrine Kiberlain). Filmed in the striking Alpine location of Annecy, the film presents picture-postcard locations as the backdrop to Carole's seemingly endless labours, as she endeavours not only to run the family's paper manufacturing plant, previously managed in dictatorial fashion by her domineering father, but also to avoid having to put Claude in a care home.

In the process, Carole inevitably suffers from her father's cognitive decline and behavioural challenges. This is most apparent in her relationship with her boyfriend Thomas (Laurent Lucas), who falls victim to an unprovoked hammer attack by Claude and leaves soon afterwards. The situation also brings her into conflict with her son Robin (Clement Métayer), who rebels against her eventual, and wholly reluctant, decision to put her father into a nursing home. In order to maintain his grandfather's independence, the young man uses the funds in his savings account – set up for him by Claude, with instructions never to touch the money "except for something important" (*sauf pour un truc important*) – in order to pay for the old man's long dreamed-of trip to Florida. The viewer consequently sees an alternately delighted and bewildered Claude at various stages of the flight to Miami, and then follows his arrival and taxi journey to the former home of Alice, his other daughter, actually long deceased. However, it remains unsure whether the whole episode is merely a figment of his increasingly troubled imagination. This ambiguity derives primarily from the protagonist's exiting the Florida villa by a door that leads directly into the care home in the company of one of its staff members.

Elsewhere, in his own chateau-style residence, as in other privileged locations used by Le Guay, the dapper Claude's adventures and misadventures are alike framed by genteel domesticity. Thus, as in Rochefort's previous films, including notably *L'Homme du train*, which is similarly set in a rambling bourgeois townhouse, this production conveys a general absence of material deprivation in its depiction of ageing. Freed from mundane hardships, Rochefort's character may take on an apparently ageless and even timeless quality. This has been likened specifically by clinical gerontologists to that associated with the later Gabin, notably in Jean Delannoy's comedy *Le Baron de l'écluse* (The Baron of the Locks, 1960; Calvet and Clément 2019, 3). However, it is important not to understate the concretely disagreeable aspects of the figure of Claude Lherminier, most obviously his variously deceitful, insulting and even bullying treatment of his long-suffering daughter Carole. It is a tribute to Jean Rochefort's skills that the actor is able to redeem this frequently repellent character by deploying his distinctive playfulness and self-deprecating humour, not least in the regularly intercalated scenes of the real or imagined flight to Florida.

Building on the theme of Americanized "senior" travel is the nostalgic car trip that Lherminier takes with his daughter in the vintage sports model that Carole has had lovingly restored for him. The old man's genuine joy is apparent from his first sight of the open-topped two-seater, and then in its passenger seat, as his daughter takes him for a spin through the region's stunning scenery. However, an occasion that starts so well will end in a pointless altercation with Thomas, an engineer at the family paper factory and Carole's new boyfriend, whom her clearly resentful father has met for the first time earlier that day. Belligerently initiated and stoked by Lherminier, this dispute – about technical aspects of the plant's manufacturing process – occurs at an idyllic lakeside restaurant, thereby ending the intended festivities.

Earlier in this episode, an apparently passing reference hints at the contextual specificity of this and other depictions of ageing masculinity on the French screen. For, at the start of the day's celebrations, Claude's grandson offers an observation that, while seemingly insignificant in itself, leads us back to the *Trente Glorieuses* and thereby to the period's obsession with the motorized mobility of its putative "new man." More specifically, Robin corrects his grandfather's Romanian carer Ivona (Anamaria Marinca), an empathetic figure and an astute observer of the old man and his family, when she mistakenly assumes that the car is an American model. The vehicle is, in fact, a Floride, as in both the film's title and the French name for the American state. Launched by the nationalized manufacturer Renault in 1958, the car prominently featured Brigitte Bardot in its advertising, thus linking the vehicle to cinematic representations of gender and sexuality, and by association to the vaunted glamour of Saint-Tropez and the Côte d'Azur. However, for all its aggressively sporty styling, the car relied on the basic technology of the company's mass-market models. As Éamon Ó Cofaigh points out: "By updating an older, lighter car, the Floride was left woefully underpowered and, hence, referred to as 'a sheep in wolf's clothing' by the media in its early years" (2022, 152). The same characterization might apply to Claude Lherminier, as to many of the variously fragile male protagonists brought to life by Jean Rochefort over the course of his long and distinguished career.

In *Floride*, his final screen role, and at the age of 85, Rochefort offered a masterclass in the depiction of ageing. As one critic commented for *Le Nouvel Observateur*, Le Guay's sympathetic direction

> enables Rochefort to play delightfully on the vagaries of growing old. By turns light-hearted, playful, embittered and withdrawn, the actor displays a flexibility of nuance and a range of qualities that continually revive a narrative that risks sinking into the abyss of old age.
>
> (Malausa 2015)

We might simply note that key elements of this remarkable culminating portrayal have their roots in the star's earlier work, and in the films considered in this chapter. As we have seen, Rochefort's leading roles extended from the depiction of professional decline and terminal illness in Schoendoerffer's *Le Crabe-Tambour*, through cumulative contributions to Leconte's extended reflection on the vicissitudes of the life course, as highlighted by both male-female and male-male relationships, to his depiction of aesthetic endeavour and ethical engagement in later life in Trueba's *L'Artiste et son modèle*. Perhaps most concretely, Rochefort the lifelong equestrian is unlikely ever to have forgotten his humbling experience of personal infirmity during his ill-fated collaboration with Terry Gilliam. Whether as Gilliam's Quixote or Le Guay's Alzheimer's patient, filmmakers looked to Rochefort as an actor uniquely able to combine pathos with the widest variety of comic forms. These ranged from slapstick, as when British director Steve Bendelack cast him opposite Rowan Atkinson in *Mr Bean's Holiday* (2007), to the verbal jousting of the 17th-century French court in Leconte's *Ridicule* (1996). Encouraging audiences throughout his career to look critically at themselves and their relationships, together with the broader society within which their lives played out, this remarkable actor's humour could range from gentle to acerbic. However, as epitomized by his masterly depiction of dementia in *Floride*, Rochefort's comic talents were at their sharpest when they were most ingeniously transgressive, allowing the ageing star to "extract laughter from us that is all the stronger because we are well aware that there are things at which we should not laugh" (Sotinel 2015).

Jean Rochefort stood out in a generation of enduring male stars who, each in their own way, grew old together on the French screen. He distinguished himself from his variously illustrious contemporaries by making personal fragility a trademark of his cinematic persona over half a century. While Rochefort was only in his forties when this process began, his own ageing would serve to expand the range of his on-screen characterization, giving ever greater depth and poignancy to his patented brand of self-deprecating humour. Indeed, the star may be said to have been old before his time as regards the roles that he took on as he matured, with Patrice Leconte's *Tandem* proving to be a pivotal moment in his later career. In that film, made when he was in his mid-fifties, Rochefort convincingly played a character transparently based on the real-life figure of Lucien Jeunesse in his late seventies. The depiction of physical and mental decline underpinning that performance was built upon in subsequent appearances, which together reveal a process of personal investment and professional dedication culminating in the remarkable *Floride*, just two years before the actor's death.

In addition, Rochefort engaged with representations of ageing not only for longer than his more celebrated peers, but also in a manner that made his on-screen persona distinctive in terms of the representation of "national" manhood that it offered. Notwithstanding the increasing subtlety of their performances as they too aged, conventionally macho stars like Belmondo and Delon remained within an established tradition of genre-based – and, indeed, gender-based – storytelling that allowed its male stars to grow old gracefully (Austin 2003, 31). They were consequently able to continue to present fundamentally reassuring iterations of their star personae and, through them, of the characteristic brand of cinematic masculinity that had been forged in the modernity-obsessed France of the *Trente Glorieuses*. In contrast, Rochefort built a career out of ageing more or less disgracefully. Whether playing a dishonoured naval officer, a cavorting sexual obsessive, or a homicidal Alzheimer's patient, his work gestured throughout to the comic element within the human condition, even – and perhaps especially – in the face of tragedy.

Notes

1 A further member of this long-lived acting generation, Jean-Louis Trintignant (1930–2022), also contributed distinctively to novel constructions of French masculinity at this time. His case is discussed by Éamon Ó Cofaigh in Chapter 7 of this volume.
2 The intrinsic similarity of the pair to Don Quixote and Sancho Panza lends additional interest to their variously fantastic halts, which include an emergency stop by Rivetot to avoid a collision with a non-existent giant red dog and the lengthy harangues directed by Mortez at roadside picnickers.
3 Like Jean Rochefort, the novelist and screenwriter Jean-Claude Carrière (1931–2021) was in his eighties at this time.

Works Cited

Adriaensen, Brigitte. "Getting Lost in La Mancha: The Unma(s)king of Gilliam's *The Man Who Killed Don Quixote.*" *International Don Quixote.* Ed. Theo D'Haen. Rodopi, 2009. 251–269.

Austin, Guy. *Stars in Modern French Film.* Arnold, 2003.

Calvet, Benjamin, and Jean-Pierre Clément. "Regards critiques sur les représentations de la vieillesse au cinéma." *Lettre de psychogériatrie* (2019): 1–5.

Degroult, Nathalie, Michèle Bissière, and Caroline Beschea-Fache. "Bilan cinématographique 2012–2013: A Holy Year!" *The French Review* 87.3 (March 2014): 15–33.

Downing, Lisa. *Patrice Leconte.* Manchester UP, 2004.

Evans, Claude. "Fantasies and Ambiguous Sexuality in Patrice Leconte's *Le Mari de la coiffeuse* and *La Fille sur le pont.*" *Studies in French Cinema* 4.2 (2004): 135–146.

Guardian [Staff and agencies]. "*Lost in La Mancha*'s Jean Rochefort, veteran French actor, dies at 87." *The Guardian,* 9 Oct. 2017. www.theguardian.com/film/2017/oct/09/lost-in-la-mancha-jean-rochefort-french-actor-dies-terry-gilliam

Guérand, Jean-Philippe. *Jean Rochefort, prince sans rire.* Robert Laffont, 2017. [non-paginated, electronic edition; citations in main text from Ch. 35 and Ch. 30 respectively].

Harang, Jean-Baptiste. "Portrait: Lucien Jeunesse." *Libération,* 24 May 1995. www.liberation.fr/portrait/1995/05/24/lucien-jeunesse-depuis-trente-ans-sur-france-inter-l-animateur-cabotin-fait-rimer-le-jeu-des-mille-f_132393/

Kermode, Mark. "The Artist and the Model – Review." *The Guardian,* 15 Sept. 2013. www.theguardian.com/film/2013/sep/15/artist-and-the-model-review

Loiselle, Marie-Claude. "La vie rêvée" [Review of *Le mari de la coiffeuse* by Patrice Leconte], *24 images* 53 (January–February 1991): 64.

Malausa, Vincent. "*Floride*, un film magistral et délicat. Jean Rochefort n'a jamais été aussi émouvant." *Le Nouvel Observateur* [website L'Ops avec Le Plus], 14 Aug. 2015. https://leplus.nouvelobs.com/contribution/1405012-floride-avec-jean-rochefort-et-sandrine-kiberlain-un-voyage-onirique-et-deroutant.html

Marques, Sandrine. "'L'Artiste et son modèle': un film semblable à une nature morte." *Le Monde,* 12 Mar. 2013. www.lemonde.fr/culture/article/2013/03/12/l-artiste-et-son-modele-un-film-semblable-a-une-nature-morte_1846096_3246.html

Ó Cofaigh, Éamon. *A Vehicle for Change: Popular Representations of the Automobile in 20th-Century France.* Liverpool UP, 2022.

Powrie, Phil. *French Cinema in the 1980s: Nostalgia and the Crisis of Masculinity.* Clarendon Press, 1997.

Ross, Kristin. *Fast Cars, Clean Bodies: Decolonization and the Reordering of French Culture.* MIT Press, 1995.

Sotinel, Thomas. "*Floride*: voyage avec un esprit qui se perd." *Le Monde,* 10 Aug. 2015. www.lemonde.fr/cinema/article/2015/08/11/voyage-avec-un-esprit-qui-se-perd_4720267_3476.html

Swinnen, Aagje. "Ageing in Film." *Routledge Handbook of Cultural Gerontology.* Eds. Julia Twigg and Wendy Martin. Routledge, 2015. 69–76.

Tinker, Chris. "Rock 'n' Roll Stardom: Johnny Hallyday." *Stardom in Postwar France.* Eds. John Gaffney and Diana Holmes. Berghahn, 2007. 67–93.

7 From Mustang to 2CV

Ageing in Claude Lelouch's *Un homme et une femme* Trilogy

Éamon Ó Cofaigh

Winner of the Palme d'Or at the 1966 Cannes film festival and Academy Awards for Best Foreign Language Film and Best Original Screenplay, *Un homme et une femme* (A Man and a Woman; 1966) brought director Claude Lelouch firmly into the limelight. Lelouch's story of racing driver Jean-Louis Duroc (Jean-Louis Trintignant), who falls in love with Anne Gauthier (Anouk Aimée), was also a considerable financial success, saving Lelouch's film company from the bankruptcy which threatened it immediately prior to its release. Trintignant and Aimée subsequently reprised their roles in two successful sequels: *Un homme et une femme: vingt ans déjà* (A Man and a Woman: 20 Years Later; 1986) and *Les plus belles années d'une vie* (The Best Years of a Life; 2019), the latter reuniting the two main characters 53 years after their first iconic outing.

This trilogy of films, all written and directed by Lelouch, offers a singular insight within French cinema into the theme of ageing both thematically and in real time (the ageing actors). This chapter examines the troubled relationship between ageing, masculinity, and identity, as experienced through the eyes of the central character of Jean-Louis, particularly in the final film. Displaying early signs of dementia, Jean-Louis lives in memories of the past with constant nostalgic flashbacks to scenes from *Un homme et une femme* which focus on his earlier racing career and his seduction of Anne. While contemporary theories of gender consider masculinities as multiple, fluid, and open to change over the course of an individual's life, Jean-Louis' refusal to come to terms with his present is indicative of an inability to move on from a traditional, normative view of masculinity rooted in his youth. As I hope to show, an analysis of the trilogy as a whole highlights his incapacity to embrace another model of masculinity as he ages and despite his evident physical and mental decline.

Ageing and Masculinity

The study of masculinity is generally traced to the emergence of "men's studies" in the 1980s when scholars questioned the concept as natural or essential or singular (Reeser 2015). Over the last several decades research

DOI: 10.4324/9781003306146-7

on masculinities has consolidated the principles that there are multiple masculinities and that there are hierarchies within masculinities, which in turn often define a dominant pattern of behaviours for a particular society (Connell 2015). The concept of hegemonic masculinity (Connell and Messerschmidt 2005) argues that traditional views of masculinity are rooted in patterns of practice associated with the subordination of women and very often involving physical strength, sexual prowess, and power. Such embodied elements are traits which are associated with youth and thus very often disappear with old age; therefore ageing may be seen as a process that is fundamentally de-gendering (Twigg 2018). Indeed, much literature on gerontology focuses on loss and perception of loss (Migliore and Dorazio-Migliore 2014). This, in part, is due to the perception of the ageing body as an ill body, a misconception that has been contested by cultural gerontologists and age critics (Phoenix and Smith 2011; Gullette 2015). With regard to ageing masculinities, this can be seen in terms of a loss of a socially dominant model of masculinity closely associated with youth.

However, given that masculinities do not pre-exist social behaviour, they come into existence as people act. In fact, all gender identities have "constantly to be reaffirmed and publicly displayed by repeatedly performing acts in accordance with the social norm" (Cameron 1997, 49). Judith Butler articulates the idea that gender identity is above all a performance, something that we do as opposed to something that we are (Butler 1990), and this concept has had a strong influence on masculinity studies. Men have to assume their "maleness"; it is not innate in their genes or blood, but "their gendered acts implicitly refer to or cite innumerable actions that others have already undertaken – actions that provide authority, meaning and stability for the current act" (Reeser 2015, 31). Masculinity as an identity, therefore, is not fixed; it is constantly shifting and open to reconstruction. And crucially, it is open to change over an individual's life course.

Gendered approaches to ageing can in general be traced back to de Beauvoir's *La vieillesse* (The Coming of Age, 1970; Armengol 2018). De Beauvoir acknowledges the disempowering effect of ageing on men, and this is echoed by Friedan's *The Fountain of Age* (1993), which similarly considers the powerful effect that growing old has on diminishing masculinity. While in recent times the ageing gendered body has been afforded more space, it has been argued that this has largely fallen under the remit of women's studies (Fleming 1999). As such, "men and masculinity have been ignored, particularly into old age" (Wiersma and Chesser 2011, 246). This has been addressed more recently by a number of articles that have looked at perceptions of the ageing male in popular culture (Twigg 2020; Armengol 2018; Dolan and Hallam 2017; Christou 2016).

There has been an underrepresentation of older characters in popular film. According to Swinnen, this is not restricted to Hollywood: "European cinema is almost as reluctant as Hollywood to grant significant roles to older characters" (2014, 73). Correspondingly, much has been made of the "conspiracy of silence" with regard to ageing in French cinema. However, it is not the same situation for men and women. Martine Beugnet argues that not only are "men on screen granted a longer life-span as sexual beings," but they also "retain a status as individuals, defined in terms of (actual or past) activities, professional, cultural, or political." In contrast, ageing women's roles are reduced to "a restrictive framework of stereotypes and allegorical visual tropes" (2006, 18).

There are however increasing and notable exceptions to such observations in recent examples of French cinema. Jean-Louis Trintignant died in 2022 at age 91. His long career and stardom date back to his on- and off-screen liaison with Brigitte Bardot during the shooting of *Et Dieu créa . . . la femme* (And God Created Woman; 1956) and is perhaps best known in recent years for his role in *Amour* (2012; Vincendeau 2000; Gaffney and Holmes 2008). Convinced by director Michael Haneke to come out of retirement, Trintignant plays the octogenarian husband to Emmanuelle Riva's Oscar-nominated role as a woman suffering from dementia. In *Amour*, Trintignant's old age, paired with his wife's steep physical and mental decline, leads to a gradual imprisonment within their apartment in both temporal and spatial terms (Quinodoz 2014; Garbarz 2012). The lesser-known *Happy End* (2017), also directed by Haneke and with Trintignant and Isabelle Huppert reprising their roles as father and daughter, explores a bourgeois family in Normandy as well as the subtext of Trintignant's character who is now, himself, suffering from dementia. In 2021 Gasper Noé wrote and directed *Vortex*, a film with many similarities to *Amour* but which offered a bleaker treatment of the final stages of life for an aged Parisian couple. And *Tout s'est bien passé* (Everything Went Fine; 2021), directed by François Ozon, is a recent reflection on ageing masculinity in which well-known French actor André Dussollier plays the role of a man incapable of accepting his physical decline and who subsequently asks his daughter, played by Sophie Marceau, to help him to commit suicide.

These contemporary cinematic depictions of ageing – and ageing masculinities in particular – in French cinema portray a difficulty or refusal to come to terms with declining health as the characters age. They show how the characters try to negotiate the meaning of masculinity as they age and highlight how challenging it can be to embrace shifting gender scripts. Ethnographic research has shown how very complex negotiations of the meaning of masculinity can occur in the normal flow of everyday life (Gutmann 1996), and in the context of these films this is particularly poignant.

In the discussion that follows, I wish to explore how the character of Jean-Louis Duroc, who initially embodies many of the typical characteristics associated with youthful and normative masculinity, ultimately fails to negotiate an alternative model as he ages. It presents his understanding of his masculinity as trapped in time through the character's constant draw to the past where the normative identities associated with being male are still intact. A narrative of decline is meanwhile established across the trilogy, which underlines fragility and transience of masculinity and the emptiness of male ageing. An ongoing and repeated struggle between remembering the past and adequately participating in the present highlights an inability to deal with the perceived loss of masculinity and as a result it generates the need to take flight into make-believe. Finally, the subversion of hegemonic masculinity to a status where ageing men have less sexual "worth" than their female counterparts is apparent in Lelouch's trilogy, where Anne is still contemplated (at least by Jean-Louis) as a sexual being.

Jean-Louis' attempts to grapple with the loss of his physical ability are intrinsically linked to his youth and masculinity. In struggling against decline, Duroc's nostalgia provides him with a means of dealing with his inability to participate in society as an older man. While *Un homme et une femme* is a plea for its protagonists to live in the present, *Les plus belles années d'une vie* is a rejection of the present, as physical and mental decline push the protagonist to take refuge in the past rather than live an emasculated present.

The *Un homme et une femme* Trilogy

The idea of an actor-character growing older on screen is not unique to Lelouch in French cinema. It has a celebrated antecedent in *Les Aventures d'Antoine Doinel* series by Francois Truffaut, filmed over 20 years. But while Truffaut's series focused on the coming of age of its young male protagonist (played across five films by Jean-Pierre Léaud), Lelouch is focused on the adult ageing of its central male character Jean-Louis Duroc (Jean-Louis Trintignant). The Duroc cycle pushes far beyond the life stages captured by Truffaut and simultaneously captures the negotiation of the ageing process of its protagonist and its central actor as they become older together.

The first film, *Un homme et une femme*, introduces the audience to two recently widowed parents in their thirties as they meet for the first time in Normandy, where their respective children are at boarding school. Trintignant's character (also called) Jean-Louis offers Anne (Anouk Aimée) a car ride to Paris, as she has missed her train. Thus begins the first of many car journeys, with the basis for their relationship formed in Jean-Louis' powerful Ford Mustang. Duroc is a well-known car racer and, in this film, his race, as is seen in the last scenes, is to beat the train from Deauville to Paris to win the woman he loves. Having been abandoned at the train station, Trintignant's character jumps into his Mustang and drives directly from Deauville to Paris to meet Anne as she gets off the train.

While it is possible to trace a rather explicit narrative of ageing and decline through the three films studied, it is also important to remember that the second and, certainly, the third films were not planned during the scripting and shooting of *Un homme et une femme*. Thus, while the first film sets out a particular version of masculinity through traditional elements of post-war French masculinity, these elements were not included with the aim of later using them to chronicle a transition to old age. It is, however, important to examine a certain number of these in order to fully understand Jean-Louis' draw to this version of desirable masculinity.

The first and most obvious example is Jean-Louis' profession, as well as the choice of car in *Un homme et une femme*. The attraction of men to "muscle cars" has long been discussed, and indeed 1960s France was the decade during which youth began to indulge in the freedom offered by the car. Jean-Louis is a racing-car driver and drives a high-powered sports car in which he effectively seduces Anne on their trips from Paris to Deauville to see their respective children. At no stage is there ever the suggestion that Anne may take the wheel. Jean-Louis' Mustang is effectively a prop used to reinforce normative masculinity. This, allied to the use of speed, is central to *Un homme et une femme*. Jean-Louis' powerful Ford Mustang is symbolic of a masculine identity defined by youth, good looks, virility, and success. However, as in her study of the role of the motorcar in the transformation of French culture during "les Trente Glorieuses" Kristin Ross argues that in this introduction of American technology France is nostalgic, as the Mustang reinforces the idea of singularity. Ross also argues that the film itself is almost nostalgic, as the myth of speed had already been "waning" for a number of years when it was released (1995). In *Les plus belles années d'une vie* the Mustang is replaced by a Citroën 2CV, reflecting both the physical decline of its driver and the sympathetic yet tired regard held for the 2CV today.

Un homme et une femme: vingt ans déjà was released in 1986, exactly 20 years after the original. With Jean-Louis Trintignant and Anouk Aimée reprising their roles as Jean-Louis and Anne, we discover what has become of them in the intervening years. We are first reintroduced to Trintignant, who is no longer a racing driver. Jean-Louis' son, Antoine, is now a powerboat racer managed by his father. Thus, there is the suggestion that Jean-Louis may now be living out his need to express hegemonic masculinity scripts through his son. This shift in power with another competing male is spelled out quite literally on the sports jacket that he wears, which announces this partnership with his son. Anne, who owns a film production company, approaches Jean-Louis with a view to making a film version of their love story. The two protagonists rekindle their romance, and the film has a rather open ending where it appears as though they remain together.

Jean-Louis' efforts to thwart his perceived loss of masculinity may be seen in his attempt to relive his youth in an awkward attempt to seduce his daughter-in-law's sister. When hegemonically masculine traits such as physical strength are in decline, men resort to strategies to avoid being "othered." One such strategy is to enter into a relationship with a much younger woman (Swinnen 2015). Anne suggests that Jean-Louis has less aggression than when younger: "I find you more chilled out" ("je vous trouve plus relaxe"), to which he replies, "I am ageing well, I'm good, older, but good. I don't race anymore, but I'm happy" ("je vieillis bien, je suis bien, vieilli, mais bien. Je cours plus, mais je suis heureux"). For Jean-Louis, being a motor-racing driver is synonymous with youthful masculinity, so while he claims to be happy, this is less than convincing.

A certain nostalgia for their younger days is played out in *Un homme et une femme: vingt ans déjà* as Anne, in her profession as a scriptwriter and producer, obtains permission from Jean-Louis to create a film version of their love story. Interested in this reminiscing of their story, Jean-Louis is regularly on set as Anne's production company sets about creating a musical version of the original film, which stars, this time, Anne's daughter. This recreation of their youthful relationship allows a joyful reflection on memory and rekindles their romance with them engaging in a brief affair. When Jean-Louis informs his significantly younger girlfriend about this affair, she states that "I always knew that we wouldn't grow old together" ("J'ai toujours su qu'on ne vieillirait pas ensemble"), to which he responds, "I'm already getting old." The film version of Anne and Jean-Louis' love story is finally rejected, however, as it is not seen to be believable enough, particularly since so much has changed over the preceding 20 years. This is a further comment on the ageing process, as not only does it underline the fact that their relationship is firmly rooted in the past, but it is also implied that such a relationship would not be possible in the present.

Les plus belles années d'une vie was released in 2019, some 53 years after the original *Un homme et une femme*, and, interestingly, it forgets that the 1986 sequel ever existed. We are therefore picking up the story a half century on from where the original left off; at the train station after Jean-Louis has beaten the train to Paris from Deauville. In an interview, Lelouch explained the impetus for the creation of this film stemmed from a reunion to celebrate the 50th anniversary of *Un homme et une femme*, and he was struck by how much his two stars had changed and also how much they were still the same. Thus, from the outset, Lelouch's aim with this film was to reflect upon life and the ageing process for both actors/characters, but in particular for Jean-Louis Trintignant's character, whose transformation from a young, headstrong racing driver to the confused resident of a nursing home is much starker than that of his female counterpart. The title of the film originates in a quotation from Victor Hugo: "The best years of a life are those not yet lived" ("Les plus belles années d'une vie sont celles que l'on n'a pas encore vécues"). This epigram is placed on-screen at the beginning of the film and is indicative of the tone of the film that Lelouch wants to create. Shot quickly over 13 days, the film is a remarkable reflection on the ageing – both on-screen and off – of its actors/characters.

The first image we encounter is that of Jean-Louis. In a nursing home, he is surrounded by women and men who may be the same age as him yet seem to be more alert and capable than he now is. Now aged 89, he is extraordinarily frail-looking, incapable of movement other than in a wheelchair (which he ironically refers to as his "voiture de course"). Duroc's mental decline is made explicit during a memory-building game for nursing home residents in which all participants are asked the dates of significant events in French history. Jean-Louis is very obviously incapable of remembering any of the questions, and we quickly discover that his mental decline is worse than the more obvious physical decline. The nursing home symbolizes Jean-Louis' loss of self-sufficiency, one of the markers of masculine identity throughout the ageing process (Wiersma).

As in both previous films, a link between masculinity, age and speed is again drawn early on (Varet 2019). Jean-Louis' son, Antoine (Antoine Sire), drives an Alpine sports car. While Antoine is in his late fifties at this stage, he is able to maintain some semblance of youth through his ability to access speed and excitement in his powerful car (Spector-Mersel 2006). In the most explicit of contrasts, Jean-Louis' decline is underlined by yet another car. In this third film, the central male and female characters drive along together as they did during their first adventure. However, instead of the male racing driver at the wheel of his powerful Ford Mustang, we find Anne driving Jean-Louis in a Citroën 2CV and, in a highly ironic twist, they are pulled over by the police for driving too slowly! After letting a long line of cars go past, they are both warned that driving slowly is just as dangerous as going too quickly. This rather hyperbolic scene highlights the decline of Jean-Louis to a complete loss of the forms of masculinity that he values. When Jean-Louis does actually take the wheel of the 2CV and proceeds to be pulled over for speeding, it turns out to be a dream.

The use of the 2CV and indeed the wheelchair as allegories for Jean-Louis' ageing masculinity/declining in speed are both evoked towards the end of the film. During their "escape" from the nursing home, after helping Jean-Louis climb gingerly into his wheelchair, Anne asks him if she is going too quickly ("je vais pas trop vite?") when referring to the speed at which she is pushing him in the wheelchair. Jean-Louis' response is immediately a reference to racing, "not fast enough to win a race, but fine" ("je sais pas si on va gagner la course, mais ça va très bien"). While just a pithy response to her question, this repeated comparison of his wheelchair to a racing car, particularly when Anne is helping him leave the nursing home, is indicative of an inability to accept any new form of masculinity where his dominance is diluted. Indeed, it is hard to imagine Jean-Louis being content with any form of present in which he is dependent. Upon transferring to the 2CV, the film ends with them finally arriving in Deauville and driving along the promenade before walking along the beach in the sun.

In this trilogy of films, a narrative of decline associated with the male protagonist is framed in terms of hegemonic masculinity and particularly in relation to themes of speed and (auto)mobility. Jean-Louis initially was young, carefree, and aggressive, but these charactcristics have diluted and, later, abandoned him the older he gets. This transient style of masculinity is contrasted with Anne's femininity. Not only does she maintain a role in society, as de Beauvoir theorized, but she is also treated as an object of attraction. As they age, Anne is the person "at the wheel," driving the relationship. Connell (2005, 76) reminds us that hegemonic masculinity should not be seen as "a fixed character type, always and everywhere the same," but instead as "the masculinity that occupies the hegemonic position in a given pattern of gender relations, a position always contestable." In this instance, Anne contests and succeeds in securing the dominant position.

The use of the flashback is a key tool used in *Les plus belles années d'une vie* to underline Jean-Louis' nostalgia and longing for youthful attractiveness. As Swinnen has theorized, the flashback contrasts the younger with the older self. This preference for the younger self makes appropriate engagement with the present much more challenging (Swinnen 2015). In his flashbacks, Jean-Louis reminisces or daydreams about Anne and the time they spent together. These flashbacks are scenes taken from the original 1966 film and placed directly into the final film, offering a strong counterpoint between the life stages. The young Jean-Louis, the handsome, confident racing-car driver, has now become someone incapable of steering his own wheelchair. Jean-Louis' attempts at grappling with his own mortality reflect his inability to uphold society's ideals of ageing, where he must abandon any thoughts of attractiveness or worth, and thus he embarks on fleeting flights of fancy into the past where he considers himself to be desirable. Jean-Louis is forced to resort to nostalgia in order to once again experience the feeling of hegemonic masculinity, as his present is one where he has become emasculated.

The strong link that Jean-Louis draws between youth and speed is underlined once again with a flashback to yet another Lelouch film. Jean-Louis reminisces about the last time that he went fast ("la dernière fois que j'ai couru"), but what we see is in fact an infamous short titled *C'était un rendez-vous* directed by Lelouch in 1976, in which the director himself travels in a sports car at high speed through Paris, thus producing a triangular link between the ageing of the central character, the actor, and the director himself. This *court métrage* is an eight-minute shot taken by one camera positioned on the front bumper of what was claimed at the time to be a Ferrari, driven at high speeds in the early morning by Lelouch. Jean-Louis uses the past once again as he describes how he crossed Paris to be in time for a date with a woman, "Paris was mine" ("Paris m'appartenait"). This last flashback superposes scenes of the couple from *Un homme et une femme* onto the scenes in this short. As we have a mixing of speed and seduction, this culminates in the superposition of the lovemaking scene from the original film onto the arrival of the speeding car at Montmartre. This close association of speed with seduction and ultimately lovemaking/conquest reflects the protagonist's own narrow definition of youth and virility. The ability to control and steer a high-powered car through the narrow, sinuous streets of Paris is placed in parallel with the challenge posed by the need to possess Anne.

The choice of the 2CV, or *deuch*, as it is affectionately called in *Les plus belles années d'une vie*, is highly significant as, while it is actually older than the original film, and it is (rather obviously) much less powerful than Jean-Louis' Mustang, the car has a special place in French popular memory. As a key symbol of the "les Trente Glorieuses," the car is associated with a period that provokes strong nostalgia, the moment when the nation became reconstituted and reaffirmed in the aftermath of war and the capitulation of the Vichy regime (Fantin 2015; Dauncey and Tinker 2015). Similarly, Jean-Louis is nostalgic for a time in the past when he believed himself to be more alive than he is now. Indeed, upon the couple's arrival in Deauville, Jean-Louis is haunted by visions of his white Mustang. This most resonant of symbols of youth for Jean-Louis, the one by which he defined his youthful masculinity and his desirability, now feeds his nostalgic longing to the extent that he sees it in front of him.

Jean-Louis feels a constant need to escape into the past through daydreams. Ageing distorts the power relations associated with hegemonic masculinity as Jean-Louis is unable to find any self-worth in his present and relies on his past to maintain a certain form of dignity in the face of social expectations. The tension between the nostalgia and the present where decline is so explicitly experienced underscores the transience of a normative version of masculinity (closely associated with youth) and leaves a masculinity trapped in time. Jean-Louis is strongly nostalgic for his youth, a time at which he considered himself both physically athletic and desirable. It is these characteristics that he craves in his reminiscences. Nostalgia associated with remembering the past is indicative of the pain of having to accept a present where Jean-Louis is "less of a man." For Jean-Louis, nostalgia is a sanctuary from frustration as a result of the loss of hegemonic traits. It is the response of a man who is unwilling to change, afraid of the present and/ or the future (Kibby 1998).

The span of 53 years for the three films highlights a gradual, yet inexorable perceived emasculation by Jean-Louis. Indeed, it is Jean-Louis' incapacity to live in the present that provides the impetus for the third and final film. In a striking counterpoint to its predecessors, Anne becomes the dominant person in their relationship. Anne enters this new film upon the request of Jean-Louis' son, Antoine, who has spent a lot of time trying to find her. He informs her that his father's memory comes and goes and that she is Jean-Louis' best memory ("vous êtes son meilleur souvenir"). Antoine convinces Anne to visit Jean-Louis, even though we discover that the reason that they didn't stay together was because of Jean-Louis' infidelity ("il était pas seulement coureur d'automobiles il était coureur tout court"). This wordplay in French between racing-car driver and skirt-chaser once again brings us back to the masculine character that Jean-Louis incarnated in the first film. Jean-Louis' perceived ability to seduce women, just like his ability to drive a (powerful) car, has ebbed away over the years as a further emasculating effect of ageing. On a number of occasions while in his current plight in the nursing home, Jean-Louis attempts to flirt with his nurses ("vous voulez toujours pas coucher avec moi?"). While these requests from Jean-Louis may be made in jest, they are couched in tones of nostalgia and regret. Jean-Louis' advances are always received in good humour, however, the gentle rebuttals in the form of a joke are further confirmation to Jean-Louis that his aged self has been stripped of the dominant masculinity by which he defined himself. While Jean-Louis' loss of memory may be a medical reality, it can also be seen as a reaction to his physical decline and a subsequent refusal to engage with the present.

The first time that Anne visits Jean-Louis at the nursing home, he does not recognize her. In the conversation that ensues, we learn a great deal about Jean-Louis' and, by extension, Lelouch's vision of ageing and death. Jean-Louis refuses to participate in any activities organized in the nursing home, preferring to while away time in nostalgic reverie. He does not live in the nursing home so much as he awaits death there ("on ne vit pas, on attend la mort"). Therefore, while he is not dead, Jean-Louis does not consider ageing/old age to be living. Death, for Jean-Louis, is the tax imposed on life ("la mort c'est l'impôt de la vie"); however, he only experiences life now through his vivid flashbacks to his youth. This constant draw to the past reflects an inability to accept or to reconcile himself to his ageing reality, one where he is no longer dominant. Jean-Louis' existence now consists of being bored during the day ("je m'ennuie") and having either nightmares or very beautiful dreams at night-time ("des cauchemars ou de très beaux rêves") – although it would be hard to imagine a nightmare worse in Jean-Louis' eyes than being trapped in an emasculated present.

Jean-Louis' vision of his life does not include ageing or old age. We see a protagonist consistently seeking to transcend and escape the present. This rejection of his current existence is summed up in his constant use of the past-tense to refer to his masculinity ("j'étais très joli quand j'étais jeune. J'étais coureur d'automobile et j'étais très joli"). Therefore, the two means by which he measures himself are physical strength, the ability to drive a high-powered sports car, and also physical desirability, which according to him have all abandoned him now. His inability to accept his older self is reinforced when Anne tries to convince him otherwise by telling him that he is still desirable ("vous êtes toujours joli"), however he accuses her of lying and goes on to say that Anne must surely too have succumbed to the ravages of time: "now she must be old and ugly" ("maintenant elle doit être vieille et moche"). Thus, for Jean-Louis, ageing is not only emasculating, but it also strips women of their desirability. However, this does not seem to be borne out in reality, as not only is Anne independent but she is also considered attractive by Jean-Louis, as the way that she plays with her hair reminds him, once again, of a transient masculinity.

The version of older masculinity presented in Les plus belles années d'une vie is one which denies any form of existence which Jean-Louis can find meaningful. He is trapped in a masculinity based on dominance, one which he believes has abandoned him with old age. Jean-Louis' physical and mental deterioration are closely linked, with the suggestion being that his physical decline means that in order for him to achieve any form of fulfilment he must abandon the present and reside in the past of his memories. The linking of ageing to dementia in effect rules out even the possibility of a fulfilling or complete life as an older man.

Conclusion

This chapter highlights the strong link in the films discussed between the pathologization of disability and pathologization of ageing (Chivers 2011). In particular, ageing masculinity is pathologized. A tension exists between the nostalgia experienced when remembering the past and the present in which decline is made explicit through physical and mental infirmity. While in many ways these films succumb to a narrative of decline, they also poignantly depict the depths and pain of this struggle and the complex and fluid intersections between identity, masculinity, ageing, and disability. Through these struggles, masculinity is depicted as trapped in time, as having no place in a painful present which the protagonist consistently seeks to transcend and escape.

While these films highlight the complexities of ageing, it cannot be said that they allow ageing masculinity to really exist. Society's (and Jean-Louis') ideals of masculinity do not seem to have a place in older age. In the second and particularly in the third films in this trilogy, Jean-Louis is pushed by mental and physical decline to take refuge in the past as the elements which defined a desirable form of masculinity for him dissipate. With the reintroduction of Anne into Jean-Louis' life we see that French post-war masculinity seems to have a time limit that femininity does not, as she can now distort the power relations associated with hegemonic masculinity. Rather than reinforcing this hegemonic masculinity, Jean-Louis Trintignant's character ultimately shows us how this form of normativity is pointless and how it is trapped in time.

Through the trilogy, the ageing process of the male protagonist, over a period of 53 years, highlights a fragility and a transience related to post-war French masculinity, which is dependent on social expectations and ultimately empty once these expectations are no longer met. Jean-Louis' inability to cope with these pressures leads him to retreat into memories of the past. Rather than a film series that celebrates masculinity or nostalgia, it is a trilogy that underlines a failure to identify an alternative model capable of competing with traditional views of masculinity. It is arguably a cinematic depiction of a crisis of masculinity, which further raises the question as to what social and cultural norms preclude the reconstruction of masculinity for ageing men.

Works Cited

Armengol, Josep M. "Aging as Emasculation? Rethinking Aging Masculinities in Contemporary US Fiction." *Critique: Studies in Contemporary Fiction* 59.3 (2018): 355–367.

Beauvoir, Simone Lucie Ernestine Marie Bertrand. *La Vieillesse*. Gallimard, 1970.

Beugnet, Martine. "Screening the Old: Femininity as Old Age in Contemporary French Cinema." *Studies in the Literary Imagination* 39.2 (2006): 1.

Butler, Judith. *Gender Trouble: Feminism and the Subversion of Identity*. Routledge, 1990.

Cameron, Deborah. "Performing Gender Identity: Young Men's Talk and the Construction of Heterosexual Masculinity." *Language and Masculinity*. Eds. Sally Johnson and Ulrike Hanna Meinhof. Blackwell, 1997. 328–335.

Chivers, Sally. "Introduction: The Silvering Screen." *The Silvering Screen: Old Age and Disability in Cinema*. U Toronto P, 2019. xi–xxii.

Christou, Anastasia. "Ageing Masculinities and the Nation: Disrupting Boundaries of Sexualities, Mobilities and Identities." *Gender, Place & Culture* 23.6 (2016): 801–816.

Connell, Raewyn. "Masculinities: The Field of Knowledge." *Configuring Masculinity in Theory and Literary Practice*. Brill, 2020. 39–51.

Connell, Raewyn, and James W. Messerschmidt. "Hegemonic Masculinity: Rethinking the Concept." *Gender & Society* 19.6 (2005): 829–859.

Dauncey, Hugh, and Chris Tinker. "Media, Memory and Nostalgia in Contemporary France: Between Commemoration, Memorialisation, Reflection and Restoration." *Modern & Contemporary France* 23.2 (2015): 135–145.

Dolan, Josephine, and Julia Hallam. "Introduction: Screening Old Age." *Journal of British Cinema and Television* 14.2 (2017): 119–124.

Fantin, Emmanuelle. "Mémoire et nostalgie des Trente Glorieuses dans la publicité française." *Modern & Contemporary France* 23.2 (2015): 147–161.

Fleming, Alfred Andrew. "Older Men in Contemporary Discourses on Ageing: Absent Bodies and Invisible Lives." *Nursing Inquiry* 6.1 (1999): 3–8.

Gaffney, John, and Diana Holmes. "Stardom in Theory and Practice." *Stardom in Postwar France*. Berghahn, 2008.

Guidez, Guylaine. *Claude Lelouch*. Vol. 72. Seghers, 1972.

Gullette, Margaret Morganroth. "Aged by Culture." *Routledge Handbook of Cultural Gerontology*. Routledge, 2015. 43–50.

Gutmann, Matthew C. *The Meanings of Macho: Being a Man in Mexico City*. Vol. 3. U California P, 2006.

Haneke, Michael. *Amour*. Les Films du Losange, 2012.

Haneke, Michael. *Happy End*. Les Films du Losange, 2017.

Kibby, Marjorie D. "Nostalgia for the Masculine: Onward to the Past in the Sports Films of the Eighties." *Canadian Journal of Film Studies* 7.1 (1998): 16–28.

Lelouch, Claude. *C'était un rendez-vous*. Spirit Level Film, 1976.

Lelouch, Claude. *Un homme et une femme*. Les Films 13, 1976.

Lelouch, Claude. *Un homme et une femme: vingt ans déjà*. Les Films 13, 1986.

Lelouch, Claude. *Les plus belles années d'une vie*. Les Films 13, 2019.

Migliore, Sam, and Margaret Dorazio-Migliore. "Aging and Narratives of Loss: A History of Social Suffering." *Anthropologica* (2014): 415–422.

Noé, Gaspard. *Vortex*. Rectangle Productions, 2021.

Ozon, François. *Tout s'est bien passé*. Mandarin Films, 2021.

Phoenix, Cassandra, and Brett Smith. "Telling a (Good?) Counterstory of Aging: Natural Bodybuilding Meets the Narrative of Decline." *Journals of Gerontology Series B: Psychological Sciences and Social Sciences* 66.5 (2011): 628–639.

Quinodoz, Danielle. "Amour." *The International Journal of Psychoanalysis* 95.2 (2014): 375–383.

Reeser, Todd W. "Concepts of Masculinity and Masculinity Studies." *Configuring Masculinity in Theory and Literary Practice*. Brill Rodopi, 2020. 11–38.

Ross, Kristin. *Fast Cars, Clean Bodies: Decolonization and the Reordering of French Culture*. MIT Press, 1996.

Spector-Mersel, Gabriela. "Never-aging Stories: Western Hegemonic Masculinity Scripts." *Journal of Gender Studies* 15.1 (2006): 67–82.

Swinnen, Aagje. "Ageing in Film." *Routledge Handbook of Cultural Gerontology*. Eds. Julia Twigg and Wendy Martin. Routledge, 2015. 91–98.

Truffaut, François. *Les Quatre Cents Coups*. Les Films du Carrosse, 1959.

Twigg, Julia. "Dress, Gender and the Embodiment of Age: Men and Masculinities." *Ageing & Society* 40.1 (2020): 105–125.

Vadim, Roger. *Et Dieu créa . . . la femme*. Iéna Productions, 1956.

Varet, Florent, et al. "Désirabilité et normes sociales dans les comportements automobilistes impliquant une vitesse excessive: une étude quasi-expérimentale des différences entre hommes et femmes." *2e Rencontres Francophones Transport Mobilité (RFTM)* (2019).

Vincendeau, Ginette. *Stars and Stardom in French Cinema*. Bloomsbury Publishing, 2000.

Wiersma, Elaine, and Stephanie Chesser. "Masculinity, Ageing Bodies, and Leisure." *Annals of Leisure Research* 14.2–3 (2011): 242–259.

8 Ageing Male Melodrama and Post-Soviet Generational Conflict in Contemporary Estonian Cinema

Teet Teinemaa

The representation of masculinities in the Eastern European cinemas has lately received considerable academic attention (Teinemaa and Unt 2022; Király 2021; Györi 2021; Durys 2021; Kalmár 2017; Mazierska, Mroz, and Ostrowska 2016; Goscilo and Hashamova 2010). The reasons for this interest are manifold and include a dearth of scholarship around gender on the screens of the European East, where, in turn, gender relations have gone through significant changes due to the dissolution of the Soviet Union and the rapid implementation of the logic of market economy. The most dominant themes within this work centre on the contemporary "crisis" of masculinity, intergenerational conflict, and male melodrama as a key site via which the former two anxieties are played out. However, a significant lack in research remains regarding the connection between ageing and male melodrama and its regional examples.

The small national cinema of Estonia, which has thus far not been studied in this regard, offers an important opportunity for adding to this corpus. Writer-director Andres Puustusmaa's 2017 film *Rohelised Kassid* (Green Cats; hereinafter *Green Cats*) brings conflicts in Eastern European masculinities to the fore via the lens of ageing. The film focuses on two men who are released from prison after serving a 20-year sentence and their difficulties of adjusting to life on the outside. While both are older men,[1] each approaches life on the outside with different dispositions and ambitions. Eduard (Sergei Makovetsky) is a gentle romantic, while Markus (Tõnu Kark) is an aggressive and self-centred pragmatic; the first is looking for love, the other his stashed Nazi gold. Yet, both are similarly alien in the world and have little success in creating meaningful relationships, especially with younger generations. *Green Cats* explores such generational differences in relation to the regime change, as the men confined during the late Soviet period emerge from a time capsule of sorts into contemporary Estonian society. The film's melodramatic effect is primarily achieved by the depicting the men as thoroughly "out of time" and unable to age "successfully" in accordance with the state's new liberal discourse of self-sufficiency.

To further highlight the social and ethnic tensions common to the region one of the main characters, Markus, is a native Estonian (played by veteran

DOI: 10.4324/9781003306146-8

Tõnu Kark), and the other, Eduard, is a Russian (played by the popular Ukraine-born actor Sergei Makovetsky). Reversing the stereotypical conception about Russians upholding the norms of domineering masculinity, the film shows the Estonian, played by a beloved local actor, to be the aggressive one. While the protagonists themselves see no problem in their bilingual union, the characters around them indicate a shifting attitude towards the Russian language. Puustusmaa[2] (b. 1971), an Estonian who has studied, lived, acted, and directed a number of films in Russia, is an ideal director to bring these rarely represented themes to the big screen. However, the relative lack of attention that the film received in Estonia (and the fact that uncommonly the film is not available on DVD) may be a consequence of its playful approach to language and nationality that goes against the state's official discourse.[3] The film nonetheless stands out for not shying away from exploring present-day themes and challenges and for including complex topics such as social segregation based on one's first language, corruption, the rise of right-wing populism, and the moral anxiety regarding the European migration crisis.

In addition to its national specificities, discussion of *Green Cats* is of value in the broader context of how ageing masculinities are represented on screen. Firstly, for stressing how age is socially constructed. While Markus still feels energetic and displays a number of "youthful" characteristics, the people the men encounter outside prison treat them as relics and has-beens. Secondly, the attention to age highlights not only intergenerational conflict, but the tensions, anxieties, and instabilities within the formation and performance of masculinities (exemplified by different generations of men in the film aspiring towards drastically different masculine ideals). While the post-Soviet context has made a "crisis" in masculinity particularly evident because of the rapid pace at which social changes have taken place over the last three decades, this chapter suggests that such instabilities, which ageing and intergenerational relations accentuate, are by no means specific to Eastern Europe.

Masculinities in the Post-Soviet Context

While an ongoing crisis of masculinity is at the forefront of many East European cinemas – often expressed through fraught relationships between fathers and sons, grandfathers and grandsons, or via all three generations (see also de Cordova 1987, 260) – the intersectionality between masculinities and ageing has not received the attention that it deserves (see also Teinemaa and Unt 2022). This is all the more problematic given that themes of generational difference illustrate the unstable nature of masculinities in general. Although, as Michael Kimmel argues (1990, 100), masculinity (as an ideological construct) can never be fully demonstrated and is always subject to endless doubt, masculinities in flux become especially visible when different generations aspire towards different models. This is particularly apparent in the post-Soviet setting because of the pace and significance of socio-cultural change since the 1990s.

Many authors have cautioned against over-emphasizing the turn to the West and the supposedly sudden break from the ways of living during the State Socialism, stressing that there remain "as many continuities as discontinuities between these two epochs" (Mazierska, Mroz, and Ostrowska 2016, 11). However, any wider discussion on the "crisis" of masculinity in the region – as *Green Cats* as well as other texts suggest – is regularly and explicitly tied to the regime change. Although some gender scholars (Negra and Tasker 2013, 345) have warned about the ease with which (usually white, middle-aged) masculinity is often termed to be in "crisis," others would still claim that "perhaps no group of modern individuals has experienced so great a collective identity crisis as Russian men in the late 20th century" (Thornhill 1997, 1). While such a dramatic generalization might be applied to post-Soviet societies more broadly and supported by statistic comparisons of men's lives between Western and Eastern Europe (see *Statistics Explained*), it is also important to recognize the regional differences regarding images of masculinities in popular culture such as film.

Heroism and Missing Fathers

Given that age(ing) is today widely recognized as having a social and relational, as well as biological, dimension (Calasanti and Slevin 2013), it might be argued that people in the post-Soviet context potentially start to "perform" old age earlier than in the West. On the one hand, due to the significantly lower expected life years of most Eastern European populations (and especially of men) when compared to the EU average, individuals may feel "old" earlier than their Western peers (*Statistics Explained*). On the other hand, age(ing) can be accentuated because, as Goscilo and Hashamova point out, the Soviet system attributed extraordinary discursive and political power to age and to various symbolic fathers (2010, 20). As such, performing old age was tied to one's respectability in the Soviet society.

Green Cats plays with both of these expectations: Markus is seen dressed in a USSR sports jumper and demands respect from the younger characters directly, while the more than ten years younger Eduard is depicted as frail and struggling with a severe form of dementia. Despite their shared history, however, there are significant differences between the Russian and Estonian contexts in performing old age. While the former has repeatedly expressed regret in the official discourse regarding the collapse of the Soviet Union (with catastrophic consequences in the case of the invasion of Ukraine), Estonia has understood the Soviet era as an occupation and loss of independence. These perspectives make adjusting to life on the outside difficult for the two men in *Green Cats* – especially Eduard as a minority Russian speaker – as their 20-year sentence coincides with the transition period of independent Estonia.

While Soviet era masculinity models might be perceived differently in Russia and Estonia, their shared past also suggests similarities in cinematic representations of masculinity in crisis, notably regarding themes of fatherhood. Eduard is the confidant of a prisoner Zek Tolik (Igor Rogatshov) who wants to re-establish contact with his estranged daughter Varya; Eduard then acts as a symbolic father bringing to her a message of love from her biological father. Markus is likewise unable to nurture a meaningful relationship with his daughter – simply credited as "Markus' daughter" (Hele Kõrve) in the end credits – and opts instead to influence his (nameless) grandson (Sass Visnapuu) who had considered Markus to be dead and is too young to understand the full extent of Markus' (grand-)fatherly neglect. The lack of proper names for Markus' daughter and grandson and their being referred to via kin in the titles emphasizes the film's focus on Markus' absent parenthood, but also reduces the duo to mere satellites of Markus and supports the film's male-centred narrative model.

Goscilo and Hashamova argue that the troubled negotiations between generations of males is characteristic of recent Russian cinema and that the cause is tied to missing fathers with a "metaphysics of absence" and "legacy of lack" being key phrases used to describe fatherhood in the post-Soviet context (2010, 1–3). A similar evaluation is made by Hajnal Király and Zsolt Györi regarding the Visegrád group of countries (Czech Republic, Hungary, Poland, and Slovakia) and Romania, who state that the crisis of masculinity is "regularly portrayed as a trans-generational confrontation with the haunting spirit of dead or missing fathers or grandfathers" (2021, xviii).[4] In both cases these authors identify the films in the corresponding countries, similarly to the Estonian example of *Green Cats*, to point towards more than a cinematic representation of a potential social issue and see this paternal absence as the symbol for the lack of generational continuity of values in the post-Soviet context.

Intergenerational Conflict in the Male Melodrama

The recurring theme of missing fathers suggests melodrama as the ideal dramatic mode via which to explore these concerns, as the family is traditionally considered to be at the centre of melodrama's interests (see Elsaesser 1992, 512–535). Király notes that "although traditionally melodrama has been considered a female genre, that is, presenting a female subjectivity and addressing a predominantly female audience . . . a striking predominance of male melodramas can be detected" in both Hungarian and Romanian cinemas (2021, 85). This is true also for Estonian cinema where a variety of recent films can be considered male melodramas, such as *Klass* (The Class; Raag 2007), *Magnus* (Kõusaar 2007), *Rain* (Jürgens 2020), and the UK-Estonian co-production *Firebird* (Rebane 2021). Additionally, and notably many such films foreground a theme of male ageing. The Estonian-Georgian *Mandariinid* (Tangerines; Urushadze 2013), but to a lesser extent also *Elavad pildid* (Living Images; Volmer 2013), *Üks mu sõber* (A Friend of Mine; Kivastik 2011), and *Minu näoga onu* (The Man Who Looks Like Me; Maimik and Maimik 2017), all have melodramatic elements and have an old man or older men as lead character(s). The prevalence of such characters not only brings out the generational conflict of masculinities more clearly but also suggests that the films attach a certain tragic tonality to male ageing in Estonia. These elements are also prevalent in *Green Cats*.

Nevertheless, as Steve Neale has argued, melodrama was not always associated with female audiences and the women's film category in the Hollywood studio system; rather it was a "cluster genre" that often centred around a Manichean battle between good and evil as that seen in films such as *Die Hard* (McTiernan 1988; 2000, 190). The melodramatic imagination of moral clarity is likewise behind the appeal of the genre in the post-Soviet context, yet in settings that do not always provide the necessary social glue for such clarity (Larsen 2000, 494). This desire for moral clarity is clearly present in *Green Cats* which at times conveys a nostalgic desire for the supposedly simpler Soviet period and strong male leadership.

Finally, it is important to stress the connection between age(ing) and male melodrama, because the intersectionality between age and masculinity often finds itself in a peculiar double bind. As Kristen Springer and Dawne Mouzon put it: "Most research on hegemonic masculinities focuses on younger men and most datasets of aging adults do not include measures of masculinity. This two-pronged omission renders older men relatively invisible" (2019, 183). Yet, as the following analysis will exemplify, masculinity is no less of a concern in old age. As such, the ageing male melodrama and its regional examples merit further study.

The Melodramatic Imaginary

As noted, *Green Cats* centres on two older male characters, Markus "the Coach" and Eduard "the Pike", who are released from prison after a 20-year sentence. Markus was sentenced for a bank robbery, intimidation, and physical attacks against the officers of the Soviet militia, while Eduard was convicted for white-collar crimes such as money laundering and dealing with counterfeit bonds. The men's crimes are an indication of their different natures where Markus' crimes are physical and Eduard's are intellectual. Yet, acting as a Chekhov's gun to validate Eduard's later physical outburst, he has also been charged for a stabbing that he firmly alleges was for self-defence. In short, while the film suggests that the men are capable of serious harm, the gravity of their past deeds is lessened by the fact that many of their crimes were aimed against the Soviet system, notably the militia that was largely seen as an enforcer of the state oppression. As such, the melodramatic tonality is there from the start because Markus and Eduard can be seen as partial victims of the past regime.

Their nicknames derive from prison jargon and refer to Markus being a boxing champion in his youth while Eduard is suffering from dementia ("having the memory of a pike" is the Estonian expression for having no memory), which in his case means considerable memory problems and later even partial immobility. Eduard is shown unintentionally agitating other prisoners by telling them the same things several times and being aware of his problem by querying from others if he has already mentioned something and promising to do certain tasks if he can remember them. To an extent Eduard's severe forgetfulness works as a plot device to motivate his later aimless wandering and his involuntary participation in the dealings of organized crime (Eduard later drives away with a car which the mafia wanted to destroy along with the dead body on the backseat). On the other hand, the film explores the problem seriously, illustrating how Eduard's situation quickly deteriorates when he no longer has access to his medicine and by often showing the situation from his point of view, creating a sense of confusion and helplessness that one might feel in such instances. On a more symbolic level, it could be argued that as a Russian Eduard is expected to forget the Soviet past in order to assimilate to the new system. On a more basic level, Eduard's cognitive disability accentuates the generational difficulties of adjusting to the new system and that older people have often been the silent victims of the post-Soviet "adjust or perish" progressivism and ageism. Thus, Markus and Eduard are not only the potential melodramatic victims of the past, but also the current state system.

A determinism around a certain type of masculine (criminal) identity is presented from the very outset as Markus and Eduard prepare to leave the prison and re-enter a much-changed Estonia. Here the emphasis is on competing styles of masculinity. Markus' voice-over narration, as his head is clean-shaven before the release in the opening scene, relates the well-known fable about the frog and the scorpion, in which the scorpion cannot resist attacking the frog even though the latter is transporting the scorpion over the river on her back. Indeed, the film will end with Markus' violent death as he is gunned down by the police during a failed heist. To further emphasize Markus' hard-man masculine image (Kark is one of the few Estonian actors who could believably depict an old macho), he is shown wearing a green tank top, connoting army apparel. As Markus narrates the story, we get to understand who the "frog" of the story is as the camera zooms out to reveal Eduard. To enhance a sense of depth and difference between the fates of these men, Markus is in the foreground of the frame, while Eduard is further away and blends into the darker background. While Markus does not directly cause Eduard's death as in the parable, it is the comparable type of aggressive masculinity expressed by the younger generation that later causes Eduard's mental collapse.

The film ends with Eduard in a psychiatric institution calling out for his mother, mumbling about the need to accept things that are beyond one's power to change, and retelling the parable about how both the scorpion and frog perish to the depths of the river. This proposes a rather defeatist message, unhelpfully reducing its larger social concerns to the individual psyche. This fatalistic ending can be considered uncharacteristic for a melodrama because traditionally the unjust forces dwarfing the characters (social injustice, bigotry, social class differences, forbidden love, etc.) are meant to create a bittersweet outrage, but not acceptance. However, *Green Cats*' hesitation in taking a strong position regarding domineering and ageing masculinity indicates the broader infancy regarding these debates in contemporary Estonia.

Further accentuating the difference between the men, we see Eduard pondering what type of flowers to get to his partner after being released, while Markus explains that he never needed close relationships because men and women have different goals in life. It has been argued that stressing gender differences serves patriarchy (Greer 1993, 30), and Markus' self-image as a "real" man likewise makes him distance himself from all that is feminine. As Niall Hanlon puts it: "Men must continually deny all things feminine including emotions, connection, and intimacy in order to prove their masculinity to others and to reassure self" (2012, 56). Yet, the self-harm that a domineering masculinity can cause is indicated by Markus' sad and thoughtful expression when Eduard states that he feels this way because he has never truly loved a woman. Indicating the unusual nature of Eduard's gentle masculinity in a prison setting, we see him dreaming of the ways in which to make his partner happy, whereas other prisoners verbally attack him and start prison fights.

After introducing and differentiating the main characters, the theme of generational difference is introduced by having the rugged old men reviewed for release by teenage-looking officials who are in constant need of having the specifics of the Soviet period explained to them by the prison warden. Further suggesting their lack of understanding, they are unable to comprehend why Markus (the ethnic Estonian) had regular conflicts in the past with Soviet militia. The antagonism should be all the more apparent given that Markus explained that his chances of competing in the Mexico Olympic games were stymied by the Soviet regime and that his father was deported to Siberia. Mass deportation is the most recognized trope of Estonian suffering under the Soviet regime.[5] Implying that a language-based difference is less pronounced among the older generation, Markus and (ethnic Russian) Eduard talk to each other in constant code-switching, where Estonian phrases are followed by Russian ones and vice versa. Talking to the young officials, however, Markus begins the discussion by speaking in Russian, as was customary during the Soviet time, but quickly realizes his mistake and changes to Estonian. It is as if he is suddenly verbalizing the intervening regime change and that the younger generation of Estonians might not even properly understand Russian.

The men are then released into a new alien world. Their being out of place is first depicted via their personal belongings, which are all worn out and dated; Eduard's Nokia mobile phone looks like it belongs in a history museum. Markus' distrust towards the state (a common attitude during the Soviet period), is indicated when he is being dismissive about the social housing in which he will be situated. The film also repeatedly suggests, by the device of fading out the soundtrack or diegetic sounds, that the new type of bureaucracy with its official jargon is largely incomprehensible for them. This first happens when the prison doctor discusses Eduard's medical treatment for dementia and the men have passed a rehabilitation programme for seniors and thus should be ready for reintegration into the society. As Malgorzata Bugaj pointedly puts it: "In capitalism the body is left to its own devices" (Bugaj 2016, 210). Yet, this is a double-edged sword in the post-Soviet context, as in addition to the liberal belief in the necessity of encouraging self-reliability, the post-Soviet subject can often demonstrate great distrust towards state institutions. The film illustrates this by showing how the two men, upon their release from prison, repeatedly steal things and lean against walls, or carefully inspect their surroundings like trapped animals.

Later in the film, there is a Kafkaesque situation suggestive of the new type of bureaucracy when Eduard discovers that his home no longer physically exists but the state official argues that the house is still in the register and explains the lengthy bureaucratic procedure that Eduard has to follow in order to make a complaint. Other suggestions of a new – more depersonalized – society are the need to take a registration number in a population register and a pharmacist refusing to provide Eduard with his medicine due to a soiled prescription. However, by far the most direct depiction of a new and colder society is presented when Eduard comes across a situation where a pastor does not have time for a young man who desperately needs to talk to him and eventually engages in self-harm.

Countering the stereotypical image of fragility traditionally associated with old age, Markus is regularly seen as a physically threatening presence. Markus first pushes over and threatens to beat up the son of his former criminal associate when he goes to collect his Soviet motorcycle that the young man has been using as his own. The motorcycle is important to Markus not only for supporting his masculine image, but also because it hides gold bars that he had stashed away before being arrested. In this scene, there is another implication of a generational conflict as it becomes evident that Markus had not betrayed his associate to the police, while the young man, on the other hand, instantly goes to inform the local underworld of Markus' release. Soon after, the mafia tracks down Markus as they are also interested in his gold, but Markus uses the image of old age and pretended ill health to his advantage by unexpectedly attacking them and escaping.

Eduard, in contrast, is not interested in continuing the criminal ways of the past and steals only items that he finds necessary to impress his love interest, such as women's earrings and clothes from a fancy boutique, while Markus steals his clothing from a thrift store. Eduard has increasing difficulties in any kind of duplicity because of his deteriorating mental faculties and at one point the men are almost caught because Eduard immediately forgets Markus' elaborate plan about how to cheat a cafeteria. While Aagje Swinnen states that "if we have late-life romances at one end of the film spectrum, on the other we find plots propelled by the impact of dementia on individual lives" (2008, 71), this film appears to offer both. Similar to the trope of missing fathers, dementia in the current "hyper-cognitive" era (Post 1995) appears to suggest a strong connection to the melodrama genre. The melodramatic anxiety over dementia is most clearly played out when Eduard relives the shock of finding out that his love interest has passed away, a circumstance he has forgotten.

Once Markus is placed in social housing, he immediately begins to organize things and thus creates a sharp contrast with the younger generation of men there. Markus takes over control from the ineffectual Kirill (Kirill Käro) in charge of the place, and makes an alcoholic Pjotr (Mait Malmsten) sober up and act as his personal secretary. It has been noted that the post-Soviet Russian cinema of the 1990s was interested in finding a new "hero of our time" and that these models were "emphatically masculine, casting paternal and fraternal bonds as vital threads in the tattered post-Soviet fabric of Russian national identity" (Larsen 2000, 493). Goscilo and Hashamova similarly note that Russian cinema has been in search of new moral and historical authorities (2010, 16), whereas Zoran Samardzija states more broadly about the EU and the rise of populistic far-right movements that nostalgia for a "strongman leader" is indicative of its political deadlock (2020, 2). Yet, in the contemporary Estonian case, where individualism and liberalism are highly valued, *Green Cats* depicts such a display of domineering masculinity in a somewhat comical way. The film implies that in Estonia the conflation of masculine authority with national identity is common only to right-wing populism and as such it depicts a certain irony in Markus, wearing the official Soviet sporting jersey, outplaying the head of the conservative party (Indrek Taalmaa), wearing the state tricolours. Markus then ends up using the conservative party's funds to provide clothing for the asylum seekers placed at the social housing estate, instead of transporting them to Sweden as he had promised.

Nonetheless, the film does not naively picture Markus, who has been spending most of his life in prison for various criminal activities, as suddenly changing for the better. Markus seeks out his daughter only after escaping the ambush by the mafia and with the goal of stashing some of his gold at her place. He befriends his grandson with the aim of getting him to translate a text in English for him. Markus also immediately becomes verbally abusive towards his love interest (Ülle Kaljuste) after he wrongly accuses her of deceiving him. Most cynically, Markus creates a conflict between the right-wing populists and asylum seekers to offer cover for a heist that he has organized. As such, Markus' decision to give away his trusty watch and a bar of gold to a young asylum seeker at the end of the film is more pragmatic than sentimental. Likewise, his death is an accident and not a sacrifice for the greater good: while Markus is fighting off the mafia's henchman intervening with his robbery, he is shot by the police attempting to suppress the racial conflict. Though *Green Cats* is much more critical of a domineering "hard-man" masculinity than many current Hollywood examples, and Markus' death could be seen as a symbol of an end of era for Soviet-time "scorpions" of domineering masculinity, the film downplays some of this criticism by concluding with the more problematic and fatalistic Eduard's story arc.

The film's scepticism towards the emergence of potentially new and less domineering forms of masculinities is echoed in Eduard's storyline. A fellow social housing resident who realizes Eduard's declining mental capabilities, convinces him to help at a job involving arduous physical labour. More dramatically, Eduard witnesses a group of youngsters attacking a father in a park who was walking his child and had scolded the group for misbehaving. Upon seeing the gruesome beating, Eduard loses all self-control and fiercely assaults the young men, resulting in his confinement to a psychiatric institution. The importance of paternal relations is stressed again when Eduard sees *The Kid* (Chaplin, 1921), a film about a father living in poverty and holding on to his foster child against all odds. This happens prior to Eduard checking into a homeless centre similarly to the scene he had seen in the film. Given that Markus has no luck at emotionally connecting with his daughter and Eduard is not only reluctant to serve as a father figure to a drifter he encounters but also finds out that Tolik's daughter does not want to hear about her father, *Green Cats* implies that emotional wounds are too deep to be healed within a single generation. While Győri has suggested that in the Hungarian and Romanian context the relationship between grandfathers and grandsons suggests the broken lineage of masculinity (2021, 120), in the Estonian case it is also the sight of hope. It is in relation to his grandson, the youngest generation, that Markus' outdated masculine notions are most evident. His grandson prefers painting to boxing and has no desire to skip school and run away from home, as Markus suggests.

Conclusion

This chapter has shown the regional similarities and differences in the representation of post-Soviet masculinities and generational conflict as depicted in the male melodrama *Green Cats*, addressing the significant gap in research that currently exists regarding these concerns in the cinemas of the Baltic States. The protagonists' emergence from a "time capsule" of 20-year prison sentences allows *Green Cats* to artistically analyse the generational differences in the fast-moving post-Soviet Estonian society. Despite Markus' background as a professional boxer and his staying fit in the tough prison environment, his prized Soviet-era motorcycle and USSR sporting jersey firmly render him as an "old-timer" in the eyes of the characters outside the prison and consequently those of the viewers. Additionally, while the problematic of the missing father is a common theme in many male melodramas of the region, the Estonian case study offered here questions the authoritarian model, showing through Markus' violent death the dangers attached to clinging to an outdated model of masculinity. *Green Cats* thus underlines the relationality and socio-cultural dimension of ageing and goes beyond any glib notions of how to age "successfully." With this, the film runs counter to Estonia's official liberal discourse of the primacy of self-reliance.

The generational conflict in the film is further accentuated by showing the younger generation of men to be ineffectual when compared to the older generation, who because of the experience of living during the Soviet regime have been rendered more resourceful. However, while some might look up to Markus' life experience, the younger generation, born after the restoration of independence, are shown to have little interest in his masculine theatrics. As such, the film not only highlights the social construction of ageing at any given moment, but also stresses how the acknowledgment of such an idea highlights the insecurities at the very heart of (domineering) masculinity. Markus' fixation on leaving a strong impression of himself and his drive towards getting the most money for his gold ends with his tragic death. Furthermore, his mistrust towards others and negligence towards his daughter deprives him of any meaningful relationships. His inability to realize this is perhaps the most touching – and melodramatic – aspect of the film.

The chapter has argued via *Green Cats* how a consideration of age functions as an important means of exploring present social realities, as well as wider questions about how "to do" masculinity in post-Soviet Estonia. The film's focus on the contrasting types of ageing masculinities that are equally inadequate in adjusting to the present-day Estonia emphasizes the complexity of ageing in an ambitiously forward-looking, market-driven state. The film's melodramatic mode thus functions to explore Estonia's contemporary problems regarding ethnicity, age, gender, and disability. Via these concerns *Green Cats* is also able to raise larger questions about the current state of (ageing) masculinities that are relevant far beyond the regional context.

Notes

1 The retirement age of 65 is used as the (arbitrary) marker of old age here; this applies to both the actors and their on-screen characters.
2 The 2022 Russian invasion of Ukraine indicates the complex role that Puustusmaa played as a mediator between the two cultures and media industries, as he has since the invasion moved back to Estonia and terminated his career in Russia.
3 A focus group interview that Kadri Aavik conducted among older (70- to 80-year-olds) Estonian male audiences regarding *Green Cats* immediately resulted in a bafflement of the old men as to why they are shown these Russian-speaking criminals.
4 It is plausible that the issue of missing fathers and the concomitant intergenerational distress is related to the looser understanding of the breadwinner model in the Soviet Union compared to the West. Scholz claims: "In socialist countries,

masculinity was also associated with paid employment, but, thanks to the almost complete integration of women into the workforce, it was less connected to the position of breadwinner [when compared to Western Europe]" (2016).
5 See Näripea (2018) for an overview of the topic in Estonian cinema.

Works Cited

Bugaj, Malgorzata. "Corporeal Exploration in György Pálfi's *Taxidermia*." *The Cinematic Bodies of Eastern Europe and Russia: Between Pain and Pleasure*. Eds. Ewa Mazierska, Matilda Mroz, and Elżbieta Ostrowska. Edinburgh UP, 2016. 207–221.
Calasanti, Toni, and Kathleen Slevin. *Age Matters: Re-aligning Feminist Thinking*. Routledge, 2013.
Chivers, Sally. *The Silvering Screen: Old Age and Disability in Cinema*. U Toronto P, 2011.
Cordova, Richard de. "A Case of Mistaken Legitimacy: Class and Generational Difference in Three Family Melodramas." *Home Is Where the Heart Is: Studies in Melodrama and the Woman's Film*. Ed. Christine Gledhill. BFI Publishing, 1987. 255–267.
Durys, Elżbieta. "Cop Cinema and the Cinema of National Remembrance: The Case of *I'm a Killer* by Maciej Pieprzyca." *Postsocialist Mobilities: Studies in Eastern European Cinema*. Eds. Hajnal Király, and Zsolt Györi. Cambridge Scholars Publishing, 2021. 124–145.
Elsaesser, Thomas. "Tales of Sound and Fury: Observations of the Family Melodrama." *Film Theory and Criticism*. Eds. Gerald Mast, Marshall Cohen, and Leo Braudy. Oxford UP, 1992. 512–535.
Elsaesser, Thomas. "Statistics Explained: Healthy Life Years Statistics". *Europa.eu*, 2021, https://ec.europa.eu/eurostat/statistics-explained/index.php?title=Healthy_life_years_statistics. Accessed 19 Mar. 2022.
Goscilo, Helena, and Yana Hashamova. "Introduction. Cinepaternity: The Psyche and Its Heritage." *Cinepaternity: Fathers and Sons in Soviet and Post-Soviet Film*. Eds. Helena Goscilo, and Yana Hashamova. Indiana UP, 2010. 1–28.
Greer, Germaine. *The Female Eunuch*. Flamingo, 1993.
Györi, Zsolt. 2021. "Ruralising Masculinities and Masculinising the Rural in Márk Kostyál's *Coyote* and Bogdan Mirică's *Dogs*." *Postsocialist Mobilities*: 101–123.
Györi, Zsolt, and Hajnal Király. "Introduction: Broken Mobilities in Eastern European Cinemas." *Postsocialist Mobilities* ix–xxiii.
Hanlon, Niall. *Masculinities, Care and Equality: Identity and Nurture in Men's Lives*. Palgrave Macmillan, 2012.
Kalmár, György. *Formations of Masculinity in Post-Communist Hungarian Cinema*. Palgrave Macmillan, 2017.
Kimmel, Michael. "After Fifteen Years: The Impact of Sociology of Masculinity on the Masculinity of Sociology." *Men, Masculinity, and Social Theory*. Eds. Jeff Hearn, and David Morgan. Unwin Hyman, 1990. 93–109.
Király, Hajnal. "The Text of Muteness in Contemporary Hungarian and Romanian Family (Melo)Dramas." *Postsocialist Mobilities*: 82–100.
Larsen, Susan. "Melodramatic Masculinity, National Identity, and the Stalinist Past in Postsoviet Cinema." *Studies in 20th Century Literature* 24.1 (2000): 85–120.

Mazierska, Ewa, Matilda Mroz, and Elżbieta Ostrowska. "Introduction: Shaping the Cinematic Bodies of Eastern Europe and Russia." *The Cinematic Bodies*: 1–28.

Näripea, Eva. "Shadows of Unforgotten Ancestors: Representations of Estonian Mass Deportations of the 1940s in *In the Crosswind* (2014) and *Body Memory* (2011)." *Journeys on Screen: Theory, Ethics, Aesthetics*. Eds. Louis Bayman, and Natália Pinazza. Edinburgh UP, 2018. 103–117.

Neale, Steve. *Genre and Hollywood*. Routledge, 2000.

Negra, Diane, and Yvonne Tasker. "Neoliberal Frames and Genres of Inequality: Recession-era Chick Flicks and Male-centred Corporate Melodramas." *European Journal of Cultural Studies* 16.3 (2013): 344–361. Web. 19 Mar. 2022.

Post, Stephen G. *The Moral Challenge of Alzheimer Disease: Ethical Issues from Diagnosis to Dying*. John Hopkins UP, 1995.

Saar, Ellu. "Different Cohorts and Evaluation of Income Differences in Estonia." *International Sociology* 23.3 (2008): 417–445. Web. 19 Mar. 2022.

Samardzija, Zoran. *Post-Communist Malaise: Cinematic Responses to European Integration*. Rutgers UP, 2020.

Scholz, Sylka. "Everyday Socialist Heroes and Hegemonic Masculinities in German Democratic Republic, 1949–1989." *Extraordinary Ordinariness. Everyday Heroism in the United States, Germany, and Britain, 1800–2015*. Ed. Simon Wendt. F Campus, 2016. 185–216.

Springer, Kristen W., and Dawne M. Mouzon. "One Step Toward More Research on Aging Masculinities: Operationalizing the Hegemonic Masculinity for Older Men Scale (HMOMS)". *Journal of Men's Studies* 27.2 (2019): 183–203. Web. 19 Mar. 2022.

Swinnen, Aagje. "Ageing in Film." *Routledge Handbook of Cultural Gerontology*. Eds. Julia Twigg and Wendy Martin. Routledge, 2008. 69–76.

Teinemaa, Teet, and Marge Unt. "Contradictions of Hegemonic Masculinity and the (Hopeful) Potential of Old Age and Caring Masculinity in Estonian Society and in Films *A Friend of Mine* (2011) and *Tangerines* (2013)." *Journal of Aging Studies* (2022). https://doi.org/10.1016/j.jaging.2022.101034

Thornhill, John. "Ivan the Terribly Lost." *Financial Times* 29–30 Nov. 1997: 1.

9 Restitution and Ageing Masculinities in Post-1989 Czech Cinema

Matthew Sweney

To discuss portrayals of ageing masculinity in Czech films, some explication is in order. Czech films are not usually intended for export, so knowledge of the socio-political context(s) of the films is assumed, rather than explained. So first, some history. For a small country, Czech film production has been robust ever since its inception in 1898. Feature films are the norm, and their early models were mostly Hollywood, French, and German films up until the end of World War II, when German films fell out of favour for obvious reasons. For a few years, Czech films were "Czech," until the communist takeover in 1948, at which point pro-Soviet proletariat films continued to be the norm even after Stalin died. With the totalitarian thaw of Prague Spring and the Czech New Wave of daring, iconoclast filmmaking in the late 1960s, film and politics became inseparable, the one shaping the other. Then, with the Normalization period of the 1970s, stricter state control prevailed until the Velvet Revolution of 1989.[1]

Although post-1990 Czech filmmakers could be daring again and not worry about state censorship, profit and the box office replaced party ideology in terms of self-censorship. While these filmmakers had to gauge their films against audience expectations and could not compete against the juggernaut of Hollywood blockbusters, they could still make a decent profit due to the preference of Czechs for comedies (the young) and dramas (older audiences) that dealt with everyday Czech situations. Older audiences have – unsurprisingly – appreciated older actors (some of whom were banned after 1970) who have lived through the same times and political changes and embody their generational experience. Ageing male actors thus represent more than familiar faces on the Czech screen; they are totems for audiences.

While some of the films I will be discussing would be hard to distinguish from Hollywood films in terms of their production values (dozens of Hollywood films have been shot in Prague's Barrandov Studios, due to the high production values, lower costs, and photogenic shooting locales), their content is wholly Czech. As mentioned, these are not films made for export, not even to their closest neighbours such as Poland, Germany, and

DOI: 10.4324/9781003306146-9

Austria (the exception being Slovakia, which avidly consumes Czech films and television). They can be baffling even to viewers in these neighbouring countries – a fact underlined by the fact that the Polish equivalent of the English idiom meaning incomprehension, "It's Greek to me," is *czeski film* (Janovec 318).

Czech men who entered into middle age (or over) after 1989 were significantly affected by a tumultuous half century of being at the centre of Europe: the political and social upheavals of World War II and Czech complicity in both the Holocaust and as the expulsion of ethnic Germans after the war; the communist takeover of the democratic country in 1948, and complicity in that; the "freedom" of Prague Spring in the mid-1960s; the 1968 Russian invasion which ended Prague Spring; the subsequent period of heavy Soviet-style Normalization in the 1970s–1980s; and the overthrow of the communist regime in 1989. Located between Western European and Russian geopolitical spheres of influence, the Czech Republic has belonged to one empire or another for centuries, with brief periods of self-determination. The Czech male mindset reflects that: often feeling ineffective against the forces of history or outside powers, an "absurd" reaction to socio-political events – just like those of the characters in works by writers such as Hašek, Kafka, Hrabal, or Havel – is perceived as normal, perhaps even healthy.

This chapter identifies eight feature films released since the overthrow of the authoritarian regime in 1989 (the Velvet Revolution) where ageing Czech masculinities are not only topical but also central to the films' themes. Six of these films are by Czech directors, and for comparison, one by a Polish director and one by a Slovak director. The films are listed here in the order in which I will be discussing them:

> *Revival* (2013, dir. Alice Nellis), a dramatic comedy about a group of late middle-aged men who decide to revive their old rock band.
> *Kolja* (Kolya; 1996, dir. Jan Svěrák), the Oscar-winning comedy about a middle-aged Czech music teacher and confirmed bachelor who "marries" a Russian woman in exchange for money but who ends up briefly raising her 5-year-old son.
> *Babí léto* (Autumn Spring; 2001, dir. Vladimír Michálek), a dramatic comedy about a couple in their late seventies wherein the wife suffers her husband's flights of fancy.
> *Vratné lahve* (Empties; 2007, dir. Jan Svěrák), another comedy by Svěrák, also written by his father Zdeněk Svěrák, who also stars in the film as an ageing secondary school literature teacher nearing retirement who quits and gets a new job in the returnable bottles section of a supermarket.
> *Odcházení* (Leaving; 2011, dir. Václav Havel), a self-reflexive comedic drama about a country's chancellor who, after his term is finished, is forcibly asked to leave his official summer residence.

Obsluhoval jsem anglického krále (I Served the King of England; 2006, dir. Jiří Menzel), a comedy based on the novel by Bohumil Hrabal about the pivotal 1935–1960 period in Czech history as narrated by an "everyman" waiter who manages to acquire riches by stealth before his fall.

Tlmočník (The Interpreter; 2018, dir. Martin Šulík), a Slovak "dramatic comedy" about a Holocaust survivor who decides to assassinate his parents' killer and instead ends up as an interpreter for the Nazi's son.

Šarlatán (Charlatan; 2020, dir. Agniezka Holland), a Czech-Irish biopic about the real-life healer Jan Mikolášek and his trial for fraud in the 1950s, including criminal charges regarding his sexual orientation.

Film critic Ewa Mazierska notes that the majority of the male characters in Polish, Czech, and Slovak national cinemas frequently come across "more as products of . . . histories and ideologies, than as independent agents" (225). This is even more true of representations of older men. Thus, contemporary Czech films featuring men of retirement age – even ostensible comedies like *Revival* – cannot help but reference and reflect on the political changes of the 20th century which shaped the lives of such men and made them who they are.

It is tempting to equate mid-20th-century Czech history with a series of life passages:

1 Childhood (1950s): Upbringing in a totalitarian regime (unquestioning socialization, strict schooling).
2 Adolescence (1960s): First tastes of freedom (sexual awakening, questioning of the regime).
3 Early adulthood without dependents or existential cares (1960s): Prague Spring, Czech New Wave.
4 Adulthood, responsibility, the disappointment of the normalcy of adult life and middle age (1968–1989): Soviet invasion, Normalization, intellectuals being forced to do menial labour.
5 Retirement and the possibility of transformation (1989): Velvet Revolution.
6 The onset of old age and memory loss (2000s): The ability to forget the past (selective amnesia) or gloss over the past (selective nostalgia) in order to cope with the shifting sands of the present.
7 Advanced senility/Alzheimer's (2010s): The inability to cope with the present.

Too tempting? Czech filmmakers have repeatedly used such tropes as a kind of shorthand. Very few Czech films are made even thinking about export, so the domestic socio-cultural–political background and the allegorical implications of certain narratives that foreground ageing do not have to be explained to local audiences – hence my explications here.

Revival

Czech writer-director Alice Nellis's film *Revival* (2013) centres on a group of late middle-aged men who decide to revive their rock group after a hiatus of 40 years – yes, another let's-get-the-band-back-together-and-put-on-a-show film, but with a socio-political twist. The film starts with a television clip reporting the break-up of a rock band made up of young men in their early twenties. The date is 1972. The band is Czech, but the television announcer is speaking Slovak, a purposeful reminder to today's viewers that this was still Czechoslovakia, when broadcasting was deliberately bilingual, in Czech and Slovak. The reporter compares the band's break-up to that of the Beatles, but this band did not break up, in the words of Paul McCartney, "because Yoko sat on an amp."[2]

As the announcer states, they chose to break up their Czech band – with the English name "Smoke" – rather than submit to the orders of the regime to sing in their native tongue. The problem was that they sang exclusively in English, the language of the Western imperialists. This was the cultural milieu of Normalization, the period following the 1968 invasion of some 200,000 Warsaw Pact troops into Czechoslovakia to crush the Prague Spring, after which about 75,000 standing Soviet troops remained in the country (Černá 114, *fn* 2) and Western, non-Socialist influences were banned. While the members of the band insist throughout the film that they were not dissidents, Czech audiences are well aware that the Velvet Revolution of 1989 which brought down the communist regime had its roots in Charter 77, the 1977 appeal for human rights under the Helsinki Accords, which itself was touched off by the jailing of the members of a real rock band, the Plastic People of the Universe – who, like the fictional Smoke, sang in English and fell foul of the law because of it.

When Smoke gets back on stage to a sell-out crowd of late middle-aged former fans (and 20-year-old fans of one of their children, a budding rock star himself), the band members each get back their self-respect, the respect of their spouses and children, their self-confidence, and, last but not least, female adulation. As the crowd goes wild, it is as if the last 40 years never happened.

However even in *Revival*, the comedy gives way to tragedy. While the film concludes with their big concert, during the closing credits we are shown the newspaper headline "Rediscovered legend of Czech dissident rock dies," and we see scenes of the front man's funeral as the band plays "I'd Rather Be in Honolulu" – *czeski film*.[3]

Kolya: Restitution

The most successful post-1989 Czech film internationally was *Kolja* (Kolya; 1996, dir. Jan Svěrák, screenplay by and starring Zdeněk Svěrák; 1996 Academy Award for Best Foreign Language Film). International audiences may remember it as a cute film about a middle-aged bachelor who is forced to grow up by taking care of a young boy; for domestic audiences, however, it is clearly anchored in the socio-political milieu of Czechoslovak communism and set in the pivotal year 1989, ending with the Velvet Revolution and the chance for its ageing male protagonist to start anew. Reading the film from the Czech perspective, it is tantamount to a national allegory: the bachelor reluctantly agreed to a marriage for money with a Russian woman (pressured collusion and invasion) who arrives in the country and then leaves him, saddling him with her child (Russian occupation and Normalization). Russian soldiers stop at the bachelor's mother's house when their transport vehicle breaks down and ask to use the toilet. They are refused (passive resistance). The bachelor listens to the Voice of America, clandestinely (passive resistance and Western-leaning politics). The end of the film coincides with the Velvet Revolution, mixing real documentary footage of the end of Soviet domination and the rebirth of self-determination with the fiction of the bachelor celebrating in the streets, his Czech lover (real domestic partner) suddenly very pregnant, the Russian "wife" and child leaving the country, and a secret policeman giving him a thumbs-up. The protagonist re-enters adult life; the Czechs and Slovaks get their country back.

After democracy was restored in 1989, the new regime in Czechoslovakia offered restitution to families and individuals who had their property confiscated and nationalized during the Victorious February communist takeover in 1948 – to some, but not all. Also, persons who were dismissed from their professions (especially teachers) for not signing a compulsory statement saying they agreed with the 1968 Soviet invasion were offered their jobs back – some, but not all. Fiscal compensations were not given individually, nor could many afford repairs on buildings returned to them after 40 years of abuse and neglect. Literally, some things were returned, but broken. Metaphorically, freedom was returned to those still living – but not one's youth, virility, aspirations, health, job, money, or sanity.

Some financial restitution *was* offered to all Czechoslovak citizens in 1991 in the form of voucher privatization, when the state issued vouchers to allow citizens to purchase shares of companies which had been nationalized during communism. Instead, vulturous mutual fund companies were set up, most notoriously Viktor Koženy's Harvard Investment Fund, which promised a 1000% return on investments if you signed over your vouchers to his Ponzi scheme. Kožený bought shares in companies, liquidated his assets, and escaped to first Ireland and then the Bahamas, leaving millions of Czechs and Slovak citizens with nothing.

To capture that zeitgeist, Věra Chytilová (1929–2014), the director of such Czech New Wave classics as *Sedmikrásky* (Daisies; 1966), directed and co-wrote *Dědictví aneb Kurvahošigutntag* (The Inheritance or Fuckoffguysgoodday; 1992), a sort of parable where the protagonist (played by Bolek Polívka, who also co-wrote the screenplay) is a young man who inherits a huge sum of money from restitution owed to his uncle who dies. However, the jobless working-class protagonist does not know how to manage his windfall; the film is a scathing send-up of the non-worldliness of those raised behind the Iron Curtain.

Autumn Spring: Up?

Certainly the post-1989 economic playing field was not completely level, and pensioners – those who had lived and suffered through the most turbulent times – were hit the hardest by entering the free market, and given back their freedoms at an age where they are not fully able to take advantage of them, be they reasons fiscal or physical. Perhaps the most interesting post-1989 Czech film centring on ageing masculinity is *Babí léto* (Autumn Spring;[4] 2001, dir. Vladimír Michálek, screenplay Jiří Hubač [1929–2011]), a very black comedy on the economics of retirement. It begins with the arrival of a New York Metropolitan Opera maestro to a manor house in Bohemia. The first we see of him is his cane, poking out of a limousine. "Very shabby," he says, in English, looking at the manor. He and his male secretary are inspecting the property before purchase, as he is looking to return to his homeland to retire. He taps the stucco in the interior with his cane. It flakes off. He leaves, undecided, followed by the realtor all the way to the Prague Hilton, where he ascends in a glass elevator.

In the next scene he arrives at a different kind of dwelling, a shabbier, socialist-era housing estate, by way of the Garden of Eden Prague Metro stop. "Old men should be rich," he declares, returning the cane to his "secretary," who congratulates him on his role: "Fanda, you were marvellous . . . and tasting the wine, only to send it back was a masterstroke!" This time, Fanda ascends a battered lift to a worker's flat, entering on his knees with a bouquet for his wife, who berates him: "Where have you been? Five people waited to celebrate your birthday and you were out drinking? Have you forgotten your own birthday?" We soon find out that it is Fanda's 76th birthday – shared with his wife – and "very shabby" could be a description for his own situation in life. Fanda is played with bravura by veteran actor Vlastimil Brodský (1920–2002) in one of his final roles (his film debut was in 1937).[5]

The official description from the film's distributor reads in part:

> Tragicomic story of a young seventy-five-year-old, eternal dreamer, *pábitel* and prankster who – as opposed to his beloved, worrying wife – refuses to accept his fate and be resigned to his life as an old man, instead living his life as a never-ending challenge in which every day becomes a wonderful opportunity for new adventure. . . . In a number of comically-rewarding situations, full of delicate and black humour, he is at odds with his wife regarding his carefree nature and independence, through which he always shows anew just what the ART OF LIVING is.[6]

The word *pábitel* in the description is a word coined by writer Bohumil Hrabal (who I will discuss later) as "a person . . . who says things that practical people say are nonsense, and does things that polite people do not do, losing the border between reality and dreams."[7] Michael Henry Heim – probably the most prominent literary translator from Czech to English – translated it as "palaverer";[8] however, that word does quite capture the dreamy nature of the original, which Hrabal had to invent to describe a curious aspect of Czech masculinity. In contrast with traits associated with other Slavic nations and nationalities, Czech masculinity is not so much concerned with being *macho*.[9] Literary examples immediately come to mind: the chubby, beer-guzzling Good Soldier Švejk (Jaroslav Hašek's Czech national anti-hero), who bullshits his way out of sticky situations; and any of Kafka's male protagonists trying to navigate their way out of perplexing bureaucratic/police procedural/hexapodal nightmares. In both cases, the men's problems are not of their creation (at least, not according to them), and they must use their wits to get themselves out. For ageing Czech males the situation is not markedly different: they are trapped in societal/political situations where they must use what's left of their wits, rather than what's left of their brawn.

In *Autumn Spring*, the character of Emílie, Fanda's wife (played by Stella Zázvorková, 1922–2005), the realist, might have a different point of view: an older woman married to a man who is rarely home, sometimes for days at a time, who seems to do nothing but squander their money. In fact, she starts divorce proceedings against him, until a judge convinces her to drop her petition.

Money – the lack of it – is the constant theme of this Central European black comedy. For example, one of the plot details is that the son gets a bargain on a used grave for his parents' birthday. Another is that after finally getting his hands on (i.e., borrowing) enough money to settle a huge debt, the pensioner's entire purse is stolen by a "fake blindman" (is injustice, then, blind?). The film ends with Fanda going up in a balloon – by himself – and showering his wife on the ground with gold coins tossed from above. This is clearly a fantasy sequence, representing the possibility of Fanda flying from his reality, realizing his dreams, and providing for his wife. We know this happy, restitutive ending is an impossibility. The real-life ending to this film about money would be that their son will sell their flat out from under them and put them in an old folks' home.

Empties: The Myth of Increasing Returns

Vratné lahve (Empties; 2007, dir. Jan Svěrák, screenplay by Zdeněk Svěrák; the same son-and-father team behind *Kolya*). In many ways the film seems like a counterargument to *Autumn Spring*: money is no problem, and the ageing male is an active agent who improves people's lives. The English title is a terrible translation; the original means "Returnable Bottles": the important metaphor being that one gets multiple chances to refill (restitute) the vessel of one's life.

Its author and star Zdeněk Svěrák, best-known outside the former Czechoslovakia as the lead actor in *Kolya*, is a beloved national figure, synonymous with the face of the ageing Czech male (think Clint Eastwood or Sean Connery, if they were also songwriters and three-time winners of the national book award). He is such an icon that his son made a feature-length documentary about him;[10] and during the first COVID-19 lockdown, Czech Television launched a new channel for older adults, choosing Svěrák to inaugurate it by singing his song "Není nutno."[11] The song was simulcast not only on television but on radio, via Internet, and significantly via the "village radio" – the loudspeaker systems, mostly in small towns and villages, set up during socialist times to broadcast news – still in use and still an important source of local and emergency information for older adults. Svěrák is also co-creator (with Ladislav Smoljàk) of the "Jára Cimrman" franchise. Jára Cimrman is a Zelig-like figure (created decades before the Woody Allen film), a faceless personality who is responsible for inventing nearly everything, as well as being on the spot at pivotal moments in history. Cimrman is the perfect example of Czech *mystifikace* – usually translated as "mystification," but properly it is more like "mythification." In the Cimrman world, the little man is the kingmaker and catalyst that holds the world together.

Empties can be read as a similar type of mythification, the story of a middle-school Czech literature teacher of retirement age who, instead of being laid off well before retirement (sadly, the norm), decides to quit. He immediately finds a series of menial jobs, first as a bicycle messenger. After his frustration with using the two-way messenger radio and a bike crash, he takes another job at the returnable bottles window in a supermarket. There he becomes a matchmaker, first between his daughter (raising a child on her own) and one of his former co-workers, and then for the other men who work with him in the returnable bottles department. He also helps other older customers, including one shut-in older woman for whom he gets the medical care she so desperately needs.

Although he and his wife are no longer intimate, he still has sexual fantasies (depicted throughout the film, and even in the closing credits), though he does not really act upon them. In one case, however, he tries and miserably fails: the woman (a former co-worker) wrote him a note saying she was home alone every Thursday afternoon, but he forgets and arrives on a Wednesday when her husband is there. But this film is clearly a fantasy where this seemingly ageless Czech male works behind the scenes making life fun and worth living – much like Svěrák's creation Cimrman, who makes Czech history funny and harmless.

In the film's balloon ride ending, the husband and wife go up together, and end up (soft) crashing together in a field, falling on top of each other in a laughing, physical jumble that suggests they might rekindle their own romance, as if to say: "While our dreams may come crashing down to earth, we still have each other to fulfil us." Love remains triumphant – echoing the passage he forces his secondary school students to memorize against their will at the beginning of the film, by "an old man who finally realizes what is important in life." One smart alec pupil in the class sarcastically says, "Wow, that poet was really great – so great, they should have made a movie about it." *Empties*, of course, is that film, and the student's sarcasm turned to success: the film won the Czech Lion (Czech Oscar) for Best Screenplay, Best Director (Jan Svěrák), and the Audience Award; and the Polish Eagle 2009 for Best European Film. Svěrák won Best Actor at the Tallinn Black Nights Film Festival 2007, and *Empties* was the highest grossing Czech domestic film in 15 years – doing even better domestically than *Kolya*.[12]

Leaving: King Václav

In discussing the links between post-1989 Czech culture and society, one must mention Václav Havel – the playwright turned president. Havel had, in fact, always wanted to be a filmmaker (Bernard 393, 401).[13] Born into a very prominent, affluent Prague family, he was denied entrance to film school for being too bourgeois. In a characteristically Czech irony, his uncle Miloš Havel had owned Lucernafilm, the biggest producer of films in the first Czechoslovak Republic, until he was forced to sell the studio to the Germans during the Nazi Occupation. Miloš and his brother Václav (father of the future president) developed the area of Prague called Barrandov, after which the famous Barrandov Film Studios were named. As a youth, Havel's friends included future directors such as Miloš Forman and Ivan Passer – the three of them even wrote a treatment they sold to Barrandov in 1964, which was never produced.[14] So Havel, the failed filmmaker, became a playwright instead. Writer-director Václav Havel's film *Leaving* (2011) is thus in itself an act of restitution. Havel, now a world figure with definite name recognition, finally got his funding and his chance, and like the central character in the film, it is obvious he did not want to give it all up. (The behind-the-scenes documentary on the making of *Leaving* shows Havel behind the camera, on a crane, rehearsing complicated scenes, having a whale of a time.)

Leaving is the story of an ageing Chancellor (played by Josef Abrhám, 1939–2022) of a nation who has completed his term but does not want to surrender the chateau provided to him by the state as his country residence. Havel wrote the piece first as a play, but with a film in mind. Well-versed in drama, Havel could not help but quote in both play and screenplay from Chekhov's *The Cherry Orchard* and Shakespeare's *King Lear*. *The Cherry Orchard* is invoked here for its setting at a time of political/economic change, embodied by the family and its hesitancy to sell the orchard (nature, past) in order to move into the present; *King Lear* is invoked for its ageing masculine sovereign who is unsure about his future and what may happen to him when he loses the power of the throne and his fate is left up to his family.

The ageing Chancellor is constructed in relation to a variety of women: humoured by his wife, ridiculed by his eldest daughter, ignored by his youngest daughter, and pursued by a young political scientist who has written her dissertation on his political writings. In the film the political scientist (played by Barbora Seidlová) repeatedly walks on the water of the chateau's reflecting pool, Venus-like, her hair flowing about her. A clandestine kiss is witnessed by his wife and then things fall apart: his wife wants to leave him, and the political scientist later repeats the same lines about how much his speeches have meant to her to the Chancellor-elect (the latter portrayed as being younger and more virile than the protagonist). The only people even remotely interested in what the Chancellor has to say turn out to be self-serving: the political scientist/opportunist, the paparazzo, the tabloid journalist – all seeking to monetize their access to the Chancellor.

While the film is less explicit about its literary origins than the play (for instance, the sound of the chainsaws cutting down the cherry orchard in the film is lost in the mix and barely noticeable, whereas the sound of chainsaws in the theatre is just the opposite; Havel's voice acting as a narrative "chorus" in the play – but absent in the film – specifies Chekhov's *The Cherry Orchard* by name), it is more obvious about its personal origins and resonances for the ageing playwright/politician. Havel leaves no room for doubt that the film is somewhat autobiographical, casting his wife (actress Dagmar Havlová-Veškrnová) in the role of the Chancellor's wife, and even casting his own brother as one of the chateau hangers-on.

Like Lear, like the Chancellor, President Havel was not able to pass his kingdom into good hands. As an ironic retelling of Chekhov's play, the old way being razed for the new is democracy. And though Havel is considered an "absurd" playwright,[15] the cherry orchard in this play being razed to put up a complex incorporating a multiplex cinema, casino, tattoo parlour, butcher shop, petrol station, dance hall, tabloid offices, and so on pales in comparison to Alexei Navalny's subsequent real-life revelations about "Putin's palace,"[16] nor are real-life examples of heads of state who refuse to leave their offices difficult to find.

As a coda to the film, Havel himself emerges from the chateau's murky reflection pool to say: "Thank you for turning off your mobile phones. Truth and love must prevail over lies and hatred. Turn your phones back on." This must seem like a *czeski film* moment to non-Czechs; the motto sandwiched in between the mobile phone talk is Havel's motto as president: it was adapted from the Czech national motto, "Truth will prevail," originally coined by Tomáš Garrigue Masaryk, the first president of Czechoslovakia, with Havel's addition of "love." The motto placed therein seems to make the maxim, like the photoplay, just an interlude of an hour and a half spent offline in today's world. In this coda, Havel is also taking on the role of the *vodník* or *hastrman*, the "water-man": a Slavic folklore creature from the black lagoon who can be either frightening – the playwright, catching unsuspecting people and submerging them into his world – or comical, a bemused, pipe-smoking grandfather type (i.e., the elder statesman).

I Served the King of England: And Got the Leftovers

Obsluhoval jsem anglického krále (I Served the King of England; 2006, dir. and screenplay Jiří Menzel, based on the novel by Bohumil Hrabal). Hrabal's sprawling novel about Czech mid-20th-century history – encompassing the heyday of the 1930s (good economic years in the country), through the Nazi Occupation and Holocaust, Liberation, and then to the communist takeover and forced labour years of the 1950s, as told by a very unreliable narrator – was finally brought to the screen by Jiří Menzel after decades of financing and pre-production problems. Menzel and Hrabal had previously worked together on the classic *Ostře sledované vlaky* (Closely Watched Trains; 1966; 1967 Academy Award, Best Foreign Film), *Skřivánci na niti* (Larks on a String; 1969, but shelved for political reasons until 1990, when it won the Golden Bear in Munich), and three other films.

This, their final collaboration, is a complex work.[17] The film is divided into lavish tableaux of the opulence of pre–World War II Prague, endless Technicolor banquets of food and drink while one-upping Busby Berkeley with bevies of female beauties; the decadence of the Nazi Occupation; and finally the grey squalidity of post-1948 communism. The "beauty" of the Nazi past is Menzel's attempt to pictorially depict the unreliability of the book's narrator – it was a beautiful time for those who profited off the misery of others. The drab tones of the 1950s represent the moral reckoning of the narrator and additionally a visual commentary/counterpoint to Czech films made in the 1950s, which depicted everything as a socialist paradise.

While some critics[18] have noted resemblances between the two actors who play the young/old main protagonist Jan Dítě, I would argue that there is more of a resemblance between the actor who plays the young Dítě (Bulgarian actor Ivan Barnev) and Menzel as a young man, and between Oldřich Kaiser (who plays the old Dítě) and Hrabal as an old man. Read this way, it represents a deeply personal film for Menzel: a nostalgic farewell to the follies of Menzel's youth as a young actor/director, and a sober goodbye to his aged and drink-ravaged friend Hrabal, with nothing left except his memories over a pint.

If there's any doubt this is a very personal film, the production itself was prefaced by Menzel's infamous "special guest appearance" at the 1998 Karlovy Vary International Film Festival, when he struck another Jiří – producer Jiří Sirotek – with a cane, Sirotek having somehow bought and sold the film rights to Hrabal's novel out from under Menzel just months after Hrabal's death. I have never seen Menzel use a cane in any film or paparazzi photo, and Menzel said himself that this was something he planned. Since the producer was within his rights legally, Menzel "had no other recourse but the rod"[19] – an intentional, symbolic caning for a moral transgression: the older generation punishing the younger.

Menzel refocused the novel's narrative by starting with the narrator's later fate: the film begins by irising out from the red star adorning a prison gate: the colour palette is grey on grey, except for the communist red of the star. Scenes taking place in the communist present of the film are bleak, reminiscent of Menzel and Hrabal's earlier *Larks on a String*, but instead of *Larks*' junkyard (Hrabal himself studied law, but was sent to work in a junkyard as a forced labourer in the 1950s), the setting is another wasteland: Sudetenland, purged of its ethnic Germans, its once-handsome buildings left to rot.

Hrabal's narrator's first conscious step on what will be his life path is a misstep: a feigned slowness to deliver the change from a large banknote which a rich train passenger gives him on the platform to buy a hotdog from the window of the train. As the train takes off, Dítě pockets the money, thinking he will never see the man again. But fate does not work that way, according to Hrabal, and he will see this man again and again throughout the next fateful decades of Nazification, the appropriation of Jewish concentration camp victims' wealth, Czech complicity in the Holocaust, and the expulsion of Germans from Czechoslovakia. Our narrator whistles to himself while counting his money, seemingly inculpable, but failing to tote up his moral debts – which come paid after the war during the communist takeover and privatization of property, after which Dítě is sent to prison and then released to a labour camp in the former Sudetenland.

Like Jaroslav Hašek's novel *The Good Soldier Švejk*, *I Served the King of England* is the "little man" version of history (hence the protagonist's name Dítě, which means "child"), as opposed to the "Big Man" narratives – which is perhaps another reason why American, British, and Polish critics found it hard to fathom (Svěrák's Jára Cimrman also falls into this category). But unlike Švejk, Dítě is not a rebel, and though he is popular with the ladies, he is complicit with the occupier, lacking a masculine spine: as director Miloš Forman stated in a documentary about Havel's inauguration, "Poles fight, Czechs bend."[20] Dítě's ill-gotten gains eventually mount to astronomical sums, enough for him to purchase his own villa. Here, far from shabby, it is the exact same manor house used in the film *Autumn Spring* – precisely to illustrate its later state confiscation (Czech filmmakers often reuse the same actors and locales; viewers can play the game of constructing elaborate alternate plots linking them all together to create a Czech film metaverse).

This villa, however, will never come back in restitution. Instead, Dítě will be "reformed" in prison and "returned" to society – as a broken man. Peter Bradshaw's review in the *Guardian* begins with a comment about Menzel's age, as if he were too old to direct, but actually (and again), this is an old man's movie – and the age of the director is crucial to understanding the film's point: the virile past is a colourful tableau you can replay endlessly in memory, while the ugly, drab impotent present can be tolerated with only

Restitution and Ageing Masculinities 113

a smile from a young woman and ruminations over a glass of beer ("Ah, if only I hadn't married a big city Nazi fanatic and found myself a nice Moravian country girl").

The film ends by irising in on a pint of beer – and while it might be tempting to relate it to the Beer Hall Putsch, it is likely more a paean to Menzel's friend Hrabal, who not only made the famous *U zlatého tigra* (Golden Tiger) pub in Prague his court where he received heads of state (such as Bill Clinton) over a beer but was even alleged to have been born in a pub. And cliché though it may be, there *is* a connection between *pivo* and Czech masculinity.[21]

The Interpreter: Something Gained in Translation

In contrast to their Czech counterparts, Slovaks do not seem to have such a fairy-tale view of history, casting a much colder eye on World War II. Writer-director Martin Šulík's *Tlmočník* (The Interpreter; 2018, winner of seven 2019 Slovak Film & Television Academy Awards including Best Film, Best Director, Best Screenplay, and Best Actor) is a serious, uncompromising film set in the present about a translator named Ali Ungár (played by director Jiří Menzel, 1938–2020), an ageing Slovak Jewish Holocaust survivor who takes matters into his own hands when, via a job translating the memoirs of an SS officer named Graubner, he realizes that this officer was responsible for his parents' deaths. He investigates the whereabouts of the officer and takes a train to Vienna, packing a pistol to shoot him. When the officer's son (played by Peter Simonischek of *Toni Erdmann* fame) answers the door and explains that his father is dead, Ungár leaves, but not before calling the son a Nazi swine and carving a swastika on his mailbox. At home he puts a pistol to his own head, but his daughter's voice on his answering machine interrupts the suicide attempt.

In Bratislava a few days later, he has a visitor: the son. The younger Graubner says that the visit made him think, and he wants to visit the "idyllic" country which he knows only through his father's letters to his mother. And he wants Ungár to see for himself "whether or not [Graubner is] an antisemitic swine," adding that he wants to also see whether or not Ungár is a "Jewish übermensch." Ungár says that he is retired and no longer an interpreter, but reluctantly agrees to the idea as a paid job – for a man in his eighties, this means decent money. On the subsequent road trip, we find that Ungár does indeed become an interpreter, interpreting not only casual conversations but also the culture and the history of Slovakia during World War II, as he takes Graubner to visit other Holocaust survivors and to the Banská Bystrica archives, where along with Graubner, we watch real documentary footage of Holocaust survivor testimony.

The film is neither sentimental nor heavy-handed, and is full of nuances of past and present identities, such as the fact that Graubner is a retired English and French teacher (the language of the victors), or Ungár's visit to his daughter's boarding school for Ukrainian refugee children where he notices the rows of shoes. Unlike the exhibit at Auschwitz, these shoes belong to living children, who are being cared for. While Graubner styles himself as a ladies' man and there is frank talk of sex – Graubner telling the older Ungár that one is never too old – we see that women rather see Graubner as a father figure. Finally, Graubner admits to Ungár that he is not actually blasé – his devil-may-care attitude is not that of an arrogant son of a Nazi SS officer, but that his sister suffered from trauma due to the sins of the father, and Graubner swore that he would never do the same.

Restitution, restoration of one's birthright, requires one to confront the past, and implies some kind of moral accounting or balancing of the scales. The real definition of masculinity in the film is having to come to grips with history and your place in it, and defining your role as to how you deal with it – now and in the future (this is the read-between-the-lines moral of *I Served the King of England* as well, though Slovaks do not pussyfoot around). In this case, one son indeed must come to grips with the sins of the father, the other son with revenge. And both sons are fathers themselves, trying to deal with the weighty problem of raising their own children with respect for the past while not letting the past weigh upon them as much as it did on them. Graubner says that when his father returned home from prison after the war, he was unrepentant, and in later years when he tried to make his father face his sins, it was too late; he had advanced Alzheimer's and remembered nothing. The film thus nicely raises the question: Is forgetting possible? While restitution for Slovakia's Holocaust victims is not possible, the film suggests that (some) form of retribution is.

Charlatan: Physician Not Allowed to Heal Himself

Finally we turn to *Šarlatán* (Charlatan; 2020, dir. Agnieszka Holland, b. 1948;[22] screenplay by Marek Epstein). This is another film by Agnieszka Holland on real-life Czech historical figures,[23] this one featuring the healer Jan Mikolášek, whose property was confiscated by the state after a communist show trial in 1959, when Mikolášek (expertly played by Ivan Trojan) was aged 69. Epstein's screenplay infers that the trial over whether Mikolášek was a charlatan or not was more a combination of then President Antonín Novotný's enmity that Mikolášek successfully treated his predecessor, Jan Zápotecký, and that Mikolášek was gay – homosexuality was literally defined as a "crime against society" between 1950 and 1961 (Sokolová 278; qtd. in Mazierska 183). Eva Mazierska, writing in 2008, laments the lack of portrayals of homosexuality in Czech films at length (182–190). Although the Czech Republic has recognized same-sex registered partnerships since 2006, full spousal rights have not been granted to same-sex partners, and depictions of same-sex relations remain rare on screen. To Holland and Epstein's credit, there are semi-graphic scenes of male homosexuality in the film between an older and much younger man that still have shock potential for audiences in the Czech Republic today, and the film raises questions over whether the state should have had the power to intrude on private lives, including one's sexuality. Mikolášek, at 69, was a man of means, a successful man at the top of his profession, who treated the poor and rich alike, with friends in very high places, only to have everything taken from him. The film stops with his conviction, leaving viewers to ask themselves what happened to him – what about his restitution?

In fact, Mikolášek was released from jail in 1963, a year after same-sex sexual activity in Czechoslovakia was decriminalized. This *non-czeski film* is pointed, and its conclusion does not leave international viewers scratching their heads but rather examining their own thoughts and prejudices. This is a film about masculine ageing which deals with one's reputation, standing in the community, sexual potency, and even sexual orientation: a true-life story where one's convictions lead to conviction. It was almost immediately picked up by Netflix, doubtless partly due to the Covid pandemic, but moreover proof of its international nature and ability to get its message across borders, including into neighbouring Poland. It is a Czech film for the 21st century, which interestingly goes back into Czech history and politics in order to present a story to mature, contemporary global audiences.

Afterword: King of May

Post-1990 Czech films tend to portray their ageing male characters as victims of fate forced to use their wits to get through adversity. The next generation will out of necessity produce a range of different masculinities, influenced by images and memes, the vast majority international and some of them home-grown, allowing the possibility of self-curated, self-created, rather than any narrowly defined, masculinity/ies.

During the Prague Spring of 1965 American beat poet Allen Ginsberg (1926–1997) was famously made *Král majáles* (King of May) for the first celebrations of the traditional university student spring festival since the communist takeover in 1948. He was paraded through the streets of Prague but ultimately stalked by secret police and deported for "public outrage" (Blažek 45) – a euphemism for public displays of homosexual affection, which although recently decriminalized, still did not fit the idea of Czech masculinity of the time. Writing one of his key works, the poem "Kral Majales," on the plane to England afterwards, Ginsberg lamented that although he was king (aged 40, at the height of his powers), he was "paranoid," because he feared the Kingdom of May could last only one month – a metaphor encompassing literally Prague Spring, but also freedom in general, plus his potency as man and poet (Ginsberg 1987).

The king was sent into exile: Ginsberg was banned from Czechoslovakia until after the Velvet Revolution. When he did return, he was given restitution in a way, symbolically restored as King of May again in 1990. Twenty-five years after being King of May in 1965, Havel was president, the kingdom was restored, but in his poem "Return of Kral Majales," Ginsberg laments the ravages of age: high blood pressure, gout, palsy, kidney and liver problems, diabetes, etc. (Ginsberg 2010). Too old to rock n' roll, what good is having a kingdom? Restitution comes too late to be of much use.

"Ah!" commented Ginsberg, as a final breath, with Buddhist acceptance – or as Czech males would sigh, "Ach, jo."

Notes

1 For more depth see, e.g., Hames, Hulík, Szczepanik, and Herzogenrath.
2 The now-classic quote by Paul McCartney in Peter Jackson's *Get Back* (2021), the re-edit of Michael Apted's footage for *Let It Be* (1970).
3 Of much less interest is the similarly themed Czech-Luxembourg-Finnish-Slovak co-production *Klauni* (Clownwise; 2013, dir. Viktor Tauš, screenplay Petr Jarchovský) about a trio of clowns in their sixties, one of whom emigrated to France during the Normalisation period and then returns home. The clowns suffer from various age-related problems including colon cancer, but they never quite get back together – until after the closing credits, when they do no clowning but simply wait motionless for a bus as the sun sets behind them. It is a pan-European *czeski film* panned even by Czech critics. See Fuka, "Recenze: Klauni – 40%."
4 *Babí léto* is the period of warm, summer-like weather in autumn known as "Indian summer" in the United States. *Babí* means "grandmother" and *léto* means "summer." The phrase *babí léto* also means "gossamer," which may have relevance to the film.
5 The film is notable for also casting Zita Kabátová (1913–2012) in a minor role as a former film star – which she was. Born in Prague when it was still Austria-Hungary, her film debut was in 1936, with her biggest triumph in the film *Muži nestárnou* (1942): "Men Don't Age" (!). Although this volume is about men, women too were victims of politics and history: Kabátová played in German language films during the Occupation, and she was briefly banned from acting after the war because of that but was reinstated. However, she was denied a visa out of the country to be with her first husband, head of Zeiss in India; eventually, they divorced. Her second husband was sent to do forced labour in the uranium mines after the communist regime began in 1948; Kabátová was banned again from acting in films from 1948–1989. Although this book focuses on masculine ageing, we must remember that women are usually longer-lived – and longer-suffering.
6 The translation is mine, as well as all other quotes from Czech in this chapter. www.csfd.cz/film/6679-babi-leto/prehled.
7 *Slovník cizích slov* [Dictionary of Loan Words]. https://slovnik-cizich-slov.abz.cz/web.php/slovo/pabitel-pabitele.
8 Bohumil Hrabal, "Palaverers," in Hrabal, *The Death of Mr. Baltisberger*.
9 Of course, there are exceptions where *machismo* is important in the Czech lands: these include Roma communities, Silesia (the area near the Polish border), football hooligans, nationalist/fascist/Nazi groups, etc.
10 *Tatínek* (Dad; 2004, dir. and screenplay Jan Svěrák and Martin Dostál). When asked by his son to produce a fifth version of the screenplay for *Betlémské světlo* (The Light of Bethlehem; to be released in 2022), Zdeněk Svěrák explodes. His wife kindly rebukes, "Remember that s.o.b. is the father of your grandchildren." He must have written several more versions in the nearly 20 years since.
11 The words to "Není nutno" (No Matter) go something like this: "No money? No matter. / No heart? That matters. / Experiencing failure? No matter. / Experiencing

boredom? That matters. / Experiencing failure? No matter. / etc., no need to be outwardly happy. / The main thing is not to be so sad that you shed tears." It has that Slavic ring to it.
12 See Česko-Slovenská filmová database (Czecho-Slovak Film Database), www.csfd.cz/film/221006-vratne-lahve/zajimavosti/. Zdeněk Svěrák and Daniela Kolářová (b. 1946), who plays his wife in the film, will again play a married couple in a new film also written by Svěrák and directed by his son Jan: *Betlémské světlo* (The Light of Bethlehem), scheduled for release in March 2022.
13 Havel, quoted in Bernard 393, 401.
14 The screenplay was a comedy called "Rekonstrukce" (Reconstruction), about remodelling Kafka's "castle" into a Kafka-themed tourist attraction. The Václav Havel Library has published an entire book on Havel's pre-1989 forays into the cinema, including his part in the Czech New Wave of the 1960s. See Bernard 176–181.
15 See, e.g., Esslin 324–326.
16 See Alexei Navalny, "Putin's Palace: The Story of the World's Biggest Bribe" and "Dvorets dlya Putina" (Palace for Putin).
17 Hrabal and Menzel had been working on various versions of the screenplay since the late 1960s. Hrabal died in 1997; Menzel's final version of the screenplay is his own.
18 See, e.g., Stephen Holden's review in the *New York Times*.
19 See https://archiv.hn.cz/c1-955915-sirotek-bude-vyzadovat-za-vyprask-od-menzela-omluvu.
20 *Proč Havel?* (Why Havel?; 1991, dir. Vojtěch Jasný). Jasný won Best Director at the 1969 Cannes Film Festival for *Všichni dobří rodáci* (All My Compatriots), a classic of 1960s cinema.
21 To quote feminist critic Eva Hauserová, "Beer apparently acts like the female hormone progesterone – it has a calming influence. And consuming fatty foods apparently reduces testosterone – the male hormone which causes aggression – levels by thirty percent. Now is it clear why Czech men are as peaceful as lambs?" Hauserová 78.
 There also may be a personal connection here – Menzel, unlike Hrabal, was not a beer drinker, although the internationally acclaimed, Oscar-winning director had to make ends meet in the 1990s by playing a recurring character on the Czech television series *Hospoda* (The Pub).
22 Holland is Polish, but she studied film at Prague's Film and Television School of the Academy of Performing Arts (FAMU) and was in Prague in 1968 when the tanks rolled in, and was even jailed for protesting the invasion. See, e.g., Wikipedia, https://en.wikipedia.org/wiki/Agnieszka_Holland.
23 E.g., Holland's HBO television series *Hořící keř* (Burning Bush; 2013) about Jan Palach, the Czech student who set himself on fire in 1969 to protest the Soviet invasion. She previously did a film on *Janošík* (2009), the "Slovak Robin Hood," and as this goes to press, Holland, aged 78, is in pre-production on the film *Kafka*, also written by Epstein.

Works Cited

Bernard, Jan, ed. *Václav Havel a film. Scénáře, analýzy a úvahy z let 1957–1989 [Václav Havel and Cinema. Screenplays, Analyses and Reflections, 1957–1989]*. Knihovna Václava Havla, 2018.
Blažek, Petr. "The Deportation of the King of May: Allen Ginsberg and the State Security." *Behind the Iron Curtain 2*. Review of the Institute for the Study of Totalitarian Regimes, 2012. 34–47.
Černá, Marie. "From 'Occupation' to 'Friendly Assistance': The 'Presence' of Soviet Troops in Czechoslovakia after August 1968," trans. Derek and Marzia Paton.

The Hungarian Historical Review 4.1: *Everyday Collaboration with the Communist Regimes in Eastern Europe* (2015). 114–143.

Česko-Slovenská filmová databaze [Czechoslovak Film Database]. https://www.csfd.cz

Esslin, Martin. *The Theatre of the Absurd*. 3rd ed. Vintage Books, 2004.

Fuka, František. "Recenze: Klauni – 40%" [Review: Clownwise – 40%]. *FFFILM*. https://www.fffilm.name/2013/11/recenze-klauni-40.html.

Ginsberg, Allen. "Kral Majales. May 7, 1965." *Collected Poems 1947–1980*. 1985. Penguin, 1987. 353–355.

Ginsberg, Allen. "Return of Kral Majales." 25 Apr. 1990. *Collected Poems 1947–1997*. 2006. HarperCollins e-books, 2010.

Hames, Peter. *The Czechoslovak New Wave*. 2nd ed. Wallflower/Columbia UP, 2005.

Hauserová, Eva. "Muzi mými očima [Men, in My Eyes]." *Lapače času [Traps of Time]*. Votobia, 2000.

Havel, Václav. "Rekonstrukce [Reconstruction]." *Václav Havel a film. Scénáře, analýzy a úvahy z let 1957–1989 [Václav Havel and Cinema. Screenplays, Analyses and Reflections, 1957–1989]*. Ed. Jan Bernard. Knihovna Václava Havla, 2018. 176–181.

Herzogenrath, Bernd, ed. *Barrandov Studios: The Hollywood of Central Europe*. Amsterdam UP, forthcoming.

Holden, Stephen. "Hot Dogs to Haute Cuisine, Then Back Down Again. Movie Review: 'I Served the King of England.'" *New York Times* 29 Aug. 2008. www.nytimes.com/2008/08/29/movies/29serv.html.

Hrabal, Bohumil. "The Palaverers." *The Death of Mr. Baltisberger*, trans. Michael Henry Heim. Doubleday, 1975. 23–34.

Hulík, Štěpán. *Kinematografie zapomnění [The Cinema of Oblivion]*. Academia, 2011.

Janovec, Ladislav, ed. *Svět v obrazech a ve frazeologii: World in Pictures and in Phraseology*. Pedagogická fakulta Univerzita Karlova, 2017.

Mazierska, Eva. *Masculinities in Polish, Czech and Slovak Cinema: Black Peters and Men of Marble*. Berghahn Books, 2008.

Navalny, Alexei. "Dvorets dlya Putina [Palace for Putin]." https://palace.navalny.com.

Navalny, Alexei. "Putin's Palace: The Story of the World's Biggest Bribe." www.youtube.com/watch?v=T_tFSWZXKN0. Documentary.

Slovník cizích slov [Dictionary of Loan Words]. ABZ.cz. https://slovnik-cizich-slov.abz.cz.

Sokolová, Věra. "Representations of Homosexuality and the Separation of Gender and Sexuality in the Czech Republic Before and After 1989." *Political Systems and Definitions of Gender Roles*. Ed. Ann Katherine Isaacs. Universita di Pisa, 2001. 273–288.

Szczepanik, Petr. *Továrna Barrandov. Svět filmařů a politická moc 1945–1970 [The Barrandov Factory. A World of Filmmakers and Political Power 1945–1970]*. Národní filmový archiv, 2016.

10 The (Im-)Possibility of Solidarity

Narratives of Ageing, Masculinity, and Intergenerational Relationships in the German Comedies *We Are the New Ones* (2014) and *Granny Nanny* (2020)

Lisa-Nike Bühring

Narratives of Ageing, Masculinity, and Intergenerational Solidarity

The increase in public and academic attention to older age in recent years is largely the consequence of the markedly extended life span in industrialized countries, which will result in a 188% worldwide increase in people aged 65+ and a staggering 351% rise in people 85 or older between 2010 and 2050 (WHO 2011, 8). In Germany specifically, over 20% of the population was 65 or older in 2011, and in 2060 this share is predicted to make up nearly 30 million of the entire German population of 77 million (Hoffmann et al. 2015, 2–3). Nonetheless, the percentage of old-age poverty in Germany has been relatively low to date, and percentages of purchasing power, as well as life satisfaction, compare favourably to other EU countries (Hoffmann et al. 2015, 6–7; OECD 2015, 32–43).

This does, however, not prevent public media discourse in Germany from painting a rather bleak picture of older age and retirement characterized by a loss of economic as well as cultural capital whilst tirelessly warning the public that the increase in older people will drain the social security system so that the pension for future generations cannot be guaranteed (Sinn and Uebelmesser 2003, 153–158). Such discussions are predominately framed in terms of generations or generational cohorts which tie specific behaviours and characteristics to defined age groups. However, it has been argued that stereotypical attributes informed solely by preconceived ideas about chronological age and linked to clear and seemingly unassailable differences between the generations do not capture the multitude of individual life-course narratives and tend to promote the impossibility of intergenerational solidarity, which is often contextualized as toxic (Cruikshank 2013, 25–28).

The negativity which characterizes the portrayal of intergenerational relationships is majorly grounded in conceptions of older age based on notions of decline, dependency, and a lack of social and economic capital, ideas which have dominated socio-cultural understandings of ageing in the West for a long time (Wilson 2000, chap. 2; Gullette 2004, chaps. 1 and 2). However, more recently this socio-cultural understanding of older age has been replaced by narratives of successful or active ageing. While the successful ageing paradigm is undoubtedly much more positively connoted than understandings of older age as a time of demise preceding death, the concept of successful ageing has been identified with transferring gender-specific neoliberal conceptions of success to older age (Gergen and Gergen 2000, 281–306), with corresponding implications for constructions of gender hierarchies.

Thus, successful ageing for women in the West is widely evaluated on their success at retaining their looks and their ability to continue fulfilling their socio-cultural role as carers for their families (Dolan 2018, 1–29; Cruikshank 2013, 37–53). Older men, on the other hand, are often portrayed as ageing successfully when they continue to maintain control of themselves and their surroundings, which is, as discussed by Raewyn Connell (2005) and other scholars (Bourdieu 2001; Cheng 1999), the prerequisite for their dominance over women and other men who do not fulfil the criteria of hegemonic masculinity. The resultant attempts of older men to retain dominance by subordinating younger generations, particularly younger men, and force their will on them, may seriously impede possibilities for intergenerational solidarity and cooperation (Bühring 2020, 160–162; Jackson 2016, 27–38).

This gender-specific conception of older age is also evident in the increasingly prominent depiction of older characters between 60 and 80 years in films and TV series produced for the international mass market (Dolan 2018, 31–71). Women continue to be the dominant focus of representations of older age, while male ageing and the analysis of the hegemonic narratives of masculinity and older age have generally received less attention (Arber, Davidson and Ginn 2003, 2–5; Nilsson, Hagberg and Grassman 2013, 59–76). However, given the inextricable relationship between constructions of femininity and masculinity, an exploration of the media representations of older male age adds a valuable perspective to discussions of socio-cultural frames available to older people to build acceptable and positive identities. At the same time, as a number of cultural gerontologists argue, it could complicate current binary, stereotypical, and often ageist conceptions of ageing to foster much-needed fruitful intergenerational cooperation (de Medeiros 2016; Gullette 2011; Moglen 2008; Twigg and Martin 2015; Gill et al. 2016, 726–736).

While films which focus on older characters are still rare in Germany (GfK *Filmhitliste 2020 (National)* 2021), two recent German films featuring older (male) protagonists are the comedies *Wir sind die Neuen* (We Are the New Ones; 2014) [hereinafter *We Are the New Ones*] and *Enkel für Anfänger* (Granny Nanny; 2020) [hereinafter *Granny Nanny*]. The respective directors of these films (Ralf Westhoff and Wolfgang Groos) previously enjoyed success with family-themed comedies which were successful in their native territory but not distributed beyond German borders. While Ralf Westhoff's previous films have tended to focus on relationship problems between middle-aged men and women, such as *Der letzte schöne Herbsttag* (The Last Beautiful Autumn Day; 2010) or, more recently, *Wie gut ist deine Beziehung?* (How Good Is Your Relationship?; 2019), Wolfgang Groos has gained a reputation for directing films for children and young adults, such as *Die Vampirschwestern* (Vampire Sisters; 2010) or *Kalte Füße* (Cold Feet; 2018). The actors featured in both these films are well known in Germany and have appeared in a variety of genres including thrillers, drama, independent film, and, though less frequently, comedies. Nowadays however, these actors are seen less since, as mentioned above, there is a considerable dearth of German media products which feature older protagonists (Was-war-wann.de 2022).

We Are the New Ones features three former hippies who shared a flat during their studies. Some 30 years later one of them, Anne (Gisela Schneeberger), due to limited financial means, asks her former flatmates, Eddie (Heiner Lauterbach) and Johannes (Michael Wittenborn), to move in together again so that they can split the rent and relive their past. However, the worldview and lifestyle of the aged hippies quickly collides with a group of young students who live above them as they prepare for their final exams. This younger generation – Katharina (Claudia Eisinger), Barbara (Karoline Schuch), and Thorsten (Patrick Güldenberg) – are portrayed as ambitious, arrogant, and totally selfish millennials who are diametrically opposed to the three fun-loving and free-spirited older adults.

Granny Nanny (2020) similarly centres around three older people in their seventies: Karin (Maren Kroymann), Gerhard (Heiner Lauterbach), and Philippa (Barbara Sukowa). At the beginning of the film, Karin is bored by her life as a retiree with her husband Harald (Günther Maria Halmer), who spends most of his time with his miniature trains. Gerhard, an acquaintance of Karin, finds life without his deceased partner unbearable. Philippa, Gerald's sister and Karin's sister-in-law, on the other hand, lives unconventionally in a caravan in a hippie community and appears to enjoy her life immensely. This is not only the result of her rebellious lifestyle but also due to her work as surrogate grandmother for families which need support in childcare and in which biological grandparents are absent. She convinces her sister-in-law, Karin, to also work as a "grandmother-for-rent," or a "granny nanny." Karin then talks Gerhard into joining them in their job as surrogate grandparents. As the story develops, these "grandparents-for-rent," the children they take care of, and their parents are challenged by a multitude of problems including bullying, alienation between parents and children, and marital problems which, in the end, they can only surmount by collaborating with each other. As such their work as grandparents-for-rent not only enriches the protagonists' lives but also the lives of their "rented" grandchildren and their parents.

Considering that comedies are among the most commercially successful genres in Germany and that both films were clearly targeted at older generations, it is not particularly surprising that both films were well received by the German audiences and particularly by the age group from 50+ onwards. *We Are the New Ones* was among the five most popular films in the age group 50+ in 2014 in Germany (GfK 2015), while *Granny Nanny* took eighth place on the national film hitlist of 2020, and the spectatorship was predominantly made up again by the age group 50+ (GfK *Top 35 Film Titles 2020* 2021). Both films rely strongly on the contextualization of socio-cultural problems perceived as characteristic for Western and specifically German society, such as gender relations and roles, deficits of the German educational system, and, of course, ageing and age-related issues, such as Alzheimer's disease.

Often these comedies utilize common stereotypes linked to the theme precisely to contradict such preconceptions. Using humour to conceptualize problematic issues allows film producers to increase the chances for critical praise, all the better to attract specific groups of spectators without losing audiences who are simply looking for entertainment and relaxation. While this strategy is certainly not only utilized in German films, given the national preference for comedies, it might be an approach that is particularly effective in Germany.

On the surface both films suggest that older people can be at least as dynamic and unconventional as younger generations and indeed often more so. A closer look at the construction of gender and intergenerational relationships in both films, however, shows that their narratives are informed by often reductive and stereotypical understandings of generational differences that may in fact reinforce ageist attitudes and hamper the possibility for constructive intergenerational relationships. Likewise, both films rely on conventional views of gender-specific attributes, which prevents them from exploring and envisioning alternative understandings of gender performance in older age. Within this context, the narrative construction of older male characters is particularly revealing since it is based on the adoption and reproduction of current socio-cultural scripts of Western hegemonic masculinity. These scripts rely on the ability to dominate not only women and non-hegemonic men but also younger generations, which precludes the possibility of fruitful intergenerational cooperation on equal terms (Cheng 1999, 297–298; Coston and Kimmel 2012, 97–99; Hall 2002, 35–61; Gullette 2004, 41–60).

Narratives of Chronological Age and Masculinity

One main cornerstone of Western capitalist societies and accordingly social understandings and constructions of ageing is chronometric time (Segal 2014, 214–222; Baars 2015, 397–403). Chronological time majorly contributes to the categorization of generations or age cohorts and the related conceptions of what is considered age-appropriate (Baars 2013, 143–165; Baars 2015, 397–403). The consequent homogenization and simplification affect not only older people but all age groups and inhibit intergenerational relationships (Grenier 2012, 79–98; Gullette 2004, chaps. 1 and 2).

That stereotypical understandings of age and age-appropriate behaviour play a crucial role in the films *We Are the New Ones* and *Granny Nanny* becomes obvious in the first scenes. At the beginning of *We Are the New Ones*, we see Anne handing over her former flat to the landlord's daughter, who needs a place to stay during her university studies. Clearly unhappy about the situation, Anne finally expresses her frustration and exclaims: "Why don't you move into a shared flat like other students?" The daughter replies: "What on earth do you want? Third floor without an elevator – you won't be able to handle that for much longer anyway" (Westhoff 2014).[1] *Granny Nanny* begins with a rapid succession of scenes in which older people are shown in situations representative of the new generation of seniors who age actively using every chance to enjoy life by travelling, by dancing at rave parties, or by being sportive, with brash, modern music playing in the background. During these scenes, we hear Karin's voice:

> In advertisements seniors are always in an extremely good mood and daring. The generation gold. The Silver Surfers. We travel, love adventure, and enjoy our freedom. We are slim, agile, and well-dressed. We dance and party without limits and give our lives the thumbs up, but reality, of course, is not like this.
>
> (Groos 2020)

In *We Are the New Ones*, "toxic intergenerationality (Gill et al. 2016, 3) precludes a fruitful cooperation of different generations since it is "characterized by conflict and divisions that can't be surmounted" (Gill et al. 2016, 3). This sets the tone for the entire film. In fact, the film appears to reproduce both the entire array of age stereotypes of younger and older age and the (im-)possibility of intergenerational cooperation and understanding perpetuated by socio-cultural agents such as the media, educational institutions, the law or politics (Gullette 2004, chaps. 2 and 3). However, *We Are the New Ones* flips the predominantly positive portrayal of younger generations and the often negative depiction of the older generation (Cruikshank 2013, chap. 3). When common stereotypes of older age are expressed by the members of the younger flat share in a particularly crude, pointed and arguably exaggerated way, one cannot help siding with the older flat sharers who are the target of these comments.

As such, throughout most of the film, audiences are asked to sympathize and identify with the older protagonists. In fact, when compared to the younger characters featured in *We Are the New Ones*, the older protagonists display many more characteristics typically associated with chronologically younger people, with Eddie, Johannes, and Anne not only much more in control of themselves and their lives but also living a much happier life than Katharina, Barbara, and Thorsten. This becomes especially obvious in the second half of the film when the younger characters' lives spiral totally out of control: Katharina cannot memorize all information relevant for her final exam in law, Thorsten suffers from a slipped disc and can hardly move, Barbara is heartbroken, and none of them has sufficient financial means to go grocery shopping or to order takeaway food.

This comically turns conceptions linked to younger and older age upside down. By a freakish turn of destiny, it is not the old ones who have lost their autonomy and depend on the young ones for financial and emotional support but the young ones who need help from Johannes, Eddie, and Anne. As funny as this may be, the film also suggests that alliances between generations only work on the basis of a clear hierarchical and quite conventional structure in which the elders have the say and are on top of the pecking order, whilst the younger generation need to respect and learn from the older protagonists even if in certain areas, such as technological advances, they might be more knowledgeable (Calasanti and King 2005, 3–23).

Granny Nanny not only utilizes typical and binary conceptions linked to the portrayal of older adults but also relies strongly on stereotypical perceptions of younger generations (Gullette 2004, chap. 3). Karin, Gerhard, and particularly Philippa embody many of the attributes linked to the concept of successful ageing, while Karin's husband mirrors many conceptions linked to depictions of ageing as decline. He is portrayed as a rather grumpy, conservative, and inflexible man who has little interest in meeting new people or making new experiences and who lives a rather dull and boring life.

On the contrary, Karin, Gerhard, and Philippa are physical and mentally fit, open-minded, adventurous, and autonomous. Their healthy bodies and minds allow them to continue staying productive members of society by taking on a job which marks one of the few socio-cultural roles available to older people: being a grandparent.[2] This is particularly noteworthy since only the lack of close relationships within a family and the disintegration of a societal system based on neoliberal values, in which several generations live together under the same roof and support each other, allow the older characters to find a meaningful occupation and to stay valued members of society (Cruikshank 2013, 163–178). Thus, the deficiencies of a system which is based on evaluating people on market value system, such as productivity and consumption power, and which is at the bottom of the often rather negative societal view of older age, ironically enables the protagonists in *Granny Nanny* to find a meaningful occupation which raises their societal value.

At the same time, the portrayal of the children and the parents who Karin, Philippa, and Gerhard meet as grandparents-for-rent offers insight into common narratives related to both younger generations and parents in the 21st century (Valiquette-Tessier et al. 2019, 299–329). The parents of Leonie (Luise und Julia Gleich), for whom Philippa replaces the grandmother, are contextualized as a picture-perfect example of helicopter parents – a behaviour their daughter suffers from immensely, since this inhibits her desire to enjoy a carefree childhood (Somers and Settle 2010, 2–9; Coburn 2006, 299–329). Karin's fosterling Jannik (Julius Weckauf) is portrayed as hyperactive and addicted to technological devices which provide him with constant entertainment and stimulus. His parents, Kai (Dominik Raacke) and Britt (Lavinia Wilson), are portrayed as representatives of a generation whose main focus is their professional career and who therefore can offer their children an abundance of material benefits but who are totally overburdened by both the psychological and emotional needs of their children and also of their partners. Their children, Jannik and Antje (Paula Kalenberg), Kai's daughter from his first marriage, react to this emotional deprivation in rather stereotypical ways: Jannik seems to have some form of attention deficit hyperactivity disorder and Antje, a teenager, rebels against everything and everybody (Neal and Hammer 2017, chap. 1; Paulin, Lachance-Grzela and McGee 2017, 463–476). Elena (Palina Rojinski), the mother of Gerhard's grandson-for-rent, Victor (Bruno Grüner), is constructed on the basis of common socio-cultural narratives linked to single-parent motherhood (Nelson 2006, 781–795). Elena is shown as a mother who feels overchallenged by being a single mother. Finding a partner would raise her social value and provide her son with a male role model in his life, the latter being one of the reasons for her interest in a grandfather-for-rent. Simultaneously, her depiction is constructed on the template of Eastern European understandings of motherhood and family, which is rooted in socialist ideology and purports intergenerational support and solidarity, while simultaneously informed by an apparently outdated ideal of the man being the breadwinner and protector of the family currently perpetuated in Russia (Tang and Cousins 2005, 527–550; Saralieva, Petrova and Egorova 2015, 255–261) – a concept her son has taken on and fails to fulfil.

The older protagonists of *Granny Nanny* are likewise constructed as much more likeable than the representatives of the always stressed but productive parents who grew up in a neoliberal political-economic system whose values and standards they have internalized (Chomsky 1999, chap. 1; Harvey 2007, chap. 3). However, contrary to *We Are the New Ones*, intergenerational cooperation and solidarity and a relationship between the older and the younger generation as equals seems imaginable in *Granny Nanny*. This is possible since the youngest generation serves as intermediary between the age group 65+ and the age cohort between 30 and 40 years of age. This becomes particularly obvious in the portrayal of the developing relationship between Gerhard and his fosterling Victor and Victor's mother, Elena. Victor and Elena strongly influence Gerhard's worldview and the value system he followed throughout most of his life since he accepts and supports Victor's wish to stand up to the boys who bully him – a behaviour which is contrary to his former conviction that the best strategy to defend oneself from attacks is invisibility. In addition, through his relationship to Victor and his mother, Gerhard learns both to express his feelings and to apologize for past mistakes – a behaviour which is largely at odds with masculinity constructions based on the dominance and subordination of others (Hall 2002, 35–61) and which indicates that older age can lead to a more flexible understanding of masculinity.

Narratives of Older Masculinity in *We Are the New Ones* and *Granny Nanny*

We Are the New Ones draws on stereotypical perceptions of what men who came of age in Germany during the 1960s are like. Both Johannes and Eddie, now in their mid-sixties, were students and part of the students' revolt and the hippie or "flower power" generation (Brown 2013, introduction). When their generation realized the extent of their parents' and generally the entire older generation's part in the horrors of the Nazi regime, the Holocaust, and World War II, this led to an overwhelming feeling of disappointment and distrust in older adults. This stirred up an attitude of resistance which found its expression in the student revolt of the late 1960s. As in other parts of the world, the student revolt and other civil rights movements resulted, on the one hand, in the development of hippie communities fostering tolerance, equal rights, and sexual freedom and, on the other hand, in the emergence of extremist left-wing organizations such as the Red Army Faction (RAF), which terrorized Germany in the 1970s. Although the 1970s were thus a time of socio-cultural upheaval and insecurity, they also paved the way for a more flexible and tolerant understanding of gender relations (Brown 2013, chaps. 6 and 7). Conservative views of what it meant to be a man were questioned and replaced by alternative understandings of masculinity. Suddenly, German men were expected to show emotions, be loving to their children, take part in their upbringing, take on household tasks, and respect women as their equals (Gotto 2017, 142–156; Baur and Luedke 2008, 7–30).

Johannes (played by Michael Wittenborn, b. 1953), seems to be a picture-perfect example of this type of post-war German male. He is soft-spoken; spends his time with reading, meditation, and yoga; shows his emotions without reservations (at least when dancing); and clearly dislikes conflict and aggression. At the same time, the film implies that Johannes has never had a stable and long-lasting romantic relationship and that his approach towards courting was and remains largely unsuccessful (Westhoff 2014).

Along with hegemonic masculinity, Connell identifies three additional masculinity constructions present at any particular moment in time in a specific society: complicit, subordinate, and marginalized (Connell, 2003, chap. 3). Within this framework Johannes can be seen as a complicit male. Complicit men often live a life which in many respects (e.g., status, physical appearance, sexual orientation, or lifestyle) does not comply with the hegemonic understanding of masculinity. Predominantly, however, they do not challenge the socio-cultural view of being a man but rather admire men fulfilling these standards. Subordination, on the other hand, characterizes the status of men who cannot and/or do not want to accept the current view of masculinity such as homosexuals or effeminate men. The "wrong" race, low economic status, and a low educational level determine the marginalization of men (Connell 2005, chap. 3). These constructions of masculinity are as context bound as hegemonic views of masculinity, and as such, they are not only affected by historical developments but, throughout their lives, men possibly embody and enact different, hegemonic, and less hegemonic narratives of masculinity (Cheng 1999, 297–298; Connell 2005, chap. 3).

Within this context, Eddie, on the other hand, appears to fulfil many of the criteria tied to hegemonic conceptions of masculinity in the 20th and 21st centuries in Western cultural settings. It is Eddie, for instance, who charms a female estate agent into providing them with a flat – even though they are at the end of the waiting list – by referring to his affair with the estate agent's mother. When the estate agent calls her mother, she says of Eddie: "He was an asshole . . . but one of the better ones" (Westhoff 2014). It is also Eddie who ends up having sex with Anne, their flatmate who, according to Johannes, "drove us all mad" (Westhoff 2014) when they lived together during their college years. And it is also Eddie who throughout most of the film refuses to talk about his past, his relationship with his sons, the break-up with his wife, or any other emotional issues.

In many ways Eddie's behaviour is shaped by his internalized understanding of the idea that "real men" are self-reliant, dominant, autonomous, and in control. From earliest childhood, any supposed feminine connoted conduct is immediately penalized in primary and secondary social groups by ridiculing the inability to be manly, while media products, socio-cultural institutions, and politico-economic structures enforce socio-cultural understandings of appropriate masculine and feminine performance (Bourdieu 2001, chap. 2; Butler 2011, 1–47). Breaching the socio-cultural standards linked to hegemonic constructions of masculinity will lead to immediate exclusion from male privilege (Cheng 1999, 297–298; Connell 2005, chap. 3; Kimmel 2001, 97–99). Eddie's portrayal thus mirrors that: "Male privilege is also a trap, and it has its negative side in the permanent tension and contention, sometimes verging on the absurd, imposed on every man by the duty to assert his manliness in all circumstances" (Bourdieu 2001, 50).

Coincidentally, the same actor who plays Eddie in *We Are the New Ones*, Heiner Lauterbach, plays Gerhard in *Granny Nanny*. His role in this film is, however, a far cry from his previous incarnation of hegemonic masculinity: Gerhard is homosexual and, although not overly emotional, he is clearly shaken by the death of his husband and, more recently, his dog. At the beginning of the film, he has lost almost all joy for life and feels that he has little to live for anymore, reflecting a common perception linked to older men perpetuated in public discourse (Tarrant 2010, 1580–1591; King 2007, 57–81). Although Gerhard matches some criteria linked to constructions of hegemonic masculinity, such as being financially well-off and his former prestigious job as a medical doctor, he clearly feels that his homosexuality inhibits his access to male privilege which is evident in the interaction with his fosterling Victor (Cheng 1999, 297–298; Coston and Kimmel 2012, 97–99). He seems to have accepted and even embraced his marginalized male status, which becomes clear when Gerhard witnesses Victor being bullied, and Victor expresses his wish to learn how to fight. Gerhard initially advises Victor strongly against defending himself and instead teaches him how to stay as invisible as possible, since this was the strategy he successfully used throughout his life to avoid conflicts and harassment.

However, as mentioned above, it is Karin's husband Gerald who fulfils many more of the attributes linked to marginalized masculinity constructions and conventional stereotypes linked to male ageing (Chivers 2011, chaps. 5 and 6; Jennings and Oro-Piqueras 2016, 71–89; Moore and Reynolds 2016, 88–105). As Jackson notes:

> The threatening loss of socio-economic productivity, social status, fears of sexual impotence and the disorientating shocks of physical disruptions and discontinuities . . . often create a destabilising, social contexts where dominant ideals of masculinity and gendered expectations are weakened.
>
> (2016, 54)

Indeed, Gerald appears rather asexual and does not seek to subordinate his wife or anybody else. Contrary to his wife, Karin, he longs neither for adventure and challenges nor for pitting his wits and/or physical strengths against other men to establish his superiority (Bourdieu 2001, chap. 2; Meuser 2008, 33–44). Instead, Gerald is quite content to spend time with his miniature/model trains and his garden – settings he can control without having to compete with other men, or so he thinks. In fact, his inability to comply with crucial benchmarks characterizing hegemonic masculinity drives his wife Karin right into the arms of Kai, the chronologically rather old father of Karin's grandson-for-rent, Jannik – a man who more closely matches attributes linked to dominant constructions of masculinity (Groos 2020).

Kai is the only male character in *Granny Nanny* who is still professionally active. He seems to be rather successful in his (unspecified) profession and financially well-off, is married for the second time to a much younger woman, and although he does not come across as overly dominating, he does not hesitate to court Karin and tries to persuade her to start an extramarital affair with him. Although charming and likeable, Kai feels little loyalty or responsibility for his family and puts his own wellbeing above everybody else's. Kai, thus, seems to embody what Connell describes as "transnational business masculinity" (Connell 1998, 16), a gender script "marked by increasing egocentrism, very conditional loyalties (even to the corporation) and a declining sense of responsibility for others (except for the purposes of image-making)" (Connell 1998, 16).

In their contextualization of gender hierarchies and performances, *We Are the New Ones* and *Granny Nanny* both use progressive strategies to move beyond earlier clichés and character stereotypes and aim for a more differentiated and realistic depiction of population groups and individuals. However, I would argue that this supposedly critical exploration of hegemonic narratives remains superficial and shallow. On closer inspection it becomes clear that both films still majorly rely on one-dimensional conceptions of gender-specific attributes and public images of masculinity, and aged masculinities in particular. In fact, despite appearing to do the opposite, the portrayal of the older male protagonists in the discussed films does not allow for a more flexible understanding of gender performances but stabilizes and confirms gender hierarchies (Dolan 2018, chaps. 4 and 5).

Conclusion

The contemporary German films *We Are the New Ones* and *Granny Nanny* offer audiences comedies which, on the surface, appear to question and ridicule conventional socio-cultural narratives of ageing, gender, and intergenerational relationships. This chapter has argued however that their narratives are informed by often reductionist and stereotypical understandings of generational differences that, in fact, foster ageism and thwart the possibility for constructive intergenerational relationships. Likewise, both films rely on conventional views of gender-specific attributes, which prevents them from exploring and envisioning alternative understandings of gender performance in older age. Consequently, these films maintain and reproduce socio-cultural narratives deeply infused with neoliberal conceptions of the self and/or that value individual efforts over societal interdependence even though they appear to do the opposite. While this is not uncommon in many media constructions of older age and/or gender performances, what is specific to these films is the portrayal of masculinities informed by the specifics of post-war German gender norms.

Hegemonic conceptions of German masculinity are characterized by ultra-conservative views of gender roles established during the industrialization in the 19th century by the developing bourgeoise (*Bildungsbürgertum*), which regained popularity in post-war Germany as a result of the general insecurity felt after World War II and have largely endured until today. An essential part of this conception of hegemonic masculinity in this context is a clear separation between the private and the public sphere, in which men are conceptualized as the breadwinners and women as taking take care of the family and in which attributes such as discipline, emotional and cognitive control, and rationality are crucial benchmarks of manhood (Bühring 2020). Both films discussed here conform to such cultural constructions/practices, guaranteeing men a high position in the male pecking order, while men who do not conform to these standards are ridiculed and portrayed as less successful in life.

Ultimately, both films utilize narratives infused with neoliberal concepts, and neither narrative manages to move beyond generalized and stereotypical understandings of generational characteristics. Both resist the development of intergenerational relationships unless the youngest generation and/or somebody from a different socio-cultural background mediates between them. Thus, although both films offer a welcome increase in representations of older characters in German national cinema, they remain rooted in cliché and two-dimensional characterizations which support neither a more differentiated view on generational attributes nor a more flexible and imaginative understanding of gender constructions in older age.

Notes

1 All direct quotes from the German films were translated by the author.
2 Granny nannies or grandparents au pairs is a rather new concept, in which older people are employed to take care of children they are not related to. As such, being a grandparent-for-rent is one of the few opportunities of employment for older people above retirement age. There are numerous agencies in Germany which match older people with people who need support with childcare and housework (Hostmum 2022).

Works Cited

Arber, Sara, Kate Davidson, and Jay Ginn. *Gender and Ageing: Changing Roles and Relationships*. McGraw-Hill Education, 2003.

Baars, Jan. "Critical Turns of Aging, Narrative and Time." *International Journal of Ageing and Later Life* 7.2 (2013): 143–165.

Baars, Jan. "Time in Late Modern Aging." *Routledge Handbook of Cultural Gerontology*. Eds. Julia Twigg and Wendy Martin. Routledge, 2015.

Baur, Nina, and Jens Luedke. "Männlichkeit und Erwerbsarbeit bei westdeutschen Männern [Masculinity and Employment Among West-German Men]." *Die Soziale Konstruktion von Männlichkeit: Hegemoniale und marginalisierte Männlichkeiten in Deutschland [the Social Construction of Masculinity – Hegemonial and Marginalized Masculinities in Germany]*. Eds. Nina Baur and Jens Luedke. Barbara Budrich, 2008. 81–104.

Bourdieu, Pierre. *Masculine Domination*. Stanford UP, 2001.

Brown, T. S. *West Germany and the Global Sixties: The Anti-Authoritarian Revolt, 1962–1978*. Cambridge UP, 2013.

Bühring, Lisa-Nike. "The Social Construction of Ageing Masculinities in Neoliberal Society – Reflections on Retired German Men." Doctoral Thesis. Media School, 2020.

Butler, Judith. *Gender Trouble: Feminism and the Subversion of Identity*. Routledge, 2011.

Calasanti, Toni, and Neal King. "Firming the Floppy Penis: Age, Class, and Gender Relations in the Lives of Old Men." *Men and Masculinities* 8.1 (2005): 3–23.

Cheng, Cliff. "Marginalized Masculinities and Hegemonic Masculinity: An Introduction." *The Journal of Men's Studies* 7.3 (1999): 295–315.
Chivers, Sally. *The Silvering Screen: Old Age and Disability in Cinema.* 2011.
Chomsky, Noam. *Profit over People: Neoliberalism and Global Order.* Seven Stories Press, 1999.
Coburn, Karen Levin. "Organizing a Ground Crew for Today's Helicopter Parents." *About Campus* 11.3 (2006): 9–16.
Connell, Raewyn. "Masculinities and Globalization." *Men and Masculinities* 1.1 (1998): 3–23.
Connell, Raewyn. *Masculinities.* 2nd ed. Polity Press, 2005.
Coston, Bethany M., and Michael Kimmel. "Seeing Privilege Where It Isn't: Marginalized Masculinities and the Intersectionality of Privilege." *Journal of Social Issues* 68.1 (2012): 97–111.
Cruikshank, Margaret. *Learning to Be Old: Gender, Culture, and Aging.* Rowman & Littlefield, 2013.
de Medeiros, Kate. "Narrative Gerontology: Countering the Master Narratives of Aging." *Narrative Works* 6.1 (2016): 63–81.
Dolan, J. *Contemporary Cinema and 'Old Age': Gender and the Silvering of Stardom.* Palgrave Macmillan, 2018.
Enkel Für Anfänger [Grandchildren for Beginners]. 2020. Feature Film. Jakob Claussen and Ulrike Putz.
Gergen, Kenneth J., and Mary M. Gergen. "The New Aging: Self Construction and Social Values." *Social Structures and Aging.* Ed. K. W. Schaie. Springer, 2000. 281–306.
GfK. *Kinobesucher Deutscher Filme 2014 – Strukturen und Entwicklungen auf Basis des Gfk-Panels.* German Federal Film Board, 2015.
GfK. *Filmhitliste 2020 (National).* German Federal Film Board, 2021.
GfK. *Top 35-Filmtitel 2020 Nach Soziodemografischen sowie Kino- und filmspezifischen Informationen auf Basis ses Gfk-Panels.* German Federal Film Board, 2021.
Gill, Rosalind, et al. "Intergenerational Feminism and Media: A Roundtable." *Feminist Media Studies* 16.4 (2016): 726–736.
Gotto, Bernhard, and Elke Seefried. *Männer mit "Makel": Männlichkeiten und gesellschaftlicher Wandel in der frühen Bundesrepublik ['Flawed' Men and Social Change in the Early Federal Republic of Germany].* De Gruyter, 2017.
Grenier, Amanda. *Transitions and the Lifecourse: Challenging the Constructions of 'Growing Old'.* Policy Press, 2012.
Gullette, Margaret Morganroth. *Aged by Culture.* U Chicago P, 2004.
Gullette, Margaret Morganroth. *Agewise: Fighting the New Ageism in America.* U Chicago P, 2011.
Hall, S. "Daubing the Drudges of Fury: Men, Violence and the Piety of the 'Hegemonic Masculinity' Thesis." *Theoretical Criminology* 6.1 (2002): 35–61.
Harvey, David. *A Brief History of Neoliberalism.* Oxford UP, 2007.
Hoffmann, Elke, et al. *Living Situations of Older People in Germany.* Research Information Systems of the German Centre of Gerontology (DZA), 2015.
Hostmum. "Granny Nannies." 2022. Web. Accessed 26 Apr. 2022.
Jackson, David. *Exploring Aging Masculinities: The Body, Sexuality and Social Lives.* Palgrave Macmillan, 2016.
Jennings, Ros, and Maricel Oro-Piqueras. "Heroine and/or Caricature? The Older Woman in *Desperate Housewives.*" *Serializing Age: Aging and Old Age in TV*

Series. Aging Studies, Vii. Eds. Maricel Oró-Piqueras and Anita Wohlmann. transcript, 2016. 71–89.

Kimmel, Michael. "Global Masculinities: Restoration and Resistance." *A Men's World? Changing Men's Practices in a Globalized World*. Ed. R. Pease. Zed Press, 2001. 21–37.

King, Neal. "Old Cops: Occupational Aging in a Film Genre." *Staging Age: Performance of Age in Theatre, Dance, and Film*. Palgrave Macmillan, 2007. 57–81.

Meuser, Michael. "Ernste Spiele. Zur Konstruktion von Männlichkeit im Wettbewerb der Männer [Serious Games. About the Construction of Masculinity through the Competition of Men]." *Die Soziale Konstruktion von Männlichkeit: Hegemoniale und marginalisierte Männlichkeiten in Deutschland [the Social Construction of Masculinity – Hegemonial and Marginalized Masculinities in Germany]*. Eds. Nina Baur and Jens Luedke. Barbara Budrich, 2008. 33–44.

Moglen, Helene. "Ageing and Transageing: Transgenerational Hauntings of the Self." *Studies in Gender and Sexuality* 9.4 (2008): 297–311.

Moore, Allison, and Paul Reynolds. "Against the Ugliness of Age: Towards an Erotics of the Aging Sexual Body." *Interalia: A Journal of Queer Studies* 11a.2016 (2016): 88–105.

Neal, Margaret B., and Leslie B. Hammer. *Working Couples Caring for Children and Aging Parents: Effects on Work and Well-Being*. Psychology Press, 2017.

Nelson, Margaret K. "Single Mothers 'Do' Family." *Journal of Marriage and Family* 68.4 (2006): 781–795.

Nilsson, Magnus, Jan-Erik Hagberg, and Eva Jeppsson Grassman. "To Age as a Man: Ageing and Masculinity in a Small Rural Community in Sweden." *norma* 8.1 (2013): 59–76.

OECD. *Pensions at a Glance 2015*. OECD Publishing, 2015.

Paulin, Mélanie, Mylène Lachance-Grzela, and Shawna McGee. "Bringing Work Home or Bringing Family to Work: Personal and Relational Consequences for Working Parents." *Journal of Family and Economic Issues* 38.4 (2017): 463–476.

Saralieva, Zarethan Khadji-Murzaevna, Irina Eduardovna Petrova, and Nadezhda Yurievna Egorova. "Parenthood and Parenting in Modern Russia." *Asian Social Science* 11.3 (2015): 255–261.

Segal, Lynne. "Temporal Vertigo: The Paradoxes of Ageing." *Studies in Gender and Sexuality* 15.3 (2014): 214–222.

Sinn, Hans-Werner, and Silke Uebelmesser. "Pensions and the Path to Gerontocracy in Germany." *European Journal of Political Economy* 19.1 (2003): 153–158.

Somers, Patricia, and Jim Settle. "The Helicopter Parent." *College and University* 86.2 (2010): 9.

Tang, Ning, and Christine Cousins. "Working Time, Gender and Family: An East-West European Comparison." *Gender, Work & Organization* 12.6 (2005): 527–550.

Tarrant, Anna. "'Maturing' a Sub-Discipline: The Intersectional Geographies of Masculinities and Old Age." *Geography Compass* 4.10 (2010): 1580–1591.

Twigg, Julia, and Wendy Martin. *Routledge Handbook of Cultural Gerontology*. Routledge, 2015.

Valiquette-Tessier, Sophie-Claire, et al. "A Literature Review of Cultural Stereotypes Associated with Motherhood and Fatherhood." *Marriage & Family Review* 55.4 (2019): 299–329.

Was-war-wann.de. "Schauspieler a-Z [Actors a-Z]." 2022. Web. Accessed 14 Feb. 2022.
We Are the New Ones (Wir Sind Die Neuen). 2014. Ralf Westhoff Filmproduktion, DRIFE Productions, Bayerischer Rundfunk (BR).
WHO. *Global Health and Aging*. World Health Organization (WHO), 2011.
Wilson, Gail. *Understanding Old Age: Critical and Global Perspectives*. Sage, 2000.

11 Ageing, Masculinity, and the Absurd in *Toni Erdmann* (2016)

Michael Stewart

At the Cannes Film Festival in 2016, Maren Ade won the FIPRESCI (International Federation of Film Critics) award for her film *Toni Erdmann*. While it didn't win the Palme d'Or (that was won by Ken Loach's *I, Daniel Blake*), it achieved the highest-ever score in the history of *Screen International*'s Cannes Jury Grid, which aggregates the ratings of a host of international critics (Gant 17). *Toni Erdmann* also went on to win five major awards at the 29th European Film awards (Best Film, Best Director, Best Screenwriter, Best Actor, and Best Actress) and numerous other accolades at European and international festivals. The UK distribution rights to the film were acquired at Cannes by Soda Pictures, who had previously distributed Grímur Hákonarson's *Rams* (2015), another film dealing with ageing men, which was well received but turned out to be much less successful than *Toni Erdmann* at the box office and in international competitions. As with *Rams*, Soda was unsure how best to promote *Toni Erdmann*. Partly led by the initial responses of audiences and critics, they settled for the less-than-snappy tag line of "near-three-hour German comedy" (Gant 17).

The distribution company was not alone in struggling to define *Toni Erdmann*'s genre or capture what distinguishes it. The film has been described as screwball (Haskell), tragedy (Wheatley), left field (Bradshaw), and the following in one review alone (Kermode): pathos-laden, surreal, melancholic, black comedy, understated tragedy, absurd, scathing satire, unbearably cruel, and a pilgrimage. And while the film is probably most often called a comedy-drama, Wheatley notes that Ade herself was unsure about it being categorized as comedy at the British Film Institute London Film Festival, insisting she'd "made a love film, not a laugh film" (Wheatley 88). Along with these descriptions, a number of critics see in *Toni Erdmann* familiar tensions between the generations, and an attack on liberal or neoliberal values depending on whose perspective we might adopt: "Winfried's baby-boomer hippy ideals clashing with Ines's 21st-century cynicism" (Kermode).

In this chapter, I'm most interested in *Toni Erdmann* as an expression of ageing masculinity. More than this, in what follows, I'll argue that *Toni Erdmann* is an intensification and to some extent reconciliation of discourses of ageing masculinity. In combining and perversely pushing at the residual and

DOI: 10.4324/9781003306146-11

emergent discourses, *Toni Erdmann* attempts to find a new language and way of being in the world. One way to understand this is via Bryan Turner's concept of world openness, where a growing and acute sense of passing time and death results in a desire to move beyond nostalgia and melancholia to test the boundaries of one's ontological security. This is partly expressed in the film, I'll argue, by Winfried's growing dissatisfaction with waiting and his fashioning of a new alter ego whose modus operandi is ambush. Additionally, a dissatisfaction with waiting is articulated in the film's use of time and space. Frequently, we and the film's characters are made to feel in-between, a state of suspended animation given form variously (e.g., by the film's distinctive pattern of enunciation), shot duration, character performance, and edit, as well as by the late modern non-spaces in which the central characters frequently find themselves. This in-betweenness, I'll argue, is ill-fitting and uncomfortable – a sensation, I'll suggest, that is at the heart of *Toni Erdmann*'s attempt to re-imagine ageing masculinity. This is expressed through Toni's body and performance, the embarrassment and irritation he repeatedly causes Ines, and the increasingly splenetic and barbed relationship between father and daughter.

Toni Erdmann begins by introducing us to Winfried Conradi (Peter Simonischek), a 65-year-old divorcee who lives alone in Aachen, Germany. In the opening parts of the film, we learn that Winfried enjoys an underplayed alter ego – thinly disguised via shaggy wig and crooked teeth – and low-key pranks; teaches piano at home and at a school; and has a mother and former wife who live nearby, as well as a daughter who is a businesswoman and is currently working in Bucharest. Viewers are given little indication of the state of Winfried's relations with these characters, except that his relationship with his daughter Ines, when she visits him briefly in Aachen, seems strained. Winfried is unimpressed by the way work dominates Ines's life, and Ines is equally unimpressed by Winfried's (only slightly tongue-in-cheek) suggestion that she should live closer in order to perform her duty of care to her ageing father. When Winfried announces that soon he will visit Ines in Bucharest, neither he nor Ines appears to believe it.

However, soon after this, Winfried is deeply affected by the death of his dog, Willi. This moves him to make good on his promise/threat to visit Ines in Bucharest. Ines is clearly unsettled by her father's unannounced arrival but does her best to include him in the beyond-the-office parts of her job, which are largely about courting a major oil company in an attempt to secure an outsourcing contract. Winfried seems out of place at drinks receptions and semi-social gatherings, but he does his best to fit in. At points, though, he fails, and tells Ines straight what he thinks about the nature of her job. Exchanges between father and daughter become increasingly tense, and when Winfried tells Ines it's best that he goes home, her relief is palpable.

On the evening of Winfried's departure, Ines is seen expressing her relief to friends in the bar of a restaurant when she is ambushed by her father's new, excessive, and spectacular alter ego: "Toni Erdmann, Life Coach." What then follows is a series of bizarre, excessive, and sometimes cringeworthy episodes, where Winfried seems intent on doggedly pushing his new persona into the personal and professional spaces of Ines in ambiguous attempts to provoke and/or communicate. These eruptive performances – at nightclubs, hard-nosed construction sites, and various domestic spaces – generally don't go well, with Ines becoming increasingly angry at Winfried's presence, and Winfried becoming only more tired and melancholic. However, in the final parts of the film, Ines seems to move away from the frequently ugly demands of corporate business towards the absurd world occupied by Toni. She gives up on the social niceties of the birthday party she has arranged in her apartment, deciding to admit only guests willing to be naked; and then runs out after her father – who is sweating to the point of collapse in a hairy all-encompassing *kukeri* (traditional Romanian) suit – when he leaves the party, to give him a hug, the first unequivocal sign of love she has shown him. Returning to Aachen for the funeral of Winfried's mother – Ines's grandmother – father and daughter have a quiet moment of reflection and, at last, transparent and kind communication in Winfried's garden. Ines makes no promises to change her career path or to be closer to her father; but the pair seem to reach a tentative understanding and acceptance, signalled, among other ways, by Ines unceremoniously putting her father's set of crooked teeth into her mouth.

What this synopsis indicates is an episodic film low on narrative event and trajectory, but not without its excesses and points of punctuation – birthdays, deaths, journeys, parties, and business deals. It tends to conceal, though, both the centrality of Winfried/Toni's performances and the often bizarre turns they take. In this respect, the film can be split into three parts: Winfried in the German domestic; Winfried in Bucharest; and Toni in Bucharest. When we first encounter Winfried at home in Aachen, he presents a familiar version of an ageing male as identified by Josephine Dolan and draws on a "performative repertoire" (155) of masculinity. He is a man who both wants to extend his middle years and return to the playfulness of his youth. In a key section of her study of ageing masculinity in contemporary cinema and culture, Dolan notes that jokes and humour are central to male homo-sociality and a primary way of doing masculinity. This is underlined by male celebrities, and Dolan looks in particular at the performances of old age by Rob Brydon and Steve Coogan in *The Trip* (Winterbottom, 2010–2020). Part of the humour of Brydon and Coogan's performance of old age derives from their anxiety about growing old and the threat this poses to masculine strength. Their performance of age adopts two familiar strategies in its attempt to dispel this anxiety: verbal dexterity and rejuvenation via physical challenges. Brydon and Coogan are brilliant and ingenious at the former and laughably poor at the latter – but the latter, Dolan argues, is no less a brilliant performance and no less about underlining dominant meanings of ageing masculinity. Firstly, in the repertoire of ageing masculinity,

Ageing, Masculinity and the Absurd 137

it connects with film stars (e.g., Clint Eastwood and Bruce Willis and an increasing number of others) who lament their aching bodies in a precursor to impossible action, thus underlining the value of experience and transcending the discourse of age as failing bodies. Brydon and Coogan can't use high action and violence to transcend this discourse, Dolan notes, but they can use their bodies. They reproduce the performances of silent comedians (e.g., Chaplin, Keaton, Laurel and Hardy) whose use of bodies and slapstick and pratfall represents its own, distinctively masculine comic genius. So in their brilliant performances of ageing masculinity, Dolan argues, Brydon and Coogan reproduce dominant comic discourses of doing masculinity, thus dispelling anxieties around the failing, ageing male body. More than this, Dolan suggests that this emphasis on the performance of age increasingly can be understood as a key way to shore up fragile masculinity. If, in British culture and elsewhere, rigid gender norms are decreasingly supportable, then discourses of ageing seem more entrenched, more evident and less easy to undo across a number of cultural and political domains, and are also more firmly attached to the idea of the failing body.

In the German-domestic part of *Toni Erdmann*, it is not clear who Winfried is impersonating. With minimal props (mostly, but not only, the crooked teeth), his personas have a general resonance. Ade (in Myers) notes she had two people in mind when she conceived Winfried/Toni: her father and the actor Andy Kaufman. The teeth, I would suggest, are so basic and effective a prop that they produce multiple memories and resonances for viewers, regardless perhaps of age or background. For a British man in his fifties (i.e., me), they recall Dick Emery's clergyman and Barry Humphries' Sir Les Patterson. However, when Winfried first puts in his teeth (out of shot) and returns to the door to fool around with the delivery man, the character he most reminds me of is the drummer in *The Banana Splits*, Bingo.[1]

What Winfried perhaps most impersonates, though, is an ageing male. While his character seems familiar, in the early part of the film he is both very singular and slightly sad. It's not clear why he impersonates or for whom. No one laughs at his jokes, but neither are they surprised by them. While he has a heart monitor wrapped around his naked upper body during his first (Bingo) impersonation, it's not clear if this is serious or part of the act. However, as the German-domestic scenes unfold, these questions begin to be answered, and Winfried becomes slightly more recognizable. His impersonating, performing body is an ageing body. This first is indicated by the heart monitor, and the slow and at times breathless way in which he carries his large frame. As Dolan (152) indicates, this performing body plays into a network of associations of ageing masculinity and can be taken in a number of directions, including recognizable celebrity, humour, and a deferral of or anxiety about the "fourth age of decline" (152). As a performing body, Dolan points out, it can also signal ageing itself and all that might, culturally, imply: "Age as well as gender can be viewed as performative, in that each of us performs the actions associated with chronological age minute by minute" (6). What Winfried's performance also manifests in these opening scenes is an enigmatic singularity and underlying dissatisfaction, which at times comes close to melancholia. The singleness of Winfried is reflected partly in the difficulty of placing this film generically, but also in the absence of close character relations and drama. Initially, Winfried seems to be cast as a piano teacher – a private piano teacher and the local school's music teacher. Having learned little of Winfried's domestic environment, we go with him to the school. Before his visit to the school, Winfried paints a ghoulish death mask on his face. Visiting his older and infirm mother en route, he tells her (in prankster fashion) that he has a job in an old people's home killing residents: "50 euros per killing." Subsequently, Winfried leads a large group of school children onto the stage in an assembly hall, where they perform a farewell song for a retiring teacher, Mr Dudinger. All the children are likewise face-painted as ghosts and ghouls. Winfried leads them on the piano: "We're dead sad that you're leaving Mr Dudinger. Here today, gone tomorrow. Just arrived, gotta go." This is a curious sentiment, given Mr Dudinger is in his sixties and has been at the school for 34 years. He, clearly, doesn't know what to make of the performance, and it's as if Winfried and the children are in on a joke that neither Mr Dudinger nor we can quite understand. It might be specifically about Mr Dudinger; or it might also be about the passing of time and death. In any case, this is the first and last we'll see of the school and the last time in the film we'll encounter Winfried the music teacher.

Likewise, Winfried as a son and his relationship with his mother are given very little screen time, and we are similarly left guessing when, briefly, we meet Winfried's wife for the first and last time. The quite short scene at Renate's (Ruth Reinecke) home, though, points to the significance of Winfried's daughter Ines and the journey on which we'll soon embark. Two aspects of their relationship are signaled at the start of the scene. Firstly, despite the fact that Winfried and his ex-wife are meeting to celebrate their daughter's birthday, Ines is absent, or at least not with them in the house. We're given brief shots of her through the windows, in a business suit and on the phone in the garden. Secondly, when Winfried is at last able to properly see and get close to Ines, he, in a sense, gets too close and contaminates her – leaving some of his ghoulish school-visit mask behind on Ines's jacket. This scene and the relationship between Winfried and Ines is quickly marked by absence, irritation, regret, and contamination. When the family moves out into the garden, further tension is evident between Winfried and his daughter. Winfried jokes, or half-jokes at least, that Ines, by being both in another country and preoccupied by work, is neglecting her duty of care to her ageing father. This receives short shrift from Ines, but what the exchange animates is a pervasive understanding of age as a "fiscal and emotional burden of care to be borne by the state, by families and by individuals" (Dolan 3). Winfried then makes a suggestion – that he'll come and visit Ines in Bucharest, where she currently lives and works – which in the context of strained father-daughter relations feels like soft provocation and idle threat. He decides to act on it, though, when shortly afterwards he experiences a loss.

The death of Winfried's dog both underlines the singularity of his status as an ageing male and serves as a punctuation mark in the film. The dog was the sum of his commitments, the only living thing keeping him at home in Germany. More than this, Willi's death and the way in which it's treated in the film brings Winfried a little more into the realm of the lonely, melancholic ageing male, and makes Elias's observation that modern mores and institutions mean that living alone and dying alone are entirely predictable but never inevitable, all the more real and poignant: "The special accent taken on in the modern period by the idea that one dies alone matches the accentuation in this period that one lives alone" (Elias 48). This may be particularly true of ageing populations in Western cultures. These populations, Gilleard argues, are frequently represented as male, white, affluent, and single. Much then is absent from these representations, including any sense of loss or collective experience. This, Turner argues, is exacerbated by the increasing museumization of the past, where older people's experiences and memories are decreasingly available to them via immediate members of the same generation and increasingly given reality or legitimacy via highly circumscribed and ironically similar aspects of popular culture. This in a sense brings a premature death to the pasts of ageing people – the past as museumized, not lived and remembered – and also serves to speed up ageing as "a process whereby we become singular, separated into our oneness" (Turner 253). As a single, white, middle-class male, this may be part of the singularity that Winfried wants to avoid when he departs for Bucharest. However, the loneliness and singularity of Winfried in this scene also serve to amplify and generalize death. That is, not only did Winfried and Willi only have each other, but there is some degree of sameness or homology between them. If we accept the homology, then at some level, Willi's death is also Winfried's death. It both prefigures death – later in the film Winfried will come close to dying when dressed as a furry creature he collapses, breathless in the heat – and represents what I'll call, below, going into death.

What the lonely moment and the homology also prefigure is a doggedness on Winfried's part. As the story or episodes unfold, Winfried/Toni's unwillingness to let go or give in on his ambiguous project becomes part of his character and the film's points of excess. Willi's death, in a minor key way, sets Winfried off on his journey. In the initial stages of his Bucharest odyssey, as with the film's early German scenes, Winfried seems a relatively conventional ageing male. Winfried to Ines is mostly a burden and an embarrassment. The full weight of his presence and the tension it produces for his daughter are made clear when she meets her friends for a drink and expresses her huge relief at her father's departure.

This is when Toni Erdmann makes his entrance. His appearance is so unexpected, absurd and grotesque, that it produces a type of humour that is highly affective – bodily, shocking, uncomfortable, and very funny. The entrance is an acute and powerful declaration of Winfried and the film's intention to provoke, embarrass, and discomfort, to produce what Muriel Cormican calls *fremdschämen* (114).[2] Briefly, the scene: when Ines stands at the bar recounting to her friends "the worst weekend in my life," sharp-eyed viewers might have spotted, over Ines's shoulder, the back of an indistinct, large, black-jacketed figure, about 3 meters away. It's important both that the figure is indistinct and that he keeps his back to us – because my untested hypothesis is that however obvious it is that this Winfried in disguise, this is only obvious on second viewings of the film. In keeping with his (for us and Ines) very thin disguise, and with the equally thin line between Winfried and Toni, part of the power of Toni emerges from a certain crass or willful obviousness. He wants his presence to be both seen and felt and has no interest in hiding and pretense. His performance is not calculated. He wants certain things, not necessarily clear to him, to be exposed, and refuses to recede or be cast as the burdensome, lonely, embarrassing father. A certain blundering obviousness is then heightened with the hindsight of second viewing. The large black figure moves even closer to the three chatting women, still indistinct and with his back to them, but only about a meter away, opening, it seems, a bottle of wine. Then, in a movement that is both subtle and extravagant and timed to perfection – both in the very close arrangement of the scene, and in the course of the dialogue as Ines laments her father's character and behaviour in cringingly cruel terms – the black-backed figure turns and, from nowhere it seems, enters the conversation, with a crooked smile and generous offer of champagne. In terms too basic for this remarkable moment, what's produced here is slightly unsettling shock and humour for Tatjana (Hadewych Minis) and Steph (Lucy Russell), hilarious shock and vicarious discomfort for viewers, and extremely unsettling shock and embarrassment (because of what Winfried must have heard) for Ines.

Like Ines, we could not have predicted this reincarnation of her father. The earlier Bucharest scenes with Winfried and his daughter focus on Winfried's perspective and can be characterized as a movement from a certain openness of enquiry and expectation to melancholy and disappointment. When we first see Winfried in Bucharest, in the foyer of a corporate building, his spirit seems light, as he anticipates the imminent arrival of Ines. He looks glad to be back in joking-and-impersonating-dad-and-ageing-male mode. Appearing to look forward to Ines's reaction to his unexpected appearance, he slips his crooked teeth into his mouth and rises to blend himself into the group of Ines and her colleagues. By the time Winfried is ready to leave, though, the teeth are not to be seen, the arguments with Ines have increased in frequency and grown in tension, and at a later stage (in an upmarket shopping mall), he looks at his daughter in disappointment and disbelief and asks: "Are you really a human?!"

Winfried's journey at this point seems only to have confirmed his earlier assumptions – that Ines's high-powered corporate life is soul-destroying and a form of disassociation. However, the spectacular entrance of Toni Erdmann soon after this is less of a gear change than this suggests. There is evidence of not just continuity but an intensification of Winfried's plan and persona as we move from Winfried to Toni. What we see is an increasingly powerful combination of ageing masculinity and the absurd. This is evident in *Toni Erdmann*'s treatment of space, time, and bodies. Firstly, by the terms of Rinhaug, the spaces Winfried finds himself in in Bucharest are absurd. They are also what Augé calls late modernity's non-places. When we first see Winfried in Bucharest, he is in the foyer of a corporate building, waiting. A young woman is curious about him/attends to him, reminding us and Winfried that this space might seem anonymous and public, but is not. The spaces Winfried then finds himself in include a drinks reception in a hotel; an ostensibly less formal drinks meeting, poolside at a hotel; poolside again in an upmarket leisure club; an upmarket shopping mall; and the gentrified rooftop of a corporate building. What Winfried mostly does in these spaces is wait and observe. The absurd, argues Rinhaug, is characterized by waiting, boredom, and suspension. Winfried's face and body tell us not only that he is increasingly disappointed in Ines but also that he's increasingly unimpressed by what he sees and hears. He does not speak much during these early Bucharest episodes. Mostly he has uncomfortable exchanges with Ines. His biggest speaking part in these corporate non-places is when he meets Ines's client and a number of her colleagues.

The evening poolside scene occurs in the film's storyline before the remarkable entrance of Toni Erdmann. This scene is less spectacular than the Toni's entrance scene, but it is equally brilliant in its arrangement for and of discomfort – of Cormican's *fremdschämen*. There is little humour in this scene, but Ines's discomfort nonetheless is heightened by the very close presence of her father, whom her boss has insisted should join them. Winfried sits close and stands out due to his age and lack of smart, corporate appearance. He is also the only one to drink beer rather than wine. The scene is about many things, but in the first instance, it is about masculine and corporate power in the era of late capitalism. Ines is one of seven people sitting in very comfortable and expensive surroundings, relaxing after a day's work. The only people who are not colleagues of Ines are her father and her boss's wife (the only other woman). Although the first language of these people is variously German, French, or Romanian, the conversation is conducted in English. It's quickly evident that Ines is easily the least relaxed in the group; she is on the edge of her seat and looks drawn. The blocking and editing of the scene make it clear how tense Ines is, as does Sandra Hüller's performance and the fact that Winfried can't take his eyes off his daughter. His expression, more than at any other point in the film, mixes curiosity and concern.

While Ines feels compelled to make small talk with her boss's wife, he (Henneberg) wants to draw her into a conversation he's having with two young male colleagues. Henneberg puts Ines on the spot as a "specialist" while one of the young men enjoys contradicting Ines's expert opinion in a way that belittles her in the group and in front of her boss. As Ines rallies to regain a foothold and credibility the other young man asks her, "What is it you actually do for Tech-oil?" In an exchange that is already very uncomfortable for her Ines proceeds, as it were, to dig herself more deeply into a hole. She describes herself as a consultant assessing the value to her client (Tech-oil) of outsourcing services. Henneberg leaps on the word *outsourcing* and makes it very clear how unimpressed he is by this term. Ines is once again put in her place by a dominant male, and the viewer is left to squirm and seethe. Henneberg then decides to lighten the mood by turning to/on Winfried. He pokes fun at him in a way that, at best, is intended to make Winfried look like an amusing, ageing oddity. Henneberg does not know that he is replaying an earlier exchange between Ines and Winfried in the garden at Aachen. "But it's Ines's father, he says, who has a great business idea for Romania. The idea is to hire a daughter, as his own is never there and he needs someone to cut his toenails." Ines feigns amusement and must think that things, surely, can get no worse, at which point Winfried slips his ever-present crooked teeth into his mouth and declares to Henneberg: "Don't you dare steal my idea!" The group is dumbfounded, sniggers, and does its best to suppress further laughter. Winfried senses he may have crossed a line of some kind, takes his teeth out, and makes a conventional fatherly gesture: "Of course we're remarkably proud of her, what she's done here and stuff."

After the group disbands Ines and Winfried are left alone, grim-faced. Winfried asks, "What was all that about outsourcing?" Ines, unsmiling and refusing to meet her father's eye, explains in simple, blunt terms the reality of her job – the consultant who recommends transferring (i.e., laying off) large numbers of employees in order to absolve responsibility and liability, perhaps even guilt, from the client. Winfried stares at his daughter, who stares into the middle distance. The medium-close shot of the two characters is held for discomfort – discomfort at the tension between father and daughter; discomfort about the realities of late capitalism. Along with this, though, we're invited to read and feel Winfried's searching look. The poolside scene ends with Winfried cruelly teasing Ines about the ageing-father burden he represents for her. Still not looking at him, Ines asks how long he plans to stay. Winfried answers that he's taken a month off and lets this revelation hang in the air – looking, still, closely at Ines, who does all she can to control her features. After four or five painful seconds, Winfried chortles and remarks: "That was real fear!" Ines says nothing. Winfried drinks his beer. The medium-close shot and silence are held. The two characters look into space, and eventually the scene ends.

This scene treads a fine line between comedy and *Toni Erdmann*'s critique of global capitalism. The scene also communicates the absurd, as "bastard form of reason" (Rinhaug 49) and the absurd as a mode of language. Winfried initially waits and observes. As I noted earlier, Bryan Turner argues that to be human is to be conscious of the passing of time and the inevitability of death. This consciousness is heightened by age and is nowhere more evident than in the ageing body. The ageing body, Turner argues, is both anticipatory and nostalgic. It is constantly aware of and planning for an unknown and contingent future, but it also cannot help but look back and take meaning and perhaps comfort from "completed time" (Turner 249). This heightened consciousness and cruel irony, Turner shows, can produce different responses. It can led to a deep need for ontological security, a firm feeling of boundedness and recognition of where one is and what one can and will do. It can also result in boredom, anxiety, and melancholia. This, as I've noted, clearly affects Winfried when he's left to wait in numerous in-between spaces. This quality of suspension, I suggested earlier, can also produce a certain type of world openness:

> The essential idea is that human beings are not determined by specific drives or instincts to function in a specific or given environment. Human beings are open to the world, because they are not born with genetic structures which point them in the direction of a specific environmental habitus. In an expression which is now very familiar to us, human beings are forced to construct socially their own cultural environment which mediates between them and the natural habitat.
> (Turner 247–248)

This partly explains Winfried's spectacular re-incarnation as Toni Erdmann; his creation of a bizarre habitus that is nonetheless recognizable – is indeed a grotesque but thin disguise for Ines and for us – as both a life coach and an ageing male. Winfried does not simply want to learn about and temporarily enter Ines's sharply defined cultural environment and habitus. He wants to prod it, confront it, test it, and feel it. He is well aware that his age and presence alone will prompt feelings of irritation, patronizing humour, and discomfort – and all of these are evident, not just in Ines but in her personal assistant, her friends, and the man for whom she currently works. These close associates of Ines express a degree of sympathy, an unspoken recognition of the "burden of old age in contemporary society" (Featherstone and Hepworth 357). The basic fact of chronological ageing, Featherstone and Hepworth argue, has been made unattractive in Western cultures to the point where it can even become a source of disgust – which is precisely how Steph describes Toni shortly after his entrance to the film in the restaurant. This to an extent represents what Dolan calls the "pathologisation of old age" (4), where it is understood primarily as a burden and sign of ugliness and decline. The neoliberal antidote to this, Dolan notes, is the discourse of "successful ageing" (4), where emphasis is placed on lifestyle, choice, and individual self-improvement. *Toni Erdmann*, then, combines these discourses of age and ageing, pushing them both into the realms of perversion or pathology. Toni's persona, however, is not as perverse as the figure I compared it to above (Barry Humphries' Sir Les Patterson). Neither is it quite Shary and McVittie's "elder kitsch" (in Dolan 15), which might be more in keeping with my other comparison (Dick Emery's clergyman). While Toni/Winfried's quest from the outset has been unclear, it is defined by his body, his physicality and affective encounters. In this respect, he both subverts and intensifies concepts of ageing masculinity.

Returning to Turner's theory of the body and ageing, Winfried's reincarnation and grotesque and laughably thin disguise can be thought of, in the first instance, as "a canopy to ward off chaos, disaster and death" (248). His visit to Bucharest has produced only disappointment and uncertainty. If the death of his dog only removed ontological security and reminded him of his own perhaps not-too-distant death, then his visit to Ines has heightened these feelings, not diminished them. His new colourful persona, then, is an extension of the masks he wore in the opening parts of the film in an attempt to subvert or banish these unsettling emotions. As Featherstone and Hepworth suggest, many older people experience an unsettling disjunction between their inner and outer selves. As their bodies accumulate signs of ageing, so do the groups and cultures they belong to respond to and construct them as ageing beings. One result of this can be a sense of disassociation from the ageing body that appears to determine how others perceive them. In this respect, Featherstone and Hepworth suggest, the outer body becomes if not an illusion then at least "a kind of mask" (358). Whether Winfried has experienced precisely this feeling in the opening episodes of his Bucharest visit is debatable. His large presence, however, is at best unexpected, at times amusing to patronizing business leaders, and increasingly for Ines unwelcome. Like the persona or mask Winfried is about to put on, he is ill-fitting, awkward, a burden. Toni is a grotesque and absurd incarnation. The absurd, Wartenberg suggests, is bodily and frequently about a lack of fit – between body and being, sense and nonsense, the rational and irrational. This seems writ large across the figure of Toni – the ill-fitting wig, jacket, monster suit; the breathless, lumbering body, erupting (farting audibly) on rooftops, contaminating his daughter, overheating and collapsing in the park; and especially the ever-present crooked, cunning, suggestively venal teeth.

Winfried's adoption of Toni is both an extension of the mask theorized by Featherstone and Hepworth and a rejection of it. In a sense, it is an exploitation of the gap between what others expect him to be and what he might in reality be. In this respect, Winfried's choice of occupation for Toni, however much it seems like clumsy improvisation, is no coincidence. He introduces himself as Toni Erdmann, life coach. This choice connects with what he perceives to be the perverse, absurd world of his daughter, as well as with contemporary discourses of ageing. In Bucharest he gets an insight into the life of a younger person (Ines) who is a virtuoso in self-management and improvement. Ines, in various settings, has shown herself to be a master of bodily self-control. As part of this, and in a relentless desire to do better, she continues to employ and consult a life coach.

In this respect, it's important that we recognize Toni's entrance as a physical, affective, and psychological form of ambush aimed specifically at Ines. Within the dominant expectations of ageing, it is no surprise that Winfried has mostly been a burden and problem for Ines during his Bucharest visit, that what he's mostly been expected to do is wait. Ade figures Winfried frequently as slumped, heavy, waiting, bored – in shopping malls, leisure clubs, corporate buildings. The waiting, though, is frequently accompanied or followed by ambush – the hilarious and shocking ambush of Toni Erdmann's entrance, which prefigures various unexpected appearances of Toni/Winfried when Ines is with colleagues; the equally shocking ambush of Ines in her own apartment when Winfried is forced to hide in her wardrobe; the more metaphoric but equally cruel ambush of Ines when Winfried insists she sings one of his favourite songs from her childhood in front of a room full of strangers; and Winfried's anonymous appearance as a huge, hairy monster at Ines's birthday party – providing a hilarious shock to disrobed and disarmed guests, but not, by this stage in Winfried's odyssey, to Ines.

Toni Erdmann's episodes, then, can be characterized, from primarily Winfried's perspective, as a series of splenetic or barbed upping of the stakes. This game begins in Winfried's ex-wife's garden, when Winfried accuses Ines of neglecting him and threatens to visit her in Bucharest. It appears to reach a splenetic and uncomfortable conclusion in the back of a cab, when Ines tells her father in no uncertain terms that he's naïve and foolish and doesn't understand what he's playing with (i.e., the harsh economic realities of neoliberal capitalism), which nonetheless doesn't stop Winfried pushing Ines into her glorious, angry, and then, for Winfried, melancholic Whitney Houston moment. The game, then seems to be over; but typically, Winfried has one last, hairy, dogged go, which appears to nearly kill him, but does indeed produce absurd sharing and a loving hug from his daughter.

Toni Erdmann, like other of Ade's complex family melodramas, is episodic and produces a series of ironic counterpoints. The film, though, as I suggested at the beginning of this chapter, also has its own distinctive and powerful rhythm. As Cormican notes, Ade's body genre articulates an aesthetics of presence, awkwardness, and discomfort – *fremdschämen*. In part, this is produced by an evident "lagging rhythm" (Cormican 115), where shots and looks and proximity and difficult exchanges are held and extended and felt. This is evident throughout *Toni Erdmann*, one of the most pointed examples being the poolside scene described above. Working with this, increasing both the discomfort and the pain and often the humour, is the rhythm of the absurd. As Rinhaug notes, the absurd frequently can be understood as a sensation and rhythm – a bodily sensation that can be linked to the spleen, emotion, embarrassment, and pain. This helps explain Winfried's bodily provocation, his movement between waiting and ambush, and his infuriating unwillingness to let go and recede, despite the ill-feeling and discomfort produced by his experiment and game. It is a complicated game with no one motivation or outcome. It is for sure compelled by nostalgia (the Whitney Houston moment) and the loneliness and melancholia of singleness and loss; and by the need for ontological security in a world Winfried no longer understands, and in which increasingly he's perceived as aged, eccentric, and even infirm. This eccentricity, though, is not simply a clinging onto the joking-dad figure expected and sometimes derided by others. It is an embrace and a going-into – a going into death[3] (sometimes with a death mask on) and into the world; a world entirely real (where a prank can cost a job) and entirely absurd. It is also a test, a testing of the limits of Ines's striving, cultivated habitus, and of the social relations produced by contemporary capitalism. These relations to Winfried seem both deathly and absurd ("Are you really a human?!"), and in this respect he seems to repeat Camus's belief that to evade the absurd is to commit a type of suicide. But Winfried/Toni does not try to save Ines, and Ines does not need saving. Instead, he pushes his daughter – doggedly and physically, perversely, and grotesquely – to re-think the terms, or the language in which the burden and embarrassment of ageing is understood; the slippery terms of father-daughter memories and relations; and more broadly but no less absurdly, the broken promises and failed contracts of neoliberal capitalism.

Notes

1 *The Banana Splits* was a US television show which ran on NBC from 1968 to 1970 and was then syndicated internationally from 1970 to 1982. That Winfried not only looks like Bingo but has a banana in his hand in the film's opening scene I assume is coincidence, not design.
2 *Fremdschämen* is the German for feeling embarrassed on someone else's behalf. Cormican uses it in her article on Ade's films to mean this and something a little more. She argues that Ade has introduced a new body genre to German cinema that produces an aesthetics of presence and discomfort.
3 I haven't got space to expand on the idea of going into death here, but it crystallizes a number of *Toni Erdmann*'s themes and questions. It is about Winfried's own death and his apparent ability to countenance it via humour ("50 euros per killing"; "Here today, gone tomorrow") but not medical reality – the heart monitor and his unwillingness to discuss it. Also, when he scrutinizes Ines, he equally asks, "Is there a beating heart in there?" (as in "Are you human?!"), and this I think is where Albert Camus's deep distrust of over-management and bureaucracy meets Robin James's thesis of neoliberal resilience and melancholy. James discusses "going into the death" (20), and by this she means both the unviability of a project (i.e., neoliberalism led by a re-tooled patriarchy) oriented to domination via destruction, and the subversion of this via intensified modes of melancholy and resilience.

Works Cited

Augé, Marc. *Non-Places: Introduction to an Anthropology of Supermodernity*. Verso, 1995.
Bradshaw, Peter. "*Toni Erdmann* Review: Long German Comedy is Slight, Biting Little Miracle." *The Guardian* 13 May 2016.
Camus, Albert. *The Myth of Sisyphus*. Penguin, 2005.

Camus, Albert. *Personal Writings*. Penguin, 2020.
Cormican, Muriel. "Willful Women in the Cinema of Maren Ade." *Camera Obscura* 33.3 (2018): 103–127.
Dolan, Josephine. *Contemporary Cinema and "Old Age": Gender and the Silvering of Stardom*. Palgrave Macmillan, 2017.
Elias, Norbert. *The Loneliness of Dying and Humana Conditio*. U College Dublin P, 2010.
Featherstone, Mike, and Mike Hepworth. "Images of Ageing: Cultural Representations of Later Life." *The Cambridge Handbook of Age and Ageing*. Ed. Malcolm L. Johnson. Cambridge UP, 2005. 354–362.
Gant, Charles. "The Numbers: Oscar Contenders." *Sight and Sound* 27.4 (2017): 17.
Gilleard, Chris. "Cultural Approaches to the Ageing Body." *The Cambridge Handbook of Age and Ageing*. Ed. Malcolm L. Johnson. Cambridge UP, 2005. 156–164.
Gloag, Oliver. *Albert Camus: A Very Short Introduction*. Oxford UP, 2020.
Gurung, Ruchika. "Fatherhood, Narcissism, and Indulging in the Absurd in *The Life Aquatic with Steve Zissou*." *Quarterly Review of Film and Video* 34.8 (2017): 746–764.
Haskell, Molly. "Making the Case: What Films Rose to the Top and Why they Should Endure." *Film Comment* 53.1 (2017): 46.
James, Robin. *Resilience and Melancholy: Pop Music, Feminism, Neoliberalism*. Zero Books, 2015.
Kermode, Mark. "*Toni Erdmann* Review: Talk about Embarrassing Parents . . ." *The Observer* 5 Feb. 2017.
Myers, Emma. "My Father the Hero: Maren Ade on *Toni Erdman*." *Brooklyn Magazine*, 11 Jan. 2017.
Rinhaug, Aino. "Is the Absurd a Male-Dominated Terrain? Pessoa and Beckett as Case Studies." *Portuguese Studies* 24.1 (2008): 41–55.
Turner, Bryan. "Aging and Identity: Some Reflections on the Somatization of the Self." *Images of Aging: Cultural Representations of Later Life*. Eds. Mike Featherstone and Andrew Wernick. Routledge, 1995. 245–260.
Wartenberg, Thomas. *Existentialism: A Beginner's Guide*. Oneworld, 2008.
Wheatley, Catherine. "*Toni Erdmann*: Review." *Sight and Sound* 27.3 (2017): 88–89.

12 "What Makes Us Alive"
The Ageing Artist in Paolo Sorrentino's *The Great Beauty* (2013) and *Youth* (2015)

Manuel Barberá

Introduction

At the beginning of *Youth* (2015), retired classical composer Fred Ballinger (Michael Caine) is visited by an emissary for Queen Elizabeth II conferring a knighthood, who asks him to perform at Prince Philip's birthday. Despite the honour, he rejects the invitation. Later, when asked about his reasons by his lifelong friend Mick Boyle (Harvey Keitel), he laconically answers: "I'm retired, I'm done. With work and with life." The reason for his refusal is that the work that he is required to play, "Simple Song #3," was written specifically to be performed by his wife, who as we learn towards the end of the film is now in an asylum. In the last scene, however, Fred does perform the song in a final concert at the Prince's birthday. He never expresses his decision directly, but we come to understand, thanks to his interactions with Mick, his family, and younger characters over the course of the film, the reasons that contribute to his change of heart.

With *Youth*, Paolo Sorrentino (Naples, 1970) achieved wide critical and commercial success through the astute casting of two of cinema's most talented and bankable older actors. However, we can see in it themes he has always been passionate about: the loss of status and power in the lives of male protagonists nostalgic for their earlier lives. Thus, Fred's journey as an artist is comparable to that of Jep Gambardella (Toni Servillo), who, at the commencement of Sorrentino's previous film *The Great Beauty* (2013), has been experiencing writer's block for four decades. There is an abyss between the life we encounter in the present and the long past time around the publication of his first and only novel, *The Human Apparatus*, a novel so successful that it immediately established him among the members of the Roman jet-set. This gap between then and now separates the 26-year-old Jep, who arrived in Rome and "didn't just want to attend parties, [he] wanted the power to make them fail," from 65-year-old Jep, who feels empty and frustrated in view of the daily parties he attends or hosts.

At the beginning of these complementary films, Sorrentino's protagonists Jep and Fred are older male artists who feel disenchanted, lonely, and apathetic of their earlier success and acclaim. This chapter aims to track and

DOI: 10.4324/9781003306146-12

explore the meaning of their portrayal at three levels. Firstly, I purport to explore Jep and Fred's experiences of old age and their attitudes towards death. Both are marked by the loss of someone long before the beginning of the respective narratives. I argue that there is a relation between these losses and how both men become artists once again: Jep reconnects with his younger self by facing up to the trauma of losing a lover, while Fred loses his friend and is trying to recover his daughter. It is only when they solve these issues that they are at peace and can once again perform their art. Contact with younger characters and the contrast with a worldview marked by ageing and the passing of time are essential to the change.

Having established the central importance of the protagonists' experiences of ageing and old age in both films, I address the dichotomy exposed by a younger character, actor Jimmy Tree (Paul Dano), at the climax of *Youth* when he expresses that, as an artist, he wants to focus on desire, not horror, as the former is "what makes us alive." I aim to show how Jep's and Fred's healing processes culminate only when they recover desire and leave horror behind, thus becoming able to express themselves artistically once again. Interestingly enough, it is when the protagonists embrace the discourse of a middle-aged man (i.e., young but already conscious of old age) that they change. Following Margaret M. Gullette's (2004) theory on decline and progress narratives, Sorrentino's protagonists eventually rebel against horror and refuse to build their identity on a declinist discourse.

Finally, I argue that Paolo Sorrentino, too, chooses desire as he creates his films in such a way that desire can beat decline. The director presents art as a tool to frame old age in a positive way, as a moment when one is still alive, inhabiting the world, and with an identity of one's own. This results in the creation of a modern, positive vision of older age, offering new and necessary models of older men. Consequently, Sorrentino creates films that enable him to induce, in a supportive, collaborative manner, the audience's empathy and resilience. He does so not by means of denying decline but through the presentation and resolution of conflicts in his films, which restore ageing as a process of growth and old age as a rich, fertile moment in life to find answers to such conflicts. In this way, he dissociates chronological and essential age by making his old, male protagonists retain or recover elements such as activity and hope, which have traditionally been associated with youth.

Old Artists Looking for an Identity

The opening of *The Great Beauty* shows Jep Gambardella smiling proudly at his bizarre, rampant birthday party. He seems to be a successful artist who has achieved everything in life: power, money, respect, friends. However, we soon discover that he is not as happy as one might think; he is tired, confused, and hurt by his past and his present. We learn that he wrote one novel decades ago, and we sense his frustration about his lack of productivity. Two events trigger a change in him: Jep learns that his first love, Elisa de Santis (Annaluisa Capasa), has died, and he starts a romantic relationship with a woman who suddenly dies as well. Jep seems to connect both events, so that they serve to heal the first, original wound – the fact that his first love left him decades ago, which appears to be the reason for his writer's block, and he eventually starts a new novel.

Similarly, in *Youth*, Fred Ballinger is a retired orchestra conductor who is spending time in a spa after being diagnosed with apathy. Having rejected Queen Elizabeth's invitation to perform at her husband's birthday, he spends his days reflecting on life, walking and talking with his daughter Lena (Rachel Weisz) and his friend Mick Boyle. These relationships produce contrasting outcomes: the improvement, at last, of his troubled relationship with Lena and the suicide of Mick towards the end of the film. We also learn that his wife and muse has been in an asylum for years, and he eventually is ready to visit her and consequently agrees to play the concert.

The failure to secure a conventionally masculine identity is a frequent characteristic of Sorrentino's protagonists. In his debut feature *One Man Up* (2001), Antonio Pisapia (Andrea Renzi), the soccer player, reaches the conclusion that he cannot be a coach because "I'm a sad man, and soccer is a game." We find the theme in Cheyenne's (Sean Penn) Peter Pan syndrome and depression in *This Must Be the Place* (2011) but especially in his "androgynous appearance, passive mannerisms, and affected vocal patterns [that] contrast sharply with his wife, Jane [Frances McDormand], who beats him at handball and works as a firefighter while Cheyenne languishes in indolent retirement" (Kilbourn 55). It also resonates in the conflicts and internal negotiations suffered by Pius XIII (Jude Law) in the mini-series *The Young Pope* (2016) and *The New Pope* (2020). All of them are insecure about the role other people attribute to them (soccer coach, rock star, pope) and are, more often than not, overwhelmed by expectations of what it means to be a successful and fulfilled man.

This theme also appears in Sorrentino's semi-autobiographical *The Hand of God* (2021), which again centres on a male protagonist who undergoes a serious identity conflict. The 17-year-old Fabietto Schisa (Filippo Scotti) is an alter ego of Sorrentino himself, and while the film shows the same conflict with identity as the films centring on older characters, it focuses on the beginning of the painful, long journey to find an identity as an individual and creator. "I don't like reality anymore. Reality is lousy," says Fabietto. However, this specific film contains a different shade of hope, sheltered by the idea of having time ahead. When at the end of the film Fabietto meets the Neapolitan filmmaker Antonio Capuano (Ciro Capano), the latter tries to force an epiphany on the teenager, asking him about his artistic and vital needs and desires, and concludes that he needs "balls" and "pain" in order to make films. Although *The Hand of God* (2021) deals with a young and still developing character, it can be seen as an earlier life stage expression of what Russell Kilbourn refers to as a "Sorrentinian subject":

> The recurring figure of a middle-aged (and in the later films, older) man, typically in a creative profession, such as a singer, writer, or filmmaker, who, while often defined by the measure of social or political power he wields, is equally defined by an underlying impotence. . . . If he lacks any tangible power at the outset, the story deals with his redemption, whether through his metaphorical or actual death or through a comparably ambiguous revelatory experience, especially one involving an encounter with memory, mediated through a specific person or event from his past.
>
> (38)

While *The Hand of God* seems to contain a statement by the filmmaker on his motivations and his first steps as a filmmaker, *The Great Beauty* and *Youth* offer more distanced, philosophical perspectives. Unlike young Fabietto, the protagonists do not have faith in their future. Jep Gambardella, who has just turned 65 years old – considered as a conventional marker of the onset of old age for men in Western industrialized societies – says he has spent his life "making plans" and now all he does is "remember the past." He admits to having been drinking, but only to forget his birthday, to forget that time keeps passing while he does not achieve anything new. "What's wrong with feeling nostalgic?" he asks. "It's the only distraction left for those who've no faith in the future."

In *Youth*, Fred Ballinger is diagnosed with apathy, and he lacks Jep's spicy fake humour: he is incapable of finding joy in life. Both seem to live in a psychic place separated from the rest of people and conform to Robert Kastenbaum's assertion that "we tend to think of a person as 'old' (i.e., manifesting the effects of process or processes known as 'aging') when this person has relatively little exchange with their environment" (165). As Kastenbaum reminds us, "'oldness' is implied by an apparent lack of attention and response to the full range of stimuli" (165), a situation illustrated by Fred's "I'm retired, I'm done. With work and with life."

In "The Double Standard of Aging," Susan Sontag stated that in industrial societies "the most popular metaphor for happiness is 'youth' (I would insist that it is a metaphor for energy, restless mobility, appetite: for the state of wanting)" (31). In a way, these older artists crave anything that can heal their feelings of being left out and their apparent lack of appetite (sexual, interpersonal, creative), but they do not know what it is. Their problems stem rather from the fact that they do have such an appetite, but they fail to understand what it means or is for, which exacerbates their feelings of frustration and impotence. Only when they identify or recover their creative needs will they counter the negative implications of old age.

There is a second gap, one between the success of Jep and Fred as artists, perceived by everyone around them, and their failure in achieving happiness in their personal lives. In a way they feel like impostors, living off their past and their royalties and receiving acknowledgment for something created by a person they feel alienated from. As a consequence, they need closure with their past in order to look ahead and accept who they are. In the case of Fred, he states that he cannot perform his masterpiece for Queen Elizabeth for personal reasons, which we later learn means that he composed it when he "still loved" and it was to be sung by his wife specifically. This links Fred to Jep Gambardella, who wrote his one and only novel while young and also "deeply in love" (Kilbourn 192). No longer the successful artists they once were, they now perceive themselves as old and artless.

In both films, the protagonists are overwhelmed by situations that escape their masculine control. Four decades were not enough for Jep to come to terms with the loss of his first love, who left him in his youth. In a way, he buried this trauma, and it is only when he learns of her death that those feelings appear again in him, forcing him to face his past. In *Youth*, Fred is accompanied by daughter and assistant Lena, who is in the middle of a divorce, and he berates himself for his failure to understand her emotional issues as his wife did. He pities himself, feels old, and thinks it is too late to change and be a caring father, which he never was.

Both men are attractive and successful. However, there is a contrast between their professional success and the effect they create on the audience and strangers and their failure on the familiar, private level. This is similarly reflected in the effect they have in terms of love relationships. While Jep is 20 years younger than Fred and has emotional and sexual relations with other women, Fred does not seem interested in any woman other than his wife. Although aged, Jep exudes enough elegance and sex appeal to be with much younger women such as Ramona (Sabrina Ferilli). However, their successes in their professional areas or with women are futile, useless for the new conflicts appearing in the films: facing death, gaining affective responsibility, or coming to terms with their past. We thus perceive a special emphasis on the men's powerlessness, a divergence between what society expects from them and their actual behaviour. To a lesser extent, there is yet another clash, that between Jep and his male friends, who cannot manage to have functional relationships, and that of Fred with Mick, his lifelong best friend but from whom he still keeps secrets: "We only ever told each other the good things."

In turn, these conditions question the idea of success itself. Is success a professional issue (being acknowledged as the author of a masterpiece, being requested by the Queen)? Is it social (Jep's big, bizarre parties)? The answer in the films seems to be that success, just like masculinity, is fluid and complex, so that these so-called successful men are not happy because they did not achieve success when it comes to being truthful to themselves, to the personal sphere, to artistic creation. Sorrentino presents a model of hegemonic masculinity as a social construct, but he also suggests the idea that hegemonic masculinity clashes with the personal concerns and desires of the individual, and by representing this clash he is problematizing the concept itself and its obsolescence.

Ultimately, Sorrentino creates a complex and contradictory image of masculinity in old age: protagonists who are successful in their professional but not their personal lives, who are unhappy and experiencing extreme emotional strain due the pressure of gender performance that is predicated on external and quantitative success (sales, audience, popularity) and not personal and qualitative (based on intimacy, friendship, love, and family relationships). This is the starting point from which Sorrentino imagines his ageing protagonists.

Choosing Between Horror and Desire

As I have noted, *Youth* takes place in a Swiss hotel-spa where Fred Ballinger is spending his retreat with his good friend Mick Boyle. Among many other picturesque characters, such as the Tibetan monk, a retired Argentinian soccer player (who is a clear representation of Diego Maradona), or a young former Miss Universe, we get to know Jimmy Tree, an actor in a personal and professional crisis who spends his days thinking about the point of his career and its legacy. Jimmy is in his thirties and cannot stand the idea of being remembered for a minor role. Not only was it for the lesser art form of television instead of cinema, but it was the role of a robot, which is also contrary to what the mission of an actor is supposed to be: to express human emotions, nuances, the human spirit, and experience.

Miss Universe (Mădălina Ghenea) compliments him on his famous role, to which he responds sarcastically. She ignores his barbed response on her looks, says she is happy to have taken part in the Miss Universe contest, and inquires: "Are you happy you played [the robot] Mr. Keith?" This is the first time we see Jimmy shocked by having his worldview confronted unexpectedly. Later, a teenager compliments him on a different role, one in a movie he thought "nobody saw" but that she remembers for a dialogue in which Jimmy told his son that he thought he was not sufficient as a father. She says she understood something important from his role: that "no one in the world feels up to it. So there's no reason to worry."

After these conversations, a subtle change takes place in Jimmy though this is not made explicit. At the climax of the film, we see Jimmy, dressed as Adolf Hitler, the role he has been secretly preparing for, delivering a solemn, passionate monologue:

> I've been studying all the hotel guests for weeks now. I have been meticulously observing you, and Fred . . . Lena, the Russians, the Arabs, the young and the old. . . . And I have finally come to a conclusion . . . I have to choose. I have to choose what is really worth telling, horror or

desire. And I choose desire. You, each one of you, you opened my eyes, you made me see that I should not be wasting my time on the senselessness of horror. I can't do this, I can't play Hitler. I wanna tell about your desire, my desire. So pure, so impossible, so immoral, it doesn't matter; because that's what makes us alive.

I would argue that this is Sorrentino speaking through Jimmy. Consequently, it seems that both Jep and Fred choose desire, instead of horror, at the end of their personal growth journeys, in their experience of old age, and this is what allows them to heal, to be creative and productive again. Immediately after the monologue, the film music reaches a peak in its intensity and we see the back of the Tibetan monk, only to discover, after a slow zoom-out, that he is in fact levitating.

We find a similarly magical climax in the final scene of *The Great Beauty*, which consists of a combination of images of the centenarian Saint crawling up the stairs while we hear Jep's monologue explaining his conclusion after the recent events in his life and his firm will to "believe," perhaps in a more prosaic sense, but a *will* to believe directly linked by Sorrentino to a previous *necessity* to believe in order to find oneself. In *The Great Beauty* "male ageing is a question of redeeming soul and memory, in which the male melodrama of Jep's suffering, as Catherine O'Rawe describes . . . becomes 'the gateway to the sublime'" (qtd. in Kilbourn 172).

In *Youth*, Fred Ballinger's interactions with young people similarly make him change his mind about his current predicament: Miss Universe, the masseuse, Jimmy, and especially the young man he meets who is playing the song he wrote for his wife. Fred, who does not like to discuss his work, denying his past, promptly gives a couple of tips to the kid. This seems to have an effect on Fred, making him think that his work can still have continuity, be alive, played and listened to through time, even after he is gone.

Sorrentino conveys this message of hope by means of images and photography, and this seems to lead audiences to understand that the films, even though they deal with trauma and death, are beautiful, optimistic, or hopeful; indeed, the film's title *Youth* is all about focusing on desire over horror. At the Cannes Film Festival the director explained that the film is about how the future always "offers a possibility of liberty, and that liberty is a state inherent to youth," liberty meaning "to live knowing that in theory you could do anything – without necessarily doing it" (Zoritch n.p.).

Thus, Fred starts appreciating time and life again after a series of events, including the kid playing his song, his friend Mick's death towards the end of the film, and the fact that his relationship with his daughter starts to develop positively as a consequence of their time spent together. He decides to visit his wife in the asylum, as a request for redemption, and accepts the invitation to perform, which his daughter asked him to do at the beginning of the film. This way, he restores his relationships both with his wife and his daughter, reconnecting with the women in his life and becoming empathic and affectively responsible towards others and himself, being saved.

Nevertheless, as much as *Youth*'s message is the need to focus on desire, it also shows an example of what happens when one does not manage to do so. That is the fate of Mick Boyle, Fred's best friend, who fails to find the necessary vitality and desire in writing his final screenplay. His friend and muse, the actress Brenda Morel (Jane Fonda), confronts him directly when she refuses to take part in his new film, which he considers to be his artistic testament: "You're the one who doesn't understand [cinema] anymore, because you're old, you're tired, you don't know how to see the world anymore, Mick. All you know how to see is your own death, which is waiting right around the corner for you." As Edelstein and Palomares put it,

> Mick's efforts to retain artistic agency and relevance in old age are eventually shown as futile, leading to desperately tragic consequences. Perhaps this is the other side of the coin . . . Mick turns to the horror of suicide rather than contemplate a life of unfulfilled desire – in his case, his desire for artistic legacy.
>
> (n.p.)

While Mick fails when it comes to negotiating with his past, Fred's reconciliation with his *oeuvre* (created when he was a younger man) reinstates him as an artist who is connected to all of his life and work and does not turn his back on either.

The Great Beauty and *Youth* as the Catalysts of Sorrentino's Message

Monologues and dialogues in Sorrentino's films are often extremely literal, in such a way that we feel as though the author is talking through a specific character. During the final climax of *The Great Beauty*, Jep Gambardella concludes: "This is how it always ends. With death. But first there was life." He has finally found what he calls "flashes of beauty," finely illustrated by shots in which his face is repeatedly illuminated by the lighthouse on the beach where he experienced his first kiss with his first love Elisa de Santis. In the words of Mimmo Cangiano:

> Only when the character gains her/his own identity, life and reality itself become meaningful, and only then, reality stops being a fluid heap of unrelated facts (a "spectacle," in a Debaurdian sense), and turns into something that can be interpreted and judged.
>
> (340)

In the end, it is the potential of reflectiveness in later life that enables Jep to set his life events in order and integrate as a new "I," which is something every male protagonist in Sorrentino needs to do. The message seems to be that such characters need to keep learning and growing, contrary to hegemonic, ageist discourses.

In this sense, Jimmy Tree's monologue coincides with the director's message and links both the form and content of the film. However, Sorrentino does not hide what he does not like but makes contradictions visible and combines humour and nostalgia, with a final result that bypasses the horror of death and the fear to old age in a way that does not feel artificial. He is not disguising pain, but rather openly shows it as a natural part of life while telling us that we have tools to accept and overcome it. These films are inspired by the idea that art is a source of hope:

> I do like to talk about these characters who are caught at the moment of their decline and they tend to develop a melancholic outlook. They are afraid of death and they inevitably make the wrong decisions and it's something that does happen when in aging they have one last burst of vitality and this can become pathetic and ridiculous. These kinds of modes and feelings are very much in tune with how I feel, and I like talking about them. It is true that I've focused on male characters and older male characters.
>
> (qtd. in Mariani, Introduction xvii)

Sorrentino is not impartial. During *Youth* we see several conversations about people saying that they saw the Tibetan monk levitating, and Fred is sceptical. As a consequence, the shot of the levitating monk comes as a statement of the idea that if art wants it so, a monk can levitate. Sorrentino uses filmmaking as a tool to make the miracle possible, transforming his will into reality or imposing it to demonstrate the power of art to modify the world. In a similar manner, inasmuch as he puts artistic creation at the centre of his works – writing in *The Great Beauty*, musical performance, and cinema in *Youth* – he produces a manifesto about such creative capacity, and by extension about his own conception of the art of filmmaking and his own *oeuvre*, these constituting a meta-reflection on his own activity – a reflection that has recently been amplified and further justified in *The Hand of God*.

In a way, Sorrentino is equating artistic creativity and activity to "youth." The protagonists become "young" again through their art: even though they are not young in terms of chronological age, they are active and productive again. The way to recover that creative energy is to recover hope, it is going back to that liberty, in the words of Sorrentino, or the "state of wanting," in terms of Susan Sontag: the prevailing idea is that life is ahead of them, instead of behind, and there are always new things to be done.

A line that summarizes all this appears at the end of *Youth*. The doctor tells Fred he is perfectly fine. Fred looks disappointed and asks, "My prostate, at least?" Finally, the doctor tells him: "Do you know what awaits you, outside of here? Youth." He seems to explain that Fred's discomfort comes from his thoughts, feelings, and situation but that it is not physical. Fred is tied to a prejudice by which he is supposed to feel weak at the age of 70, after living through many things, but he is completely fine and there are no objective reasons for him to abandon his career or identity or to stop living.

Conclusion: What Makes Us Young

In *The Great Beauty* and *Youth*, Paolo Sorrentino explores themes of alienation and nostalgia through his ageing male protagonists. As they reflect on the events earlier in their lives, they realize they still, or can again, have a future. He pictures older age not as a final stage in life but as a starting point in which hope for the future is what allows people to go on. He creates a sense of hope and beauty that bypasses the horror and negative connotations of old age and the spectre of impending death.

Jep Gambardella and Fred Ballinger change as artists when they go past the "horror" (imagined as emotional pain and heartache) accumulated through their lives and decide to focus on desire in order to make beauty a reality. At this point, old age is essential for the conception of the message. If, as Margaret M. Gullette argues, "aging is a narrative" (2011, 5), Sorrentino exploits this narrative and catalyses it, making the most of the vital load of older characters. Desire feeds desire, and it needs to be kept alive. The issue here is not to stay physically young but to stay alive and with a passion for the future. A positive future is in fact enabled by the contact with the worst things, such as isolation and death. Art expresses the restoration of hope and happiness: Jep starts a new novel, while Fred performs his most famous piece. However, there are slight differences to their new situations: Jep's restoration is about being productive again without a lover by his side to inspire him, Fred's about performing his special piece without his wife. Jep needs inspiration, while Fred needs reconciliation.

Sorrentino chooses these older artists as representative of the human and seems to suggest that we all share a common experience:

> Sorrentino explains that the reason why *Youth* may affect the younger audience is because the anguish and worries of older and younger people are pretty much the same. He elaborates: "The film speaks more about this fatigue which is to live in this world," which is felt both by the young and the elderly.
>
> (Zoritch n.p.)

It seems that the fatigue perceived by the director in life is stressed by the lack of prospects and time. However, while Sorrentino seems to offer a vision that encompasses human experience regardless of age, it is unclear whether this includes the experience of women properly, as they seem to remain in a secondary level.

As a result of his personal vision, Paolo Sorrentino's films can be understood as progress narratives, thus contributing to what has been referred to as a culture of positive ageing (Featherstone and Hepworth 31), a notion that might be misleading. In *Agewise*, Margaret M. Gullette talks about the inevitability of death and how these "resistant fictions" (209) she calls *progress narratives* make the audience stronger against it. She contends that "anti-ageist literature challenges the gruelling negativity and automaticity of decline but not by facing away from loss" (209). I would argue that the cinema of Paolo Sorrentino, and more specifically *The Great Beauty* and *Youth*, are representative of these resistant fictions: they let grief, sadness, and obsolescence into the narrative, and this seems to be more effective when it comes to building resilience than invisibility. They expose fears and pains connatural to life and illustrate how protagonists come to terms with them. Sorrentino is, I would argue, trying to make a point and to offer a lesson for ageing artists and non-artists: creation and activity might be key. Sorrentino creates works that discuss the need for such attributes and the painful processes that might lead to change.

Works Cited

Cangiano, Mimmo. *Against Postmodernism: Paolo Sorrentino and the Search for Authenticity*. Mariani, 2021. 24–36.

Edelstein, Gabriella, and Claudette Palomares. "The Way We Will Be: Sorrentino's Youth." *Erratic Dialogues*. Nov. 2015. 15 Jan. 2022. https://erraticdialogues.com/2015/10/29/youth-2015/.

Featherstone, Mike, and Andrew Wernick, eds. *Images of Ageing: Cultural Representations of Later Life*. Routledge, 1995.

García Navarro, Carmen. "Joy Harjo's Poetics of Memory and Resilience." *ATLANTIS: Journal of the Spanish Association of Anglo-American Studies* 41.1 (June 2019): 51–68.

Gullette, Margaret Morganroth. *Aged by Culture*. U Chicago P, 2004.

Gullette, Margaret Morganroth. *Agewise: Fighting the New Ageism in America*. U Chicago P, 2011.

Kastenbaum, Robert J. "Habituation as a Model of Human Aging." *International Journal of Aging and Human Development* 12.3 (1980–1): 159–170.

Kilbourn, Russell J. A. *The Cinema of Paolo Sorrentino*. Wallflower, 2020.

Mariani, Annachiara. "The Antithetical Coherence in Sorrentino's *Youth*: Visual (Ab)use and Male Dominance." *South Central Review* 35.2 (Summer 2018): 117–132.

Mariani, Annachiara. *Introduction: The Creative and Artistic Trajectory of Paolo Sorrentino*. Mariani, 2021. xvii–xxx.

Mariani, Annachiara, ed. *Paolo Sorrentino's Cinema and Television*. Intellect Books, 2021.

Sontag, Susan. "The Double Standard of Aging." *The Saturday Review* 23 (Sept. 1972): 29–38.

Sorrentino, Paolo, dir. *One Man Up*. Indigo Film, 2001.

Sorrentino, Paolo, dir. *This Must Be the Place*. Indigo Film, Lucky Red, Medusa Produzione, 2011.

Sorrentino, Paolo, dir. *The Great Beauty*. Indigo Film, 2013.
Sorrentino, Paolo, dir. *Youth*. Indigo Film, 2015.
Sorrentino, Paolo, dir. *The Young Pope*. Wildside, Sky Italia, Canal+, HBO, Mediapro, 2016.
Sorrentino, Paolo, dir. *The New Pope*. Sky Italia, HBO, Mediapro, Wildside, Haut et Court, Canal, 2020.
Sorrentino, Paolo, dir. *The Hand of God*. The Apartment, Netflix, 2021.
Vilalta, Ton. "Paolo Sorrentino: 'Hacer una película es una cosa de locos.'" *Jotdown*. Nov. 2020. 20 Nov. 2022. www.jotdown.es/2020/11/paolo-sorrentino-entrevista-director-cine/
Zoritch, Katia. "On Paolo Sorrentino's Latest Film, 'Youth', and its Place Among Earlier Works." *Medium*. 5 Dec. 2015. 26 Jan. 2022. https://medium.com/@katiazoritch/paolo-sorrentino-perhaps-youth-depends-on-a-walk-around-the-lake-dc077f088cd2.

13 Masculinity, Creativity, and Successful Ageing in Pedro Almodóvar's *Pain and Glory* (2019)

Heather Jerónimo

Introduction

Pedro Almodóvar's 2019 film *Dolor y gloria* (Pain and Glory; hereinafter *Pain and Glory*), a thinly veiled reflection of Almodóvar's life that touches on his childhood, career, relationship with his mother, and ageing, has been described as "sobria, reposada, madura, reconciliadora" ("restrained, collected, mature, conciliatory"; Solórzano 68) and "an old man's confessional" (Brooks). At the centre of the film is Salvador Mallo, an on-screen "alter-ego" (Solórzano 69) of the director played by the internationally recognized and recognizably ageing Antonio Banderas, who has been a presence in the films of Pedro Almodóvar over nearly four decades. *Pain and Glory* follows Salvador as he confronts masculine fears of ageing into irrelevance; overcoming physical and emotional pain (tied to his relationship with his mother and growing up as a queer child) through mental fortitude and allowing Salvador to engage once again in the creative task of filmmaking. In converting his memories into a feature film, Salvador transforms himself once again into a productive member of society, thus reinforcing the belief that older people should strive to achieve "successful ageing," a term proposed by gerontologists John Rowe and Robert Kahn (1987). The three components of successful ageing include "low risk of disease and disease-related disability; maintenance of high mental and physical function; and continued engagement with life" (593). Rowe and Kahn's term has been criticized, however, for its limited definition of ageing and the impossible physical and health standards it promotes (Martinson and Berridge 62). While *Pain and Glory*'s message about the redemptive nature of creativity is positive, Almodóvar's depiction of "successful ageing" as the goal for Salvador – and for Banderas, who has incorporated successful ageing into his public persona – should therefore be interpreted critically, as it does not consider a wider range of ageing experiences.

As the film opens, we learn that Salvador Mallo has retired from his work and the public eye due to various chronic illnesses. When a film group hosts a screening of his decades-old film *Sabor* (Flavor), Salvador reaches out to the film's lead actor and estranged friend Alberto Crespo (Asier Etxeandia),

DOI: 10.4324/9781003306146-13

to mend their relationship in the hope that they can attend the screening and Q&A session together. During Salvador's visit to Alberto's home, they use heroin, a habit which Salvador increasingly relies upon to assuage his physical pains, which range from migraines to back problems to "dolores del alma" ("pains of the soul") such as depression. Salvador lives with "el insomnio, la faringitis crónica, la otitis, el reflujo, la úlcera, y el asma intrínseca. Los nervios en general y el ciático en particular y todos tipos de dolores musculares: lumbares, dorsales, tendinitis, ambos rodillas y hombros" ("insomnia, chronic pharyngitis, otitis, acid reflux, ulcer, and asthma. Nerves in general and the sciatic nerve in particular and all types of muscular pains: lumbar, dorsal, tendonitis, both knees and shoulders"). In addition, Salvador is diagnosed with Forestier's disease, an ossification of the bones in his throat that causes him great difficulty in swallowing, leading to terrifying choking scenes.

Salvador uses heroin to manage his pain and facilitate flashbacks to childhood memories,[1] primarily scenes that permit him to reflect on growing up as a queer child, examining his relationship with his mother or his encounters with Eduardo (César Vicente), the young painter who first stirred Salvador's homosexual desires. Salvador's reliance on the drug increases until he receives a visit from Federico (Leonardo Sbaraglia), his former lover whose struggle with addiction during the drug-filled years of *la Movida* in 1980s Madrid[2] led to the unravelling of their relationship. After Federico's visit, Salvador disposes of his illegal drugs, enlisting the help of a doctor to manage his pain to a point where he can become physically active again. *Pain and Glory* ends with a flashback to Salvador's childhood. As Salvador's mother tucks him in, the camera zooms out to reveal that this is a movie set rather than a memory, and Salvador (the adult) is again directing a film, presumably based on his childhood memories. The audience learns that flashbacks throughout the movie, believed to have been Salvador's memories, are actually scenes from the new movie Salvador is directing. Although viewers mistake them for memories until the end of the film, seemingly reinforcing a narrative of ageing as decline (Morganroth Gullette, *Decline* 8), Almodóvar is concurrently crafting a narrative of productive ageing in which art plays a central and redemptive role through Salvador's return to filmmaking and through his own film.

Ageing, Gender, and Society

These two narratives of ageing, as either a process of decline and retreat or as a continued engagement with life,[3] form the uncomfortable binary of ageing permeating Western culture. Both present challenges and establish stereotypes. At the beginning of *Pain and Glory*, Salvador exemplifies the narrative of ageing as decline, living a closed-off half-life and refusing the many invitations he receives to attend gallery openings, theatre productions, and parties due to the physical pains he experiences daily. By the end of the film, as Salvador transforms his memories into artistic creation, he becomes an example of successful ageing. By managing his pain to the extent that he can write and direct a new film, Salvador reclaims his vitality and sense of purpose. Salvador's life experience is thus posited as a positive character arc, the inspiring story of an older person who has overcome the physical demands of ageing, but his struggles to stay relevant obscure any potential narrative about alternative ways in which to address the anxieties surrounding ageing masculinity. Ageing men may feel pressured to uphold an image of themselves as productive and physically strong, as those men who cannot do so are at risk of being marked as part of the narrative of ageing as decline, which is "often linked to femininity through an emphasis on (embodied) frailty, dependency, and passivity, [while] positive-ageing discourses are notably masculinist through stressing productivity, autonomy, activity, and control (Sandberg 2013a)" (Sandberg 25). When Salvador admits that his bodily limitations are hindering him from resuming the work of filmmaking, he senses the potential shame of being perceived by his male peers as weak or feminine, for whom masculinity is "a homosocial enactment . . . fraught with danger, with the risk of failure" (Kimmel 129). Instead of adapting as a filmmaker while considering the realities of his older, changing body, *Pain and Glory* suggests that Salvador has willed away all markers of ageing and disability from his body through mental fortitude; what he describes as his "voluntad férrea" ("iron will").

In addition to physical changes, individuals are "aged by culture" (Morganroth Gullette 2004, 3), and Western culture establishes different standards of ageing for women and men. Society arguably has subjected women to a more intense patrolling of ageing, either criticizing any signs that their bodies are changing or cloaking the ageing, "disappearing female body" (Woodward 163) in invisibility. More than women, men have been allowed to age naturally without the societal message that they must hide all signs of ageing, as masculine "youth and its associated sub-cultural adornment is something to be outgrown in favour of a privileged maturity" (Dolan 85). Older men are permitted to gain weight and go grey (often celebrated as "silver foxes"), as society is not concerned with older men's appearances, instead demanding demonstrations of power, "money, status and social dominance, so that early signs of ageing such as grey hair are read as marks of maturity and authority" (Twigg 62). Banderas, for example, who is known for his Latin heartthrob roles in Hollywood films that have positioned him as an ideal of hegemonic masculinity[4] and as a handsome male movie star, has been allowed, even encouraged, to age. Despite visible signs of ageing – his grey hair styled to resemble that of Almodóvar – Banderas' performance of pain emanates a quiet dignity and charismatic appeal. By transforming his memories into a consumable product (a film), Salvador regains the respect of his peers and society, viewed once more as masculine, active, and youthful. Salvador's return to the director's chair offers an optimistic portrayal of ageing where his passion for creativity and productivity conquer all challenges of ageing, instead of questioning successful ageing's insistence on productivity and strength.

While male stars

> are closely scrutinized for attempting to hide signs of ageing, particularly hair loss; . . . women are routinely maligned if they *fail* to hide the signs of ageing. Indeed, popular culture is able to accept, even celebrate an ageing man, but quite the opposite is the case in relation to women.
> (Fairclough-Isaacs 363)

Banderas' ex-wife Melanie Griffith – only three years older than Banderas but described by him as "a victim of aging" (Chivers xii) – has struggled to sustain a career or find fulfilling work, even as Banderas' popularity has continued to grow. His role in *Pain and Glory* earned him the Best Actor award at the 2019 Cannes Film Festival and a Best Actor nomination at the 2020 Academy Awards (Crisolago), demonstrating that audiences and critics are far more open to representations of ageing men rather than women on-screen.

Disability, Queerness, and Ageing

Despite societal aversion to any suggestion of the narrative of ageing as decline, Salvador must embrace decline before reclaiming his masculine agency as a successfully ageing person. Salvador experiences a triple social marginalization due to his age, queerness, and various disabilities and illnesses. Robert McRuer compares queerness to disability, asserting that both "have the potential to disrupt the performance of able-bodied heterosexuality" (24). Salvador does not use his queerness or disability in a subversive way, though, and is controlled by the dictates and norms of successful ageing. Salvador spends most of his time alone in his apartment, partly due to pain, but also because he does not want to reveal any indication of decline or weakness in public, his ageing and physically limited body stymieing his social and work life. Most individuals will eventually experience some form of illness or disability as they grow older, as "able-bodied status is always temporary" (McRuer 30). Even so, Western society continues to marginalize both disabled and older people, two groups "constructed as bodily, threatening, and signaling failure" (Chivers 23). Salvador assumes he will be socially rejected for his ageing and disabled body, so he stigmatizes and marginalizes himself.

In addition to laying the groundwork for a plot line that epitomizes the narrative of ageing as decline, Salvador's struggles with ageing and pain are reflective of Almodóvar's own experience with these same concerns.[5] Almodóvar confirms having endured many of the pains and illnesses that Salvador lives with, stating that while he has never used heroin, *Pain and Glory* allowed him to imagine himself as a character who would do so to deal with his back pain (Sánchez-Arce 299). Disability and illness appear frequently in Almodóvar's oeuvre, as does the inclusion of scenes in hospitals (Sanderson 472), presenting themes that often claim a meaning "that goes beyond the purely physical and affects the emotional" (Huici Módenes 104). In *Pain and Glory*, physical pain correlates to emotional distress about ageing, as the dissipation of Salvador's pain is linked to his rejection of ageing as decline through renewed engagement in his social and work life. Emotional and physical states of wellbeing are connected for Almodóvar, as well, who recounts that he falls ill before beginning to film each movie, claiming that these illnesses, now a "tradition," indicate that it is time to begin filming (Almodóvar 450). While preparing to shoot a film is physically demanding, the ritual illness Almodóvar describes is imbued with emotional import. Audiences should not interpret Salvador as a purely autobiographical representation of Almodóvar, who characterizes his work "not [as] autobiography. It is autofiction in its origins" (Sánchez-Arce 293). Nonetheless, Salvador is a character who reveals and then resolves a filmmaker's anxieties about maintaining a creative life while experiencing disability and ageing; he masters his physical and emotional pain more through mental determination than medical interventions.

Over the course of the film, Salvador transitions from a narrative of ageing as decline to one of successful ageing, which requires both a low risk of disease and disability, as well as maintenance of mental and physical function (Rowe and Kahn 593). When the film begins, Salvador has withdrawn from writing scripts and directing films due to migraines and other debilitating pains. He remains isolated in his apartment cared for by his housekeeper, Maya, and his assistant, Mercedes. Maya recounts Salvador's many physical struggles to Mercedes, explaining that he wears only slippers because he cannot bend over to tie his shoelaces, and he is too proud to ask Maya for help. Salvador's embarrassment for others to see his physical limitations delay his attempts to achieve the third requirement of successful ageing, continued engagement with life (Rowe and Kahn 593).

Even though Salvador has witnessed the addictions fostered by the exuberant, drug-fueled years of *la Movida*, he turns to heroin consumption late in life for pain relief rather than pleasure. Eager for more social engagement, he promises he will attend a screening of his earlier film *Sabor*, produced during those heady early years of Spanish democracy when the death of Franco also meant the end of an ageing tyrannical patriarchy. However, before the event, Salvador uses heroin to control his pain and nerves, ultimately deciding not to attend, as he does not want the audience to see him in a drugged state. Salvador's shame at not being able to maintain peak physical function keeps him from participating more fully in his life.

The subsequent visit of his ex-lover Federico represents a turning point for Salvador. When Federico appears outside his building, Salvador decides to use heroin to calm his physical pain. Spectators witness Salvador's emotional and physical struggle as he places a pillow on the floor before slowly kneeling to get the drugs out of a cabinet. An over-the-shoulder shot hides Salvador's face but still establishes empathy for this moment of vulnerability. A close-up of his hand preparing the drugs, which then zooms out to include his face blowing the drugs away, reveals a quick but poignant moment of decision. Salvador flushes the drugs down the toilet, and after Federico leaves, asks Mercedes to take him to the doctor. Salvador admits to his heroin use and asks for help with his addiction, turning to prescription drugs to manage his pain and correcting his Forestier's syndrome through surgery. *Pain and Glory*'s portrayal of ceasing drug use is undoubtedly unrealistically optimistic, as Salvador does not struggle with withdrawal but instead easily reincorporates himself into his work, revealing the mindset that physical or emotional distress can be vanquished largely through willpower. Before he feels able to rejoin society, Salvador seeks out ways to "correct" his body and eliminate signs of weakness or ageing, substantiating Robert McRuer's argument that able-bodiedness is culturally produced as the societal norm, and all those who are not able-bodied must affirm that able-bodiedness is the preferred state of being (9). Salvador craves both able-bodiedness and the elimination of physical pain, but Federico's visit has also permitted him to resolve the residual emotional pain from their relationship.

Federico's visit stirs up in Salvador a conflation of emotional reconciliation and the desire to be societally affirmed as once again able-bodied, drawing attention to the fact that queer relationships and emotions have caused Salvador pain throughout his life, in addition to illness and ageing.[6] Queer characters abound in Almodóvar's oeuvre, often "linked to art, creation, music, drugs, death, clairvoyance, religion, acceptance, and the need to be admired" (López-Font et al. 56). The impact of Salvador's queerness on his identity is most fully understood through his childhood memories, since he does not have a romantic partner in the present. When Federico offers an opportunity to explore their connection again, Salvador rejects him – not from lack of desire, as Federico comments that he can feel Salvador's arousal – but most likely from fear that his physical limitations will keep him from enjoying a sexual experience with Federico. For all of Salvador's physical disabilities, sexual virility is not one of them, even though loss of sexual vigor is one of the "Western cultural fears about aging and sexuality" (Wentzell 70). Perhaps it is telling that Almodóvar allows his cinematic alter ego to exhibit physical but not sexual vulnerability, or decline, carefully measuring the extent to which audiences may consume representations of his frailty.

Federico is a complicated figure in Salvador's life, revealing the interconnected nature between his anxieties about his physical disabilities and his queerness while still serving as a beacon of creative potential. The ex-lovers' names reference two Spanish icons of creativity, the painter Salvador Dalí and the writer Federico García Lorca, "en un guiño emocionado a ese espacio de creación, juventud y amor imposible" ("in an emotional gesture to that space of creation, youth, and impossible love"; García Catalán and Rodríguez Serrano 107). Salvador and Federico's relationship is marked by both consumption of drugs and creative production, demonstrated in "Adicción" (Addiction), the monologue Salvador wrote about their relationship, which is also a love letter from Salvador to the cinema, as he describes the impact going to the cinema had on him during his childhood. Salvador ultimately sets aside romance to focus on his other love, filmmaking, which will lead him to achieve greater societal acclaim.

Revisiting childhood memories for his film, particularly those featuring his mother, reveals Salvador's sexual orientation as a site of emotional pain. Their relationship is marked by both love and misunderstanding. Queerness or "otherness" is an underlying current of Salvador's childhood, rarely addressed directly. As a child, Salvador's sexuality is first awakened when he sees the naked, desirable male body of Eduardo, a young man who is painting Salvador's family home. As Eduardo disrobes to wash himself in plain view of Salvador, queer desire combined with too much sun exposure causes Salvador to faint. Just as his physical limitations will later play a role in his rejection of Federico, Salvador's body shuts down at the onset of desire. When Salvador's mother returns home to find him in bed, she accuses Eduardo of not watching him closely enough. Although it is uncertain whether Salvador's mother understands the emotional causes for Salvador's body's physical response, Salvador's earliest memory of queer desire is linked to his mother's anger. When both Salvador and his mother are older, she tells him that he has not been a good son, to which he responds, "Te he fallado simplemente por ser como soy" ("I have failed you simply by being how I am"). Neither of them directly refer to his queerness, but his sexuality is part of the otherness that has caused a rift in his relationship with his mother. The connection between Salvador's queerness and the alienation he feels from his mother is visually evoked as the camera traces a long scar running up Salvador's back as he floats in the pool at the beginning of *Pain and Glory*. In the next shot, Salvador is a young boy sitting on his mother's back as she does laundry in the river. The presence of water in both scenes, and even Salvador's mother's insistence that he stand in the water instead of sitting on her back due to the pain he is causing her, establishes a connection between physical and emotional pain in Salvador's life, his main psychic trauma the relationship with his mother and the ways in which she has rejected his otherness. The film Salvador writes and directs serves as a method to work through the painful aspects of his relationship with his mother, allowing him to rewrite their relationship.

In *Pain and Glory*, the relationship between ageing, disability, and queerness is convoluted; Salvador is plagued by an expansive list of physical and emotional pains connected to the ways in which society has marginalized him because of these identity categories. Many of Salvador's health concerns, however, are not related to his age, but audiences are expected to conflate Salvador's long-term health concerns as problematic by-products of ageing. This, as Chivers and others have noted, is because Western society interprets even the appearance of age as disability. "By this logic, healthy aging is an imitation of youth and so images that reveal wrinkles suggest ill health. As a result, silvering screen films rely on illness or disability narratives to convey the social burden of growing old" (Chivers 8). While ageing and disability do intersect, Salvador's body first fails him when, as a young boy, his desire for Eduardo causes him to faint: Salvador has had a lifelong relationship to physical vulnerability. His illnesses may not all be effects of growing older, but they impact how he lives as an ageing person and how he enacts his sexuality.

The portrayal of Salvador as a queer man with disabilities does not engage with a critically disabled position, a concept established by Robert McRuer that "would call attention to the ways in which the disability rights movement and disability studies have resisted the demands of compulsory able-bodiedness and have demanded access to a newly imagined and newly configured public sphere where full participation is not contingent on an able body" (30). Through Salvador, Almodóvar expresses anxieties about continuing a creative, "productive" life while ageing and living with pain and the desire to conform instead of imagining an alternative way of expressing agency as an older individual. In an interview promoting *Pain and Glory*, Almodóvar was asked whether he is afraid this will be his last film, and he responded by reflecting on the physical demands of filmmaking, asserting that he struggled as much with "los dolores de espalda que sentía como el miedo a no poder rodar" ("the back pains I felt as the fear of not being able to film"; Reviriego). Salvador reflects the same sentiment; when his doctor asks him what he is working on, he responds that he is currently unable to work, as filmmaking is a very physical job. *Pain and Glory* narrowly envisions a definition of fulfilling work for older individuals who can successfully control and master their bodies.

Ageing as a Public Persona

Salvador's struggle to rise above signs of ageing is mirrored in the attitude of Banderas, for whom successful ageing has become a significant aspect of his public persona.[7] The image of successful ageing that Banderas sells in his media interviews is part of his public persona, the consumable good that is his stardom. In Western culture, stars who do not want to "be found sexually undesirable, socially irresponsible and culturally invisible" must look healthy, which is "increasingly about being youthful" (Hurd Clarke and Bennett 134). In Banderas' interviews, he shapes his stardom into an easily digestible package, presenting a narrative of overcoming illness, reinventing oneself, and staying active as the only ways to age well. Deborah Chambers explains that celebrities create two versions of themselves for public consumption, both linked to their physical bodies. Fans are presented with both "a contrived image of the celebrity as 'personality' [that] is presented in the popular media" and the "'real person' behind the projected self [that] is, paradoxically, constructed for public consumption" (Chambers 163). In both the public personality and "real" self, audiences are accustomed to seeing flawless bodies. Stars may hide their illnesses or disabilities, as they detract from the fantasy of fame constructed through photos, interviews, and endorsements.

Older stars help shape our cultural construction of ageing through the topics they address in interviews and the products they choose to endorse. Like many actors, Banderas has his own line of cologne and perfume, in addition to his association with the high-end clothing retailer Marks & Spencer. In contrast to these elegant endorsements, Banderas voiced the Nasonex bee, representing a product that is not particularly sexy or youthful. Perhaps a questionable choice, Banderas did not attach his face to the product, just his voice, showing the overall care he has taken to maintain his public persona as an attractive consumable product (neither old nor ill). The film roles that stars accept are crucial in how they present themselves as products, but endorsements and interviews are other ways of "making themselves into commodities; they are both labour and the thing that labour produces. They do not produce themselves alone" (Dyer 5). Hollywood and Western society contribute to the packaging of stardom. While ageing male stars have generally had more longevity as consumable goods than their female counterparts, even male stars like Banderas must be cautious not to present themselves as old or ill.

Banderas' continued appeal to audiences is surely connected to his "successful" navigation of the ageing process. Speaking with NPR, Banderas discussed the heart attack he experienced in his mid-fifties, saying,

> We are all conscious that we are going to die since we, you know, can use our reason in our brain. But when you see it very close, when you see the face of death very close to you, it change [sic] completely the meaning of your life. The priorities order change completely.
>
> (Inskeep)

Banderas' recovery from his heart attack and his ability to continue acting position him as someone, like Salvador, who challenges the physical limitations of his ageing body. Almodóvar has stated that he chose Banderas for the role of Salvador because of his brush with mortality, "porque el actor también ha lidiado con problemas de salud y porque quería que el personaje fuera más guapo que él" ("because the actor has also dealt with health problems and because he wanted the character to be more handsome than him"; Solórzano 69). Almodóvar thus values Banderas' struggle with (and ultimate conquest of) health issues, as well as his ability to make ageing appear sexy and strong to audiences. Almodóvar and Banderas are not alone in their investment in the narrative of successful ageing. Banderas' interview with *Zoomer* reveals the pervasiveness of the social desire to promote successful ageing. Beginning with a question about his heart attack, the interviewer goes on to discuss Banderas' work, ending with the question, "What advice can you offer for staying fit and healthy and active as you age?" (Crisolago). Banderas offers a standard response, urging readers to follow their doctors' recommendations, take aspirin, and limit their alcohol consumption. Although his advice offers no revolutionary insights, Banderas' response is a telling affirmation that older individuals must fight any signs of physical or mental ageing to be considered worthy and productive members of society instead of a burden for younger generations.

Creativity, Productivity, and Successful Ageing

Almodóvar's casting of Banderas contributes to the film's emphasis on the narrative of successful ageing, revealing the correlation between Salvador's and Almodóvar's views on ageing and artistic production – or more particularly, their anxious use of filmmaking to remain visible as contributing members of society. Salvador finds a path to successful ageing by overcoming physical and emotional pain to turn his memories into a creative product that can in turn be consumed by audiences who will validate Salvador's self-worth. Various individuals in Salvador's life reaffirm the redemptive nature of creativity, encouraging him to resume his artistic pursuits. His assistant, Mercedes, feels that he has "demasiado tiempo libre para pensar en [sus] dolencias" ("too much free time to think about his ailments"), and his doctor affirms that it would do him good to stay busy. Other artistic characters in the film highlight the importance of creativity in their own lives, including Alberto, who begs Salvador for permission to turn the "Addiction" script into a performance. Zulema, an actress with whom Salvador has worked in the past, expresses surprise that Salvador is no longer working, proclaiming that "Sin rodar, mi vida carece de sentido" (Without filming, my life lacks meaning"). The importance these characters place on creative work reveals filmmaking and living in the spotlight to be a form of addiction; Salvador has replaced heroin with his creative work. Almodóvar admits that his relationship with film is that of an addict, saying,

> I rely on it, it's an addiction, the need to tell stories. If anything, my relationship with film has become more tense, more of a problem, because there is always that question: When will my time be up? Will this be the last film I make?
>
> (Brooks)

Even though *Pain and Glory* has established the creative production of films as an ideal instance of successful ageing, Almodóvar himself seems to be acutely aware of the precarious social position dictated for him by such narratives, which can only be maintained so long as he and his characters control the physical manifestations of ageing.

Salvador is saved, not by embracing his queer identity and his former lover Federico but through the creative (and commercial) work of filmmaking and the cinema. *Pain and Glory* has been described as "the story of how Salvador (a name that means saviour in Spanish) is literally saved from himself, returning to writing and filmmaking at the end of *Dolor y gloria* to make a new film" (Sánchez-Arce 294). The film's final scene returns to Salvador's childhood. As he and his mother sleep in Paterna's train station during their journey to their new home, the camera zooms out to reveal one worker holding a boom microphone and another worker with a clapperboard, confirming that the audience is viewing a film set, not Salvador's memories. Only at the end of the film do viewers realize that what they believed to be flashbacks to Salvador's childhood are actually scenes with actors from Salvador's latest movie, *El primer deseo* (First Desire).[8] While audiences thought they were accompanying Salvador on his journey to defeat his physical limitations and age successfully throughout *Pain and Glory*, they realize that Salvador's struggles had already been resolved by the time they viewed the film. Mise en abyme works here to distance Salvador from the narrative of ageing as decline, presenting audiences with exactly the vision of male ageing that Almodóvar wishes them to consume. While "objects, pictures, and wounded childhoods are important clues to Almodóvar's self-presentation, . . . the core of identity in Almodóvar is often expressed specifically in terms of films" (Mira 93). Through his filmmaking, Salvador once again engages with society and transforms into a productive member of society, denying his age in order to continue producing cultural products of worth.

As the film's title suggests, those aspects of life that bring joy and glory will most likely also be intertwined with pain. Immediately before entering the operating room for a surgery to correct his Forestier's syndrome, Salvador receives an image of a painting of himself as a boy that Eduardo made for him many years ago. He will later find and purchase the actual painting in a gallery. Although the painting is simple, its meaning is multifaceted for Salvador. First, it is a memory of the day of his sexual awakening. It is also a work of art, a joyful expression of the creativity that Salvador prizes and hopes to unleash in his own life again. Finally, it is a reminder of his past, of the passage of time, and the distinct temporal location that Salvador now occupies. The return of the painting as Salvador is receiving medical help for his physical pains foreshadows the return of his creativity and productivity. Although Salvador cannot deny his ageing, he recognizes his ability to create has not been lost to him. Confronting his ageing body has led Salvador to consider "the issue of creativity and its relationship to the life course: does old age bring a new way of thinking? If so, is its effect positive (achievement) or negative (decline)?" (Wallace 395). Through childhood memories, Salvador finds a way to maintain his creativity, although he has not adapted to reflect on the ageing life stage he inhabits.

Conclusion

Pain and Glory reveals the masculine anxieties about ageing shared by director Pedro Almodóvar, actor Antonio Banderas, and the character of Salvador. Instead of embracing the potential to celebrate the queer, disabled aspects of Salvador's character by examining alternative forms of growing older however, the film endeavours to minimize outward signs of ageing in order to position Salvador within the productive mould of successful ageing. Fears of ageing out of relevance propel Salvador back into the director's chair. By overcoming physical and emotional pain and refusing a narrative of ageing as decline, Salvador accesses his creativity again. The film remains firmly planted in the Western binary of ageing that views the only alternative to successful ageing as a narrative of decline and death. Salvador's ageing masculinity is defined by productivity, as well as the creation of goods and stardom that will be consumed by others. Despite the many legitimate anxieties Salvador might have about ageing – physical pain, unresolved relationship issues with his mother, romantic relationships – these concerns are set aside so that Salvador might succeed by the masculine requirements of ageing successfully. Almodóvar's anxiety about ageing is evident in *Pain and Glory*, as well as in his interview with AARP, where he shares, "I'm producing things every day and I don't have a positive view of getting old [and slowing down]. So, I'm trying [to keep active]. Just making this movie helps me feel much more comfortable with the passing of time" (Hoyt). Viewers of *Pain and Glory* absorb Almodóvar's anxious message about growing older. While the film is to be celebrated in bringing a queer, disabled representation of ageing to the silver screen and demonstrates the powerful potential of creativity, Salvador is a character who struggles against being perceived as old or ill, rather than critically investigating and rejecting negative stereotypes of male ageing in the early 21st century.

Notes

1 In her article "El Atragantamiento en el cine de Pedro Almodóvar: Análisis de *Dolor y gloria*" (2021), Eva Hernández Martínez analyses the ratio of flashbacks to present time in *Pain and Glory*, finding that flashbacks occupy 36 minutes of the 113-minute film (Hernández Martínez 250).
2 *La Movida*, a countercultural movement in Spain arising after dictator Francisco Franco's death in 1975 and developing throughout the 1980s, was a youth-led reaction to the dictatorship's harsh limitations. *La Movida*, "a period marked by collective affects of freedom and creativity, in which culture played a central role" (Fernández de Alba 119), explored nightlife and drug culture, as well as increasing freedom of sexual expression.
3 Linn Sandberg, in her 2013 article "Affirmative Old Age – The Aging Body and Feminist Theories on Difference," challenges the dichotomy of ageing as decline versus successful ageing through the addition of affirmative old age, which suggests that physical changes brought on by older age should neither be ignored nor necessarily construed negatively.

4 While some might question Banderas' presence as an ideal model of heteronormative hegemonic masculinity in Almodóvar's films, where he has often played gay men, Banderas usually embodies "macho" (Perriam 57) gay characters who are strong, handsome, and imbued with masculine authority.
5 Numerous scholars have established autobiographical connections between Almodóvar's work and his life. Among extensive scholarship on the topic, see Alberto Mira's chapter in *A Companion to Pedro Almodóvar* (2013), Ana María Sánchez-Arce's *The Cinema of Pedro Almodóvar* (2020), and Paul Julian Smith's *Desire Unlimited: The Cinema of Pedro Almodóvar* (2000).
6 Both queerness and autobiographical elements are ubiquitous in Almodóvar's work. Some critics have labelled Almodóvar as gay, and he "is known (outside of Spain at least) as a gay-identified man, who appeals to the queer-coded registers of kitsch and camp; yet his filmic career can be read as a progressive disavowal of homosexuality, whether masculine or feminine" (Smith 2). Almodóvar himself has never spoken directly and definitively about his sexuality, a vagueness that reflects the often-ambiguous message about queerness in his films, which are staunchly loved and defended by some queer and feminist theorists and harshly criticized for their representation of queer characters by other critics.
7 Antonio Banderas and Pedro Almodóvar have a long working relationship. Their first collaboration was *Labyrinth of Passions* (1982), where Banderas played a gay terrorist with an exceptional sense of smell. Banderas had roles in five of Almodóvar's first eight films (D'Lugo and Vernon 2). *Pain and Glory* is the first film the two men have worked on together since *I'm So Excited* in 2013.
8 The film's title is an autobiographical nod to Almodóvar's production company, called El Deseo (Desire), which he established with his brother Agustín in 1986.

Works Cited

Almodóvar, Pedro. "Coda: *Volver* A Filmmaker's Diary." *All about Almodóvar: A Passion for Cinema*. Eds. Brad Epps and Despina Kakoudaki. U Minnesota P, 2009. 446–463.

Brooks, Xan. "Pedro Almodóvar: 'I Can No Longer Hide.'" *The Guardian*, 11 Aug. 2019.

Chambers, Deborah. "Sexist Ageing Consumerism and Emergent Modes of Resistance." *Aging, Performance, and Stardom: Doing Age on the Stage of Consumerist Culture*. Eds. Aagje Swinnen and John A. Stotesbury. LIT, 2012. 161–176.

Chivers, Sally. "'Move! You're in the Way': Disability and Age Meet on Screen." *Revue Canadienne d'Études cinématographiques/Canadian Journal of Film Studies*, 17.1 (2008): 30–43.

Chivers, Sally. *The Silvering Screen: Old Age and Disability in Cinema*. U Toronto P, 2011.

Crisolago, Mike. "Antonio Banderas Turns 60: Talking Aging and the Heart Attack That Changed His Life." *Zoomer*, 10 Aug. 2020.

D'Lugo, Marvin, and Kathleen M. Vernon. "Introduction: The Skin He Lives In." *A Companion to Pedro Almodóvar*. Eds. Marvin D'Lugo and Kathleen M. Vernon. John Wiley & Sons, 2013. 1–18.

Dolan, Josephine Mary. *Contemporary Cinema and 'Old Age': Gender and the Silvering of Stardom*. Palgrave Macmillan, 2017.

Dolor y gloria. Directed by Pedro Almodóvar, El Deseo, 2019.

Dyer, Richard. *Heavenly Bodies: Film Stars and Society*. St. Martin's Press, 1986.

Fairclough-Isaacs, Kirsty. "Celebrity Culture and Ageing." *Routledge Handbook of Cultural Gerontology*. Eds. Julia Twigg and Wendy Martin. Routledge, 2015. 361–368.
Fernández de Alba, Francisco. *Sex, Drugs, and Fashion in 1970s Madrid*. U Toronto P, 2020.
García Catalán, Shaila, and Aarón Rodríguez Serrano. "La pantalla fetiche: deseo y sublimación en *Dolor y gloria* de Pedro Almodóvar." *Journal of Spanish Cultural Studies* 22.1 (2021): 95–110.
Gullette, Margaret Morganroth. *Declining to Decline: Cultural Combat and the Politics of the Midlife*. UP Virginia, 1997.
Gullette, Margaret Morganroth. *Aged by Culture*. U Chicago P, 2004.
Hernández Martínez, Eva. "El Atragantamiento en el cine de Pedro Almodóvar. Análisis de *Dolor y gloria*." *Miguel Hernández Communication Journal* 12.1 (2021): 243–266.
Hoyt, Anne. "Pedro Almodóvar on Aging, Mom and 'Pain and Glory.'" *AARP*, 4 Oct. 2019.
Huici Módenes, Adrián. "The Liquid Man: Between the Old and the Postmodern." *All About Almodóvar's Men*. Ed. Juan Rey, translated by Francisco Uceda. Peter Lang, 2017. 101–112.
Hurd Clarke, Laura, and Erica V. Bennett. "Gender, Ageing and Appearance." *Routledge Handbook of Cultural Gerontology*. Eds. Julia Twigg and Wendy Martin. Routledge, 2015. 133–140.
Inskeep, Steve. "Antonio Banderas on 'Pain and Glory.' Working With Pedro Almodóvar." *NPR*, 4 Feb. 2020.
Kimmel, Michael S. "Masculinity as Homophobia: Fear, Shame, and Silence in the Construction of Gender Identity." *Theorizing Masculinities: Research on Men and Masculinities*. Eds. Harry Brod and Michael Kaufman. Sage Publications, 1994. 119–141.
López-Font, Lorena, Carlos Fanjul-Peyró, and Cristina González-Oñate. "Queer Masculinities: Evolution of Homosexual, Transsexual, and *Queer* Characters." *All About Almodóvar's Men*. Ed. Juan Rey, translated by Francisco Uceda. Peter Lang, 2017. 49–58.
Martinson, Marty, and Clara Berridge. "Successful Aging and Its Discontents: A Systematic Review of the Social Gerontology Literature." *The Gerontologist* 55.1 (2015): 58–69.
McRuer, Robert. *Crip Theory: Cultural Signs of Queerness and Disability*. New York UP, 2006.
Mira, Alberto. "A Life, Imagined and Otherwise: The Limits and Uses of Autobiography in Almodóvar's Films." *A Companion to Pedro Almodóvar*. Eds. Marvin D'Lugo and Kathleen M. Vernon. John Wiley & Sons, 2013. 88–104.
Perriam, Chris. *Stars and Masculinities in Spanish Cinema: From Banderas to Bardem*. Oxford UP, 2003.
Reviriego, Carlos. "Entrevista a Pedro Almodóvar." *El Cultural*, 08 Mar. 2019.
Rowe, John W., and Robert L. Kahn. "Successful Aging 2.0: Conceptual Expansions for the 21st Century." *The Journals of Gerontology: Series B*, 70.4 (2015): 593–596.
Sánchez-Arce, Ana María. *The Cinema of Pedro Almodóvar*. Manchester UP, 2020.
Sandberg, Linn. "Affirmative Old Age – The Ageing Body and Feminist Theories on Difference." *International Journal of Ageing and Later Life*. 8.1 (2013): 11–40.

Sandberg, Linn. "Towards a Happy Ending? Positive Ageing, Heteronormativity and Un/happy Intimacies." *Lambda Nordica* 20.4 (2015): 19–44.

Sanderson, John D. "To the Health of the Author: Art Direction in *Los abrazos rotos*." *A Companion to Pedro Almodóvar*. Eds. Marvin D'Lugo and Kathleen M. Vernon. John Wiley & Sons, 2013. 471–494.

Smith, Paul Julian. *Desire Unlimited: The Cinema of Pedro Almodóvar*. 2nd ed. Verso, 2000.

Solórzano, Fernanda. "*Dolor y gloria*: todo sobre Almodóvar," *Letras libres*, July 2019.

Twigg, Julia. "The Body, Gender, and Age: Feminist Insights in Social Gerontology." *Journal of Aging Studies* 18.1 (2004): 59–73.

Wallace, Diana. "Literary Portrayals of Ageing." *An Introduction to Gerontology*. Ed. Ian Stuart-Hamilton. Cambridge UP, 2011. 389–415.

Wentzell, Emily. "Erectile Dysfunction as Successful Aging in Mexico." *Successful Aging as a Contemporary Obsession: Global Perspectives*. Ed. Sarah Lamb. Rutgers UP, 2017. 68–84.

Woodward, Kathleen. "Performing Age, Performing Gender." *NWSA Journal* 18.1 (2006): 162–189.

14 Ageing Myths and Dark Romanticism in Albert Serra's *Story of My Death* (2013)

Esther Zaplana

Introduction

Catalonian film director Albert Serra (b. 1975) has become known for a highly personal *auteur* filming style, in which the audience is invited to an extraordinary and new visual narrative experience. Serra's innovative approach to film genre and storytelling strives to avoid clichés and goes against the grain of the planned script and calculated scenes that characterize cinematic conventions. The director has often explained that his films do not contain a central idea as a starting point in the filmic process, nor does he have a pre-conceived imprint of the film's end result. In this sense, Serra's films may be seen as embracing a narrative thread made up of a succession of poetic and often bewildering visual images that challenge the viewer's expectations of the film's diegetic world. Serra's camera work is laden with lyricism and a scenography imbued with allegorical elements that construct a highly personal vision which, nonetheless, bears inspiration from earlier auteur filmmaking, such as Carlos Saura, Jesús Franco, Andy Warhol, Peter Greenaway, Straub Huillet, as well as the Kubrickian use of lenses to shoot scenes only by candlelight.[1]

Emerging from a literary and artistic background, Serra has frequently opted for stories that involve a historical male figure in late life; a protagonist in his twilight years whose story is singularly re-imagined, as is the case of Giacomo Casanova in *Història de la meva mort* (Story of My Death; 2013) and the French Sun King in *La mort de Louis XIV* (The Death of Louis the 14th; 2016). We also find portrayals of older male characters in Serra's take on literary and cultural myths, such as Don Quixote in *Honor de Cavelleria* (Quixotic; 2006) and the biblical three kings in *El cant dels ocells* (Birdsong; 2008). These anti-period films refract their source texts and let contemporary thought and action represent the era rather than offering a truthful recreation of past times. Serra's films engage with the *avant-garde* to tell stories of the late stages and events in the lives of their iconic male figures and their experience as ageing individuals. In this sense, his male protagonists can be said to re-construct the experience of the male myths in late life, whilst, at the same time, their stories deconstruct the masculine

DOI: 10.4324/9781003306146-14

heroism of these legends to create allegories of ageing that resonate in our contemporary world. With the aim of investigating more closely the theme of ageing and masculinity in Serra's portrayals of male myths, this chapter focuses on one of Serra's signature works, *Story of My Death*.

Story of My Death fictionally re-creates the final journey of the eccentric and infamous figure of Giacomo Casanova (1725–1798), Italian adventurer, author and legendary lover, and is depicted by Serra as a declining, yet sexually undeterred, decadent older man determined to live to the full until his death. Casanova's life is well known and has been amply documented in his 12-volume memoirs *Histoire de ma vie* (Story of My Life), which describe his life and adventures from birth to 1774. The autobiographical work was written during the final years of Casanova's life before his death in Dux, Bohemia (Czech Republic). While Serra's film plays on the title of Casanova's memoirs, it presents a story of ageing and demise, rather than the captivating account of his adventurous life. The sense of an ending in *Story of My Death* is conveyed through protracted camera work, ominous atmospheres and the symbolism of the dark static "painting-like" quality that comes to life in the still frames. Moreover, the sense of impending death is foregrounded in the second half of the film when another legendary older man, Dracula, makes his appearance and fully engages in the plot's economies of desire.

The aim of my analysis is to examine the images of ageing and masculinity as embodied by the main characters in the film's fictional world: Casanova and Dracula. It also aims to assess the ways in which Serra's film plays with genre, fiction and reality in demystifying these iconic male characters and subverts, through what I call "dark aesthetics," the gender and cultural meanings attached to the characters' fictional personae. By "dark aesthetics" I specifically refer to a tradition in Spanish artistic expression, mainly on canvas, of *Pinturas Negras* (Black Paintings), which spans from Goya's terrifying depictions of dark ghostly characters in his *Pinturas Negras* series to the grisly, sombre visions embodied in the *España Negra* paintings at the end of the 19th century.[2] Spanish black paintings at the *fin-de-siècle* specifically connect with the *avant-garde* through Expressionism, a style whose traces can also be felt in *Story of My Death*. For example, Serra's camera work tends to focus on framing photographic detail and favours visual metonymy and synecdoche. His characters are also stripped of psychic complexity and reduced to their stereotyped essence, to their instinctual urges and desires, which aim to elicit a subjective and emotional response from the spectator. The idea of invoking the emotions through snapshots befits the Dark Romantic atmosphere re-created in Serra's anti-period film from a postmodern perspective.[3]

The older Casanova depicted in Serra's film shows a declining sexuality that does not hinder him from dissipation and forming romantic liaisons with younger women like Delfina in his Swiss mansion, as well as a female maid in the remote countryside. Despite fading prowess and deteriorating health, Casanova clings to his instincts and sexual feats and his life as a libertine. He thus holds in old age to a conception of ideal masculinity firmly rooted in patriarchy. Decadence of values and boldness prevails when Dracula enters the scene and partakes of the debauchery and masculine entitlement directed initially towards the female peasant maids in the story. While the unlikely encounter of seemingly opposing male iconic figures hinders verisimilitude within the filmic narrative, the pairing serves as pretext to re-enact a vision of the "Gothic Sublime," whose subversive power functions as a veiled critique of hegemonic conceptions of masculinity and ageing – which in turn echo down the ages. *Story of My Death* involves conceptual complexity, intricate visuals and "ugly" *avant-garde* dark aesthetics in the form of discomforting visions of senility and eschatological symbolism. The combination of these elements implicates the ageing body, masculinity, the abject, and artistic and literary intertextuality.

In readings of "successful ageing," the ageing declining body is often denied, an omission that circumvents the most distressing aspects of old age with a view to presenting senectitude in positive terms. *Avant-garde* aesthetics on the other hand dabble with radical forms of artistic expression, as well as the experimental, and do not follow a logic of exclusions. Despite the lingering virility pervading Serra's older characters, the film does not portray old age in a positive light. On the contrary, the film invites the viewer to reflect upon the implausible events in the story to gain insights into old age and masculinity, as well as the motivations for the desperate sexual feats and the experiences recounted in the film. Thus, although my approach to ageing male characters here will not pursue sociological scrutiny, it should not deter the reader from seeing Serra's aesthetically motivated portrayals of an ageing Casanova and Dracula as "ugly" renderings that critique gender conventionalism and invite ideological positioning. In other words, the experimental ways in which these two older male characters are portrayed in *Story of My Death* would be symptomatic of an *avant-garde* postmodern style that both "performs" and reifies hegemonic cultural ideas around ageing and gender. Yet the veiled purpose is to demythologize the icons and subvert hegemonic thinking, an aspect contained in the contemporary viewpoint attached to anti-period filmmaking.

Time as a Metaphor for Ageing and Death

In *Story of My Death* the spectator is faced with a cinematic experience that runs contrary to the classical utilization of time in film narrative, where efficient editing is maximized to eliminate unproductive time. Instead of focusing on the viewer's attention to the action, Serra's camera is allowed to either remain static or run through long scenes without interruptions. This slowness makes the viewer await in expectation for the narrative to move forward. Serra shares many of the premises of arthouse experimental filmmaking and has indeed emphasized the significance of aesthetics and text style in a modernist fashion. Yet, *Story of My Death* is not a documentary, despite its focus on aesthetics and the slowness of motion, both of which are aimed at strengthening the abstract qualities of the content. Serra has explained that he follows a film routine that involves several hours of shooting which is then paid close attention to and edited for the details that have likely escaped the naked eye yet were captured on camera.[4]

In the film's opening prelude, a group of country people gather around a dinner table sharing food and drinks late in the evening. Sitting on benches close to each other under the candlelight, the rustic diners are absorbed in animated conversation and sensual mannerisms whilst indifferent to the camera movements. The prelude creates dead time and sets the tone and rhythm of the film, in which the onlooker will be confronted with moments of dead time, broken occasionally by unexpected changes. The protracted prelude involves the viewer visually in anticipation for such a narrative change. In the film's first scenes, which take place in the sumptuous chambers of an 18th-century mansion, an ageing Casanova (Vicenç Altaió) peers attentively at his own image in a large mirror as if trying to identify the features of the older face reflected on the wall. Clad in pancake makeup Casanova is seen gesticulating as if trying to get his own reflection to look straight into his eyes. This caricatured encounter reminds us of Slavoj Žižek's account of "seeing oneself looking" (*se voir voyant*), which signifies a moment – for the older man – that undoubtedly stands for death (Salecl and Žižek 94). According to Žižek, the gaze "is no longer the elusive blind spot in the field of the visible but is included in this field, [thus] one meets one's own death" (94). The significance of the gaze at the moment Casanova sees his grim facial expressions and meets his own eye in the mirror thus foretells his own ending.

The mirror as explicit Lacanian gesture of identity recognition also marks a symbolic moment for the ageing Casanova, since the trope of the mirror is re-dimensioned to accommodate the sense of identity effacement in old age. In her discussion of the mirror stage and old age, Kathleen Woodward argues that we increasingly separate in old age our sense of real selves from the body. This psychological phenomenon of alienation from our bodies leads to a sense of the self being hidden inside the body and the latter being in opposition to the self (Woodward 62). In Woodward's words: "we can understand the 'horror' of the mirror image of the 'decrepit' body as having been produced as the inverse of the pleasures of the mirror image of the body of Narcissus" (62). This phenomenon of disassociation of self from the body is at work when an ageing Casanova does not seem to recognize his own image in the mirror and then asks his male servant for assurance and opinion regarding his dishevelled look. The feeling of alienation persists when the protagonist ponders on the servant's difficulties in sharing a life with a man like him, a writer who believes that if a writer does not move (through time), he is unable to write. Casanova's sense of self in old age comes with writing and he believes writing comes before the voice.

Story of My Death then takes the spectator on a journey that follows Casanova in senectitude through unspecific time and spaces burdened with symbolic and transcendental meanings: from the civilized order of the mansion where he lives in Switzerland to the untamed wilderness of the Carpathian Mountains. The film's first part takes place in the lavish, yet enclosed, setting of the Swiss chambers, where the characters are figuratively bound to and enclosed. Casanova is at the centre of the action, moving from room to room conversing leisurely with his friends, satiating his appetite and performing his bodily functions. The second part marks an ideological shift towards nature. Casanova and his loyal servant Pompeu embark on a rudimentary trip on horse-drawn cart into a forested area in the countryside, leaving behind the comfort of their interior chambers and embracing a simple existence in a farm cottage. This trip becomes an allegory for life's final journey when everyone will leave behind material possessions and confront a weakening body advocated to merge with the natural world. The film's denouement ends with the bodies of the dead scattered in the wilderness under the wolves' prying eyes.

In the film's second part unproductive or dead time is used more intently. Dracula (Eliseu Huertas) appears on the scene which marks an unexpected change in the story. Still, Dracula's interactions soon also become obscure and lengthy, a tendency occasionally broken by Dracula's own murderous activity. The most poignant moment occurs when Dracula delivers two loud screams in the forest, one after he has bitten Carmen, the first of his female victims, and then at the end of the film when he has achieved his sadistic aims and gained control over the characters' lives. Dracula's screaming saturates the otherwise silent space. Michel Chion, in his analysis of the cinematic voice, conceptualizes the scream not so much in terms of sound quality, but in terms of the "screaming point" and its placement in time. Chion emphasizes the gendered nature of the scream, inasmuch as "the woman's cry is a scream, and the man's cry a shout" (Chion 78). Dracula's masculine shouts (following Chion), have a bestial quality that inundates the land and exhibit the absolute power of the masculine fantasy of the supernatural: they are "phallic cries" that "rip through the fabric of time" and recreate the fantasy of the "auditory absolute" (Chion 77). They disrupts the film's time and overwhelm the listener, who finds it hard to make sense of the strange auditory experience. In this sense, Serra's aesthetics vis-à-vis his handling of time tread the line between auteur filmmaking and art gallery work.[5] Despite the sudden breaks in the narrative flow, the slow-motion quality of the cinematic experience is utilized as a metaphor for ageing, decline, and death, with a view to drawing the attention of the audience towards the details of an irreversible process of destruction. The film's camera work and pacing captures Dracula's deadly presence as well as Casanova's hedonistic and futile use of time in order to provide a sense of an existential ending for the characters.

Masculinities and Older Men's Stereotyping, Dichotomous Representation, and the Logic of *Mimesis*

Western representations of age, films specifically, tend to follow a cultural tradition of stereotypes and unchallenged myths of masculinity, as well as of ageing, that are deeply entrenched in our cultural imagination. Both the male protagonists of *Story of My Death*, Casanova and Dracula, one a historical figure, the other fictional, have become the embodiments of a type of predatory, dangerous masculinity from which society must ward off. Their trajectory and myth status have become inscribed in the collective consciousness and their uncanny association in Serra's film *de facto* dissolves the duality between fiction and reality. This is one of several dichotomies that are re-staged and then challenged in *Story of My Death* by way of employing artifice that can then be read from a postmodern standpoint. Although not new to postmodernism, the strategy of *mimesis* and *mimicry* as theorized by Luce Irigaray can be productively applied for a recuperative reading of Serra's re-utilization of dichotomous thinking imagery and gender stereotyping.

The film is replete with dualities, such as the one between culture and nature, mirrored in the settings of the Swiss chambers versus the open wild landscapes in which the film's two main locations are divided. The symbolic dualism of light and darkness recurs as aesthetic device in connection with life and death, day and night, as well as the duality embedded in the structure of the film's plot. Casanova's departure to the countryside is envisioned as a journey from life to death and the contrast between light and darkness is stylistically reinforced in the farmhouse and its surroundings by way of increasing the scenes shot at night. In Kubrickian fashion, some of these scenes are filmed in almost pitch blackness under a single source of light in a manner similar to *chiaroscuro* painting. The contrast between darkness and light is exemplified in extended shots at night, such as the black sky lightened up by moonlight glow, or the shadowy interior of a room illuminated only by a three lamps candlestick on the room corner.

Light, as the positive term in the hierarchy, is associated with Enlightenment and in turn the dichotomy between Rationalism and Romanticism becomes evident, in so far as the story stages a return to nature where Casanova and his companions unleash their sexual fantasies and emotions amidst a sublimated and menacing natural world. The untamed landscapes and the night become Dracula's natural space where his bewildering vampire activity is carried out: he primarily targets the three farmer's daughters who are often outdoors, although his infectious bite spreads thereafter through the women. Dracula's looks resemble those of a religious figure or a strange sect guru, and his quasi-clerical charms convince first Carmen, and then the other women, to submit and metamorphose into female vampires (there is a nod here to *Dracula*'s three vampire women, often portrayed in films). On his part, an unbridled Casanova is set to finishing up his last leisure moments and experiences the intensity of carnality and hedonism whilst oblivious to the staging of the supernatural and the sentiments of the women's vulnerability. This inauspicious activity occurs within the ordinary and the trivial; hence the filmic *tableaux* depict a romanticized vision of country life (alien to the events) that brings to mind the bucolic settings of 17th-century pastoral literature, only to recreate an anachronistic and dissident version of the Gothic Sublime.

Dracula's Gothicism is firmly rooted in Romanticism whilst Casanova, who had once embraced Rationalism, in particular its criticism of religion, shows his scepticism towards the omnipotence of reason. Early in the film, Casanova casually declares his disagreement with Voltaire with whom he used to share a friendship but ended up drawing apart. Whilst in the Swiss chambers, there is a specific instance of Casanova conversing with a poet friend when he makes reference to the times to come and presages a revolution. The conversation starts with women and Casanova's recalcitrant remarks about women not having independent thinking and needing a man to channel their thoughts. Casanova becomes an example of the contradictions of the masculine subject regarding gender attitudes at a time of profound change, given that he also presages that women will raise in the future to great social impact. He then raises a dead fish as symbol for the chaos of the (French) revolution: "there will be head-rolling"; France is about to fall and he lifts a dead goose that stands for the king, pouring a glass of red wine over the lame carcass. All this symbolism points towards Casanova's readiness to part from Rationalism and embark on a journey of dissidence that his gestures also presage as bloodstained and deadly.

The film's most deliberate re-enactment of dichotomous representation concerns the duality between the masculine and the feminine principles. The feminine, illustrated by the three country women in the story, falls into the trap of the traditional patriarchal stereotype of the consenting woman who is also subjected to the female dualism of the virgin versus *femme fatale* following her vampiric transformation. The feminine from a gender perspective is also associated with the principles of Romanticism and its obsession with the Rights of emotions as a counter strategy to the Rationalistic pursuit of the Rights of man and its assumption of a hegemonic ideal of masculinity. Despite embracing the philosophical and aesthetic principles of Romanticism, male subjects run the risk of sacrificing the privileges of their gendered identity. Indeed, Ellen Brinks has argued that in an attempt to incorporate the emotional and the feminine, Romanticism used "gothic languages and figures" to create a supernatural fantasy that threatens the coherence of the masculine subject (Brinks 12). Brinks questions the dynamics of masculine identity if males are displaced and inhabited by uncanny forces that disrupt male authority and patriarchal culture. Yet she also asserts that an alternative reading exists, wherein the effeminizing forces of the Gothic within the male subject require the feminine to complete the divergences in the narrative (12).

Casanova's (final) journey into the wilderness can be seen as a passage from Rationalism to Romanticism and prefigures also a journey into the unknown and death. By entering the mysterious confines of the forest, the effeminizing effects of the uncanny take hold of Serra's older men to dissolve the ordinary boundaries of masculinity; they will become disinhibited and displaced, yet the dialogue between Casanova and Pompeu, whilst *en route* on the horse-drawn cart, does not indicate that the men have been dispossessed of their authorial subjectivity. Casanova repeats the remark that all women are the same and asks Pompeu whether he is pleased with the dim, half-light of the forest in direct allusion to the dichotomies of light and darkness vis-à-vis gender dualism. The faint light reminds Casanova of women's lingerie, which is read as explicit connection between the forest and female sexuality.

Thus, both male characters exhibit in old age a gender duality expressed in their embracement of Romanticism linked to the feminine narrative of the passions and emotions; yet their masculine narrative is also firmly grounded in the patriarchal logic and its hegemonic gender roles. Significant to this reading is the contradictions embedded in the old men's gender identifications, given that senectitude looms heavily in constructions of prowess and virility attached to ideal masculinity, and thus the older males in the film paradoxically appear both to welcome and resist the effeminizing forces of the Gothic Sublime. This leads the older characters, in particular Casanova and Dracula, to representational *excess* which is in turn deeply connected conceptually with the feminine. Elisabeth Grosz has argued that female corporeality is constructed in terms of *excess*, inasmuch as it is inscribed as "a mode of seepage", as an uncontrollable and "formless flow", a "viscosity" and "a seeping liquid" that lacks self-containment (Grosz 203). Under the spell of Romantic and Gothic masculinity, Casanova and Dracula, respectively, embody the effeminizing effect of lack of self-containment that threatens all order. From the perspective of ideal masculinity, the older character myths strive for a model of masculine perfection that accrues sexual power and privilege, and yet this is also tainted by *excess*. Roland Barthes theorizes that the distance between the model (of perfection) and the copy is part of the human condition and to bridge this distance would mean lying "outside anthropological limits, in supernature, where it joins the other inferior transgression: *more* or *less* [perfection] can be generically placed in the same class, that of *excess*" (Barthes 71). In view of this, both myths stand for a prototypical self-entitled, authoritative masculinity in old age whose closeness to the model renders it *excessive*; hence Casanova and Dracula end up having the same status as that which is outside (the feminine and the monstrous, the instinctual).

Hence the masculine principle is illustrated through the *excesses* of the ageing Casanova and Dracula, both of whom underpin the negative stereotype of the libidinous old man, a notorious characterization of older men whose prototype is socially rejected. The effects of any stereotype of ageing, either positive or negative, can unconsciously reinforce ageism due to the fact that stereotypes remind us of the social constructedness of ageing; even positive stereotyping glosses over the complex, multidimensional heterogeneity among "older adults" (Dionigi 1). Yet, Casanova's and Dracula's ageing personae in the film and their stereotypical enactments of masculinity are mediated by Serra's subtle utilization of clichés and parody in his re-staging of Dark Romanticism and the Gothic Sublime. Both aesthetic tendencies function in the film as contemporary postmodern imitations of the genre. A parody of the biblical episode of Eve being lured by the snake in Genesis is re-worked in a pastoral setting under a tree. One of the three maids, Clara, trifles with a small snake which prompts Casanova to reference the story in the Old Testament. He sardonically observes that men lose their authority when "a stick turns into a snake." He then echoes the famous gendered biblical maxim addressed to women: "you'll crawl on your belly all the days of your life." Yet Casanova's statement sounds humdrum and hollow, lacking either emotion or conviction, and thus his assertion is quickly followed by a remark about the woman's response to the maxim, which is to stick out her tongue. We can see how this episode is intended as burlesque, not only deriding the biblical tale, but also thwarting both the patriarchal masculine and feminine paradigms through trivial and seemingly inconsequential dialogue.

If we look at the clichés of ageing and gender from one of Irigaray's model strategies, the realm of parody and *mimetic* logic, it is possible to contest dichotomies and dominant cultural representations. The parodic displays of old age and masculinity become copies that mirror the ideal original, that is, they mirror a believable showdown of old age, sexual prowess and masculine power. Yet since the dichotomous displays in Serra's film are merely *mimetic*, they just mirror an ideal "masculine attitude" within a dominant culture. Irigaray's concept of *mimesis*, which she develops for traditional models of femininity, is understood as strategy to thwart the biases of entrenched cultural representation. Irigaray believes that women have been dedicated to replicating sameness within a masculine culture of the Same and that "any move toward the other means turning back to the attraction of one's own image" (Irigaray 207). Reproducing inauthentic copies of dominant culture, as if a "living mirror," can thus provide a way to disrupt the seamlessness of its narrative.

We can see here how the *mimetic logic* can be useful to read Casanova's parodic displays of *excess*: they become replicas of ageing masculinities that exhibit an inert, "frozen," quality as passive support of representation. In other words, the film's stereotypical portrayals of masculinity and old age recast Serra's myths as copycats within a postmodern vision of dissident representation. A vision illustrated by the artificiality of the Dark Romantic figurations of the genre. Both Casanova and Dracula add nothing new to what they reflect, they are just projected images that, like a screen, stay still in performative mode – they become less substantial, caricatured versions of the same (Jones 60). Crucial to the logic of *mimetic* repetition is that the projections are not exact copies of the original ideal. In this way, the film's parody attached to the ageing male myths and the aesthetically motivated *mimetic* repetition can be seen as "unauthentic" copies that have the potential to disrupt dominant representations of old men and masculinity.

The Transgressions of Dark Aesthetics: Intertextuality, Para-visuals, and the Performative

To translate into cinema the idea of the "performative," Serra deploys his own technical vision in the process of accomplishing the film's extensive shots. As discussed, he also makes use of artistic artifice. These two dimensions are executed both in terms of the creation of visual effects that are purely artistic, as well as in terms of Serra's interest in allowing the actors the possibility to alter the script and contribute their own dialogue.[6] On the latter point, the actors' freedom to use their own inspiration is incorporated in the editing, given that their spontaneity strengthens the credibility of the character's performance. As for the dimension of the film's visual effects, *Story of My Death* creates mesmerizing scenes of pictorial quality whose artistic intertextuality reminds the viewer of a *tableau vivant*. The characters in the *tableau* construct a rich "performative" vista that utilizes artifice to conjure up the ominous and disturbing aura of the film's complex universe.

Many scenes in *Story of My Death* are framed intertextually as static *tableaux* or vignettes parallel to artworks, examples of which can be found in Casanova's gatherings around the dinner table. The diners meet under the candlelight where food and repetitive eating become metaphors for abundance and insatiable desire. Darkness reminds the viewer of Baroque still life paintings drawn from the European tradition, such as Nicola Turnier (*Feast* c. 1624), Gerrit van Hornthorst (*The Prodigal Son*, 1623) and Velázquez (*Peasants at a Table* [El Almuerzo], c. 1620). Another recurrent canvas motif in Serra's film refers to carcass painting, an imagery frequently invoked in the film's shots. Imprints of animal carcasses, in particular the ones displaying the carcass stretched and hung on wood frames, are not only signs of the grotesque and dark aesthetics, but they are also harbingers of death and become allegories for the cycles of life and death, the destruction and consumption of the flesh, regeneration and annihilation. Amongst some of these pictorial references there is Jacob Leyssens (*Carcass in a Kitchen*, c. 1690) and the famous Rembrandt's *Carcass of Beef* (1657), an image that had also emerged in Carlos Saura's seminal biopic film *Goya in Bordeaux* (1999) when the opening prelude displays a tell-tale shot of a stretched beef carcass gradually merging in a close up with the face of a recumbent Goya, ailed by advanced age. The beef carcass is intertextually used in *Story of My Death* in a long cinematic shot from evening to night when the villagers gather outside to dissect the carcass, which is then hanged on wooden posts. The carcass still shows muscular contractions when Casanova compares it with a Minotaur, an allegory that he believes brings to an end all allegories: represented as a man with a bull's head, the Minotaur is a symbol for fear of death and an allegory of masculine power. The severed animal's head is shown in separate shot where it lies festering on the ground, an image that suggests masculine disintegration and death.

Goya's Black Painting series additionally provide a well of inspiration for the Gothicism and the darkest romantic aesthetics that his paintings inaugurate. Serra's still frame of the peasants' static poses with beef carcass at night around a fire – as the only source of light – creates a Goyaesque *tableau* already engraved in the viewers' imagination (1:33:13). Goya's etching *The Sleep of Reason Produces Monsters* (c. 1799) contains a double meaning germane to Casanova's views on Rationalism in the film: when reason allows the imagination to roam free, it produces impossible evils and monsters. Yet, when it allies with fantasy, it can give birth to sensational artistic creation. Elisabeth Bronfen has pointed out the contradictions within the spirit of rationality, which was meant to eradicate superstition and cast reason as the basis of social behaviour, however, it became "the germ of psychic unease" (Bronfen 139). Bronfen argues that the spirit of the era can be best summarized as, "The more we seek enlightenment, the more alienating our world becomes: the more forcibly superstition is banned to the realm of the eternal night, the more persistently this repressed material returns in configurations of the uncanny" (Terry Castle qtd. in Bronfen 139). The film's Gothic references are thus understood as rejection of Rationalism at end of the 18th century when the blind belief in reason to explain the world starts to fracture. At this juncture, reason gives way to scepticism and a philosophy of Romanticism that contains a dark dimension of evils and monsters, Dracula amongst them, as epitome of the irrational.

The pictorial and filmic intertextuality displayed in the film's *tableaux* or vignettes function as para-visual elements which can be understood as metaphors for realistic renderings. In other words, the re-utilization of the emblematic canvases helps visualize the concepts created in the film's universe. Thus, para-visuals offer intertextual renderings of the film's narrative: they make evident the film's abstractions through performative glimpses into the intertextuality of a screenshot. Yet, the realistic renderings do not depict a true reality and respond rather to what Žižek terms "a 'flatness' of depicted reality" (Žižek 114). This refers to the lack of depth in spaces not framed along perspective lines, the pictorial vignettes in this case, as well as characters who have been stripped of depth and appear flat, displaying an "artificial quality that clings to the depicted individual" (Žižek 114).

As intimated, interspersed screenshots of dead animals such as hares, birds and fish common to still-life painting become symbols of danger, warnings of death and possible regeneration. The horror film genre is intertextually referenced in numerous photographic scenes of night shadows, as well as Dracula lurking outside the cottage window ogling a maid prior to attacking. Although the maid here is dozing off in a rocking chair, the shot replicates the classic scene of the vampire coming through the window to draw Lucy's blood. Para-visuals require the active participation of the viewer to conceptually interpret the images he is confronted with. Thus, Serra's experimental vision in depicting ageing men and masculinity in *Story of My Death* involves a culturally informed interpretation of the aesthetic mediations implicated in its para-visuals.

Towards the end of the story, the film's visuals focus on scenes of vampiric bodies and corpses lying around after vampires have defiled them. A snapshot of a weeping Casanova gathering manure inside a barn is followed by a close up of a bowl of gold, an allusion to Casanova's enthusiasm for alchemy. Casanova's act comes full circle from a scene earlier in the film when he is shown in the process of defecating in his bedchamber. The scatological images of bodily functions and appetites together with the animal carcasses and vampire-infected bodies generate an imagery linked to abjection. The threat that the images of dying bodies and animals recalls Julia Kristeva's theories on the abject and its conceptualization as "death infecting life" (Kristeva 4). In Kristeva's terms, the sight of the corpse is "something rejected from which one does not part, from which one does not protect oneself" (4). The uncanniness of the corpse is the utmost abjection; it does not respect the borders and the rules of the subject: as such, it is not the cleanliness and the infirmity in old age that is threatening, but the disturbance to the system and the subject's identity (4).

Serra's film does not spare the viewer from witnessing defecation, animalistic munching, Casanova's bloodstained hands after sex, the body of an old man whipped to death and collapse. Such images can be associated with Kristeva's conceptualization of abjection as defilement, repugnance, and spasms that protect the subject from filth or waste. Accordingly, Kristeva's semiotics of the sinning flesh and impurity as alteration of social order provides an insight into the psychological workings operating in both Casanova's and Dracula's encounters. In particular, Kristeva argues that the roots of impurity are linked to the subordination of maternal power; thus the wheel of regulatory gender power within the Symbolic order is given a turning in Serra's film to unleash *jouissance*: the erotization of abjection becomes for Dracula a means of endlessly transcending death whereas for Casanova it means "an attempt at stopping the haemorrhage: a threshold before death" (55). We can see how Casanova's ageing decaying body is placed in the film a step ahead of the corpse. His *excess* is prefigured as an impending absence that heralds the older men's eventual demise.

Conclusion

Story of My Death illustrates Serra's fascination with anti-period filmmaking which takes on the thematic of old age and mythical masculinities, whose declining final moments are revisited and re-imagined from the vantage point of a postmodern *avant-garde* aesthetic vision. The film constitutes a singular example of experimental filmmaking that re-utilizes the clichés of Dark Romanticism and the Gothic Sublime in order to reflect upon the ideology embedded in cultural representations and genre, as well as ageing old male characters and their masculine constructions.

At the centre of *Story of My Death* there is a narrative of an older Casanova undeterred in his displays of sexual prowess and on a symbolic journey from Rationalism to Romanticism. There is also an extraordinary coincidence in time with Count Dracula whose firm placement within the Gothic and the supernatural comes to represent a fantasy of the transcendence of life and death, and thus of ageing, a desire that continues to fascinate us until now. Although Serra's account of older ageing males partakes of historical considerations attached to ideological changes at the end of the 18th century, his stereotyped ageing characters can be used as a lens to understand our cultural trajectory: they are relatable to us in ways that are uncannily familiar, and their stories of decline and death bring into relief an experience of demise relevant to all of us. As Timothy Shary and Nancy McVittie highlight, ageing "is a constant factor in understanding our own conceptions of the self as well as our relationships with others" (Shary and McVittie 7).

Through a series of *tableaux vivant* containing intertextual references to pictorial artworks and films, the film reflects back to the viewer *mimetic* images of ageing stereotyping that, on one level, are reinforcing the connection of older men with constructions of ideal masculinity within the *status quo*. On another level, through the strategy of *mimicry*, the parodic replicas of ageing embed the disruptive potential of the Dark Romantic aesthetics that have inspired the film's metaphors, meronymies and poetic imagery.

Serra's film places older men's experience of decay and degeneration at the centre of the stage as protagonists. Mortality is not brushed aside, and the spectator needs to confront death in all its lacerating aspects. Casanova and Dracula, stripped of psychological depth and heralding *excess* become removed from reality to the extent that their senile acts of debauchery indicate that they have become something less than human. Thus, the viewer is not spared from the process of disintegration: the film underscores the subversive power of narratives of decline through "ugly" renderings and "dark aesthetics." Ageing is intertwined with death in the film's narrative, and the viewer is reminded of this connection at the level of the gaze. As we witness Casanova's decline and see him peering inquisitively in the mirror, missing the blind spot that announces his death, our gaze also partakes of the identificatory processes that closes the distance between the onlooker and the ageing subject, becoming observers of a filmic mirror scene that foreshadows our own mortality.

Notes

1 See Fernando F. Croce, "Festival Gems: Albert Serra's 'Story of My Death.'" MUBI: https://mubi.com/notebook/posts/festival-gems-albert-serra-s-story-of-my-death, accessed 25 July 2022. See also Emanuele Sacchi, "Casanova incontra

Dracula in un allegorico scontro di concezioni filosofiche." MyMovies.it: www.mymovies.it/film/2013/historiadelamevamort/, accessed 23 July 2022.
2 The tradition black painting, particularly its revival at the *fin-de-siècle*, was documented by some of the artists at the time. See José Gutierrez Solana, *España Negra*. COMARES, 2000 [1920] and Darío de Regoyos & Émile Verhaeren, *España Negra*. CreateSpace Independent Publishing Platform, 2016 [1899].
3 Anti-period filmmaking refers to period pieces that engage with the times from a contemporary perspective. Serra's films share this feature. See Alonso Aguilar, "Elegy for Transgression: The Anti-Period pieces of Albert Serra," MUBI: https://mubi.com/notebook/posts/elegy-for-transgression-the-anti-period-pieces-of-albert-serra, 2020, accessed 23 July 2022.
4 This point made in a masterclass given by Serra for Ji.hlava International Documentary Film Festival 2014. www.youtube.com/watch?v=2Ty7BgezZ6I, accessed 22 July 2022. Serra has often explained his extensive filming routine which has been referred to as the poetics of chaos. In *Story of My Death* he used about 400 hours of film reel, which then took two years to reduce to 160 minutes. See Sacchi, "Casanova incontra Dracula."
5 Parallel to his filmic experience, Serra has also been developing art gallery video work and has exhibited in various art centres around the world. Serra interviewed in Javier Yuste, "Albert Serra: La historia del cine no me ha marcado como creador." *El Cultural* (15 February 2019). www.elespanol.com/el-cultural/cine/20190215/albert-serra-historia-cine-no-marcado-creador/376464179_0.html, accessed 27 July 2022.
6 This point explained by Serra in Ji.hlava International Documentary Film Festival 2014.

Works Cited

Barthes, Roland. *S/Z*, trans. Richard Miller. Blackwell Publishing, 2002.
Brinks, Ellen. *Gothic Masculinity*. Rosemond Publishing &Printing Corp, 2003.
Bronfen, Elisabeth. *The Knotted Subject. Histeria and Its Discontents*. Princeton UP, 1998.
Chion, Michel. *The Voice in Cinema*, trans. Claudia Gorbman. Columbia UP, 1999.
Dionigi, Rylee A. "Stereotypes of Ageing: Their Effects on the Health of Older Adults." *Journal of Geriatrics*. 2015. http://dx.doi.org/10.1155/2015/954027. Accessed 25 July 2022.
Grosz, Elisabeth, *Volatile Bodies*. Indiana UP, 1994.
Irigaray, Luce. *This Sex Which Is Not One*, trans. Catherine Porter. Cornell UP, 1977.
Jones, Rachel. *Irigaray: Towards a Sexuate Philosophy*. Polity Press, 2011.
Kristeva, Julia. *Powers of Horror. An Essay on Abjection*. Columbia University Press, 1982.
Salecl, Renata, and Slavoj Žižek. *Gaze and Voice as Love Objects*. Duke University Press, 2000.
Shary, Timothy, and Nancy McVittie. *Fade to Grey: Aging in American Cinema*. U Texas Press, 2016.
Woodward, Kathleen. *Ageing and Its Discontents: Freud and Other Fictions (Theories of Contemporary Culture)*. John Wiley & Sons, 1991.
Žižek, Slavoj. *The Metastases of Enjoyment. Six Essays on Woman and Causality*. Verso, 2001.

15 Male Ageing and Retribution in Contemporary Action Thrillers

Thomas Britt

Introduction

The three contemporary films discussed in this chapter – the Belgian film *W. - The Killer of Flanders Fields* (2014), the Irish film *Bad Day for the Cut* (2017), and the American film *Rambo: Last Blood* (2019) – feature ageing male protagonists seeking vengeance for crimes against their families and others in their respective communities. The chapter contextualizes the ageing male protagonists of these action thrillers within their indebtedness to Westerns in terms of genre conventions and constructions of masculinity. I begin by observing the foundational influence of classical Western films, particularly John Ford's *The Searchers* (1956) and its contested portrait of an ageing masculine heroism, and explore how these have shaped the retributive action film genre. I then compare the heroes of three contemporary action thrillers and explore the functions they serve in varying circumstances of crime and punishment, with specific references to their responsibilities to young women and children. I argue that the fact that the protagonists of these films are marked as middle-aged or older is a significant aspect of these narratives, as the codes and capacities they embody seem to come from a different time, or indeed, were formed across a long span of time, and within their plots they are uniquely suited to meet the challenges they face. Jeff Hearn has written of the power signified by middle-aged men "through formal, organizational statuses as well as through physical labour-power and indeed patriarchal power" and by older-age men "not just through the historical carry over of generational and patriarchal power, but through mental labour-power and the accumulation of resources" (102). While the ageing heroes of the contemporary action thrillers lack "organizational statuses" that confer power – loners that they are – each one represents generational, patriarchal, and resourceful qualities that they utilize to protect members of a younger generation. Additionally, these ageing action heroes reflect the patriarchy itself as a less stable concept or construct than it has been for their counterparts of past generations.

The three films discussed below have not been the subject of widespread scholarly analysis, yet they are reflective of the post–*Death Wish*

DOI: 10.4324/9781003306146-15

(1974)/*Taken* (2008) action film modes involving ageing white masculinities. Though the American Western has been globally influential, this chapter explores contemporary American and European films that bear a double influence; that of the cowboy archetype generally and that of the ageing masculinity seeking retribution indebted to John Wayne's characterization of Ethan Edwards in *The Searchers* in particular. That *Death Wish* was an American film directed by an English filmmaker and *Taken* was a French film about an ageing American protagonist (played by an Irish actor) establishes the preexisting context for the fluidity of this particular type across American and European film cultures. Contemporary global issues, such as human trafficking, are also present in these films, serving as a new line of combat or a new frontier for ageing action heroes to tackle.

Western Masculinity and Myth

In fall 2021, the National Conservatism Conference assembled in Orlando, Florida, predicated on the belief that "the past and future of conservatism are inextricably tied to the idea of the nation, to the principle of national independence, and to the revival of the unique national traditions that alone have the power to bind a people together and bring about their flourishing." Though this gathering and its politics might at first seem unrelated to the subject of ageing masculinities in international film cultures, the speeches and surrounding discourse revealed the potency of certain cinema conventions in creating an ideal of masculinity that spans both generations and American and European societies. Even as the performance and meaning of that form of masculinity continue to evolve, there appears to be an ongoing appetite for and interest in ageing action stars whose international brand has spanned generations. Most notable perhaps is Clint Eastwood, who shares with John Wayne an indelible link to the American Western genre and who continues (now into his nineties) to exist within the cinematic imagination as an ageing hero from another time, rising to meet contemporary challenges. Eastwood's 2021 film *Cry Macho*, in which he was the director and star, updates its 1975 source material, N. Richard Nash's novel of the same name, to tell a story that fits within this chapter's narrative concerns, that of an ageing man protecting a child from violent, avaricious criminals.

Atlantic writer David Brooks illustrated the link between conservative politics and the ideals of masculinity shaped by the Western film genre in his article about the National Conservatism Conference. After summarizing a speech from Missouri Senator Josh Hawley, in which Hawley "[defended] manhood and masculinity" in the face of "the deconstruction of American men," Brooks dedicates a more substantial portion of his coverage to Amanda Milius, "the daughter of John Milius, who was the screenwriter for the first two *Dirty Harry* films and *Apocalypse Now*" (Brooks). As the daughter of the man who wrote the *Dirty Harry* films, as well as other male-centred Western and action films including *Jeremiah Johnson* (1972; screenwriter) and *Red Dawn* (1984; screenwriter and director), Amanda Milius is qualified to reflect on the ageing portraits of masculinity in these linked genres. Brooks characterizes her speech thus:

> She argued that America needs to get back to making self-confident movies like *The Searchers*, the 1956 John Ford Western. This was an unapologetic movie, she asserted, about how Americans tamed the West and how Christian values got brought to "savage, undeveloped land." This is about as dumb a reading of *The Searchers* as it's possible to imagine. The movie is the modern analogue to the *Oresteia*, by Aeschylus. The complex lead figure, played by John Wayne, is rendered barbaric and racist while fighting on behalf of westward pioneers. By the end, he is unfit to live in civilized society.
>
> (Brooks)

On Twitter, Amanda Milius forcefully pushed back against Brooks' take, testifying to her thorough knowledge of *The Searchers* (sparked by her father's enthusiasm for the film) and accusing Brooks of distorting and lying about her remarks in order to reduce her to a preconceived caricature. This public spat between Brooks and Milius is indicative of the contested status of Western-derived masculinity within American culture.

In general, the American Western is a genre that has aged considerably, no longer as popular as it once was, in part because its ideologies and traditions (including its portraits of masculinity) have been deconstructed and challenged through postmodern cultural reimagining. Susanne Kord and Elisabeth Krimmer link the Western genre to waning myths, reasoning that

> Because myths are by definition stuck in the past, the Western has become saddled, as it were, with a reputation for being the most backward, traditional, and un-modern of all film genres. For over thirty years now, scholarly consensus has declared Westerns to be a genre in decline.
>
> (62)

In recent years, those Westerns that have proven successful are revisionist works made for (or at least mostly seen on) the small screen: Jeymes Samuel's *The Harder They Fall* (2021) and Jane Campion's *Power of the Dog* (2021), among the most highly acclaimed films of 2021, were both distributed via Netflix, and Taylor Sheridan and John Linson's *Yellowstone* premiered on Paramount Network in 2018. A further contemporary example extending the classic Western in a limited fashion is Ed Sinclair's 2021 true crime television series *Landscapers* (HBO/Sky), which uses archival footage of Westerns, particularly sequences featuring Gary Cooper, to represent the fantasy life of a troubled woman seeking protection and a masculine hero.

Despite these revisionist or referential examples, the Western movie genre is no longer a significant commercial/box office force within national or international cinema.

Yet, as the Brooks/Milius dust-up attests, the myths reinforced and reshaped by Westerns such as *The Searchers* continue to be parsed for their meanings and their influence, decades after the fact. As an indicator of the long influence of historical texts, Brooks' reference to the *Oresteia* suggests that dramatic works with justice/revenge themes are able to remain relevant for centuries, even if widespread awareness of the source texts wanes. This is one way of considering *The Searchers'* ongoing influence on contemporary action thrillers with ageing protagonists. If the Western is considered a genre that has aged well beyond commercial viability, it is worth exploring how the heroes who populated the genre at its peak have shifted into action thrillers where their generational, patriarchal, resourceful qualities are a corrective against present-day violence, especially organized or networked violence against young people.

The Searchers and Vengeful Masculinity

The Searchers was adapted from a 1954 novel of the same name by Alan LeMay. The protagonist is 40-year-old Amos Edwards, a man "liable to be pulled back into his shell between rare bursts of temper" (335) whose "uncertainties, his deadlocks with himself, his labors without pay, his gravitation back to his brother's ranch" are all connected to his being "in love with his brother's wife" (357). In Ford's film version (adapted by Frank S. Nugent), Amos becomes Ethan Edwards, played by John Wayne, then nearing 50 years of age and with a star persona shaped by Western myth and masculinities dating back to *The Big Trail* (1932). By 1956, Wayne was uniquely identified with the masculinity of the West, but he was also middle-aged (or beyond), which adds a layer of authentic belatedness to his presence in the film and informs the character's status as an ageing man whose glories are behind him. That *The Searchers* was released post-World War II and pre-Vietnam is a historical happenstance that allows critics and audiences to further appreciate how Ethan Edwards is out of his time, awaiting whatever paradigm will replace him. Edwards fought for the Confederacy in the Civil War and in the Second French Intervention in Mexico, for which he was rewarded with a medal. His overarching goal in both the novel and the film is to find a young girl who was taken by the Comanches, and Ford's film showcases Edwards' contempt for the Comanches responsible for the abduction, leading many to perceive the character as irredeemably racist.

In his *BFI Film Classics* study of the film, Western scholar Edward Buscombe is arguably more clear-eyed than either Amanda Milius or David Brooks in assessing the complexities of Ethan Edwards. After noting John Milius' "obsession with the film, naming his son Ethan and constantly working references into his work," Buscombe observes that "The contradictions of Ethan's character, his compelling strength matched only by his repellent bigotry, cannot be easily resolved, forcing us to a more painful awareness than the pieties of more obviously liberal films" (68–69). Brooks is correct that by the end of *The Searchers*, Edwards is unfit for society, but Buscombe highlights the character's strength, which relates to the values and confidence Amanda Milius perceives.

Edwards is certainly committed to violence, a veteran who spends years tracking down and fighting the Comanches responsible for killing his family and abducting the young girl. His racism regarding the Comanches, which seems to have existed independent of the attack on his family, fuels both his retribution and his response to the girl, now a grown woman who he perceives to be corrupted by her relationship to the Comanches. Yet he also chooses, in the end, to spare the girl rather than be clouded by his hatred for the Comanches, who have claimed her as one of their own. After returning her to what remains of her loved ones, Ethan walks away into the harsh exterior, separated from home and community. This plot structure – the maverick, ageing white male seeking violent retribution over those who threaten women or children – has more recently become the province of the action-thriller film.

American films of the 1970s played a significant role in bridging the masculinities of the classical Hollywood Western and the contemporary action thriller. Writing contemporaneously, Joan Mellen, author of *Big Bad Wolves: Masculinity in the American Film* (1978), observes that:

> In the seventies the male hero is more violent than ever before, as if we in the audience, men and women, were more alienated from and discontented with our lives than were people in the past. The violence of the hero, instead of being projected into an obsolete frontier community, is now seen as the necessary weapon of the male citizen attempting to survive in the cities.
>
> (12)

Films such as the Milius-authored *Dirty Harry* (1971), directed by Don Siegel, and Michael Winner's *Death Wish* (1974), typify the violent heroes and dangerous cities covered in this section of Mellen's study. Mellen goes on to link the films of the period to a revival of Western heroes:

> With rare exceptions, when the question of male identity is at issue during the sixties and seventies, the American film returns to the male styles of Wayne and Cooper in the course of a vigorous denial that there was anything unappealing or lacking in the masculine code they proposed.
>
> (285)

Though actor and filmmaker Clint Eastwood, who played "Dirty" Harry Callahan, exists at the nexus of Western films and vengeance/justice-themed films from the 1970s onwards, *Death Wish* is a more fitting point of comparison for the protagonists of *W. - The Killer of Flanders Fields* (2014), *Bad Day for the Cut* (2017), and *Rambo: Last Blood* (2019), in part because Paul Kersey (Charles Bronson) exists outside of the law from the beginning of the narrative. Bronson, already in his fifties during the first *Death Wish*, would go on to play Kersey in a series of films that employed him through his early seventies to his final theatrical leading role, Allan A. Goldstein's *Death Wish 5: The Face of Death* in 1994 (then aged 72). To situate Bronson's age in that series relative to Wayne's age in *The Searchers*, in the first *Death Wish* Bronson was already a few years older than Wayne was when he played Ethan Edwards. Thus *Death Wish* is significant for establishing older-age characterization as a legitimate narrative element of action films indebted to Westerns. There are thematic connections as well. Brian Baker includes revenge thrillers such as *Death Wish* in his study of American films "from *Dirty Harry* to *LA Confidential*" which "inhabit and replicate the tension between the necessity for law to organize a democratic, civic society, and the extra-legal violence which the law both excludes and relies upon to discipline the community" (xi–xii). That Kersey is not a lawman and also uncooperative with representatives of the law in order to succeed distinguishes him as the lone vigilante hero his community needs, even as his actions alienate him further. Kersey's vigilantism is an outgrowth of Edwards' retributive violence, however Kersey's arc is more extreme, as he lived most of his life peacefully until experiencing a kind of wake-up call towards violence in middle age. This contrasts with Edwards' history of sanctioned violence during wartime. Both men commit to rogue vengeance when outside of institutional rules and blinded by the personal fury of atrocities committed against their families. Their older age, combined with their existing losses, also implicitly suggest that they have less to lose by their vigilante actions.

This dramatic situation of the rogue yet essential arm of justice is consistent with Will Wright's observation in *Six Guns and Society* (1977) that within vengeance-themed Westerns, "The hero must establish his independence by doing what society cannot, punishing the villains; yet in doing so he risks decisively separating himself from the values of society and becoming a calculating killer" (157–158). A calculating killer is a fitting way to describe Paul Kersey of *Death Wish*, an ageing architect who transitions from conscientious objecting Korean War veteran to firearms expert and roving vigilante. The inciting incident for this transformation is the assault of Kersey's wife and daughter, which is fatal for his wife and permanently traumatizing for his daughter.

The first few *Death Wish* films tacitly situate Kersey as a frontiersman of sorts, moving westward from New York to Chicago to Los Angeles, settling scores with gang members otherwise untouched by official law enforcement. Notably, the first *Death Wish* film includes a sequence set in Tucson, Arizona, where Kersey observes a period reenactment of justice within the Old West, extolling "honest men with dreams, who would fight to protect" those dreams and their interests. Kersey embodies the Western hero conventions of becoming detached from the individuals and values he attempts to protect through his acts of vengeance. Whenever Kersey settles into a new community, the temporary stability of his professional and personal roles there collapse through intervening acts of villainy, usually by gang members, which necessitate his response.

A generation after the *Death Wish* series began, Pierre Morel's *Taken* (2008; also a film spawning multiple installments) reiterated the vengeful action-thriller template established by *Death Wish*, featuring a hero exercising his skills as a one-man militia. *Taken* initiated Liam Neeson's emergence as an action star while in his mid-fifties, with a plot that echoes both Ethan Edwards' commitment to avenge and rescue an abducted girl and Paul Kersey's turn toward violence prompted by the murder of his wife and rape of his daughter. In *Taken*, Neeson bridges the gap between the 1970s-style action thrillers associated with *Death Wish* and the late-2000s action film mode through implicit and explicit references to intervening 1980s action films. For example, early in the film, one of Bryan's associates calls him "Rambo." Neeson's character, divorced former CIA officer and Green Beret Bryan Mills, characterizes his past profession as being "a preventer" who stopped "bad things from happening."

After his daughter is abducted in Paris, Mills travels to France to rescue her from criminals who manipulate girls into becoming drug addicts and turn them into prostitutes, selling virgins to the highest bidder. In this scenario, Mills commits to taking down a criminal network (with which the corrupt police force is in league) while attempting to preserve the honour of his daughter. Her captivity at the hands of a sheikh at the climax of the film varies "the New England Indian captivity narrative" Richard Slotkin describes in *Regeneration Through Violence* (1974): "In it a single individual, usually a woman, stands passively under the strokes of evil, awaiting rescue by the grace of God. . . . To partake of the Indian's love . . . was to debase, to un-English the very soul" (94). The sheik of *Taken* is an unsubtle update of the Comanche of *The Searchers*, threatening to irrevocably disgrace Mills' daughter.

Though the release of *Taken* directly preceded the emergence of the subgenre known as "geriaction" cinema, the film and those it has influenced, which are the subject of this chapter, are distinct from geriaction with respect to most elements but the ages of the protagonists. One of the first writers to use the term geriaction was Karen Brooks of Southern Cross University, who in 2010 wrote in the *Courier-Mail*,

> where younger actors such as Matt Damon, Daniel Craig and Shia LeBeouf get to flex their muscularity while posing a serious threat to public safety or a clandestine enemy, the geriaction film stars steer a lighter-weight vehicle altogether – one that's more likely to make fun of them while still allowing them to shine.
>
> (2010)

One significant distinction between the contemporary action thrillers discussed in this chapter and the films Brooks and other geriaction scholars often write about is that there is little levity of any sort to be found. Tonally, *RED* (2010) or the *Expendables* series (2010–present) lack the serious mode of a film such as *Taken* (2008), which could not be said to make fun of its aged star.

Isolated Heroes: Contemporary Narratives of Male Ageing and Retribution

Despite his success in rescuing his daughter, Bryan Mills does not reestablish a family; like Ethan Edwards in *The Searchers*, he begins and ends the film in social and familial isolation. This characterization of being present but detached, and waiting to be activated by violence, is characteristic of the ageing male anti-hero of retribution narratives and is also present in *W. - The Killer of Flanders Fields*, *Bad Day for the Cut*, and *Rambo: Last Blood*. In *W. - The Killer of Flanders Fields*, retired Belgian homicide inspector Witse (played by Hubert Damen, age 68) has been living alone in the city for years. His wife has left him, he has no children, and he is estranged from his sister. The murder of his young niece, described as "sexual assault with extreme violence," committed by a serial killer who preys on women being enslaved and tortured for online pornography, causes Witse to reenter the small community in which he grew up, reconnect with his sister, and even sleep in his childhood bed, surrounded by the belongings of his youth.

Bad Day for the Cut's variation on this character type is farmer and mechanic Donal (Nigel O'Neill of indeterminate middle age), who is unmarried, not dating, and lives with his elderly mother. His first appearance in the film is waking in the night to help her onto the toilet. She appears to be the centre of his life. When she is murdered by unknown assailants, Donal becomes aware of a criminal enterprise out to destroy his family as well as the lives of European women being trafficked into prostitution. His movement from ageing mother's boy to vigilante in a camper van is an isolated sort of mobility, in that he is finally free to depart his home, but his own escalating violence prevents him from being able to settle anywhere.

Rambo: Last Blood (starring Sylvester Stallone, age 73) advances the character type further by having the titular hero directly articulate the necessity to keep his loved ones out of the way, living on a ranch, away from outsiders. Like Witse and Donal, John is unmarried, has no children, and is living in an environment that is in part his childhood home. One additional narrative element defining John's ranch is his construction of an elaborate underground tunnel system, to which he retreats to create weapons and attempt to manage his trauma from war. When his teenage niece is trafficked into prostitution and killed, John makes it his mission to annihilate ostensibly the entire criminal network responsible for her death.

In *The Searchers*, Ethan Edwards left for war, was hardened by it, and returned to his extended family an older, more sentimental man, seemingly retired from fighting, only to encounter violence so savage and close to home that he seeks retribution and seals his position outside of both home and society. Likewise, Witse, Donal, and John are ageing men who have not managed to build and sustain families as social units, because their vocations, commitments, and other experiences have brought out certain competencies while neglecting or distorting others. Their displacements and vacillations, however, are more complex than those of Ethan Edwards. Unlike Ethan, each of them begins his narrative with a tenuous impression of stability. While they are ultimately destined to be wanderers, their age and routines have lulled them into a temporary sense of being settled.

Witse, a former police commissioner, has the most conventional background of the three men. He has lived a professional life, officially on the side of the law, and has been married. However, his wife's infidelity (she had an affair with his superior) prompted his move to a new city and a new life, to which *W. - The Killer of Flanders Fields* adds the narrative event of Witse's retirement. His murdered sister's house, which for a while becomes his base for investigating the serial killer, is a narrow structure, the architecture of which signifies the various "halves" Witse has lost as he has aged, such as his sister and his wife. His childhood bedroom, frozen in time at the home his sister now inhabits, remains as it was when he was a child, and his presence in it as an ageing man has the effect of wiping away his personal history since he was last in that room.

In *Bad Day for the Cut*, the middle-aged Donal is, by contrast, a case of arrested development. His attachment to his elderly mother keeps him tethered to the physical space of the family home, its domestic routines, and the needs of her failing body. An early confrontation in the film finds an antagonistic man in the pub judging Donal, asking, "How . . . is it a man your age can still live with his ma?" The response to this pointed question occurs not through dialogue, but in setting and action, as Donal occupies a camper van that becomes his one sphere of independence within a life governed by his mother's needs. Additionally, once his mother is killed, Donal could no longer be said to live with her, only with her memory. The cruel irony of the taunt Donal faced is that what was once an observation about his awkward place within the community (a middle-aged man living with his mother) is now a reflection on the loss of even that status, as his mother is gone. Her killing, however, opens an opportunity for the completion of his psychological development toward a more complete and conventional manhood.

John Rambo is so mentally and physically scarred by his experiences in numerous wars and conflicts that his family home is no sanctuary, even when no obvious enemy is present. He lives at his deceased father's ranch with longtime friend Maria (Adriana Barraza) and her granddaughter Gabriela (Yvette Monreal). John interacts with them as if they were a surrogate family, but he spends much of his time in the self-fashioned underground lair that he refers to as "the tunnels." The Arizona ranch would be an ideal setting for a Western, with John riding horses and outfitted as a cowboy. However, the underground tunnels, linked to the trauma of John's experiences in Vietnam, Burma, and elsewhere, portend that John will never achieve stability at the homestead.

Even as each protagonist's situation is more tenuous than he realizes, the temporary sense of being settled allows the viewer to initially observe and understand these men at rest, before they are drawn into violence. As ageing characters, each of them is far from peak physical condition, yet all of them have accrued competencies that will shape their individual narrative arcs: Witse is skilled in detection; Donal is a hunter and a mechanic; John is an expert tracker. Though they are figures in action thrillers, these men embody the kind of competence that Wendy Chapman Peek identifies as a key element of gender construction in the Western:

> The Western is not primarily a romance of masculinity but a romance of competence, and the man who demonstrates a range of abilities broad enough to address any perilous situation gets to be the hero. . . . Competence does not entail simply being the baddest man in town; in fact, that kind of monolithic masculinity is regularly represented as impeding success. Instead, the competent man knows when to quell his ferocity and when to let it loose. Mental acuity, which can judge from experience what needs to be done and the best way to go about it, trumps youth and physical ability every time.
>
> (208–209)

For the ageing heroes of contemporary action thrillers, their age and attendant experiences are directly linked with their competencies. Unlike in geriaction films, which are predisposed towards making fun of the decline and deficits experienced by aged characters, the contemporary action thrillers discussed in this chapter highlight the resourcefulness and abilities available to aged characters, often employed in service of the young, who are less capable by comparison. These films' attention to the psychology-linked dwellings that the protagonists temporarily occupy, as well as their distinct abilities (what *Taken*'s Bryan Mills would call "a very particular set of skills"), focus the viewer's attention on the often-underestimated position of the ageing man in society. This is a theme with a long tradition, one which Cormac McCarthy previously updated from Yeats' "Sailing to Byzantium" (1928) for his novel *No Country for Old Men* (2005), itself famously adapted into Joel and Ethan Coen's acclaimed neo-Western 2007 feature film of the same name. Yeats writes that "An aged man is but a paltry thing" likened to "a dying animal" (193). Witse, Donal, and John might appear ready to be put out to pasture, but violence close to home motivates each of them to become a rescuer of young women, in the manner of Ethan Edwards and Bryan Mills.

Crime and Punishment

The arrival of Witse's sister highlights his long-time separation from his family. When she informs him of the crime that is the catalyst for the narrative, "My daughter's been murdered," Witse responds incredulously. "You lived like a nun," he retorts, to which she counters, "You haven't seen me in thirty years." As Witse reenters the life of his sister to avenge the daughter she had long ago in secret, he takes on the emotional weight his sister cannot bear. After a career investigating crime, Witse is accustomed to seeing dead bodies. He absorbs the reality of his niece's suffering by taking in the sight of her brutalized body and then initially lying to his sister, saying that her daughter did not suffer. This compartmentalization of such tragic circumstances echoes Ethan Edwards' insistence that he alone is suited to see the ravaged bodies of the women in his family, thus sparing other, younger men from being haunted by the sight.

Witse's method of fighting back is similarly individualistic. He is too late to rescue his niece, a fact aligning with his protracted estrangement from his family. Yet he is motivated to save other young women before they are likewise tortured and killed. Complicating the situation is a contested criminal investigation involving Belgian police, French police, and crime at a British cemetery. Though several characters, on both sides of the law, comment on his retirement or his being too old to participate in the already complex investigation, Witse becomes instrumental in infiltrating the online network of pornography producers and consumers associated with the serial killer. Because Witse is not officially part of any of these institutions, he is not bound by the bureaucracy that hamstrings such cases. A police commissioner eventually reveals that Witse is not so alone, after all. There is a team working in a clandestine manner on the serial killer case, yet the force is always calculating whether the skilled Witse – an ageing outsider – is a threat to their order.

Witse validates their skepticism when he threatens the entire enterprise by becoming physically involved in the search for the killer. However, it is his virtual presence that makes advances in the case. Online, Witse's status as an ageing retiree is a nonissue, because he is able to play a variety of roles. He poses as a consumer of violent pornography to attract the killer and then later, after becoming completely immersed in such investigative roleplaying, uses a young waitress as bait for the killer. The ultimate effect of the virtual investigation is that Witse starts to regard real bodies as a means to his desired end. Even the killer, when caught, points out that Witse has forever lost his "inner peace" over the case.

Donal lacks Witse's sophistication in investigating crime, and he's not estranged from his family. However, his arc in *Bad Day for the Cut* is an extended coming to terms with secrets from his mother's past. A tragic irony of Donal is that he goes to great lengths to avenge his mother before discovering that he did not know her as well as his proximity to her would suggest.

A recurring visual motif within the film is Donal holding his shotgun, ready to shoot. This image is first associated with hunting, as he provides food for him and his mother to eat. However, after his mother is killed in a home invasion and he teams up with young criminal Bartosz (Józef Pawłowski) to rescue Bartosz's sister, who has been forced into prostitution, Donal uses his gun to face off with criminals. This characterization of Donal, as a sort of father figure to Bartosz and his sister, as a capable hero with a long gun filling the frame, contrasts with the initial impression of Donal as a domesticated caretaker. *Bad Day for the Cut* benefits from this polarity of character, as Donal alternately uses weapons associated with domestic activities, including a hot pot of beans to burn his foes and a clothing iron to beat and burn them further.

The deeper level of conflict that Donal slowly realizes he is caught within is the prospect of an ongoing generational war. After rescuing the young woman from a life of forced prostitution and in the process surviving violent encounters with several male criminals, Donal must contend directly with Frankie (Susan Lynch), the most substantial villain of the plot. Frankie admits she killed Donal's mother because decades earlier, Donal's mother killed Frankie's father. Presently, Donal attempts to avoid killing Frankie, lest he continue the cycle and leave her young daughter without a mother. Despite Donal's thoughtful restraint, Frankie's aggressive violence finally results in Donal fatally shooting her. The film ends as Donal, who has largely avoided interacting with the law throughout the narrative, dials an emergency number but says nothing to the dispatcher, his face expressing the dreadful awareness that his intervention into a criminal enterprise has produced a higher body count than individuals saved.

John's interactions with the 17-year-old Gabriela in *Rambo: Last Blood* illustrate his foreknowledge that he cannot entirely vanquish the criminal chaos that exists in the world beyond his home. When Gabriela, whom he regards as a niece, wants to go to Mexico to find the father who abandoned her, John warns her that there is nothing to be gained by venturing beyond the ranch. He reasons, "I can't control what's out there." Gabriela becomes another character like Witse's niece and Donal's mother, insofar as John is unable to save her from death caused by criminals. In this case, Gabriela is sex trafficked by a cartel in Mexico, in a plot strongly reminiscent of *Taken*. John risks his life to rescue her, in part because he is aware the police force does not even attempt to intervene into the cartel's actions.

The brutality John experiences as a result of singlehandedly battling with the cartel plays like a cinematic concession following the character's years of seemingly superhuman abilities across the *Rambo* franchise. John's time in Mexico extends his cowboy characterization, as a woman comes to his aid and nurses him back to health, or at least brings him back from the brink of death to fight another day. John's restoration is intercut with Gabriela's descent into abuse and exploitation by the cartel. She eventually dies next to John in his truck, as he attempts to bring her home to the ranch.

Unable to depend on law enforcement to bring justice, John draws upon his entire history of combat to lure the criminals across the border and into his tunnel system, where he gruesomely shoots, impales, maims, and blows them up. In this section of the film, John's version of ageing masculinity departs from the virtual disembodiment of Witse and the reluctant firepower of Donal. John beheads one individual and rips another one's heart out. With his ageing, aching, scarred body, he may be older than all of his foes, but he reduces each one of them to gory detritus. In the process, he collapses the tunnels that have offered him some semblance of refuge and becomes once again a hero without a home.

Dead Men Riding

The retribution arcs within these action thrillers dramatically affect the ageing protagonists. Not only have they meted out and endured violence, but they have further alienated themselves from the societies that benefit from their vengeance. This is a tragic, yet predictable position consistent with the "vengeance variation" Western that Will Wright identifies in *Six Guns and Society*: "If retribution is to be exacted, the hero must do it himself, alone.... Since society is weak and unable to fulfill its obligations to its members, the individual must rely only on himself if justice is to be done" (155). Furthermore, as ageing action-thriller heroes, the physical and mental toll of their actions reads as more self-sacrificial than if they were younger men who could more believably withstand such conflicts and combat. It is worth noting that both Witse and John have preceding screen histories that allow the viewer to revisit their earlier journeys and compare their past selves and the damage done.

That Witse, Donal, and John were already ageing at the beginnings of the present narratives has a special significance in light of the films' intentional variations on Western film themes and structures. Jenni Calder notes in *There Must Be a Lone Ranger* that "the Western hero is indeed obsolete" when "the frontier is tamed, the moment when the frontier no longer exists" (206). Existing long past the frontiers of Western myths, the ageing action-thriller heroes discussed here might be said to exhibit a masculinity that is particularly threatened with obsolescence and extinction. Theirs are already no countries for older men. That which lies beyond the new frontiers they encounter includes horrors such as an online network of sexual exploitation, a criminal syndicate of sex traffickers, and a drug cartel selling young, abducted women – all of which operate above the law's capabilities to intervene. These are old degradations in new forms; challenges that law enforcement and younger men fail to sufficiently confront and shut down.

Gone is the comparative simplicity of Ethan Edwards patiently tracking the Comanche villain Scar for years as his captive young relative grows into adulthood. Witse, Donal, and John make a last stand for the values they represent, specifically benefitting a younger generation of threatened women and children. This exchange of their remaining vitality to redeem the young and vulnerable is a contemporary variation of what Calder describes as a key feature of the Western, "harnessing violence in the cause of good," yet, as in many Westerns, "it is a limited solution" (207). That is, none of the criminal networks are fully extinguished by the end of these action-thriller films, and all of the avenging heroes suffer the consequences of their interventions.

Brian Baker writes that the post-classical Western is saturated with "belatedness, in that their characters have 'outlived their time' . . . and the only thing for them to do is to die, peaceably or otherwise" (134). Witse, Donal, and John, all updates on the stoic Western hero, meet such a fate. Not long after the serial killer pronounces that Witse has lost his inner peace, Witse boards a train and dies. This is a fitting end for a hero estranged from home and family, and especially for one having just navigated a complex international criminal investigation. Whatever frontier might lie ahead, Witse will not be alive to cross the border. Donal, having reluctantly killed Frankie, thus perpetuating the cycle of generational violence of which he was a victim, sits on a shore. He stares into the water, with his camper van behind him. The vehicle that initially offered a means of independence and some suggestion of a road out of the co-dependent situation with his mother has now been suffused with a series of violent acts. John's sendoff is comparatively triumphant and thoroughly indebted to Western imagery. After sitting for a moment in a rocking chair, looking at his land, he rides away on a horse. John is wounded, but the montage of all five Rambo installments that concludes the film has the effect of resurrecting the hero in the viewer's imagination. Each of these conclusions is a variation on Max Steiner's "Ride away, ride away, ride away" refrain from *The Searchers*, though only John can embody the phrase with masculine mobility. Collectively, the endings of the three narratives evoke Le May's closing image of *The Searchers'* vengeful hero: "Amos looked like a dead man riding, his face ash-bloodless, but with a fever-craze burning in his eyes. It seemed a physical impossibility that he should have stayed on a horse to get here" (554). Witse is the dead man riding, Donal's face is ash-bloodless, and John rides a horse, impossibly, towards a future installment of *Rambo*.

Conclusion

The persistence of Western film conventions in these action thrillers corresponds to the ageing stars' settling into the legacy of a past genre and breathing new life into it. In other words, it is possible that when there seem to be no new frontiers left for popular film genres, one solution for appearing to inject new vitality into them is to return to a genre that considerably diminished in popularity by the 1970s, half a century ago. Though the three films that are the focus of this chapter are not blockbuster films (*Rambo* is part of a franchise, but that is not synonymous with blockbuster), all illustrate a generative trend for ageing male actors in a post-*Taken* international cinema marketplace. The contemporary action thriller provides a space for ageing male actors and characters in both national and international cinema to return to and re-work themes of the post-classical Western model, and in so doing assert a type of outmoded masculinity that represents a fighting chance within the films, and within their careers as well.

Works Cited

Baker, Brian. *Masculinity in Fiction and Film: Representing Men in Popular Genres, 1945–2000*. Continuum, 2008.
Baugh, Chris. *Bad Day for the Cut*. Well Go USA, 2017.
Brooks, David. "The Terrifying Future of the American Right." *The Atlantic*, Atlantic Media Company, 19 Nov. 2021. www.theatlantic.com/ideas/archive/2021/11/scary-future-american-right-national-conservatism-conference/620746/.
Brooks, Karen. "New Age Laughter Lines Not Very Hip." *The Courier-Mail*, November 3, 2010. https://www.couriermail.com.au/news/new-age-laughter-lines-not-very-hip/news-story/15ee978a02398741923392e19c58ffec.
Bruzzi, Stella. *Men's Cinema: Masculinity and Mise-En-Scene in Hollywood*. Edinburgh UP, 2013.
Buscombe, Edward. *The Searchers*. London: British Film Institute, 2000.
Calder, Jenni. *There Must Be a Lone Ranger*. Hamilton, 1974.
Ford, John, dir. *The Searchers*. Warner Bros., 1956.
Grunberg, Adrian, dir. *Rambo: Last Blood*. Lionsgate/Millennium Media, 2019.
Hearn, Jeff. "Imaging the Aging of Men." In *Imaging the Aging of Men*, edited by Mike Featherstone and Andrew Wernick, 97–115. London: Routledge, 1995.
Kord, Susanne, and Elisabeth Krimmer. *Contemporary Hollywood Masculinities Gender, Genre, and Politics*. New York: Palgrave Macmillan, 2011.
May, Alan Le. "The Searchers." *The Western: Four Classic Novels of the 1940s & 50s*, Library of America, 2020.
Mellen, Joan. *Big Bad Wolves: Masculinity in the American Film*. Elm Tree Books, 1978.
Morel, Pierre, dir. *Taken*. 20th Century Fox Home Entertainment, 2008.
Peek, Wendy Chapman. "The Romance of Competence: Rethinking Masculinity in the Western." *Journal of Popular Film and Television* 30.4 (2003): 206–219. https://doi.org/10.1080/01956050309602857.
Slotkin, Richard. *Regeneration through Violence*. Wesleyan UP, 1974.
Winner, Michael, dir. *Death Wish*. Warner Brothers, 1974.
Wright, Will. *Six Guns and Society: A Structural Study of the Western*. U of California P, 1977.
Yeats, William Butler. "Sailing to Byzantium." *The Collected Poems of W. B. Yeats*. Collier Books, 1989. 193. www. https://nationalconservatism.org/about/

16 De-ageing and Denying the "Older Man" in Recent Hollywood

Timothy Shary

When we think about ageing movie stars, an inevitable veneration sets in, as we become nostalgic for their earlier roles and gain respect for anyone over a certain age who is still skilled at their craft. And of course, our views of older people have distinct differences in terms of gender, which is worthy of a lengthy argument all its own. But here I will be focusing on a number of older male stars and their roles in recent years to make the case that their status as honoured icons of the silver screen is actually quite tenuous. The "old man" in Hollywood movies is marginalized and maligned more often than he is embraced and admired. Indeed, in recent years, there appears to be an outright resistance to ageing male stars on screen.

Despite the increasing age of the American population and the lengthier careers men now enjoy with their longer lives, Hollywood would have us believe that most male stars are not worthy of much attention after the age of 60, and certainly by 70 they are not entrusted with the same prominence on screen and the same potency in their roles as they are in earlier decades. This erasure of visibility and denial of authority contradicts what we see in American political and financial circles, as so many politicians and CEOs are indeed older white men – a condition that is often derided for its demonstration of racist patriarchal elitism. Curiously, the opposite tends to be true in current mainstream American cinema, where there is little elitism in being a man over the age of 60.

Because numbers do matter with age, let me begin with some demarcation of the population about which I am speaking. After all, "growing old" is much more common now than it was just over a century ago, when the life expectancy of an American citizen born in 1900 was a mere 47 years.[1] At the same time, people born in 1900 who lived to be 48 years old were certainly not viewed as decrepit for their generation, and most still had many years of productive work and healthy living ahead of them; in fact, according to the 1900 census, nearly 70% of all men over 65 were gainfully employed (Achenbaum 15). Even when the statistically *average* person born in 1900 did not live past 50, the perception of "old age" in the last century was still more connected to cultural distinctions in appearance and ability rather than the chronological age of a person. Indeed, determining the point

DOI: 10.4324/9781003306146-16

at which age is "advanced" or when one becomes "aged" is highly ambiguous and subjective.

If the cessation of employment or the start of retirement could be an indicator of advanced age, even that number has had variable standards for the past century. Until 2002, Social Security in the United States allowed citizens to declare retirement and begin receiving full benefits at age 65, but for those born between 1943 and 1959 (who would have turned 65 from 2008 to 2024), those same benefits were not available until the age of 66. For citizens born in 1960 and since, the age is 67. Granted, the primary reasons for this two-year increase in the retirement age under Social Security are financial rather than statistical, because the system is running out of money as so many Americans are living longer and claiming more benefits.

To consider some labour statistics, the *actual* age for retirement from fulltime work for many Americans has been considerably lower than the age at which the government recognizes them as retired for Social Security benefits. While workers who are not yet retired have *expected* to retire at the age of 65 or older for many years, the average retirement age has been much closer to 60, and only reached as high as 62 for the first time in 2014 (Riffkin). One certain factor in the previous lower age of retirement included the inability of older workers to retain full-time positions in the workforce (for reasons including prejudice as well as declining health), yet in recent years factors such as financial needs and improving health have kept the aged working longer. In fact, after a steep decline in the older workforce throughout the 20th century until the 1980s, the percentage of Americans aged 65 and older with jobs (including part-time) has again begun rising, from 12.1% in 1990 to 16.2% in 2011, of which 44.3% worked full-time, so thus 7.2% of the population *after* "retirement age" was still fully employed (Kromer and Howard).[2] Thus, considering the typical ages by which characters are retiring or considering retirement, I have focused my study on films in which protagonists are age 60 or older.[3]

Studies of social representation in cinema should proceed with an awareness of the difference between reality and the movies, particularly those products of Hollywood that are designed for mass consumption with the goal of the greatest profitability. The industry has not been required to portray life in any realistic manner, yet conversely, it tends to present a fantasy of life that entertains fundamental human ambitions, such as the search for love, the accomplishment of goals, and the resolution of conflicts. Thus, on screen we see an often-preferred vision of life, however, with so many roles for older men in recent years, that preferential image is rather derogatory.

There are at least two rationales in play that explain the disempowerment of older men in American cinema: the elder audience's weakening presence as a media demographic and the social prejudice the dominant population holds against the aged. To address the first topic, consider how blatantly Hollywood tends to ignore the interests of the older audience altogether. After all, as people age, they attend movies at theaters in decreasing numbers, and furthermore, they become a less valuable portion of the consumer audience than American industries rely upon for consumption, because most older people have diminishing disposable incomes and tend to spend less on media-based products. By 2020, 24% of Americans were age 60 and over yet made up only 14% of the moviegoing audience; at the same time, 22% of the moviegoing audience was aged 12–24 despite making up only 17% of the population (Motion Picture Association of America, *THEME Report 2020*, 50). American movie studios have been able to justify their preoccupation with stories about younger characters through this economic reasoning. However, through a more pernicious cultural reasoning, the movie industry continues to promote the idea that young lives are the most worthwhile, the most fulfilling, and even the most common.

The fact is, America has been "ageing" more than ever before because people are living longer. The median age of American citizens increased by 15 years between 1900 and 2014, and the percentage of the population aged 65 and older more than tripled in that time, from 4.1% in 1900 to 13.3% in 2011 (US Department of Health and Human Services 2). This condition has resulted in numerous geriatric health concerns that have distorted perceptions of older life in media products, even though an increasing number of citizens are extending their working careers and maintaining a more visible presence in society.[4] American movies remain relatively uninterested in these particular trends nonetheless, except insofar as the expanding population of older people lends itself to familiar dramatic conventions, particularly fighting illness and death, and discovering meaning in life. The distinctions in movies about older characters are grounded in the evolved – and often limited – cultural assumptions about what we perceive to be "old age."

And those perceptions naturally cover a spectrum of negative and positive traits: in the former realm we see frail, senile, and irritable old men, while in the latter we less often see sagacity, serenity, and frugality – and even these qualities are often suspect. There are indeed certain stock character types throughout ageing narratives – such as the curmudgeon who likes no one, the old pro drawn out of retirement for one last job, and the sage who doles out wisdom – yet most older male characters are primarily identified *through* their age. Being "old" is thus rarely indifferent, though unlike youth, older age is resisted and shunned.

For much of the 20th century, Hollywood depicted elderly men through various conventions that exaggerated eccentricities and encouraged a level of reverent distrust, particularly as honoured stars of the industry's golden age themselves aged into their later years. Guarded attitudes toward older men in movies were thus evident by the 1970s in examples such as *The Cheyenne Social Club* (1970, with Jimmy Stewart and Henry Fonda), *Chinatown* (1974, with John Huston), *The Shootist* (1976, with John Wayne), *Marathon Man* (1976, with Laurence Olivier), and *Going in Style* (1979, with George Burns and Art Carney). Many of these roles were infused with criticism for what these men had become – chiselers, rapists, killers, criminals – and in most cases, they were met with ignominious fates.

By the end of the 20th century, after the nation had seen relative prosperity under the rule of a septuagenarian president (Ronald Reagan) in the 1980s, and the percentage of citizens over the age of 65 had *tripled* since the start of the century (Hobbs and Stoops 56), Hollywood attitudes toward older men became slightly more endearing, perhaps most famously with the elders who encounter aliens in *Cocoon* (1985), the bumbling romantics in *Grumpy Old Men* (1993), and the intrepid adventurer in *The Straight Story* (1999). At the same time, these roles were sparse, and few of them achieved the box office success of star vehicles in franchises. Moreover, the male stars who so often led those franchises in the 1970s and '80s – Clint Eastwood (*Dirty Harry* starting in 1971), Sylvester Stallone (*Rocky* starting in 1976), Harrison Ford (*Indiana Jones and the Raiders of the Lost Ark* starting in 1981), and Arnold Schwarzenegger (*The Terminator* starting in 1984) – would be naturally phased out of their roles to make way for younger male stars that inherited the mantle of potency once bestowed upon their predecessors.

Since the turn of the most recent century, the previously reliable box office heroes who wrought bankable products for the film industry have been systematically displaced, even as some stars over 60 have continued to earn substantial roles. Older actors like Morgan Freeman, Ian McKellen, Patrick Stewart, and even Harrison Ford have appeared in blockbuster hits of the past 20 years, though there are many famous stars whose cinematic visibility has been more limited (Robert De Niro, Clint Eastwood, Al Pacino, Arnold Schwarzenegger, Sylvester Stallone), and some who have faded away or given up acting altogether (Gene Hackman, Dustin Hoffman, and Jack Nicholson). Further, the roles for older men in blockbusters are all supporting; the industry and the audience tend to have little interest in stories *about* older people.

One of the prime examples in this regard is *The Irishman* from 2019. For as much attention as it generated with its scandalous story and the union of Oscar-winning stars Robert De Niro, Al Pacino, and Joe Pesci, the film was in many ways most notable for technically "de-ageing" the actors – aged 76, 79, and 76 respectively – so that they could play younger versions of their historical figures for much of the film. I felt the technology used for this process was an unsuccessful distraction, though the fact that it was used so extensively, and by an older director (Martin Scorsese at 77) who himself might long for his younger days, augurs the opportunity for older actors to be subject to further revisions in appearance (which, after all, have been available for decades through makeup and cinematography) that threaten to diminish their worth as performers.

Indeed, after the current generation of middle-aged stars such as Bradley Cooper (45), Leonardo DiCaprio (46), Mark Ruffalo (53), Brad Pitt (57), or Johnny Depp (57) age into their sixties and seventies, the next generation may not have as many "older stars" to appreciate. And if the industry continues to minimize their roles, older male performers may become obsolete altogether. After all, if digital effects can be used to "de-age" older actors, they can just as easily be used to "age" younger actors, who themselves may be subject to less value in their later years.

As a further demonstration of my argument, I expand the previous examples.

Harrison Ford was once the highly bankable star of the *Star Wars* films that started in 1977, the *Indiana Jones* films that started in 1981, and prestige dramas such as *Witness* (1985), *Frantic* (1988), *The Fugitive* (1993), and *Air Force One* (1997), though his visibility diminished considerably after he turned 60 in 2002. While he remained in some limelight with sequels to his past hits in the *Indiana Jones* (2008) and *Star Wars* (2015) series, and the one-off *Blade Runner* sequel (2017), his roles have otherwise been small or forgettable – *Morning Glory* (2010), *Paranoia* (2013), *The Age of Adaline* (2015) – even as he continues to appear in an average of one movie each year, and had mild success with *The Call of the Wild* during the COVID-19 crisis in 2020.

Morgan Freeman did not have much fame as an actor until he was 50, when he earned his first Oscar nomination with the small film *Street Smart* in 1987. Thereafter, his star rose with increasingly recognized roles in other Oscar fare such as *Driving Miss Daisy* (1989), *Unforgiven* (1992), and *The Shawshank Redemption* (1997), until he at last won his own Oscar in 2004 with *Million Dollar Baby* at the age of 67. Such a career peak yielded his highest-grossing films as he found smaller roles in the new *Batman* series that started in 2005, and his productivity thereafter was most prodigious: 40 films in 15 years. Alas, a decreasing number of popular titles featured him in a lead role – *The Bucket List* (2007), *Invictus* (2009), *Lucy* (2014), *Angel Has Fallen* (2019) – and most of his leading roles have been in films with marginal reputations, such as *Feast of Love* (2007), *Thick as Thieves* (2009), *The Magic of Belle Isle* (2012), *5 Flights Up* (2014), *Just Getting Started* (2017), and *Vanquish* (2021).

Ian McKellen and Patrick Stewart also achieved their greatest Hollywood fame later in life, having toiled in British film and television until middle age, when the former earned his first Oscar nomination at 59 in *Gods and Monsters* (1998) and the latter moved into movies after his successful run on the new *Star Trek* TV series (1987–94). However, their dueling forces in the *X-Men* films that started in 2000 when both were just over 60 became their blockbuster achievements, along with McKellen's roles in the *Lord of the Rings* trilogy (2001–03) and later *Hobbit* trilogy (2012–14). Success with the *X-Men* films continued for both actors across three more entries in the franchise until 2014. Along the way, McKellen continued to receive accolades for his work in smaller roles, including many short films and TV specials, though his attempts at lead roles garnered meager audiences, as in *Mr. Holmes* (2015), *All is True* (2018), and *The Good Liar* (2019). Similarly, Stewart continued to have sporadic success on television and in voice work, while his lead roles have been in minor productions such as *Match* (2014), *Christmas Eve* (2015), and *Coda* (2019).

The previous example of *The Irishman* notwithstanding, its two most famous performers – Robert De Niro and Al Pacino – have been among the most prolific and yet least profitable of all male actors in recent years. From 2000 to 2020, De Niro appeared in an astonishing 45 feature films (and ten other shorts or TV movies), with only one earning more than $100 million at the domestic box office outside of existing franchises, his Oscar-nominated dark comedy *Silver Linings Playbook* (2012).[5] In those same two decades, Pacino appeared in a more modest 24 features (and five TV movies), only two of which (*Ocean's Thirteen* in 2007 and *Once Upon a Time in Hollywood* in 2019) earned more than $100 million domestically.

To be fair, these well-regarded actors have often taken on roles in less lucrative genres, and neither built their career on the kind of tentpole franchise success that was embodied by Sylvester Stallone and Arnold Schwarzenegger. Still, even these two – the former being the biggest box office star of the 1980s with his action franchise entries of *Rocky III* (1982), *Rambo* (1985), *Rocky IV* (1985), and *Rambo III* (1988)[6] and the latter the dominant star of the 1990s with *Total Recall* (1990), *Terminator 2* (1991), *True Lies* (1994), *Eraser* (1996), and *Batman & Robin* (1997) – were met with much less success as they aged into the new century. Schwarzenegger's last serious hit was the third *Terminator* entry in 2003 at the age of 56 (at which point he left movies for nearly a decade to be governor of California). Stallone had only one hit (*Spy Kids 3-D* in 2003) outside of his ongoing attempts to exploit his *Rocky* (2006, 2015, 2018) and *Rambo* (2008, 2019) characters, although in 2010 at the age of 64 he did launch a gainful action franchise based on a mixed-age group of stars, *The Expendables*, which had sequels in 2012 and 2014.

At least these older actors continue to get work. Other Oscar-winning older stars have largely given up acting. Clint Eastwood does remain a remarkable movie-making machine into his nineties, having directed 18 films since he turned 70 in 2000, although he has only *acted* in seven movies during that time. His most recent starring role in *Cry Macho* (2021), which he also directed, had a tepid critical reception and even less financial interest. Dustin Hoffman had averaged about one film per year until he turned 70 in 2007, yet he has only appeared in two films since 2015. Jack Nicholson and Gene Hackman have retired from movies altogether, with the former not appearing since 2010 and the latter being away since 2004.

Of course, anyone in their later years may have various reasons for stopping or slowing their professional output, but if we consider the actual *roles* for older male actors alongside the actors themselves, we see a similar pattern of decline. Even though the older population remains as visible and vibrant as ever before in American history, and men by far outnumber women in lead roles within the sexist Hollywood system, very few films focus on or even feature older male characters. Of the 200 films from 2001 to 2020 in the top-ten highest-grossing box-office ranks each year, only *five* have featured a male character over 60, two of which were *X-Men* sequels. In the past 10 years, films about men over 60 have been just as scant, rarely landing in the top-20 most popular films of each year, particularly when excluding *X-Men* and other established franchises.

The following list demonstrates my point. This is the box-office rank of the highest-grossing American film featuring a male character over 60 in a lead role over the past decade (excepting co-starring roles in the *X-Men*, *Men in Black*, and *Expendables* franchises). The name and age of the older star is listed alongside the rank and amount of domestic box office income that year.

2011: *True Grit* (a 2010 release); Jeff Bridges, age 61; #34, $84.6 million
2012: *Hope Springs*; Tommy Lee Jones, age 66; #48, $63.5 million
2013: *Olympus Has Fallen*; Morgan Freeman, age 76; #33, $99 million
2014: *Lucy*; Morgan Freeman, age 77; #22, $126.6 million
2015: *The Intern*; Robert De Niro, age 72; #39, $75.6 million
2016: *Dirty Grandpa*; Robert De Niro, age 73; #80, $35.6 million
2017: *The Hitman's Bodyguard*; Samuel L. Jackson, age 69; #41, $75.5 million
2018: *The Mule*; Clint Eastwood, age 88; #49, $64.7 million
2019: *Knives Out*; Christopher Plummer, age 89; #21, $130.1 million
2020: *The Call of the Wild*; Harrison Ford, age 78; #9, $62.3 million

We can always recall the Hollywood syllogism that deduces how the most lucrative target audience for movies is young white men, and we know that many movies accordingly cater to their interests. At the same time, even *those* young men have little media exposure to what realistic older men look like, because the culture at large is engaged in an active erasure of the older population within the entertainment sphere. Once again, the public may actually *not* want to see more realities of older age on screen. We should still question if such blissful ignorance is healthy for ageing people who cannot (and may not want to) escape from their real lives, and more so for the younger population that is ageing into their elder years with fanciful distortions about what they can expect. With the current possibility of "de-ageing" actors in appearance and the ongoing neglect of older characters in prominent roles, this trend is likely to continue, and we may subsequently deny the relevance of this growing and significant section of our population. We may further corrupt the very experience of ageing that presumably all of us aspire to achieve.

Notes

1. The oldest person to ever live with recorded documentation has been Jeanne Calment of Arles, France, who died in 1997 at the age of 122 years, 164 days, although recent reports cast doubts on her claim, if only because *no* other person has lived to 120. See Robin-Champigneul. For life expectancy at birth, see *Health, United States, 2013*, National Center for Health Statistics (Washington, DC: US Government Printing Office, 2014), 82.
2. If 16.2% workforce participation for those 65 and older does not seem significant, consider that the 2012 employment rate for Americans aged 55–64 was 64.5%, and for those aged 25–54 it was 81.4%. The so-called unemployment rate in the United States (usually under 10%) is deceptive, as it only refers to those who apply for unemployment benefits in any given week (see Bureau of Labor Statistics).
3. This is the same parameter set for the study of characters in *Fade to Gray: Aging in American Cinema*, by Timothy Shary and Nancy McVittie (University of Texas Press, 2016).
4. Since 1985, the percentage of Americans working at age 65 and older has been increasing, after decreasing substantially throughout the earlier 20th century (US Department of Health and Human Services 12).
5. De Niro appeared in only four other movies to break $100 million at the domestic box office, three of which were the franchise comedies *Meet the Parents* (2000), *Meet the Fockers* (2004), and *Little Fockers* (2010). He appeared in *Joker* (2019), which was part of the DC Comics *Batman* lineage, and with a $335 million domestic gross, it remains the most successful film of his career. All box office income figures in this chapter are taken from *The Numbers*, www.the-numbers.com.
6. *Rambo* (1985) was technically the sequel to *First Blood* (1982), with the subtitle *First Blood Part II*. Because the new title was more popular than the original, the studio opted to name the next sequel *Rambo III* even though there was never a *Rambo II*.

Works Cited

Achenbaum, W. A. "A History of Aging in America." *Older Americans Almanac: A Reference Work on Seniors in the United States*. Ed. Ronald J. Manheimer. Gale, 1994.

Bureau of Labor Statistics. "Civilian Labor Force Participation." www.bls.gov/emp/ep_table_303.htm.

Health, United States. 2013 National Center for Health Statistics. Washington, DC: US Government Printing Office, 2014.

Hobbs, Frank, and Nicole Stoops. *Demographic Trends in the 20th Century*. US Census Bureau, 2002. www.census.gov/prod/2002pubs/censr-4.pdf.

Kromer, Braedyn, and David Howard. "Labor Force Participation and Work Status of People 65 Years and Older." *American Community Survey Briefs, US Census Bureau*, Jan. 2013. www.census.gov/prod/2013pubs/acsbr11-09.pdf.

Motion Picture Association of America, *THEME Report 2020*: 50. www.motionpictures.org/wp-content/uploads/2021/03/MPA-2020-THEME-Report.pdf.

The Numbers. www.the-numbers.com.

Riffkin, Rebecca. "Average US Retirement Age Rises to 62." *Gallup Economy*, 28 Apr. 2014. www.gallup.com/poll/168707/average-retirement-age-rises.aspx.

Robin-Champigneul, François. "Jeanne Calment's Unique 122-Year Life Span: Facts and Factors; Longevity History in Her Genealogical Tree." *Rejuvenation Research* 23.1 (Feb. 2020): 19–47.

Shary, Timothy, and Nancy McVittie. *Fade to Gray: Aging in American Cinema*. U Texas P, 2016.

US Department of Health and Human Services, Administration on Aging. *A Profile of Older Americans: 2012* 2. www.aoa.gov/Aging_Statistics/Profile/2012/docs/2012profile.pdf.

17 Our Fathers

Ageing Masculinities and Dementia in Contemporary Film

Tony Tracy

> "I am a very foolish fond old man"
> "O, let me not be mad, not mad, sweet heaven
> Keep me in temper: I would not be mad!"
>
> *King Lear*

One of the best known and most performed portraits of old age in the Western canon is Shakespeare's *King Lear* (1608). Inspired by multiple earlier sources (especially *The True Chronicle History of King Leir, and His Three Daughters* [anonymous 1594]), Shakespeare added original elements to his retelling of the widely circulated legend; most notably his madness and a tragic ending, both of which substantially challenged and changed its portrait of an ageing patriarch. Shakespeare's version of the story thus:

> forces us to contemplate the individual human inside the frail elder [and] Lear exemplifies the sheer mystery of ageing. The play urges us to view ageing not as a scientific rational and quantifiable process but as something vexing, enigmatic and endlessly intricate.
> (Combe and Schmader 1999, 84)

The meaning(s) of *King Lear* continue to be debated, its textual uncertainties inextricably linked to the apparent mental unreliability of its protagonist. Is Lear "mad," in a state of tragic cognitive decline, or merely old? And how fixed are these categories to begin with?

Recent productions of the play, particularly in Western societies, have approached such questions of interpretation under the influence of the growing social visibility and concern surrounding dementia. A high-profile Royal Shakespeare Company production in 2014 directed by Sam Mendes and starring Simon Russell Beale, for instance, explicitly linked the King's tragedy to the disease. In a "platform" interview (filmed during the production), Russell Beale discussed Lear's misguided desire to create a "living will," "*his condition* . . . where the seeds of sympathy should come [from the audience]" because "he's well aware of *being ill*" (Russell Beale 2014; my italics). Beale spoke of how, in preparing for the role, he had spoken to a geriatrician and discovered that a list of Lewy body dementia symptoms mapped onto King Lear's behaviour in almost uncanny fashion: physical tics, wandering, shame, anger, changes in thinking and reasoning, confusion, and an alertness that varies from one moment to the next.

While this seemed to bring a level of physiological explanation and coherence to Lear's actions, dementia activist Mark Butler was among those who noted the "go-to" function of this approach:

> A Lear for our times then. One where dementia is felt to add to the drama, to deepen the tragedy, to explain in some way an inevitable path downwards. I am shocked at how many people seem to have bought into this nonsense . . . there are real dangers in this "dementia-spotting."
>
> (Butler 2014)

A BBC/Amazon Studios adaptation followed in 2018, written and directed by Richard Eyre featuring Anthony Hopkins in the title role. Now 80 (the age that the character purports to be), Hopkins' performance was widely praised, with Mark Lawson describing the production as a "thrilling reimagining," noting that, "As has become common with modern Lears, he gives a clinically precise depiction of the onset of dementia, with which we now diagnose the king" (Lawson 2018). However, Alastair Morrison suggests that:

> As well as announcing dementia's sudden prominence as a concern, these neurotragic Lears may tell us something about how we are disposed to see it. That Lear is male, European, and a king should prompt some reflection on the highly partial nature of this supposedly universal prospect.
>
> (Morrison 2017)

These developments and observations are of relevance and of a piece with trends in mainstream Anglophone cinemas where ageing masculinities and dementia have also become "prominent concerns" in recent years. Firstly they suggest how these identities have become increasingly commonly associated – and often co-terminus – with each other. Placing ageing, men, and dementia together allows filmmakers to pursue themes they might not otherwise, most notably perhaps around contemporary social shifts in masculinity and patriarchy as well as perceptions and anxieties around dementia. Additionally, they remind us how Shakespeare's *King Lear* (itself an intertext to earlier plays and poems) continues to be a key influence in shaping the cinematic treatment of these themes, notably in the preponderance of narratives of late-life fatherhood and intergenerational/filial tensions framed in terms of cognitive decline. And finally, perhaps – to paraphrase critics such as Butler and Morrison – for all their effort to represent dementia in naturalistic and "universal" contexts, such cinematic treatments continue to offer "highly partial" cultural constructions imagined in fixed and hegemonic terms of race, gender, and class.

The Age of Alzheimer's

Dementia is defined as a syndrome associated with the decline of brain function. Alzheimer's disease and vascular dementia are the most common forms, but there are others, including Lewy body dementia and frontotemporal dementia. A number of scholars have historicized dementia as emerging as one of the "diseases of the century" during the 1980s to a situation today where it is often referred to terms of a pandemic (Fox and Petersen, 2013), with an estimated 153 million diagnosed cases by 2050 (Global Burden of Disease Study 2019). Since 2000, and coinciding with increases in life expectancy, dementia has come to occupy an increasingly prominent presence in social, political, and cultural discourses around old age. Indeed, for many it has come to be identified as *the* disease of old age, associated with an accompanying loss of sovereignty of the self, a crisis of care, and terminal decline.

Dementia is nonetheless a condition about which many misconceptions exist, and persons with dementia and their caregivers routinely face stigmatization (Werner, Goldstein, and Buchbinder 2010). As Cohen puts it, "those relegated to the victimhood of Alzheimer's [have] to bear the dehumanizing brunt of a total and questionable pathology" (Cohen 69). Many gerontologists see this as the result of an overly – or exclusively – medicalized view of the disease that ignores both individual and broader cultural contexts. "The cultural framing of dementia has resulted in a putative understanding of dementia and AD as something that is incredibly frightening: a complex, unknowable world of doom, ageing, and a fate worse than death" (Zeilig 2014, 259). Central to such framings has been the image of a nonperson – "a shell" – and "the death that leaves the body behind" (Cohen 1998; Kitwood 1997, 37).

Screening Dementia

Cinema – in terms of both its broad popular appeal and broadly naturalist form – clearly has an important role in shaping cultural understandings and social responses to dementia. Reflecting the broader diagnosis, awareness, and anxieties around the disease, the 21st century brought with it a sharp increase in feature films dealing with the topic. A first wave of representations shared notable features. Richard Eyre's 2001 biopic *Iris*, Sarah Polley's *Away from Her* (2006), and *Still Alice* (2014) focused on strong, highly intelligent women whose intellectual fortitude proves no defence against the onset of the disease. Each of these portraits also tended towards what we might term a "neuro-normative gaze" in which the protagonist is viewed through and from the perspective of supporting/supportive characters (husbands/carers, family members, medical staff) who function to underline their cognitive decline and increasing distance from everyday life. Finally, all were set in white, Anglophone contexts and the central performances were highly esteemed by critics and audiences.

In the "first systematic review" of representations of dementia on-screen, Segers (2007) identified a number of repeated elements in films released between 1970 and 2004. Among the most prominent are: an overrepresentation of highly educated people; disturbance and aggressiveness as the most often represented symptoms, and sudden – albeit fleeting – moments of insight in their disease by sufferers. Wulff (2008) has also discussed recurring features of such representations and argues that at the centre of such films is almost always a (heteronormative) love relationship; a recurring central theme of the loss of one partner's orientation; and characters who are generally from upper-middle-class backgrounds or who are engaged in artistic and scientific activities. Most Alzheimer's stories solicit the emotion of the audience and are, therefore, melodramas: "The dominant emotion [of such films] is not grief, but nostalgia" (Wulff 2008, 280). Finally, Aagje Swinnen posits three major "tropes" within such films: a focus on the caregiver with the consequence that "viewers are rarely invited to see through the eyes of the person with dementia," a narrative focus on a person "who is known to the public as someone exceptional, making the impact of the illness seem especially cruel," and a flashback structure that "contrasts the younger with the older self [and] results in the preference for the past self over the present one" (Swinnen 2015, 71).

In this chapter I wish to add to this literature in consideration of recent films centring on protagonists with dementia: *Headful of Honey* (2018), *Falling* (2020) and *The Father* (2020). While they contain a number of the features identified above, there are also distinctive and notable differences. In place of the earlier focus on female protagonists and stories taken from biography, I identify a cycle of fiction films foregrounding older men, and more specifically ageing fathers. As suggested, these portraits can be seen as of a piece with contemporary productions of *King Lear* and their framing of ageing masculinities in terms of cognitive decline. At the centre of these narratives we thus find a motif of home as both a physical and psychic space from which these increasingly isolated men – all widowers – are removed and to which they wish to return. Aligned with this theme we find a desire for reconciliation with women – whether as wives or daughters – who in different ways symbolize this lost home and heart(h). Less abstractly however, these films are notably contemporary in setting and circumstances and suggest varied cultural framings of dementia for today's audiences. While, like the representations referred to above, they remain generally situated in relation to white, middle-class settings and contexts, the protagonists are less likely to come with exceptional backstories, and indeed a sense of "typicality" is often central to their narratives. In the first two case studies in particular I shall argue that the films use dementia as a means of exploring and critiquing "typical" masculinity rather than the other way around. However, across all three films we also find ambition to move on from a neuro-normative gaze and an attempt to engage with the experiences of their ageing male protagonists via a variety of narrative and formal strategies. While the results of these efforts vary in sophistication and success, they can nonetheless be seen as expressing a broader impetus to move away from representations of dementia in clinical terms towards more person-centred constructions.

Headful of Honey (2018)

As the earliest released of the films under consideration in this chapter, *Headful of Honey* offers a point of departure and comparison and introduces a number of common thematic and stylistic elements: an ageing father figure whose robust masculine persona and authority is undermined by the onset of Alzheimer's disease; the theme of filial responsibilities and caregiving; a motif of home and domestic settings as expressions of dissonance between past and present identities; and the formal expression of cognitive decline through cinematic strategies of point of view. However, a number of film critics have noted that the film approaches these themes in often discordant and inappropriate ways as it narrates the antics of a grotesque grandfather Amadeus (Nick Nolte) and his relationship with his granddaughter Matilda (Sophie Lane Nolte). Responses to *Headful of Honey* were almost universally negative. "There's no doubting the laudable intentions to confront the realities of Alzheimer's," wrote Trevor Johnson in the *Radio Times*, "but the execution, frankly, verges on the catastrophic," while the *New York Times* judged it as "a disastrous, tonally dishevelled and occasionally offensive treatment [of Alzheimer's]" (Johnson 2018; Ebiri 2018).

Headful of Honey was financed by Warner Bros. studios as an American remake of the hugely successful *Honig im Kopf* (2014), directed by and starring Til Schweiger, one of Germany's best-known actors and most commercially successful directors (Tartaglione 2015). Although the American remake closely follows many of the elements of the German original, the film's excessively romantic plot, simplistic characterization, and fantasy-like settings did not translate well for Anglophone audiences who found its treatment of dementia flimsy, unconvincing, and patronizing.

The story centres on Amadeus (Nolte), a brawny and often bawdy retired veterinarian. As the film opens, his granddaughter Matilda (played by Nolte's real-life granddaughter) tells us in voice-over (VO):

> Grandpa has Alzheimer's. People with Alzheimer's forget a lot of stuff. I mean, I forget to do my homework, or brush my teeth, but with my

grandpa, it's different. He forgets pretty much everything. So, I'm taking him on a trip to Venice to make him better.

We see this young/old odd couple travelling on a steam-driven train in Italy. Anachronistically, Matilda is talking to her parents on a mobile phone when Amadeus abruptly jumps off the train, casting lewd glances at beautiful young women as he goes, is chased by police and generally causing mayhem. The narrative then goes back in time to the memorial service of Amadeus' wife Maggie, whose death "started everything" some months before. Stumbling to the lectern to deliver the eulogy, he tells the congregation: "My Maggie was just wonderful. She had the biggest heart . . . and breasts. Big, beautiful breasts. She always laughed at my stupid joy, jokes. Right up to the end. What bees make milk? Boo-bies." Then, and presumably in light of this behaviour, Amadeus' son Nico (Matt Dillon) and Matilda arrive at a dilapidated farmhouse somewhere in rural America, with the intention of bringing Amadeus to live with them.

Beneath the tonal and temporal shifts and inconsistencies of this quite chaotic opening sequence, there are serious points being made about Alzheimer's disease (AD): a recognition by his family that Amadeus is in need of care and can no longer live alone, Nico's embrace of his responsibilities, and Matilda's childlike perspective that continues to engage with him as a person rather than a set of symptoms. Nico's proposal that Amadeus move to live with his family also introduces a narrative element that is common to all the films discussed here, reflecting the practical challenges and realities of caring for elders in contemporary Western societies in which smaller, geographically dispersed families tend to be the norm. Despite their considerable differences, these narratives thus offer a collective contemporary portrait of older male characters who are not "at home" in physical, psychological, and social senses.

It is debatable, however, that the film is interested in engaging with AD in any serious manner and instead – I would argue – uses it as a mechanism or shorthand to represent (male) ageing in patronizing and often contradictory ways. Indeed, it might be suggested that the film mobilizes common tropes and associations around AD primarily as a means of constructing a certain version of ageing white masculinity as an identity category that is out of time and "mind" with contemporary norms and values. At the same time, it sentimentally suggests that approaching such an identity through the eyes of a (female) child can redeem such an identity, albeit only momentarily.

Although the relationship between Amadeus and his granddaughter Matilda occupies the central storyline of the film and shapes its whimsical tone (eschewing realism for a world of warm colours and picturesque locations), the secondary father-son relationship is arguably more significant to its broader social resonances and meanings. The majority of the film's action takes place in the genteel surrounds of a stylized English country setting where Nico brings his father to live (and where his eccentricities are vividly counterpointed), but their complicated dynamic has its origins in a mode of masculinity forged in the American heartland, the land of cowboys and the western. When Nico and Matilda visit Amadeus following the funeral, we find him sitting on his front porch with a rifle in hand, determined to assert his rights in the frontier tradition. When the rifle is wrestled off him by Nico, he subsequently produces a Colt 45 and starts shooting up his living room telling his granddaughter: "Honey, if the Russians came you wouldn't wanna have your gun locked up!" While the comic scene narratively functions to illustrate that, in his current mental condition he can no longer live alone, his AD associates him with a version of masculinity that is as out of date and out of place as his phallic gun collection. Linking the "frontier masculinities" of the Old West and the Cold War, the scene frames tensions between father and son in terms of the shifting social understandings and performance of white American manhood.

In contrast to patterns of representation identified earlier, Amadeus is more often constructed as a figure of sexist (rather than violent) masculinity through his inappropriate language and behaviour. Rather than being understood as part of his diagnosis, however, such behaviours serve to reveal something of his inner character and generally bring levity rather than pathos to his condition. (Even a scene where he jumps into bed with a strange woman on a train sleeper and grabs her breasts is excused by the woman's husband when Matilda explains he has Alzheimer's.) Amadeus is thus an "old-fashioned" man whose words and actions belie a longing to be romantically reunited with his deceased wife.

The final farcical scenes (which opened the film) show Amadeus and Matilda travelling to Venice – the site of his honeymoon with Maggie – pursued by a frantic and worried Nico and Sarah. All are finally reunited and return home to England. In the transposition from German to US versions, however, there is a telling and interesting change in endings. In the original film, Sarah decides to stop working so that she can take care of her father-in-law and gives birth to a baby boy nine months later, who is named after his grandfather. A sense of care and continuity prevails. In the US version, however, we learn in voice-over that Amadeus is installed in a care home (after his caregiver quit), where he lives for a short time before dying. In this ending there is no redemption, no larger sense of meaning or rebirth; Amadeus ceases to exist. This change alters not only our final response to the film but also crucially towards the meaning of dementia, which is thus positioned as a short and chaotic interlude between a full and fulfilled life (marriage to Maggie, life in the United States) and death in a strange place. In the generally comic manner of its presentation and association with a recognizably American form of (rugged, manly, dominant) cowboy/cold warrior masculinity, the film therefore links AD not only with ageing masculinity in general but with the passing of a certain type of male: superficially crude and untutored, perhaps, but also romantic, loving, and loyal (Nolte's casting is essential to this intention) – a manliness whose time has passed or, as Matilda puts it, "and then he was gone."

Falling (2020)

Although it differs radically in tone and execution from *Headful of Honey*, the critically praised *Falling* shares a narrative focused on a late-life relationship between a son and his gruff American heartland father, who also suffers from dementia. In order to secure financing for what was a tough-sell project, Viggo Mortenson wrote, directed, produced, and starred in the film and composed its score (Ryan 2021). In interviews Mortenson stressed the personal nature and origins of his long-gestating directing debut and sought to underline the accuracy of its portrait of dementia: "*Falling* is based on my experience – there's a lot of dementia on both sides of my family. . . . My parents, my stepdad, grandparents, aunts, uncles, both sides. I've seen it a lot, up close" (Ryan 2021). While the film represents the disease in more realistic and confrontational terms than *Headful of Honey*, Mortenson's comments on developing the screenplay over four years also suggest broader, and comparable, motivations: "I wanted to pose questions rather than give answers. I wanted to ask myself, among other things, 'Are there limits to communication? Are there people you can't communicate with or who don't deserve to be communicated with?'" (Zemler 2021).

While largely focused on the difficult and often eruptive relationship between a father suffering from dementia and his son keen to care for him and allay his frequent confusion and anxieties, *Falling* might be read not simply as an effort to realistically represent the condition, but a film in which AD functions as a means of exploring wider themes linked to contemporary American masculinities. In this sense it might be related to Zeilig's (2014) conceptualization (following Susan Sontag) of "Dementia as Metaphor" in contemporary culture, "Where the exploration of dementia through a central character or situation has also been a means of questioning politics, social mores, morality, and the nature of our humanity" (Zeilig 2014, 259). Specifically, we might read it as a text seeking to allegorize – and come to terms with – the bruising, bitter, and highly gendered divisions of American cultural politics.

Although emotionally knotty and formally sophisticated, *Falling* is relatively simple in narrative terms. Willis (Lance Henriksen), an 80-year-old small farmer, travels from the east coast to Los Angeles for an indefinite stay with his middle-aged son John (Viggo Mortenson). Willis is a widower (who had a long relationship with a woman not John's mother). John is a gay man married to Asian-American physician Eric (Terry Chen), with whom he shares an adopted daughter, Mónica (Gabby Velis). Willis manifests signs of dementia and has come to California on John's initiative, with the intention of relocating from his farm to live closer to his son and daughter (Laura Linney). John has organized house viewings and a medical appointment for Willis but the older man's response to these interventions is generally negative and/or confrontational. Additionally, Willis makes little effort to suppress or disguise deep-seated attitudes of bigotry, homophobia, and misogyny even – or especially – towards his own children and grandchildren. After a medical check-up that reveals he must have major surgery, John returns with Willis to the family farm where the latter will live out his remaining days.

In discussing an earlier phase of fictional film representations, Cohen-Shalev and Marcus (2011) have argued that popular Anglo-American films in which AD is featured (*The Savages, Away from Her, Iris, The Iron Lady*) tend to distance the viewer from the person with AD. Zeilig (2014) has similarly noted that the biopic *Iron Lady* (2011) encourages us

> to look (and marvel) at the myriad ways in which a once hugely dominant figure in British political life has been undermined by the processes of AD. Dementia is portrayed as it "beats" the omnipotent Prime Minister and the net effect is to distance the viewer.
>
> (Zeilig 2014, 260)

Falling, on the other hand, does not distance us; quite the contrary, we are forced to engage with Willis from the very outset. It is a notably direct and generally unsentimental portrait of neurocognitive decline, encompassing spells of confusion and memory loss as well as eruptions of an irrational and outsized temper. If – as I have suggested – *Falling* has more on its mind than just a portrait of dementia, it nonetheless endeavours to bring the audience into the experience of AD from the perspectives of both sufferer and carer.

The film opens on scene of young parents and a baby; the mother asks the father to help as she changes the child. We cut to an airplane and see an older man (Willis) get out of his seat to go to the bathroom. John realizes he has gone and jumps to assist but Willis is irascible, angry, confused, disturbing other passengers, trying to smoke, swearing, and so on. Once in the aircraft's tiny bathroom we experience sudden shifts in narrative space and time – cutting between the present and past. We see Willis and John as a boy on a lake in an idyllic rural setting. The father lets the son shoot his rifle at mallards; they return home victorious and hand the duck to his doting mother. Once they land, Willis disappears and John gets home to find he left the airport of his own accord, too impatient to wait for him. Here we encounter more narrative information: John is married to Terry, who is leaving to work a night shift at hospital. Willis is sitting on the doorstep. "'Where's the can,' he asks John without apology, 'I'm going to take an almighty crap.'"

This 20-minute opening section not only condenses a large amount of narrative information but introduces formal elements that will be repeated throughout the film and are central to its intentions and meaning. Foregrounding its central focus on the father-son relationship, the narrative unfolds through a process of piecemeal, sometimes contradictory and cumulative revelations. Although the film follows recognizable Hollywood conventions (in casting, settings, costumes, etc.), the filmmakers unsettle the viewer and disrupt a sense of narrative continuity. This is primarily achieved through editing – flashbacks of varying lengths and temporalities (sometimes flashbacks/associative edits within a single sequence) – but also through other means; point-of-view (POV) shots and frontal close-ups, a soundtrack that is by turns elegiac and discordant, and Lance Henriksen's performance as Willis which is an unpredictable blend of lucidity and confusion, quietness, and crudity. Indeed, although it is naturalistic in tone and functions largely to establish the film's characters and settings, the opening section can be seen to introduce the struggle for POV that is at the centre of the film's thematic, as well as formal, concerns.

This struggle is further explored in more explicitly ideological terms the next day. John shares an airy and comfortable home with Ted and their daughter Monica. Together they (and Willis) visit a gallery followed by lunch at an Asian restaurant. Although somewhat over-determined, these scenes function semiotically to establish a liberal, middle-class outlook that promotes tolerance and embraces difference within a non-traditional family structure. Mortenson gives a political dimension to these cues through the insertion of the Obama "Hope" poster on the family's refrigerator door, the sight of which prompts a characteristically outrageous response from Willis:

> You voted for that negro, huh?
> You voted for McCain I take it?
> He's an American hero. Did they know you were a fag in the Army?
> I hardly knew it myself.
> Maybe that's a good thing.

Initially a conversation between a caring son and his dementia-suffering father, the exchange foregrounds tensions in their relationship in terms of the displacement of a hegemonic, "Cold War" era American masculinity – in which patriotism and whiteness were often imbricated – by a less rigid gender script in which identities of race or sexuality ceased to be defining attributes. More explicitly than in *Headful of Honey*, dementia serves as a means of characterizing a masculinity that is out of time and place. This is made metaphorically explicit in a scene when as they are eating lunch at the Asian restaurant, Willis gets up to go the bathroom, then wanders out the wrong door and ends up at the beach, where he sits until the tide comes in and he has to be rescued.

Throughout *Falling* we skip between past and present, though by virtue of the film's style and identification with Willis' perspective, we are not always certain where we are or who is generating the images. If dementia functions as a core concern and stylistic element of the film, it also serves to suggest that categories of race, gender, and sexuality are social constructs that are in flux and always open to revision. But the narrative concedes that it is too late for Willis (and, by extension, his ilk) to change. Having failed to convince his father of the potential for a new life in California, father and son return to the familiar terrain of "the north country," where Willis undergoes major surgery and goes home to his dilapidated farm.

As they argue over dinner – Willis refusing to eat the food prescribed for his health – the film *Red River* (1943) plays on a portable TV on the kitchen table. It is the film's famous closing scene where Tom Dunston (John Wayne) finally catches up with his surrogate son, Matt Garth (Montgomery Clift), and sets to fight him for having stolen his cattle in an epic clash between intergenerational American manhood in the transition between the open range and market capitalism. "Won't anything make a man out of you?" yells Wayne as Matt refuses to fight him. Likewise, Willis declares

> I'm going to make a few fried eggs. . . . This is my house and I can do as I please and if you don't like it you can go back to your boyfriend and eat all the salads you want.

The parallel is clear: Wayne and Willis are old men of the mythic American West, while Montgomery Clift and John now disrupt, defy, and challenge their embodiment of white manhood.

Falling concludes with John returning to his non-traditional family in California and leaving his father – who presumably will deteriorate further in physical and neurological terms, alone on his farm. This is framed in terms of a romantic resignation: "I can see why you want to stay here Dad – it's a beautiful place . . . I've asked someone to come and look in on you – whatever you need her to do – is that OK?" The final scenes show Willis lying in the snow, nuzzled by his horse. He opens his eyes and makes crude sexualized comments, conflating past and present in an enigmatic and – it must be said – unsatisfactory closure. Is he dreaming? Is he dead? Are we to understand he is better off having been left alone by his son?

Wulff (2008) and others have argued most films that deal with dementia are melodramas in which the suffering individual and their partners are portrayed as victims of a disease that gradually causes their separation. While *Falling* also maintains this trope of separation between caregiver and patient, it resists a fully melodramatic rendering of it, as well as the often accompanying "love miracle" which precedes the journey into darkness (Swinnen 2015). While there is a measure of acceptance of Willis by John, there is no reconciliation between the son and the father, and Willis remains as cut off from his son as he always has. Dementia has changed nothing; if anything it has clarified and codified their alienation from one another. The suggestion, on both levels, is that Willis – and men like him – are unreachable.

The Father (2020)

One of the more celebrated contemporary productions of *King Lear* was the 2018 BBC/Amazon Studios version with Anthony Hopkins playing the title role. While some reviewers noted the adaptation's referencing of Donald

Trump's presidency (a backdrop that is clearly present in all three films discussed here), dementia was again accepted as the most topical touchpoint for interpreting Lear's "madness":

> Anyone who's seen loved ones grapple with the condition will flinch in recognition when Lear inappropriately touches Goneril and verbally stumbles his way toward recognizing Cordelia . . . It's a vision of rule collapsing and both individuals and institutions losing their minds.
> (Zoller Seitz 2018)

With fatherhood and dementia also being the central themes of Florian Zeller's hit stage play *The Father* (London, 2015; New York, 2016) it was perhaps inevitable Hopkins would be first choice for lead role in the screen adaptation. Hopkins inhabits the role with an understated ease and familiarity, gradually building from an avuncular middle-class politeness through periodic confusion, to moments of explosive anger and eventually palpable distress. Progressively losing a grip on his surroundings and sense of self, here was a Learian performance for the age of Alzheimer's.

As the film opens, we see Anne (Olivia Colman) walking to her father's apartment/flat where he lives alone. On the soundtrack an aria plays – one of three pieces of opera included in the film – and, as she enters, it abruptly ceases as Anthony (Hopkins) registers her entrance and takes off his headphones. We have, in other words, been hearing his soundtrack while watching her. This is our first indication of not just a disparity but a disruption in perception, formally indicated through the separation of the film's visual and aural elements. While the visual seems to afford the viewer an objective scene, the soundtrack relates to another subjectivity and indeed narrative (Purcell's opera *King Arthur*). Anne thus disrupts Anthony's world in two senses – physical and psychic – a disturbance that is also present in the aria which speaks of being roused from sleep, male ageing and a desire for release that prefigures the film's conclusion:

> What Power art thou,
> Who from below,
> Hast made me rise,
> Unwillingly and slow,
> From beds of everlasting snow!
>
> Let me, let me,
> Let me, let me,
> Freeze again . . .
> Let me, let me,
> Freeze again to death.
> (Purcell)

Although he greets his daughter with apparent clarity and calm, the scene commences an accelerating series of narrative disturbances and disruptions and hastens a loss of perspective between subjective experience and objective reality. Indeed, as a second viewing reveals, this moment represents the beginning of the end for such a clear separation.

In *Headful of Honey* and *Falling*, the sons of the gruff and increasingly unpredictable fathers insist that they come to live with them once their diagnosis becomes clear. While this care solution ends in failure of one kind or other, such late-life proximity facilitates a degree of emotional reproachment between the ageing parent and adult child. *The Father* follows a similar narrative trajectory but imbues it with complexity and pathos rather than melodrama. In the former films the widower fathers register and reluctantly agree (at least at first) to leaving their homes. In Zeller's text, Anthony does not fully register this reality or indeed the change that follows, and his refusal and/or inability to accept either is expressed by his ongoing obsession with his "flat" (a word that appears 27 times in the screenplay). Zeller draws on the paranoic tendencies characteristic of dementia to express anxieties about space and time – both of which, Anthony believes, are in danger of being stolen from him.

Throughout the drama he repeats similar phrases: "This is my flat, isn't it?"; "What are you doing in my flat"; "Let me be absolutely clear. I am not leaving my flat. I am not leaving my flat." At one point he suggests that Anne is trying to steal it from him and tells his new carer Laura:

> Well, the situation is this: I have lived in this flat for some time now – I bought it more than 30 years ago – it's a big flat – I've been very happy here. Anyway, my daughter is very interested in it. . . . Sorry dear, I may as well tell you I'm not going to leave this flat anytime soon.

The flat is thus Anthony's psycho-spatial locus of identity even if, as we discover, it's not the flat he believes it to be. Parallel to this fixation is a corresponding anxiety about time, his loosening relationship to which is expressed through the constant loss and search for his watch (a word that occurs over 30 times) and a belief that others are stealing it from him. "Has anybody seen my watch"; "I've always had this watch, you know"; "The watch must be somewhere." At one point he tells a new carer that "I have two watches. I've always had two. One on my wrist and the other in my head." It's a remark that seeks to bridge external and internal worlds and perceptions, with Anthony cheerfully insisting that even if he can't always find his watch, he knows what time it is.

Of the films discussed in this chapter, *The Father* most fully and intensely explores the meaning and experience of dementia through a motif of home/unhomeliness and pursues this on spatial, thematic, and psychological levels. Its narrative moves us – and its protagonist – through three such spaces of decreasing familiarity: the flat/apartment of Anthony (Hopkins), the flat/apartment of Anthony's daughter Anne (Olivia Coleman), and finally a residential nursing home. This progression is not linear, however, and Zeller moves Anthony in and out of times and spaces to the extent that neither he, nor the audience, are quite sure where we are. As the film progresses, space-time logic gradually collapses, culminating in a scene where we see Anthony leaving his bedroom and walking down a hospital corridor where he discovers his daughter Lucy who lies badly injured, and then eventually waking up in the nursing home where Anne has placed him.

Finally, in the present of the film the audience gains mastery over the various slippages of place and persons (the nurses he mistook for his daughter and boyfriend/husband, etc.). But Anthony does not, and we experience a "letting go" between his cognitive experience and our own. He makes one last appeal for certainty as he calls for his "Mummy" as he weeps childishly. Although its shares similarities with *Headful of Honey* and *Falling* in ending with the father alone, longing for the comfort of a female/maternal presence and a desire to "go home," it is a far more devasting conclusion than either of those films. Anthony's condition is not a metaphor; he is less a male type or outmoded ideal than a loving father who has become unmoored from his surroundings. In the place of the recollection of a romantic honeymoon or sexual union, we have only fear: "I don't know what's happening anymore – do you know? – nowhere to put my head down anymore."

Conclusion

As many revivals of *King Lear* in recent years attest, cultural constructions of ageing masculinities have become increasingly entwined with themes of dementia on both stage and screen. This reciprocity reflects, perhaps, not just the enduring value of Shakespeare's portrait of old age but its usefulness in reflecting upon two highly topical social concerns: anxieties around the growing incidence of dementia in ageing Western societies and the meaning of masculinity in old age. The films considered in this chapter offer explorations of these themes in contemporary cinema. While significantly different in their sources and approach, these texts exhibit notable points of comparison as well as contrast. As with Shakespeare's Lear, all three men are widowers who leave their homes and become care dependent on their children. All exhibit, to varying degrees, symptoms commonly associated with dementia including forgetfulness, confusion, depression, and paranoia. While, in *Headful of Honey* and *Falling*, the filmmakers add degrees of sexism and crude language to such symptoms, *The Father* offers us a gentler figure whose one moment of impropriety is to tell his new carer that she is "lovely" and confuse her with his beloved dead daughter. This difference of emphasis is also reflected in the casting, the first two deploying older American actors associated with traditional Hollywood genre masculinities such as crime films, Westerns, while *The Father* is a clear intertext to Hopkins' more literary stage origins and roles. These differences reflect competing emphases on themes of masculinity and dementia.

Headful of Honey can't quite make up its mind about how it wants to portray dementia because it isn't quite sure about what kind of man Amadeus is or what it wants to say about him as a father. Ultimately, it seems to suggest that he is simply a man of his time who is also out of time. *Falling* also presents us with a man whose style of masculinity – right-wing, racist, and misogynistic – is wholly out of step with contemporary values, but it does so in more recognizable terms. The film's treatment of dementia is recognizably constructed in relation to the contemporary "culture wars" with the ageing father associated with a post-war hegemonic, heteronormative whiteness, while his son is identified with the liberal values of recent Democratic Presidents Clinton and Obama. *Falling* is to be commended for its efforts to offer a more accurate depiction of dementia symptoms, as well as expressions of its protagonists' splintering subjectivity and suffering through sound and point of view. Nonetheless, it comes to a similar conclusion to the often risible *Headful of Honey*, to the extent that the father is deemed unfit for contemporary society and is left alone on his farm where he can care for his horses, watch Westerns and vent his disgust for women, "flag burners and cocksuckers."

Only *The Father* eschews a social purpose to focus fully on the individual and seeks to give expression to the subjective experience of dementia. It does this through a fragmented and disturbing narrative of shifting temporal and spatial settings – a "puzzle film" (Buckland 2009) that confounds repeated attempts by its protagonist – and its audience – to maintain psychological coherence. Ultimately, however, Anthony is also left by his child, when Anne reluctantly commits him to a nursing home when she goes to work in Paris. "Fetch me home," he implores, but as with Lear and the other fathers discussed here, he is left confused and alone, his dementia framed as contemporary tragedy.

Works Cited

Beale, Russell, "Talking Lear: Simon Russell Beale on King Lear." 2014. https://www.youtube.com/watch?v=xgXM0b6PaHw

Buckland, Warren. *Puzzle Films: Complex Storytelling in Contemporary Cinema*, Wiley-Blackwell, 2009.

Butler, Mark. "The Modern Lear – 'Oh Let Me Not Have Dementia.'" https://dementia.stir.ac.uk/blogs/diametric/2014-03-19/modern-lear-oh-let-me-not-have-dementia

Cohen, Lawrence. *No Aging in India: Alzheimer's, The Bad Family, and Other Modern Things*. U California P, 1998.

Cohen-Shalev, Amir, and Esther Lee Marcus. "Lifting the Lid of Pandora's Box: Alzheimer's Disease in the Cinema." 2011. www.interdisciplinary.net/wpcontent/uploads/2011/08/shalevhpaper.pdf.

Combe, Kirk, and Schmader, Kenneth. "Naturalizing Myths of Aging: Reading Popular Culture." *Journal of Aging and Identity* 4 (1999): 79–109.

Ebiri, Bilge. "'Head Full of Honey' Review: Alzheimer's Gets the Wacky Grandpa Treatment." *New York Times*, 30 Nov. 2018. www.nytimes.com/2018/11/30/movies/head-full-of-honey-review.html

Fox, Nick C., and Ronald Petersen. "The G8 Dementia Research Summit – A Starter for Eight? 9909. Vol. 382." *Lancet*, 2013. 1968–1969.

Global Burden of Disease Study. 2019. www.healthdata.org/gbd/2019

Hartung, Heike, Rüdiger Kunow, and Matthew Sweney, eds. *Ageing Masculinities, Alzheimer's and Dementia Narratives*. Bloomsbury, 2020.

Johnston, Trevor. "Review: *Headful of Honey*." *Radio Times*, 2018. www.radiotimes.com/movie-guide/b-orfq6z/head-full-of-honey/

Kitwood, Tom. *Dementia Reconsidered: The Person Comes First*. Open UP, 1997.

Lawson, Mark. "King Lear – Can the BBC's Starry Adaptation Avoid Bard Mistakes?" *The Guardian*, 28 May 2018. www.theguardian.com/tv-and-radio/2018/may/28/king-lear-bbc-anthony-hopkins

Morrison, Alastair. "Review Essay: *Forgotten*, by Marlene Goldman AND *Alzheimer's Disease Life Writing*, by Martina Zimmermann." *Age, Culture, Humanities* 4. https://ageculturehumanities.org/WP/double-review-forgotten-by-marlene-goldman-and-alzheimers-disease-life-writing-by-martina-zimmermann/

Ryan, P. "'It Feels Like a Horror Film': New Dementia Dramas 'Falling,' 'Supernova' Aim for Truthfulness Over Tears." *USA Today*, 5 Feb. 2021. https://eu.usatoday.com/story/entertainment/movies/2021/02/05/viggo-mortensen-falling-supernova-the-father-depict-dementia-realistically/4384359001/

Segers, Kurt. "Degenerative Dementias and Their Medical Care in the Movies." *Alzheimer Disease & Associated Disorders* 21.1 (Jan–Mar. 2007): 55–59.

Swinnen, Aagje. "'Everyone is Romeo and Juliet!' Staging Dementia in Wellkåmm to Verona by Suzanne Osten." *Journal of Aging Studies* 26.3 (2012): 309–318.

Swinnen, Aagje. "Ageing in Film." *Routledge Handbook of Cultural Gerontology*. Eds Julia Twigg and Wendy Martin. Routledge, 2015. 69–76.

Tartaglione, Nancy. "Strong Frame for Fox, Eastwood, Local Pics at International Box Office: Update." *Deadline.com*, 13 Jan. 2015. https://deadline.com/2015/01/international-box-office-night-at-the-museum-tomb-taken-3-american-sniper-unbroken-1201347113/

Werner, Perla, Goldstein, Dovrat, and Buchbinder, Eli. "Subjective Experience of Family Stigma as Reported by Children of Alzheimer's Disease Patients." *Qualitative Health Research* 20 (2010): 159–169.

Wulff, Hans J. "Als segelte ich in die Dunkelheit . . . Die ästhetische und dramatische Analyse der Alzheimer-Krankheit im Film [As if I Sailed into the Darkness . . . . The Aesthetic and Dramatic Analysis of Alzheimer's Disease in Film]." *Jahrbuch Literatur und Medizin*. 2nd ed. (Winter 2008): 199–216. www.derwulff.de/2-151.

Zeilig, Hanna. "Dementia as a Cultural Metaphor." *The Gerontologist* 54.2 (Apr. 2014): 258–267. https://doi.org/10.1093/geront/gns203

Zemler, Emily. "Viggo Mortensen Wanted to 'Pose Questions' by Making 'Falling.'" https://observer.com/2021/02/viggo-mortensen-interview-falling/.

Zoller Seitz, Matt. "Amazon's *King Lear* Captures the Heart of a Classic Shakespeare Tragedy." Vulture.com, 28 Sept. 2018. https://www.vulture.com/2018/09/king-lear-amazon-anthony-hopkins-review.html.

Index

Page numbers in *italics* refer to figures. Page numbers followed by 'n' indicate a note.

able-bodied heterosexuality 163
able-bodiedness 167
A bout de souffle (Breathless; 1960) 61
Academy Awards 75, 163
accountability 62
Ade, Maren 6–7, 134, 137, 145
"adjust/perish" progressivism 93
affirmative old age 3
age-defying youthfulness 26
ageing: boyhood 12–13; chronometric time 122; contemporary cinematic depictions 77; cultural construction of 168; Czech masculinities 6, 107; definition 11–12; de-gendering 76; Depardieu, candide effect 45–49; disempowering effect of 76; elderly masculinities 14–15; Estonian cinema 88–98; Fabrice Luchini and fetishization of literary culture 52–55; filmography 16; French cinema 75–85; gendered approaches 76–77; guyland 13–14; heroes 198; Johnny Hallyday, fantasizing the family 49–52; male 136; and male melodrama 92; masculinities 2–3, 6, 11, 75–78, 106, 134–146, 190; as public persona 167–169; text 60; tragic tonality 92; women's roles 77
ageism 9
Age of Adaline, The (2015) 208
age-related social withdrawal 62
Agewise 158
Aimée, Anouk 75, 78–79
Air Force One (1997) 208
Alfie (1966) 18
Almodóvar, Pedro 7, 160–171

Alzheimer's disease (AD) 70, 72, 114, 122, 215–219
American acting 35
Americanization 61
American Western 191
Amour (2012) 77
Anderson, Lindsay 34
Anglo-American films 221
Anglophone cinemas 2, 8, 214
anti-period films 8, 175
anxiety 136
Apocalypse Now 190–191
Arab dancing 66
Arthur (1981) 30, 32
ART OF LIVING 106
Atkins, Eileen 35
Atlantic 190–191
Autumn Spring (2001) 102; ageing masculinity 106; Czech masculinity 107; Emílie, character of 107; *pábitel* 106–107
average retirement age 205
Away from Her (2006) 215–216

Babí léto (2001) 102, 106–107
baby boomer generation 23
Bad Day for the Cut (2017) 189, 194, 196, 199–200
Baker, Brian 202
Ballinger, Fred 153, 157
Banana Splits, The 137, 146n1
Banderas, Antonio 7, 160, 168–169, 171
Bardot, Brigitte 77
Barrandov Film Studios 101, 109
Barton, John 34
Bates, Alan 33

Index

Batman Begins (2005) 21–22
Batman series 208
Beatles 104
Beckett, Samuel 39
Belmondo, Jean-Paul 61–62
Berkeley, Busby 111
Berlin, Normand 39
Beugnet, Martine 77
"bigs" 14
Big Trail, The (1932) 192
black comedy 107
Blade Runner sequel (2017) 208
Blethyn, Brenda 20
Blowing the Bloody Doors Off 25
Bond, James 19
boomer generation 1–2
boyhood 12–13
Boyle, Mick 153
Bradshaw, Peter 112, 134
Brideshead Revisited (1981) 32, 34
British acting profession 33
British cultural capital 31
British Film Institute classics 192–193
British theatrical acting 34
Broadbent, Jim 26
Brodský, Vlastimil 106
Brooks, David 190–193
Brydon, Rob 136–137
Bugaj, Malgorzata 95
Bullock, Sandra 20–21
Burns, George 207
Buscombe, Edward 192–193
Butler, Isaac 35
Butler, Judith 76
Butler, Mark 214

Caine, Michael 4, 148; active ageing, mythologies of 22–24; final act 25–27; as "tribal elder" 19–22
Calder, Jenni 201
Campbell, Joseph 13
Campion, Jane 30–31, 191–192
Cannes Film Festival 75, 134, 163
Capano, Ciro 150
Capuano, Antonio 150
Carcass of Beef (1657) 184
Carney, Art 207
Cartwright, Jim 20
Casanova 178–179, 182–183
Casanova, Giacomo 7–8, 175–176
Cassidy, Gary 35
Catastrophe (2000) 39
Caughie, John 33–34

Chariots of Fire (1981) 32
Charlatan (2020) 103, 114–115
Cherry Orchard, The 109
Cheyenne Social Club, The (1970) 206–207
Chinatown (1974) 206–207
chronological age and masculinity 122–126
Chytilová, Věra 105
Cider House Rules, The 19, 21
Cimrman, Jára 108
cinematic masculinity 73
cinematic representations 2
cinematic voyeurism 64–65
clandestine enemy 195
Cochrane, Claire 33
Cocoon (1985) 207
cognitive disability 93, 216
cognitive frailty 37
Cohen-Shalev, Amir 221
comedy-drama 134
complicit male 126
Connell, Raewyn 120, 126, 128
contemporary action thrillers 8, 198
Coogan, Steve 136–137
Cooper, Bradley 207–208
Cooper, Gary 191–192
Cormican, Muriel 140–141
Costner, Kevin 19
Courtenay, Tom 26
court métrage 82
Coutard, Raoul 62
COVID-19 lockdown 108, 115, 208
Craig, Daniel 195
"crisis" of masculinity 90–91
Crouse, Lindsay 35
Cry Macho, 2021 190
cultural capital 32
cultural construction of ageing 168
cultural discourses 25–27
cultural gerontology 2, 22
cultural heritage 34
cultural narrative of ageing 22–23
cultural work 9
Cyrano de Bergerac (1990) 67
Czech cinema 6, 101–116
Czech-Irish biopic 103
Czech Lion (Czech Oscar) 109
Czech masculinity 107, 113, 115
Czech *mystifikace* 108
czeski film 110

Damon, Matt 195
Daniel Blake (2016) 134
Dano, Paul 149
dark aesthetics 176
Dark Knight, The (2008) 21–22
Dark Knight Rises, The (2012) 21–22
de-ageing 8; actual age for retirement 205; cessation of employment 205; cultural reasoning 206; domestic box office income 210; guarded attitudes 206–207; Hollywood syllogism 210; middle-aged stars 207–208; retirement age 205; social representation 205
Dean, James 14
death, attitude towards 149
Death Wish (1974) 193–194
Death Wish 5: The Face of Death (1994) 194
de Beauvoir, Simone 76, 81
Dědictví aneb Kurvahošigutntag (1992) 105
deep old age 4, 25, 36–37
Delon, Alain 61–62
dementia 215–217
De Niro, Robert 209
Depardieu, Gerard 4
Depp, Johnny 208
Der letzte schöne Herbsttag 121
DiCaprio, Leonardo 207–208
Die Hard 92
Die Vampirschwestern (2010) 121
Dirty Harry (1971) 24, 190–191, 193
disability and illness 164
discomfort and comedy 7
Dítě, Jan 111–112
Dolan, Josephine 1, 23, 25, 136–137
domestication 13–14
Double Standard of Aging, The 151
Downing, Lisa 60, 64–65
Dracula 181–183
dramatic comedy 102–103
Dressed to Kill (1980) 18
Driving Miss Daisy (1989) 208
Dussollier, André 77
Dyer, Richard 17–18

Eastern European film 5
Eastwood, Clint 137, 190, 193–194
Edwards, Ethan 190, 192, 199
Ehle, Jennifer 41
Elavad pildid (2013) 92
El primer deseo (First Desire) 170

Emery, Dick 137
Empties (2007) 102, 107–109
Enkel für Anfänger 120
Entertainer, The (1957) 34
Epstein, Marek 114
Erdmann, Toni 139, 141
erotic male fantasy 65–66
Estonian cinema 88–98
Etxeandia, Asier 160
European Film awards 134
Expendables, The 15
Expendables series (2010–present) 196
Eyre, Richard 214–216

Falling (2020) 216, 220–223
Father, The (2020) 216, 223–226
Featherstone, Mike 36–37
female: feminism 1; self-sacrifice 65–66; sexuality 182
Ferilli, Sabrina 152
Filmhitliste 2020 120
Finney, Albert 33
FIPRESCI (International Federation of Film Critics) award 134
Firebird (2021) 91
First Knight 31–32
Floride (Florida, 2015) 70
"flower power" generation 126
Fonda, Henry 206–207
Ford, Harrison 208
Ford, John 8, 189
Ford Mustang 79, 81, 83
Forman, Miloš 109, 112
Fountain of Age, The (Friedan) 76
fragile masculinity 137
frail old age 4
Franco, Jesús 175
Frantic (1988) 208
Freeman, Morgan 207–208
Fremdschämen 140–141, 145
French cinema 75, 77–78
Fugitive, The (1993) 208

Gabin, Jean 61
Gambardella, Jep 151, 157
Gambon, Michael 26
Gandhi (1982) 32
Garth, Matt 223
gender identity 76, 198
gentle masculinity 94
"geriaction" cinema 195
Get Carter (1971) 18

Gielgud, John 29–41; frailty, virtuosity, and voice 36–40; heritage, theatre, and performance 31–35; as stage actor 29–30
Gilliam, Terry 67, 72
Ginsberg, Allen 115–116
Godard, Jean-Luc 61
Gods and Monsters (1998) 208
Going in Style (1979) 206–207
Good Soldier Švejk, The 112
Gordon, Robert 33
Goscilo, Helena 90–91, 96
Gothic masculinity 182
Granny Nanny (2020) 6, 121; age-appropriate behaviour 123; grandparents-for-rent 121; intergenerational cooperation and solidarity 125; older masculinity 126–129; older protagonists 125; sociocultural problems 126; stereotypical perceptions, younger generations 124
Great, The (2020–21) 41
Great Beauty, The (2013) 7, 148–158; climax 154; Jep Gambardella, frustration 150; Sorrentino's message, catalysts of 155–157
Greenaway, Peter 30, 175
Green Cats 90; ageing masculinities 89; domineering masculinity 94, 96–97; emotional wounds 97; generational conflict, masculinities 92; generational difference 88–89, 94; Kafkaesque situation 95; main characters 88–89; masculinity, crisis of 90; mass deportation 94; moral clarity 92
greying of Europe 2
Groos, Wolfgang 121
Grosz, Elisabeth 182
Grumpy Old Men (1993) 207
Guardian, The 29, 112
Guinness, Alec 36
Gullette, Margaret Morganroth 7, 22, 149, 158
guyland 13–14
Györi, Zsolt 91, 97

Hall, Peter 34
Hallyday, Johnny 4, 60–61, 67
Hand of God, The 150–151, 156
Haneke, Michael 77
Hanlon, Niall 94

Hannah and Her Sisters (1986) 18
Happy End (2017) 77
Harder They Fall, The (2021) 191–192
Harry Brown (2009) 23–24
Hašek, Jaroslav 102, 112
Hashamova, Yana 90–91, 96
Haskell, Molly 134
Havel, Miloš 109
Havel, Václav 39, 102, 109–110, 112, 115
Hawley, Josh 190–191
Headful of Honey (2018) 216–219
hegemonic masculinity 3, 76, 81–82, 92, 126, 162
Heim, Michael Henry 107
Helsinki Accords 104
Hensler, Martin 39
Hepworth, Mike 36–37
heritage films and TV 34
Herman, Mark 20
Higson, Andrew 34
Història de la meva mort (Story of My Death; 2013) 175
Hobbesian horror 12–13
Hobbit trilogy (2012–14) 208–209
Holland, Agnieszka 114
Hollywood cinema 2
Holocaust, the 111, 113, 126
Home (1970) 34
homophobia 13
homosexuality 114, 128; enactment 132; innocence 13; purity 12–14
Honor de Cavalleria (Quixotic; 2006) 175
Hopkins, Anthony 214, 223–224
Horrocks, Jane 20
horror and desire 153–155
Hrabal, Bohumil 102–103, 107, 111–113
Hugo, Victor 80
Huillet, Straub 175
Hüller, Sandra 141
Human Apparatus, The 148
human trafficking 190
Humphries, Barry 137
Huppert, Isabelle 77
Huston, John 206–207

I, Daniel Blake (2016) 134
Indiana Jones (2008) 208
Indiana Jones and the Raiders of the Lost Ark (1981) 207
Innocent 46, 47

intergenerational conflict 6–7, 91–92
intergenerational solidarity 119–122
Interpreter, The (2018) 103, 113–114
intertextuality 184–186
Ipcress File, The (1966) 18
Irigaray, Luce 180
Iris (2001) 215–216
Irishman, The (2019) 207
Iron Lady (2011) 221
I Served the King of England (2006) 103, 111–113
Italian Job, The (1968) 18

Jackson, Russell 36
Jeremiah Johnson (1972) 191
Jeunesse, Lucien 63
Jewel in the Crown, The (1984) 34

Kahn, Robert 160
Kaiser, Oldřich 111
Kalte Füße 121
Karlovy Vary International Film Festival 111
Käro, Kirill 96
Kastenbaum, Robert 151
Kaufman, Andy 137
Keitel, Harvey 148
Kermode, Mark 134
Kersey, Paul 194–195
Kid, The (1921) 97
Kilbourn, Russell 151
Kimmel, Michael 3–4, 89
King, French Sun 175
King Lear 8–9, 109, 214–215
King of May 115–116
King of Thieves 26–27
Király, Hajnal 91
Klass (2007) 91
Knocked Up (2007) 13–14
Knox, Simone 35
Kolja (1996) 6, 102, 104–106
Kolya (1996) 102, 104–106
Kožený, Viktor 105
Král majáles 115–116
Kramer vs. Kramer 14
Kubrickian fashion 180
kukeri (traditional Romanian) 136

La mort de Louis XIV (The Death of Louis the 14th; 2016) 175
La Movida 161
Landscapers (crime television series) 191–192

Lapotaire, Jane 35
Laslett, Peter 23
Lauterbach, Heiner 127
La vieillesse (De Beauvoir) 76
Law, Jude 150
Lawrence of Arabia (1962) 34
Lawson, Mark 214
Leaving (2011) 102, 109–111
LeBeouf, Shia 195
Leconte, Patrice 60
Le Crabe-Tambour (1977) 62–63, 72
Le Jeu des mille francs 63–64
Lelouch, Claude 5, 75–85
Le Mari de la coiffeuse (1990) 65
LeMay, Alan 192
Le Parfum d'Yvonne (1993) 64–65
Les Aventures d'Antoine Doinel 78
Les plus belles années d'une vie 79–82
Leyssens, Jacob 184
Lherminier, Claude 70
L'Homme du train (2002) 60–61, 67
Liar 14
Linson, John 191–192
Little Voice 20
Loach, Ken 134
Loiselle, Marie-Claude 65–66
Lord of the Flies (1990) 12–13
Lord of the Rings trilogy (2001–03) 208–209
Louis XIV 7
Lucernafilm 109
Luchini, Fabrice 4

Magnus (2007) 91
Making the Cut 197
male ageing: cinematic narratives of 189–203; crime and punishment 199–201; dead men riding 201–202; homo-sociality 136; organizational statuses 189; patriarchal power 189; physical labour-power 189; and retribution, contemporary narratives 196–198; western masculinity and myth 190–192
male melodrama: ageing 91–92; aggressive masculinity 93; dementia, "hyper-cognitive" era 96; fatalistic ending 94; generational difference 94; *Green Cats* 88–97; intergenerational conflict 91–92; men's crimes 92
male privilege 127
Mamet, David 39
Mandariinid (2013) 91

Man Who Would Be King, The 18
Marathon Man (1976) 206–207
Marceau, Sophie 77
Marcus, Esther Lee 221
Markson, Elizabeth W. 36
Marks & Spencer 168
Marques, Sandrine 70
Martin, Wendy 2
Masaryk, Tomáš Garrigue 110
masculinities 12, 60–73, 75; ageing and 75–78, 106; aggressive 93; constructions 61–62, 126–127; crisis of 90–91; domineering forms 94, 96–97; gender identity 76; generational conflict of 92; gentle 94; hegemonic 76, 81–82, 92, 120, 126–127; loss of 79–81; older 126–129; post-Soviet context 89–90; redemption 14; Soviet era masculinity models 90–91; transnational business 128
"Masculinity and Class: Michael Caine as 'Working-Class Hero'" 17–18
masquerade 60–73
Mazierska, Eva 114
Mazierska, Ewa 103
McCarthy, Cormac 198
McCartney, Paul 104
McDormand, Frances 150
McKellen, Ian 207–208
McRuer, Robert 163, 165, 167
Mellen, Joan 193
Melling, Victor 21
mental acuity 198
mental illness 37
Menzel, Jiří 111–113
#MeToo era 9
middle-class complacency 18
Mikolášek, Jan 114–115
Milius, Amanda 191–193
Mills, Bryan 196
mimesis 180
mimicry 180
Minu näoga onu (2017) 92
Miss Congeniality 20–21
Monsieur Hire (1989) 64–65
Moore, Dudley 32
moral clarity 92
Morel, Pierre 195
Morley, Sheridan 30
Morning Glory (2010) 208
Morrison, Alastair 214
Mortez, Michel 63–64

Mouzon, Dawne 92
Mr Bean's Holiday (2007) 72–73
museumization 139
mystification 108

narratives: ageing, masculinity, and intergenerational solidarity 119–122; chronological age and masculinity 122–126; older masculinity 126–129
national cinematic traditions 2–3
National Conservatism Conference 190
Navalny, Alexei 110
Nazi Occupation 68, 111
Neale, Steve 92
Neeson, Liam 195
Nellis, Alice 104
Netflix 115
neuro-normative gaze 8–9, 216
New Pope, The 150
No Country for Old Men (2005) 198
Noé, Gasper 77
No Man's Land (1975) 34
Novotný, Antonín 114

Obsluhoval jsem anglického krále (2006) 103, 111–113
Odcházení (2011) 102, 109–111
Olivier, Laurence 29–30, 206–207
Once Upon a Time in Hollywood (2019) 209
One Man Up (2001) 150
oriental dance 66
Ostře sledované vlaky (1966) 111
otherness 166
O'Toole, Peter 29, 33
Ozon, François 77

pábitel 106–107
Pacino, Al 209
Pain and Glory (Dolor y gloria) (2019) 7, 160–171; ageing as public persona 167–169; drug use 165; homosexual desires, Salvador 161; life experience, Salvador 162; masculinity 162; queerness 166–167; Salvador Mallo 160–171; Salvador's sexuality 166; successful ageing 169
Palme d'Or 75, 134
Paranoia (2013) 208
para-visuals 184–186
Passer, Ivan 109
Patterson, Less 137
performative, cinema 184–186

Index 235

performative masculinity 136
Peter Pan syndrome and depression 150
physical and vocal transformation 35
Piccoli, Michel 61–62
Pinter, Harold 34
Pitt, Brad 207–208
Pius XIII 150
Polish Eagle 2009 109
Polley, Sarah 215–216
Ponzi scheme 105
Portrait of a Lady, The 30–31, 37
post-Soviet: cinemas 5; European cinemas 5–6; society 6
Power of the Dog (2021) 191–192
Prague Spring 102–104, 115
Pride and Prejudice (1995) 41
progressive emasculation 14–15
Prospero's Books 29–30
Providence (1977) 32
provocative sexuality 66
psychological complexity 65
Puustusmaa, Andres 88–89

queerness 166
Quixote, Don 7, 175

Rae, Paul 39
Rain (2020) 91
Rambo, John 197–198
Rambo: Last Blood (2019) 189, 194, 196, 200, 202
Rams (2015), 134
Rebel Without a Cause (1955) 14
RED (2010) 196
Red Dawn (1984) 191
Red River (1943) 223
rejuvenation 136
Renzi, Andrea 150
resistant fictions 7, 158
Resnais, Alain 32
Revival (2013) 102–104
Richardson, Ralph 29–30, 34
Ridicule (1996) 72–73
Riva, Emmanuelle 77
Rochefort, Jean 5, 68–69; as ageing star 60–73; French national treasure 61; representations of ageing 73
Rogan, Seth 14
Rohelised Kassid (2017) 6, 88
Role Models (2008) 14
romanticism 8
Ross, Kristin 79
Rowe, John 160

Ruffalo, Mark 207–208
Russell, Maurice 30

Sabor (Flavor) 160
Samardzija, Zoran 96
Samuel, Jeymes 191
Sandberg, Linn 3
Šarlatán (2020) 103, 114–115
Saura, Carlos 175
Schneider, Elsa 19
Schoendoerffer, Pierre 62, 72
Schwarzenegger, Arnold 207
Searchers, The (1956) 8, 189, 191–197, 202
Sedmikrásky (1966) 105
self-conscious modernity 61–62
self-defence 24
self-discovery 64
self-fulfilment and inactivity 23
self-reflexive comedic drama 102
self-reliance 6
Serra, Albert 7, 175
Servillo, Toni 148
sex/sexual: awakening 170; boredom 13; fetishism 65; traffickers 201
Shakespeare 109
Shawshank Redemption, The (1997) 208
Sheaffer, Madame 65
Sheridan, Taylor 191–192
Shine 38
Shootist, The (1976) 206–207
sibling society 14
Siegel, Don 193
silvering 1–2
Silver Linings Playbook (2012) 209
Simonischek, Peter 135
Sirotek, Jiří 111
Six Guns and Society 194
Skřivánci na niti (1969) 111
social taboos 25
social typologies 18
Soda Pictures 134
Something's Gotta Give (2003) 15
Sontag, Susan 151
Sorrentino, Paolo 7, 148–149, 158
Soviet era masculinity models 90–91
Soviet-era norms 6
Soviet-style normalization, 1970s–1980s 102
Spicer, Andrew 18–19
Springer, Kristen 92
Stage Directions 36

stage performance in Britain 35
Stand by Me (1986) 12
Stars (1979) 18
Star Trek TV series (1987–94) 208
Star Wars (1977) 38
Star Wars (2015) series 208
State Socialism 90
Stewart, James 206–207
Stewart, Patrick 207–208
Still Alice (2014) 215–216
Storey, David 34
Story of My Death (2013) 8, 175–176;
  ageing and masculinity 176;
  avant-garde dark aesthetics 177;
  conceptual complexity 177; dark
  aesthetics 176; declining sexuality
  176; dichotomous representation
  180–184; intertextuality 184–186;
  masculinities 180–184; *Mimesis*
  180–184; older men's stereotyping
  180–184; para-visuals 184–186;
  performative, cinema 184–186; time
  as metaphor for ageing and death
  177–180; transgressions of dark
  aesthetics 184–186
Story of My Life 8
Straight Story, The (1999) 207
successful ageing 23, 160
Šulík, Martin 113
Svěrák, Zdeněk 102, 108–109
Swinnen, Aagje 3, 9, 76, 82, 96

Taken (2008) 195
Tallinn Black Nights Film Festival
  2007 109
Tandem (1987) 63–65
"the fourth age" 4
There Must Be a Lone Ranger 201
Thomson, David 30
Tichborne Claimant, The 32
Tlmočník (2018) 103, 113–114
Toffs, Laura 20
Tolik, Zek 91, 97
Toni Erdmann (2016) 6–7, 134; ageing
  masculinity 134–146; father-daughter
  relationship 136, 138–139; genre
  134; re-imagine ageing masculinity
  135; treatment of space, time, and
  bodies 141
Tout s'est bien passé 77
toxic intergenerationality 123
transgressions of dark aesthetics
  184–186

transnational business masculinity 128
Trente Glorieuses 73
Trintignant, Jean-Louis 75, 77–80, 85
Trip, The 136
*Trouble With Men: Masculinities in
  European and Hollywood Cinema,
  The* 17–18
Truffaut, Francois 78
Turner, Bryan 135, 143
Turnier, Nicola 184
Twigg, Julia 2
Tynan, Kenneth 32

Üks mu sober (2011) 92
Unforgiven (1992) 208
Ungár, Ali 113
Un homme et une femme trilogy
  78–85; ageing 75–85; car, choice of
  79; Citroën 2CV 79, 81–82; Ford
  Mustang 79, 81, 83; hyperbolic
  scene 81; *Les plus belles années
  d'une vie* 80–82; masculinity 78–79;
  masculinity, loss of 79–81; mental
  decline, Duroc 80–81; narrative of
  decline 77–78; *Un homme et une
  femme: vingt ans déj* 79–80; youth
  and speed 82
Un homme et une femme: vingt ans déj
  79–80
U zlatého tigra 113

van Hornthorst, Gerrit 184
Velvet Revolution of 1989 6,
  101–105, 115
vengeance variation 201
Venus (2006) 29–30
Viagra-related romantic comedies 25
victim of ageing 163
vodník/hastrman 110
voice-over (VO) 217–218
Vortex 77
Vratné lahve (2007) 102, 107–109

Warhol, Andy 175
Warsaw Pact troops 104
Wayne, John 13, 190, 192,
  206–207
We are the New Ones (2014) 6,
  121, 123, 125; older masculinity
  126–129; older (male) protagonists
  120; spectatorship 122; toxic
  intergenerationality 123
Wearing, Sadie 37

Welcome to New York (2014) 46, 48
Western-derived masculinity 191
Westhoff, Ralf 121
Wheatley, Catherine 134
white masculinity 9
Willis, Bruce 137
Winner, Michael 193
Wir sind die Neuen (2014) 120
Witness (1985) 208
Woodward, Kathleen 23, 178
world openness 135
Wright, Will 194

W. – The Killer of Flanders Fields (2014) 189, 194, 197
Wulff, Hans J. 216, 223

Yellowstone (2018) 191–192
Young Pope, The 150
Youth (2015) 7, 148–158; Fred Ballinger, trouble relationships 150; Sorrentino's message, catalysts of 155–157; young people, interactions with 154

Žižek, Slavoj 178
Zulema 169
Zulu (1964) 18

For Product Safety Concerns and Information please contact our EU
representative GPSR@taylorandfrancis.com
Taylor & Francis Verlag GmbH, Kaufingerstraße 24, 80331 München, Germany

www.ingramcontent.com/pod-product-compliance
Lightning Source LLC
Chambersburg PA
CBHW051354290426
44108CB00015B/2015